impossibly funky

a cashiers du cinemart collection

To Rudy Ray Moore,
the baddest mutha who ever lived.

Impossibly Funky: A Cashiers du Cinemart Collection
© 2010 by Mike White
All photos from the author's collection unless otherwise noted

All rights reserved.

Published in the United States of America by:
Bear Manor Media
PO Box 71426
Albany, Georgia 31708
www.bearmanormedia.com

ISBN 1-59393-547-1

No part of this book may be reproduced in any way or by any means, including electronic, mechanical, photocopying or otherwise, without the prior written permission of the publisher.

Book design and copyediting by Lori Hubbard Higgins
Cover design by Jim Rugg and Jasen Lex. www.jimrugg.com

IMPOSSIBLY FUNKY:
A *CASHIERS DU CINEMART* COLLECTION

By

Mike White

Skizz Cyzyk

Mike Thompson

Rich Osmond

Leon Chase

Chris Cummins

Andrew Grant

Andrea White

Clifton Howard

Edited by Mike White

ACKNOWLEDGEMENTS

So many folks have helped me over the years, it's impossible to list everyone. Certainly, my most heartfelt appreciation goes to my wife, Andrea, for always supporting my efforts in everything, including *Cashiers du Cinemart*. Likewise, I'm grateful for all of the folks who made this collection possible, from my publisher to my fellow writers to the artists and, especially, my sounding boards: Lori Hubbard Higgins, Andrea White, and Mike Thompson.

Additionally, these fine folks deserve a shout out: Aaron Finestone, Alex Winter, Alison Faith Levy, Allen Pasternak, Andrew Haupt, Andrew Gurland, Ann Gavaghan, Anthony Morrow, Ari Kahan, Atomic Books, Betsy Willeford, Brad Beshaw, Brian Frye, Brian Smith, Bryan Wendorf, Chris Smith, Chris Ungar, Clint Johns, Colin Geddes, Dan Clark, Dave Cawley, David Faris, David MacGregor, David Walker, Dennis McMillan, Derrick Scocchera, Dion Conflict, Don Alex Hixx, Doug Holland, Drea Clark, Eamonn Bowles, Ed Halter, Edmond Davis, Eric Litwin, *Factsheet Five*, Faye Kosmidis, Gary Cole, George Armitage, Gregg Babus, Herb Eagle, Howard A. Rodman, J. Hoberman, J. Rocky Colavito, Jake Austin, Jason Pankoke, Jay Edwards, Jay Wiseman, Jeff Dunlap, Jen Talbert, Jesse Nelson, Jim Trupin, Joe Bob Briggs, Joe McSpadden, John Grace, Jonathan Rosenbaum, Joseph Gervasi, Josh Hadley, Kevin Johnson, Kevin L. Christopher, Krista Garcia, Kristen Anchor, L. Rob Hubbard, Larry Yoshida, Lewis Teague, Lou Boxer, Marc Vogl, Mark Peranson, Mary Gillen, Matt Clark, Matt Lieberman, Melanie G. Dante, Michael Weldon, Mike Dereniewski, Mike Faloon, Mike Malloy, Mike Sullivan, Mike Z., Mitch Davis, Nicholas Kazan, Nick Kujawa, P. Kimé Le, Pat Drummond, Patricio Vamos, Pierre-Alexander Buisson, Renee Bulanda, Rita Su, Robin Bogie, Rusty Nails, Sam McAbee, Sarah Geren, Sarah Price, Scott Calonico, Scott Cornish, Scott Huffines, Scott Ruisch, Scott Wallace Brown, Shawna Kenney, Shepard Fairey, Steve Puchalski, Sheldon Sturges, James Jacobs, Terry Gilmer, Tim Lucas, Tim Smy, Todd Philips, Todd Rohal, Tom Fitzgerald, Val Madill, *Zine World*, the MicroCineFest crew, fellow fans of *Black Shampoo*, my family, friends, all of the readers, advertisers, and filmmakers who supported *Cashiers du Cinemart*.

TABLE OF CONTENTS

Foreword vii

Introduction ix

Part I: Tarantino 1
    The Tale of the Tape 3
    Pamphlet Publisher Treads Water 15
    Enough with the Fooling! 17
    Attention: Enemy 19
    Tarantino in a Can 21

Part II: Feature Articles 23
    The *Cashiers du Cinemart* Manifesto 25
    The Serious Moonlight: The Cinematic World of David Goodis 29
    The Dark Places of James Ellroy 45
    Madness in the 20th Century 59
    Tragically Obscure: John Paizs's (*The Big*) *Crime Wave* 73
    Oedipal Ketchup 81
    On the Road to Meifumado 87
    All the Good Guys and the Bad Guys That I've Been 99
    The Four and a Half Worlds of Parker 107
    The Prize Is Your Life 123
    A Dynamite Double Feature 133
    Double Impact: The Duplicity of Jean-Claude Van Damme 135
    The *Highlander* Returns! 137
    Psycho Vixens 143

Part III: Scripts 145
    Not So Super…*8mm* 147
    The Mouse That Roared: An Evolution of Catwoman 153
    The Uncredible Hulk 157
    The *Gremlins* That Could Have Been 165
    Digging up the Bones of Indy Jones 169
    Travis McGee and the Lonely Silver Screen 175
    The Metamorphoses of *Alien III* 183
    Return to the *Planet of the Apes* 211
    Superman: Grounded 223

Part IV: Interviews 235
Bruce Campbell: The Man Who Was Ash 237
Monte Hellman: The Interview 243
The Return of *Captain Milkshake* 249
Still Demented After All These Years: Dr. Demento 257
Off the Record with James Ellroy 261
Tales of Guy Maddin 265
From Shitter to Auteur: Keith Gordon 273
Stephen Hawking's Lab Assistant 287
Hellion 289
10 Questions for Svengoolie 293

Part V: Star Wars 297
Star Wars: The Lost Cut 299
Da Jar Jar Done Gone 303
Triumph of the Whills 309

Part VI: Black Shampoo 317
A Few Notes on *Black Shampoo* 319
Can You Feel the Love? 321
Music Is Their Way of Life 327
Have You Seen Brenda? 333
Jonathan's Right-Hand Man 337
"I Hate the Hollywood Bag" 341
Shades of Greydon Clark 347
Feel the Love…on DVD 351

Part VII: Life 353
Theater Daze 355
Ghoti out of Water 365
Andrea and Mike Go to Breakfast 367
Brendan Fraser + Monkey = Fun! 369

Part VIII: Credits 371
Afterword 373
About the Contributors 375

FOREWORD

Kinder, gentler times? Not for us.

We who toil in the dungeons of independent film production know a nasty truth: If our "product" parallels that of the major studios, we're doomed to screenings in our basements.

So we take a direction too many majors ignore—a wild grab for attention. We take chances the majors won't. We exploit as the majors never do. We pay our actors and actresses as little as we can, because nobody goes to see our movies because Joe Glutz and Heather Nudelman are the stars. We use friends and semi-pros and out-of-work oldsters as crew.

And we don't lounge in a director's chair, with an overpaid assistant who yells "Roll sound!" and "Cut!" based on a nod from us. Oh, no, we're on our feet, pulling cable and holding the microphone and operating the camera and eventually chopping up the negative or the tape.

Increasingly, we shoot digitally rather than on film. That opens another nest of buzzing hornets, because every would-be producer is out there with a digital camera, tracking the same prey we're tracking.

So we live on our wits. And I love it.

While the notion of having a hundred million dollar budget is enticing, the notion of losing fifty million of that budget isn't so enticing. And that happens with unsurprising regularity in big-budget films. Why? Because they don't think as we do—that we have to titillate, to shock, to force someone coming out of the theatre or taking a DVD out of the player to exclaim, "Wow!"

It isn't that simple, as this book points out so succinctly. We not only have to be showpeople; we have to be innovators. Lacking expensive national or international advertising campaigns, lacking simultaneous multi-theatre openings in multiple areas, lacking star names who can stumble around the talk-show circuit, mumbling, "He was, like," and "I went, like, to, y'know, like there," we either generate one-to-one word of mouth or we're failed egoists, showing our product in our basements.

So let this book be a litmus test, if you're planning to invade our sacred turf. Mike White has compiled a unique collection here, one that certainly has a place in our checkered history.

And if your intention isn't to be our competitor but just to enjoy all the work and muscle Mike has put into this volume, you're in for a sparkling good "read."

So: Welcome to our world.

OK, Mike. Now it's up to you.

—Herschell Gordon Lewis

INTRODUCTION

Cashing In

"...if I've learned anything about film critics, it's that they love to fight about movies probably as much as they love movies."
—Chris Gore

Mike White doesn't like me.

I think he hates me.

And now that I think about it...he must really *hate my guts to the core*. Mike probably wants to punch me in the face and make me bleed in the most painful way possible. A good skull-fucking is too good for me, based on what I did to him.

Seriously.

You'd hate me too if you were about to appear as a contestant on IFC's short-lived game show *Ultimate Film Fanatic*. A competition in which Mike, if he had actually been allowed to walk out on stage to participate, would have won handily. But I prevented him from doing so. I was the one responsible for destroying his dream. It's my fault.

Here's the story from my perspective. (And, uh, Mike, feel free to correct me or fill in details from your side of the story in a possible rebuttal foreword...something I've never seen in a book before.)

I was hired as the host of this "reality game show" for the Independent Film Channel in which the most hardcore movie geeks compete, testing their film knowledge and passion in three rounds. The first round of *Ultimate Film Fanatic* involved movie trivia, the second round featured a debate topic such as the greatest director of all time, and the final round was like the card game War, only played using movie collectibles. Since I'd never actually hosted a game show before, I was sent to a "game show boot camp." It was there that I learned the most effectively dramatic way to read a question. And how to create tension by restating a contestant's circumstances for the audiences' benefit; for example, "Mike...you've waited your *whole life* for *this* moment...it all comes down to *this question*. Are you *ready*?!"

During my boot camp experience, I was also informed with great seriousness about the legalities regulating game shows. These laws came into play after the quiz show controversies of the 1950s and remain today to ensure that game shows are fair. Basically, I needed to remember two important things:

First, and this one is very obvious, I could show no favoritism or do anything that might help a contestant. I could not even talk to contestants in a friendly manner, as it could be perceived to be implying some kind of bias on my part. The most I was allowed to utter would be something like, "Good luck." That was the worst part since the one thing a collection of misfit movie geeks want to do more than anything is talk about film endlessly.

Second, I could not have any prior relationship or know anyone who was going to participate on the show, for obvious reasons. And I knew Mike White.

You see, Mike is primarily responsible for all the fuss regarding Quentin Tarantino heavily borrowing from Ringo Lam's *City on Fire* as the basis for *Reservoir Dogs*. Mike's amazing video of side-by-side scene comparisons from the two films is indisputable evidence that Tarantino had lifted ideas, compositions, and whole scenes for his feature directorial debut. Through his cleverly edited video, Mike proved that *Reservoir Dogs* was more than a simple homage; it was a form of cinematic thievery. He didn't do this for money or fame, he did this for the same reasons others are attracted to expressing themselves through writing about film…he did it because he's so passionate. This was not his job, he didn't collect a paycheck for writing about whatever movie came to the multiplex that week; he did it because as a film fan, he had to. *Film Threat* magazine wrote about Mike's video, and this is how I came to know him. For this reason alone, Mike White became my hero. He had the balls to call it like he saw it and confront QT, regardless of the outcome.

Mike and I corresponded over the years in what often became heated arguments; if I've learned anything about film critics, it's that they love to fight about movies probably as much as they love movies. Mike even took the time to lambaste me personally within the pages of *Cashiers du Cinemart*, which I always took as the highest compliment since, well—love and hate…those emotions are so close.

Mike, along with the other contestants, nervously waited backstage. The audience was pumped up. Just before the show featuring the Midwest contestants was about to start, I was handed a list of names and the cities each person hailed from. I saw Mike White's name. My heart sank past my heart down to my balls…as if Mike himself had kicked me between the legs…only his leg bounced back and he kicked himself in the balls…not sure where I was going with that, but getting hit in the balls is how it felt. Anyway, I had to be honest.

Because I knew Mike, he could not appear on the show.

The producers immediately had a talk with the lawyers, and then confronted Mike backstage, who told him that he could not be on the show. That was a somber day for me, but I can't imagine how Mike must have felt. He'd come all the way out to California for nothing. We never spoke. I didn't get to say how genuinely sorry I felt. I never even got to shake his hand. Like a back-alley abortion, Mike's dream to be crowned King of Film Geeks of the United States would be tossed aside in a dumpster and left to rot.

I do believe that Mike and I will one day meet. And get into a shouting match. Which will escalate to a bar brawl. A punch might be thrown, probably hitting nothing but air. And neither of us will do anything physical; film geeks aren't really the type to do that. But we'll scream threats at each other, which will turn out to be tough guy lines from movies, like: "*You can act like a man!*" Or "*You seem a decent fellow. I hate to kill you.*" Or "*Say hello to my little friend!*"

And after this heated exchange screaming cruel movie quotes at the top of our lungs, we'll probably hug. A manly hug. To me, that hug will mean more than burying the hatchet over our tenuous relationship over the years; it will be the thanks Mike deserves for creating the film world's most original and entertaining irritants in the form of a magazine entitled *Cashiers du Cinemart*. The pages of each treasured issue exposed controversy, explored unseen cinema, and offered some of the most groundbreaking film journalism ever, always with a unique perspective. Or at least *on paper*, until the internet came along, putting print critics out of work, democratizing film "reviewing" in which anyone with a blog could be a "critic," and *completely ruined* it for all of us. But I digress. This foreword was supposed to offer some perspective as to why *Cashiers du Cinemart* is the greatest and most influential underground film journal of all time. Or at least, that's what Mike suggested I write.

Writing this foreword is the least I can do after royally fucking Mike on TV. Or at least, *off camera*, which is probably best because it would have been embarrassing for both of us if a video of us *fucking* surfaced. One thing I can count on—if a video *did* exist of Mike and I blowing each other and engaging in anal sex somehow emerged, you can count on the fact that *Cashiers du Cinemart* would cover this random Indie-Gay-Art-Core video within its pages. And for that, we all owe Mike our gratitude and respect.

—Chris Gore

tarantino

THE TALE OF THE TAPE

By Mike White

"If you must provide prose and poems the words you use should be your own, don't plagiarize or take on loan. There's always someone, somewhere, with a big nose who knows and who trips you up and laughs when you fall."

—The Smiths. "Cemetery Gates."
By Johnny Marr and Morrissey. *The Queen is Dead.* Sire, 1986.

Background

It all started back in the fall of 1993. I had become friends with Mike Thompson in my Film/Video 300 class at the University of Michigan. I knew of Thompson from previous classes (where I thought he was an obstreperous jerk—a kindred spirit), but it wasn't until F/V 300 that we actually had a conversation. It turned out that both of us were big fans of Quentin Tarantino's *Reservoir Dogs*. Sure, most of our fellow film students were enamored of that film as well, but none were as vociferous about it as we.

Certainly we knew that Tarantino was a big film geek like the two of us, and that his freshman film was heavily steeped in film history. Quentin didn't seem to hesitate in shooting off his mouth about this film or that. We spent hours talking about where Tarantino got ideas and who influenced his work. We tracked down every video he mentioned in interviews and hungrily watched them, determined to find out what made this wünderkind tick.

One fateful day, Thompson dropped a bomb on me. It was something from which I could never recover. It turned out that our hero was not all he appeared to be.

British movie magazine *Empire* broke the story. In a sidebar by Jeff Dawson, the horrible truth was laid out in black and white for the world to see (but for no one to pay attention to): "Quentin Tarantino has been hailed as the hip new messiah of film making. How strange, then, that the basic premise of his legendary movie bears a remarkable resemblance to that of Ringo Lam's 1989 Hong Kong movie *City on Fire*." Dawson provided a comparison of action from Lam's *City on Fire* that was repeated in Tarantino's *Reservoir Dogs*.

I was in shock. How could this be? How could my hero, the Horatio Alger of video store clerks, be a plagiarist? Say it ain't so!

I became obsessed. I looked in the computer system at Blockbuster Video, but only found *City on Fire* by Alan Rakoff (written by Jack Hill, director of *Switchblade Sisters*, which Tarantino re-released via his Rolling Thunder distribution company in 1996). Luckily, John Woo was coming into his American heyday and I found where gweilo could rent Hong Kong films. It took a little

The Tale of the Tape

driving and a lot of patience, but I found Lam's *City on Fire* at a Chinese grocery store after going through their hundreds of tapes, video by video.

By no means is *City on Fire* a good movie. In the years since my initial viewing, I've only managed to stomach the whole thing once. The only watchable qualities of the film are actors Danny Lee and Chow Yun-Fat and the film's familiar third act.

I waited. I was going to be patient about it. I didn't want to pass judgment over Tarantino before I had all the facts. Perhaps this information was in the press notes; common knowledge to movie reviewers. Perhaps a statement was going to be issued. Perhaps Tarantino was planning a press conference to apologize for this oversight. I was waiting for answers to all questions.

I waited for the next *Entertainment Weekly*—my bible. It had never let me down before, always providing me with the most up-to-date information about movies, videos, and music. But the formerly infallible *EW* let me down. And it wasn't just them. The media was strangely mute. It wasn't that Tarantino had lost popularity and no longer appeared in magazines; quite the opposite. While reporters were fawning over him, no one asked the question I wanted to hear.

It was up to me to press the issue.

I had shown those final precious twenty minutes to all of my housemates. Through my temerity, they all were *Reservoir Dogs* fans. Some were angry, some were indifferent, and some couldn't grasp the idea. I realized that I needed a better format with which to make my case.

I had waited six months for the media to respond before giving up hope. Finally, I took a few hours at the University of Michigan's shoddy video editing suites to make a full-motion montage of the similarities between *Reservoir Dogs* and *City on Fire*. *Who Do You Think You're Fooling* was born.

The Story of a Robbery

"I'm not claiming Tarantino wasn't influenced by other directors. I just think it's a pretty dubious assumption to say he'd even heard of City On Fire *while creating* Reservoir Dogs."

—Greg Gioia

When Tarantino wrote the screenplay to *Reservoir Dogs*, he thanked Jean-Luc Godard, Andre DeToth, Chow Yun-Fat, Lionel White, Roger Corman, and Timothy Carey. The person missing from that list is Ringo Lam, director of *City on Fire*, the movie on which *Reservoir Dogs* is based.

Like Kubrick's *The Killing* (based on Lionel White's *Clean Break*), *Reservoir Dogs* employs a fractured time frame as a narrative conceit. Tarantino's film is an unusual entry in the heist subgenre, in that the actual robbery is never shown. I used this as the jumping-off point for *Who Do You Think You're Fooling*. I subtitled the film "The Story of a Robbery" to play off the jewelry store score at the heart of *Reservoir Dogs* and *City on Fire*, while calling out Tarantino for not acknowledging Lam's film. I led into the action with Joe Tex's "I Gotcha."

I showed the robbery scene from *City on Fire* while narrating it with dialogue from *Reservoir Dogs*, cutting back to Tarantino's film to ground the narrators in time and space. I was particularly happy about cutting the "Bam, Bam, Bam" from Mr. White (Harvey Keitel) with the clerk shot in *City on Fire*.

The getaway sequence intensifies the parallels in action and is where I began inter-cutting more fervently. I went between the two crashing getaway cars and the double-gunned robbers (Harvey Keitel/Danny Lee) shooting up pursuing police vehicles. I also had a bit of fun reworking some of the editing that Sally Menke did for *Reservoir Dogs*, especially matching Mr. White removing his gun from his belt (an action shown twice in the original film) and eliminating the steadi-cam around Mr. White and Mr. Orange (Tim Roth), cutting on action to compress time.

Enfant Terrible Quentin Tarantino

The sequence that still seems to confound some viewers comes when the Tim Roth/Chow Yun-Fat characters are gut shot, killing an innocent victim to maintain their undercover status. The rapidity of the action may be what loses audiences momentarily until we enter the warehouse sequence.

After the undercover cop is accused of being a rat, he's defended by the Harvey Keitel/Danny Lee character. This begins the famous Mexican standoff finale. Moving at a more leisurely pace, this bit features some of my favorite Engrish in HK film: "You pointy gun at boss!"

Ringo Lam is known for building up major action sequences, only to abort before giving the audience any kind of proper payoff. *City on Fire* is no exception. Tarantino has to be lauded for letting the Mexican standoff play out to a satisfying conclusion. It was a blast reworking *Reservoir Dogs* to make the non-linear flow back into a straight line, compressing the action to eleven minutes.

Reaction

> *"Mike White btches* (sic) *in this "film" about how Tarantino stole from* City on Fire. *But in this "film," White doesn't have a frame of original material. Even in documentaries about other films something*

The Tale of the Tape

> *is usually shot independently. This is blatant plagerism* (sic)*, using unliscenced* (sic) *footage from not one but 2 films. So as bad as White thinks Tarantino is, he's 10 times worse. PWNED!"*
>
> —VonCouch

Things were quiet for a while. I really didn't know what to do with my tape, other than show it to friends. It never dawned on me to send it anywhere until, months later, *Film Threat* finally ran a story on the rampant similarities between *Reservoir Dogs* and *City on Fire*.

In order to show them they weren't the only people who knew of the scandal, I sent them a copy. For my troubles I got a call from Chris Gore, the editor-in-chief. The first time I talked to him, Gore ranted about how great my tape was. He rang me up a few weeks later, asking for the master copy. Since I wasn't pleased with the original VHS editing job (thanks to the crappy original editing gear), I promptly put my pal Eric Litwin to work, helping me redo it on 3/4" tape (this was the pre-digital age). We toiled long into the night, making a much more acceptable version for Gore to use on the *Film Threat Video Guide*'s free subscription video (his proposed mode of distribution).

Observant viewers of *Who Do You Think You're Fooling* may notice that the first third of the video exhibits better production values than the rest of it. You can almost pinpoint the moment when Eric had to go home. Without his capable hands and keen ear, the sound gets a little over-modulated at times. I always considered Eric my Roger Avery. He did all the work and I took all the credit.

Who Do You Think You're Fooling did what I needed it to do: it told a simple narrative while highlighting the rampant similarities between the two works. Eric and I set it up, too, with an opening narration (Eric on voice modulator to sound more "deep throat"). Yet that didn't stop the dumb questions from coming (more on this later).

After my second conversation, I've never talked to Chris Gore again. Chris now considered me *persona non grata*, though not enough to avoid showing my video at the '94 Chicago Underground Film Festival (without my permission) or sending a copy to Lisa Kennedy at *The Village Voice* ("Gore was only too happy to FedEx me a copy marked 'Evidence,'" Kennedy wrote), but enough to never return my calls, letters, or email.

Mr. White (Harvey Keitel) takes aim in *Reservoir Dogs*

It's interesting to see where Chris has gone since then. When we talked, Tarantino was the Ultimate Evil in the Universe, but in Gore's first editorial for the fourth incarnation of *Film Threat* he praised Quentin for creating a new genre of film: the Independent Movie. The fascinating aspect to this article (apart from his twisted logic, considering Indie films as a new "genre") was that he ended it with the line, "let's stir up some shit," when, only three years before, he told me that we were going to "tear shit up." Maybe it's his obsession with fecal matter that hurt his magazine.

Diary of a Malcontent

"Tarantino's adaptation (even if it goes uncredited) is nothing but a compliment to Ringo Lam. Reservoir Dogs *is an original work, while most might watch* City on Fire, *or possibly the documentary* Who Do You Think You're Fooling *(A film made by a University of Minnesota [sic] film student with the arogance [sic] to actually pursue an investigation into the topic) and consider themselves an authority on what Tarantino was thinking."*

—everythingtarantino.com

Late winter 1995. It was lightning in a bottle. Bolstered by Gore's praise of my work, I submitted *Who Do You Think You're Fooling* to the New York Underground Film Festival and it was accepted. *Pulp Fiction* was enjoying a resurgence, receiving seven Academy Award nominations. Miramax was burning through money like mad, stoking their publicity machine. To call into question Quentin Tarantino's originality during "campaign season" was akin to heresy. NYUFF was suddenly in a publicity shitstorm and they were fanning the flames…until they got burned.

February 1995. I was accepted into the New York Underground Film Festival. Todd Phillips, co-director of the fest, called me up to ask for a copy of my video sooner rather than later, since he wanted to show it at the press screening. He sounded kind of excited—as much as he could muster, I think.

March 3, 1995. I got a call from Michael Fleming of *Variety*. He asked me all about my video and told me that *Variety* was "a seed-bed for stories."

March 5, 1995. I called Todd to tell him I was coming out to NYC (my first time in the Big Apple). He told me that Miramax had called him and wanted him to stop the story from running in *Variety*. Pretty funny: a little guy like me creating such a stir!

March 6, 1995. I went over to my PO Box and found a ton of mail requesting copies of my video, thanks to my appearance in *The Joe Bob Report*!

The Tale of the Tape

March 7, 1995. I went over to Borders and picked up a copy of *Variety*. When I got back, Jami Bernard of the *New York Daily News* rang me up. She interviewed me for her new book on Tarantino (*Quentin Tarantino: The Man and His Movies*). It was pretty neat hearing her type everything I said, even if it seemed a little premature to write a book about a guy who has only made two and a quarter films (ten years later there would be over a dozen English language tomes dedicated to the auteur).

Despite her dictation she still managed to misquote me. I still chuckle when I read my discussion of "The Great Poster Defense" (discussed later) and "*The Black Shampoo*."

March 8, 1995. The *Variety* story ("Dogs Bark at Tarantino") really created some waves. I got a call from Bill Jenkins, Ringo Lam's U.S. Manager. I got the feeling he thought I was some kind of punk kid, since I was quoted as calling *City on Fire* "awful." Overall, he just wanted to touch base with me and assured me that there'd be no legal repercussions. He also refused to let me interview Ringo. Um, thanks.

March 10, 1995. Michael Fleming called to do a follow-up piece ("Quentin Cancellation"). He informed me that the press screening at NYUFF had been cancelled. That bummed me out; I was getting hooked on all this attention!

March 13, 1995. After a slow weekend, my phone started ringing again. I got a call from Gersh Kuntzman of the *New York Post*, who filled me in on the press screening a little more. The screening wasn't canceled; my film was pulled at the last moment.

When I called Todd Phillips twenty minutes later, he ducked all of my questions while sounding belabored by fielding angry calls from Miramax:

"Hey Todd, what's up? This is Mike White."
"Oh, man, I got Miramax calling me all over the place."
"Really? What are they saying?"
"Oh, man, it's just chaos around here." *(After ducking my question, I got a little suspicious.)*
"Yeah, I just got a call from a guy at the *Post*."
"Who was it?"
"I'm not really sure," I lied.
"Did he leave a phone number?"
"Yeah, why?"
"I can probably tell who it is just by the number." *(Did he want to call this reporter to "set the record straight"?)*
"So, what kind of stuff is Miramax saying?" *(I asked, still trying to find out, while changing the subject.)*
"It's just crazy; they're calling me all the time!" *(Something's fishy here.)*

March 14, 1995. I got a call from Steve Schaffer of *Entertainment Weekly* (my favorite mainstream magazine)! He told me he'll call me the next day after watching my video.

March 15, 1995. As I worked until 4 a.m., I took the phone to bed with me in case Schaffer called. The phone woke me up at 10 a.m.; it was my dear friend Jeff Dunlap on the line. He excitedly read the article from the *Post* ("'Dogs' has fur flying") and I delighted in hearing it, as well as relating the "behind-the-scenes" scoop on Gersh's conversation with me. I was on edge all day waiting for Schaffer's call.

March 16, 1995. I talked to Ann Richie from a San Diego radio show and set up an interview for the following Monday. I also got a call from Terry Mc-Cloud of Fox TV for an in-person interview when I got into New York.

March 18, 1995. I talked to high-school chum Chris McGraw for the first time in a long time. He saw a news story about me on MTV! I waited a few hours, watching *MTV News* at every break. All I saw were stories on Snoop Doggy Dogg.

March 19, 1995. Twenty-four hours later, I finally caught a repeat of the MTV story (no VCR running, of course). Man, what a rush, hearing Kurt Loder say my name! Of course, all the facts were wrong, but it was still fun!

March 20, 1995. I talked to MTV today to see if they could get me a copy of the story. The woman on the phone sent it to me, as it only ran twice. Good thing McGraw saw it, or I'd never have known it aired!

The radio show had their facts as wrong as MTV (or at least I hoped so—everyone kept saying that my video wasn't going to screen. Do they know something I don't?).

I had hoped that the radio show would take callers—I was waiting for someone to attack me. I kind of got my wish a few hours later when the copy of the *LA Weekly* arrived at my door. The article by Manohla Dargis ("West Looks East: City on Fire and Reservoir Dogs") sounds like a Miramax Press Release. Maybe Manohla saw the American *City on Fire*; that's the only way I can see that she can say, "The occasional similarities between *City on Fire* and the superior *Reservoir Dogs* are noticeable but not striking." Huh? Oh, and I found out that I am from the East Coast and have a "hard-on" for Quentin.

At least the *Daily News* article ("Charges of 'Theft' Still 'Dog' Tarantino") was nicer. It's so strange to read quotes of things I've said in the paper. I'd really like to talk to Marcy Granata from Miramax and ask her where in the hell Quentin "acknowledged the influence of a variety of movies, including *City on Fire*."

The Tale of the Tape

March 21, 1995. I packed and sent out a big pile of tapes before I left. I'm so excited to go see New York City!

March 27, 1995. Where should I begin? What a whirlwind week I had. Let me just say that New York was fun. I took a bite of the Big Apple and tried to not mind the maggots, but it was a tough fight.

My first evening in NYC was tainted by an article that Andrew Gurland gave me on the way into the dive where we saw Helmet. It was a copy of a *USA Today* article ("Dispute 'Dogs' Tarantino" by Marshall Fine) in which Todd Phillips was quoted as saying, "If you take any horror film and cut it together with something by Hitchcock, it looks like they're ripping off Hitchcock."

Not only am I mad about the complete insanity of that quote, but this is the festival's organizer, the same guy who played my best bud, saying this crap in a national newspaper. Pulling my video from the press screening was a clever move, I'll grant them that. They were responsible for all the hype around the video, but why try to deny the substance of it? Why promote a piece just to dis it—and its creator—in public? And, did they pull it from the screening as a stunt, or were they really pressured? Who can believe the back-pedaling and butt-kissing of Phillips?

Tarantino: "I just can't go on living this lie."

By this time, it seemed like Phillips and Gurland were trying to parlay their success into something "bigger" than a film festival. The *New York Post* held that Phillips "has friends at Miramax" (I heard his girlfriend/fiancée worked there). Though he denied it, Phillips appeared to be bending to the pressures of the notorious studio. If nothing else, he knows how to get publicity—good or bad. His documentaries on GG Allin (*Hated*), Al Goldstein (*Screwed*), and frat house hazing (*Frat House*) were well played in the media (though the latter was pulled from release when questions of its legitimacy were introduced).

The screening went well, though I wasn't very into the films running in the same program. (Must every new filmmaker adapt a Charles Bukowski short story?) I took part in a Q&A at the end. This was my first time in front of a crowd. Rather unnerving, but I think I handled it fairly well.

Probably the best thing to come of it was getting back to my seat and being offered a card by the guy next to me. This shaggy individual invited me to send a copy of my tape for one of his public screenings, if I so chose. That was my first time meeting Skizz Cyzyk.

After the screening, I went out and celebrated. It was only the next day that I found out that the demand had been so high that *Who Do You Think You're Fooling* was shown at the two subsequent screenings that night. Had I known, I would have stuck around to do more Q&As and to see the reaction. This was my first time as part of a film festival; getting audience reaction was critical for me. This was just one more way that Phillips and Gurland paid me a discourtesy.

Controversy

> *"Some people are turned off by Tarantino, saying that he's doing nothing more than taking from other films and areas of pop culture. There was even a even a short film made by filmmaker Mike White titled* Who Do You Think You're Fooling *where he charges Tarantino with directly copying a 1987 Hong Kong film titled* City On Fire *when he made* Reservoir Dogs. *White then made a second short film titled* You're Still Not Fooling Anyone, *where he charges Tarantino with taking from various films to make* Pulp Fiction. *To me, these reports seem to be coming from some hack who is jealous."*
>
> —Josh Gilchrist

I can't say many good things about Chris Gore, but I can say that at least he could figure out what was going on in *Who Do You Think You're Fooling*. The same cannot be said for a lot of people. I've gotten quite a few hilarious questions over the years after people watch the video:

"Where'd you get all those Asian guys to act for you?"
"Now, let me get this straight, Tarantino ripped *you* off with *Reservoir Dogs*?"
"Is Mike White your real name?"
"Why do you hate Tarantino so much?"

It seems that I just can't explain this simply enough.

I've gotten a lot of flack for "hating" Quentin Tarantino and for making a case out of "nothing." The first person who ever attacked me for hating QT had never seen *Who Do You Think You're Fooling* or spoken to me. That's a nice, unbiased attitude for someone in the "news" business, dontcha think? That person was Touré from MTV. I think he must have been some sort of flunkie or intern, because he was completely unprofessional and lacking in many of the social graces. He had gotten my name from Lisa Kennedy of *The Village Voice* and asked me to send him a copy of my video.

The Tale of the Tape

Reservoir Dogs is still one of my favorite films. I wasn't that wild about *Pulp Fiction* and really could have done without *Four Rooms*, but I enjoy Tarantino's writing (despite his horrendous spelling). He's one of the few screenwriters that can paint such a complete picture in the mind of the reader that you can practically see the film in your mind's eye before a single frame has been shot.

The issue here is not one of personal vendetta. It's about giving credit where credit is due. Think back to all the articles and interviews Quentin's given this decade:

When comparisons were made between Jean-Pierre Melville's *Le Doulos* and *Reservoir Dogs* in the July/August '94 issue of *Film Comment*, Quentin missed his chance to correct the interviewer and say that the biggest influence on the film was Ringo Lam's *City on Fire*.

When asked for a top-ten list of favorite movies in September '94 issue of *Details* and December '94 issue of *Vox*, several of the films that influenced Quentin were there, but *City on Fire* was missing.

The only mentions of Lam that Tarantino made in 1994 (two years after *Reservoir Dogs* was released) I ever uncovered during my extensive research were to say that he owns the movie poster:

"I loved City on Fire; *I got the poster framed in my house, so it's a great movie."*

—*Film Threat*, Issue 18, pg. 23

"I've got the poster right here. That's Danny Lee. Ringo Lam is like my second, after Jackie Chan, third favorite of all the Hong Kong directors."

—*The Village Voice* 10/25/94 No. 43, pg. 31

Just because you own the poster doesn't mean you can lift chunks of the plot liberally. Other than the "Great Poster Defense," Tarantino's been mute on the subject, despite what Marcy Granata of Miramax pictures says:

"Quentin has always been really open about the movies to which he was making homage, including City on Fire."

—Marcy Granata, *USA Today* 3/16/95

So, is it plagiarism or is it homage? Milton would say that since *City on Fire* was "made better by the borrower," no theft has occurred. Others would say that there is nothing new; "good artists paint while great artists steal." And then there are some that say if you don't give credit to your sources, you're a plagiarist.

Impossibly Funky

Was Vanilla Ice simply paying homage to Queen? Did this other trash-talking, material-stealing, bad-acting, "from the streets" kid make his original material better by sampling? In Quentin's case, the answer would have to be "Yes." His ability to take crappy material and make it shine is truly commendable.

I'd be even more proud of the lil' nipper if he had 'fessed up. If Tarantino had come clean right away, saying that *City on Fire* was one of his biggest influences, and then I saw Lam's work, I would have been really impressed. Instead I was pissed, because Quentin didn't feel it was necessary to give Lam his due.

Mr. Pink (Steve Buschemi) and Mr. White (Harvey Keitel) face off in *Reservoir Dogs*

It would have been nice for Quentin to volunteer the *City on Fire* information early on. But once the story was out there, shouldn't someone have gotten to the bottom of it? I have more of a problem with mainstream media than I do with Quentin Tarantino.

For a year, the only magazine to cover the story was *Empire*. *Film Threat* tried to get the story rolling again; it was dead in the water. Even during the controversy surrounding the New York Underground Film Festival, the majority of mainstream sources stayed away from the story, or downplayed it by dismissing the "similarities" as flights of fancy, never bothering to get their facts straight.

Let's compare how this story was handled by *Paper* versus *Premiere*. In her article, "Outlaw Cool," from the May '95 issue of *Paper*, Dana Dickey took the time to come out to the New York Underground Film Festival (suffering through *Raging Boil*) to see my video and talk to me. Meanwhile, Holly Sorenson of *Premiere* lives in a delusional white tower world where she believes she can trust Todd Phillips and Andrew Gurland, the directors of the NYUFF, and reports in her June '95 article, "The Subterraneans," that Gurland, unbeknownst to Phillips, planted the rumor that Miramax was putting the screws on the festival. Uh-huh. Sure.

The story flamed out quickly after Tarantino walked away with an Oscar for Best Original Screenplay at the 1995 Academy Awards. My name still pops up in the odd Tarantino biography, but authors wearing rose-colored glasses tend to overlook the story. For the best-written coverage, be sure to check out Joe Bob Briggs's *Profoundly Disturbing: Shocking Movies That Changed History*.

Andrew Gurland and Todd Phillips would go on to various film projects; Phillips definitely the more popular of the two, having helmed *Old School*,

The Tale of the Tape

Road Trip, *The Hangover*, and more. Chris Gore wrote *My Big Fat Independent Movie* before hosting IFC's *Ultimate Film Fanatic* and acting as film correspondent on G4's *Attack of the Show*. Eric Litwin became the master of offline editing and Adobe AfterEffects. Touré became a host on BET. Mike Thompson still regrets telling me about that story in *Empire*.

As a bit of a joke, Eric and I returned to the scene of the crime with a follow-up piece, *You're Still Not Fooling Anybody*. This was another experiment in editing and quite a challenge to do with our rudimentary equipment. I've since been asked to give his subsequent films the same kind of treatment but, despite accusations to the contrary, being the boy who cried plagiarism isn't who I really care to be.

Portions of this article originally ran in *Cashiers du Cinemart* #1, #2, & #3.

Just to prove that there are no hard feelings, I decided to aid my detractors in trashing my latest video release by writing an article for them. I made sure to be as rabid and close-minded as possible, not allowing little things like "facts" stand in the way of witty journalism.

PAMPHLET PUBLISHER TREADS WATER

By Anonymous

I thought things couldn't get any worse when I read a few newspaper stories about Mike White and his copyright-infringing *Who Do You Think You're Fooling*. That was until I found out that this east coast film student actually publishes his own "'zine," a primitive and cheap homemade publication. I'm sure that only White's close friends and relatives are on his mailing list but the fact that anyone has to listen to his over-opinionated and self-aggrandizing drivel is truly disturbing.

White's been spending the past two years trying to get as much as he can out of his brief "fame" with his anti-Quentin Tarantino video which claims that the Oscar-winning writer/director paid homage to Ringo Lam's *City on Fire*. White tried to pass this off as plagiarism while it is common knowledge that Tarantino had always acknowledged Lam's film as an influence even though the similarities are slight and of no great importance.

But what is even sadder is that White, who I'd wager has never had an original idea, is not content to try and ride Tarantino's coattails just once. He's at it again; announcing that he has made another creatively bankrupt video which focuses on Tarantino's critically acclaimed *Pulp Fiction*.

The "sequel" appears to be a preview but when White's fleeting underground status appears to be in jeopardy again I expect him to make a full-length feature out of *Your Still Not Fooling Anybody*. As it stands, *Anyone* begins with an *MTV News* report about White's first video being pulled from the New York Underground Film Festival. By this, White attempts to establish how important he is by "making it" to MTV where he undoubtedly felt at home among intellectual icons like Beavis and Butthead!

Then, the viewer is subjected to clips from *Pulp Fiction* shown side-by-side with other films which we are supposed to assume Quentin Tarantino "plagiarized." Three of the clips are less than ten seconds long and merely contain an incidental line of dialogue or slight visual similarity. What the dim-witted White apparently doesn't realize is that Tarantino's fondness for each of these films is common knowledge.

In one of the other clips, White tries to show that the heart-stopping Adrenaline Needle scene was actually from a Martin Scorcese documentary,

Pamphlet Publisher Treads Water

The All-American Boy, because one of the people in the Scorcese film mentioned giving an adrenaline shot to a fellow junkie.

White continues to grasp at nothing with the final comparison, claiming that Tarantino took Samuel J. Jackson's Ezekial 25:17 speech from another movie. Perhaps White has never heard of a book that's been on the best seller list in Western Civilization for the past two thousand years—it's called The Bible!

You're Still Not Fooling Anyone is a pathetic attempt at gaining notoriety by slamming a noted figure. If only White realized that he's not telling anyone anything we didn't already know no matter how inflammatory the method of presentation. His jealous vendetta against one of the world's foremost filmmakers is pitiful and his thirst for undeserved attention is remarkable.

DISCLAIMER: The preceding article was a parody inspired by Christopher B. Goldsmith, David E. Williams, and Manohla Dargis. It is not meant to be taken seriously. All errors (spelling, grammatical, and factual) are intended.

This article originally ran in *Cashiers du Cinemart #7*.

ENOUGH WITH THE FOOLING!

By Clifton Howard

In *Cashiers du Cinemart #7*, Mike White wrote a mock review of his latest effort, *You're Still Not Fooling Anybody*. I'm very saddened to say that the sentiment he falsely expressed was very real to me as I watched this unneeded sequel to his groundbreaking 1994 video *Who Do You Think You're Fooling*. *YSNFA* is a case of "too little, too late." Back when I interviewed Mike in *CdC* #3, I asked him if he was going to do a piece on *Pulp Fiction*. His reply:

> "No, that isn't my job and *Pulp Fiction* takes its inspiration from a lot of sources; at least, as far as I know. And most of the references are passing; like that Bonnie is a black nurse, just like Pam Grier in *Coffy*. Unless I turn on the TV late at night and see a story about two hitmen going after a briefcase, a twist contest, a couple of hillbilly anal sex enthusiasts, and a diner robbery done exactly the same, shot for shot, then I won't have any complaints."

So, what changed his mind?

YSNFA doesn't feature any of the above *Pulp Fiction* antics. Instead, it focuses on only five, smaller bits; a line here and an idea there. Truth be told, there's nothing of any great significance here—no great revelation like there was in *Who Do You Think You're Fooling*. Even the most naïve cinema-goer is aware that *Pulp Fiction*'s glowing briefcase is a reference to the noir classic, *Kiss Me Deadly* (or maybe it was another kiss—*KISS Meets the Phantom of the Park*'s glowing talisman case). And thus, the impact of White's original is missing from this half-hearted sequel.

I think the entire project was flawed from the beginning. When White first told me about it, I thought that the concept was pretty shaky, but with his immense talent, he might be able to pull it off.

No luck. It comes off like the bullshit criticisms that people had for White's original; you would think he would have realized this. The sequel feels like a vendetta, with White coming across as a nut with an axe to grind.

I think the only way that *YSNFA* would have worked is if White had had more references. Then he could have banged them out in quick succession with an overwhelming amount of plagiarism. But a scant five things make it seem like a pathetic attempt to make Tarantino look bad—which it does, but it makes White look even worse.

Even on a technical level, I had problems with *YSNFA*. It was done in a process White calls "Plagiarvision"—a nearly clever name for a simple split screen with overlapping dialogue. It's really kind of confusing, like those

Enough with the Fooling!

arguments Bruce Willis and Cybill Sheppard had in *Moonlighting*, each trying to talk over one another with the audience unable to understand a word.

Someone take the car keys away from this drunk—he's not only going to hurt himself, but others as well. I'm rather dismayed that he included a couple of "thank yous" at the end of this. I cringed when I read the names, thinking that, if I were them, I wouldn't want to be associated with this doomed project!

As long as White just sticks this little ego trip at the end of his video copies of *Who Do You Think You're Fooling*, then no one should get hurt. But, then again, I'm not even sure about that!

I'm hoping that this review might make Mike think twice before sending this thing off to festivals and humiliating himself: "Hey, remember me? I was in all the QT bios. Well, I'm back!" *YSNFA* might get some play, but if it does, White will be branded a kook forever. Just doing *WDYTYF* and letting it stand alone would have made for a nice little backstory to any write-ups he might get in the future—I think White has quite a career ahead of him, if only he can put Tarantino behind him and start doing original projects. If this thing gets heavy circulation, however, White will forever be "the kid who whines about Quentin Tarantino."

The original version of this article ran in *Cashiers du Cinemart* #8.

ATTENTION: ENEMY

By Mike White

"Are you an imbecile?" asked my old buddy Todd Phillips from the headquarters of the Fourth Annual New York Underground Film Festival. He was quickly joined in a conference-call berating of me by his partner, Andrew Gurland.

It was February 18, 1997, and I had just sent them a copy of my latest work, *You're Still Not Fooling Anybody*. I thought it might be fun for the boys to check it out, since *Who Do You Think You're Fooling* had been such a hit two years before.

The conversation started in a much more civil tone. Todd informed me that I was past the entry deadline and that he would be returning my check and entry fee within a few days. But then things got ugly.

Not only would they not be showing my work this year, but they said that they would never show anything of mine ever again. That's right—I'm officially banned by the New York Underground Film Festival. That was even their choice of words.

I'll attempt to relay as much information as accurately as memory allows.

Why were Todd and Andrew so mad? They felt that they had been treated unfairly by me. They felt betrayed. Didn't I have a good time when I was in New York? Didn't I get a lot of press? If so, then why did I run back to Detroit and say such nasty things about them in my little magazine?

I couldn't believe that they felt victimized by me—after they would tell me one thing and I would read something else in the papers. Why didn't they let me in on their schemes?

Or, did they even have a plan?

I had never been to a film festival before. How was I supposed to know that festival organizers will go to such great lengths to get the word out about their festival?

Obviously I was media savvy enough to make a video like *Who Do You Think You're Fooling*; why wasn't I as smart when it came to realizing that they were "playing the media" into publicizing my video and their festival?

Certainly they aren't like other festivals. They pride themselves on being different. Couldn't I figure that out? They had done so much for me. How could I be so ungrateful? How could I write such libelous things in my magazine? Granted, it doesn't have a big circulation, but saying those things hurt the festival. It hurt Todd and Andrew.

Being media savvy themselves, you would think that Phillips and Gurland might have seen that my take on the events that transpired is my own way of "playing the media." I never lied or exaggerated about what happened during this period. I presented the facts the way I saw them. The NYUFF is an institution, and they have to realize that it's fair game. And, like I always say, bad press is better than no press!

Phillips, Gurland, and I talked for a good twenty minutes. They so wished that I had talked to them about any misunderstandings while they were occurring, instead of printing such spiteful untruths. A phone call, an email, a letter…anything. How could I be so mean? So ungrateful?

To be honest, by the end of the conversation, things seemed to be smoothed over. I had thought that all the bad blood between us had passed. Not only was I not banned from this year's festival, they might even show *You're Still Not Fooling Anybody*!

But then…

On March 3rd, I got a package from the fellas. It was my tape, my check, and my press materials. No note. No letter. Just a plain manila envelope addressed to me, and sent to the attention of "ENEMY."

The original version of this article ran in *Cashiers du Cinemart* #8.

TARANTINO IN A CAN

By Mike Thompson and Mike White

The bathroom motif runs throughout Quentin Tarantino's oeuvre. In the first thirty minutes of *Reservoir Dogs*, Mr. Pink says, "Where's the commode in this dungeon? I gotta take a squirt." A word not in the common vernacular, "commode," makes its appearance again later with one of the biggest scenes of the whole damn film, where Mr. Orange is in the toilet of a train station in a bullshit story he's telling to crime boss Joe Cabot. The whole thing is a ruse used by at least one other undercover cop, and it's called The Commode Story.

Moving on to *True Romance*, where is it that Clarence confers with the spirit of Elvis? Why, the place where E met his demise, of course—the bathroom. This happens twice in the film, the first time E aids the decision to put Drexl down like a dog, and the other will remind one of *Pulp Fiction*, in the way our protagonist is missing all of the shit outside while he's taking a piss inside.

When Clarence has to find a quick change of scenery he calls his old pal Dick Richie, who is, naturally, sitting on the toilet when Clarence's call arrives. And when does that firecracker Alabama finally take her stand after getting the shit knocked out of her in her hotel room? Only after the Madsenish thug makes the mistake of throwing her into the bathroom.

The first time we go to the bathroom with anyone in *Pulp Fiction*, we go with Mia. Here, in the can, she snorts coke, a sign of the impending doom for herself and Vincent Vega.

Vincent (John Travolta) and Jules (Samuel L. Jackson) in *Pulp Fiction*

Butch and Fabian have one of the longest scenes together in the bathroom right after they shower together. It even seems to Butch that Fabian has spent all night there, brushing her teeth.

Jules and Vincent wash their hands in Jimmy's bathroom. Could it have been the kitchen, or even outside with the hose? Not with Tarantino behind the typewriter.

Vincent Vega's life would be much better (and longer) if he could just avoid using the toilet. He almost gets wasted by the kid with the "cannon" who hides in the bathroom (but, luckily, a miracle occurs). If he never had gone to "take a piss" and talk to himself, Mia wouldn't have ODed. He would have been around to handle Pumpkin and Honeybunny in their restaurant heist, and he would have avoided his own death if he hadn't been reading *Modesty Blaise* in Butch's bathroom.

Okay, we can't find any toilet scenes in *Natural Born Killers*, but it's probably due to the lack of one that makes Tarantino call *NBK* his least favorite script.

Roger Avery must have been paying attention to his pal's writing style—but who's not to say that Avery didn't conceive of all the aforementioned scenes [uncredited, of course]—for the bathroom rears its ugly head at least twice that we can think of without even trying—Eric Stoltz makes a big deal out of showering, and there is that bizarre sex scene during the overly long trippy act one that happens in the men's room in *Killing Zoe*.

Damn! That's a lot of bathrooms! We could get really deep and explore the implications of Yolanda's "I gotta go pee" line, but we'll leave that to someone more qualified. Instead we'll ask, "Why?" It's a theory that it is a combination of Barry Levinson's *Tin Men* and Monte Hellman's *Flight to Fury*.

In *Tin Men*, a character observes that no one in the TV show *Bonanza* (pop culture reference) ever goes to the bathroom. So Tarantino thinks to himself, "Hey! He's right! When I make a movie I'm definitely going to show someone in the bathroom." It looks like QT really outdid himself with *Pulp Fiction*. Monte Hellman is the seldom-mentioned producer of *Reservoir Dogs*. And if experience has taught us anything, it's that if Tarantino doesn't mention something, he's probably plagiarizing it. Okay, QT did write a big article on Hellman's *Ride in the Whirlwind* in *Sight and Sound* of February 1993, but we think he was influenced more by *Flight to Fury*.

In this film, all of the major characters are involved in an airplane crash. When the airplane has engine trouble, however, there is no obligatory shot of smoke pouring out of the propeller. Instead, the camera has followed an elderly Japanese gentleman (who has been a completely minor character and has not had one line in English) into the bathroom when suddenly the camera, the set, and the man begin to flail about, *Star Trek*-style, as the plane's engines begin to fail. It is strikingly effective, original, and even rather unusual, and we do believe it was influential to the overuse of the potty in *Pulp Fiction*.

The original version of this article ran in *Cashiers du Cinemart #2*.

feature articles

THE *CASHIERS DU CINEMART* MANIFESTO

By Mike White and Mike Thompson

Over a century before the motion picture camera was invented, the illusion of motion through still pictures was implemented in a myriad of tools with a central motivating factor: entertainment. Certainly, persistence of vision, the idea that the retina maintains an imprint of a still image, which can be connected smoothly to another still image to give the impression of motion between the two, has its roots in scientific study. Indeed, the first primitive films, from the equine experiments of Muybridge to the *actualities* of the Lumiere brothers, were rooted in the realm of study and exact representation, rather than storytelling.

However, the idle fancies of the magic lantern, zoetrope, thaumatrope, etc., quickly became fodder for film in its earliest form. The fantastic found the fancy of the public and displaced the realistic works of pioneer documentary filmmakers. The cinema has since been the playground of the public, who demanded narratives instead of naturalism.

Just as the mind connected eighteen to twenty-odd still frames into flowing movement, the work of Lev Kuleshov proved that audiences were motivated to connect disparate images and interpret them psychologically. One of Kuleshov's more famous experiments involved a shot of a man with a neutral look on his face, followed by a shot of another object. If the second object was a bowl of food, the audience, when questioned, remarked that the man looked hungry. If the second image were a dead woman in a coffin, then the man was said to look sad over the loss of his wife. Thus, montage was made possible through the audience's will to accept images and explain their connection.

The Kuleshov effect sounds rather rudimentary. But without the internal drive to find meaning and some semblance of order when presented with two different shots, the language of cinema would not exist. Tools such as close-ups, long shots, and cross-cutting were the result of an ever-increasing sophistication of both filmmakers and viewers, who evolved from the one long-shot film to the seamless "Hollywood-style" montage with relative ease. The audience comprehends that when an actor climbs a flight of stairs, the action can be fragmented, showing the actor walking up the first two steps and then cutting to the actor reaching the second floor landing. Not every step need be shown, as the mind invents the missing material.

Certainly, there have been those who have attempted to subvert the traditional Hollywood style of narrative and montage with varying degrees of success. And perhaps those plucky upstarts have laid the groundwork for the coming era.

If the viewer's retina can maintain positive after-images long enough to make still frames move, and if the viewer's mind can connect two shots into a cause–effect relationship, then certainly, after a century of cinema, viewers are prepared to evolve further in their understanding of film.

Faithful readers of *Cashiers du Cinemart*, we are proud to present a theory that shall rock the world of cinema to its basest foundations: The Persistence of Plot.

After one hundred years of formulaic genre films, audiences should be able to accept new films wherein the elements of a story are present, but it is up to the mind of the viewer to imply events that connect them. Filmmakers of the world, rejoice! You can cease patronizing the audience and allow for apparently simpler storylines, which viewers shall expand upon. Gone are the tedious days of character development and plot! These are the salad days of stock characters placed in pat situations told in episodic glimpses with which the viewer will be so familiar, all connective material will be conceived so fully as to give the illusion of a complete, thought-out film. Why bother wasting any more time with window dressing?

Reborn is the cinema into a new age of common motifs and tired plot points, such as the Now-It's-Personal device, in which the main character has been set on a path that he or she is reluctantly following for little or no reason, until someone close to them (best friend, spouse, sibling, parent, dog) is kidnapped, injured, or murdered. The Now-It's-Personal device becomes the motivating factor for the protagonist to fully engage in the task at hand. With the Persistence of Plot, the Now-It's-Personal can be presented at the beginning of the film, and the audience can decide the significance of the event and the proceeding two-thirds of the film. The Persistence of Plot heralds the end to long running times, as films can now be told in their most base elements.

As an example of the Persistence of Plot in action we offer the film *Dragonheart*, which has an overtly straightforward story of a knight, a friendly dragon, and a boy of unspeakable evil. With these elements, one can already put the plot together. Even an inexperienced cinemagoer knows that the knight and dragon will become friends, that the ultimate evil must be destroyed, and that the dragon must die. How does one know all of this? Because of the Persistence of Plot. Different actors, setting, and animals/fantasy creatures—but the plotline remains true to form.

Dragonheart is one of myriad films that embrace and relish in the Persistence of Plot. Characters are never defined, scenes never connect, and yet the film still reaches its inevitable conclusion. Never does one worry, hope, or panic that because the story isn't coming together, it won't have the expected ending. The mind has filled in the blanks, made the connection, retained not only the images upon the film's frames, but the point of the scene, carrying it to the next. The Persistence of Plot dictates that the director must simply show a clear line of implied plot, and the audience will know the rest of the formulaic storyline.

One cynical *CdC* staffer has gone so far as to suggest that the Persistence of Plot is actually well known in Hollywood, and is an insidious device used between the studios in conjunction with suppliers of refreshments. As we have shown, it's no longer necessary to watch every scene of a film, which leaves product placement more immediate. By allowing the audience the opportunity to divine the rest of the film, they won't worry about missing the next scene if they happen to want a concession item. The best example of this is Jan DeBont's *Twister*. Anybody want a Pepsi?

What's the next step? Where will Persistence of Plot take us? Oversized budgets, terrible writing, short attention spans, and home theater systems dictate that soon, trailers will take the place of feature-length films. Looking at current previews, we're well on this path. These tell-all trailers border on being five minutes in length and allow us to implement the Persistence of Plot to rearrange all the story elements into a clear linear narrative, leaving nothing left to the imagination and no plot twist untold. Fear not, cinephiles, we predict that "feature-length" films will still exist in the form of half-hour specials similar to HBO's "First Look" series, and shall be known as "Directors Cuts."

Viva La Cinema Nouvelle!

The original version of this article ran in *Cashiers du Cinemart* #8.

Cover of *The Wounded and the Slain*, Hard Case Crime edition, copyright ©2007; painting by Glen Orbik; reproduced by permission of Winterfall LLC

THE SERIOUS MOONLIGHT: THE CINEMATIC WORLD OF DAVID GOODIS

By Mike White

Living in a David Goodis world isn't easy. Consisting of losers, dropouts, and has-beens, everyone is a sad victim of circumstance. They are victims of urban angst, paranoia, and alienation. Often without a friend in the world, the only semi-stable family relationships are found among criminals, where there's always the danger of an Oedipal explosion or incestuous liaison.

His Sisyphean protagonists either start off poor or they take a hard fall from grace. Regardless, they always end up on the wrong side of the tracks, face down in the gutter. Those who fall may have it worse than those who live perpetually in poverty, for they have had a taste of the good life before it was wrenched away. More often than not, these sad souls find themselves in Philadelphia.

Lauren Bacall and Humphrey Bogart buddy up to *Dark Passage* scribe David Goodis

The life of David Goodis (1917–1967) followed the same trajectory as his main characters in *Down There* and *Street of No Return*. In these novels, a pianist and singer, respectively, have a meteoric rise to fame and spectacular swan dive into obscurity. After a rocky start with the widely panned *Retreat From Oblivion*, Goodis stuck to the pulps for a while, churning out countless stories for magazines such as *Flying Aces*, *Man Hunt*, *Dime Sports*, and *Sinister Stories*. He caught his big break in 1946 with the publishing of *Dark Passage* as a serial in the *Saturday Evening Post*. This garnered him an invitation to Hollywood, where he penned several treatments, helped with an adaptation of W. Somerset Maugham's play *The Letter*, and adapted *Dark Passage* for the silver screen.

David Goodis wasn't made for the Hollywood life. After working on several more screenplays that never saw the light of day (and seem to have disappeared from the face of the Earth), Warner Brothers ended their relationship with the author. He packed his bags and returned to Philadelphia and to the pulps, churning out novels for publishers like Appleton-Century, Lion, and Gold Medal. Between 1947 and 1957, Goodis had an incredible fifteen books published.

A biography of David Goodis guarantees more questions than answers. There are major milestones, but the grout between is rife with allegations, assumptions, and ribald rumors. He was a mystery to all those around him. Did he run away from Hollywood to escape the clutches of his overbearing first wife, or did he feel obligated to his brother, Herbert (said to be retarded in some accounts and schizophrenic in others)? Did he prowl the ghetto bars and nightclubs in Los Angeles and Philadelphia looking for large African-American women to abuse him verbally and physically? Did the bizarre family relationships of his characters reflect the dynamic of his home life?

When families weren't criminals (*Down There*), criminals often resembled families (*The Burglar, Black Friday, Somebody's Done For, Street of No Return*), with an older criminal mastermind ("father"), a blowzy, brassy gal whose shoes overflow with the fat from her calves and whose bosom threatens to burst out of her low-cut blouse ("mother"), and a ham-fisted lummox ("brother"). The most intriguing "family" member was the mousy gal who invariably captures our protagonist's heart (if not, at least, his attention). She should be considered the "sister." And, from there, our hero acts out a quasi-Oedipal scenario. He often sleeps with the mother figure while really wanting the sister. To get her affection, it may be necessary to eliminate the father.

Was the time spent living back with his parents just too much? Was it this closeness that caused Goodis to crack up and pass away a mere six months after his mother died? Again, we have many more questions than answers.

During the last decade of his life, the spark seemed to disappear from Goodis. There was a dearth of books being published: *Night Squad* in 1961, and *Somebody's Done For* published after Goodis' demise on January 7, 1967. The opening of *Somebody's Done For* (also known as *Raving Beauty*) finds the main character lost at sea and in danger of drowning. This is one of Goodis's common themes, with protagonists drowning (or nearly doing so) in *The Burglar* and *The Wounded and The Slain*. Meanwhile, many of his characters could be seen as drowning themselves in alcohol (*Street of No Return, Fire in the Flesh, The Wounded and The Slain*) and all of them are adrift, hoping for purchase.

Retreat into Obscurity

While Goodis toiled in his little room at 6305 N. 11th Street in Philadelphia, filmmakers mined his ever-increasing wealth of material. *Of Missing Persons* was made in Argentina and *Nightfall* in Hollywood. Warner Brothers' television division used one of his stories for an episode of their *Bourbon Street Beat* series, and Goodis adapted a Henry Kane story for *The Alfred Hitchcock Hour*. The closest Goodis came to reigniting his Hollywood flame came in 1957, with the film adaptation of *The Burglar*. Shot in the streets of Philadelphia by his friend Paul Wendkos, Goodis helped write the screenplay based on his own work for this inventive film noir. Delayed after completion and overlooked upon release, *The Burglar* didn't fulfill the promise of a Wendkos/Goodis creative partnership.

Goodis may have labored in the penumbra of obscurity in the United States, but his existential and essentially bleak portrayal of the empty American dream caught the attention of European intellectuals in general and the French Nouvelle Vague in particular. In 1960, *Cahiers du Cinema* writer-turned-director Francois Truffaut brought Goodis's *Down There* to the cinema as *Shoot the Piano Player*. This lauded film was the first entry in the European appreciation of Goodis. Even as Goodis's novels quickly went out of print in his native country, they would remain available in French and British editions throughout the years.

Of Goodis's nineteen novels, ten of them have thus far been adapted for the silver screen—one of them, *The Burglar*, has been adapted twice. His story "The Professional Man" was adapted for television for both HBO (*The Edge*) and Showtime (*Fallen Angels*). Also, the ABC series *The Fugitive* was based on one of the author's early novels, *Dark Passage* (a heated court case upheld this claim after Goodis's demise).

David Goodis in Hollywood

Too often, the films based on Goodis's work fail because they're too concerned with crime. Even in a book like *The Burglar*, the heist is secondary. Sometimes there are some larcenous activities, but there are few crimes to be found in a Goodis book. Likewise, without the constant paranoid narrative voice that slides from third person to second to first and back again, it's difficult to identify with the tortured Goodis protagonist. Utilizing voiceover narration, *Shoot the Piano Player* and *Street of No Return* come closest to capturing the Goodis voice. By not showing Vincent Parry's face for the first act of *Dark Passage*, and by reading aloud the writing of Alan Kolber in *Descent into Hell*, the audience is given insight through other means.

Goodis on Film

Dark Passage *(Delmer Daves, 1947)*
Dark Passage *(Messner, 1946)*

Wrongly convicted of murdering his wife, when Vincent Parry (Humphrey Bogart) escapes from San Quentin, he acquires a new face and new hope for the future. The use of a semi-subjective camera in the opening act was utilized far more effectively here than it had been months earlier in Robert Montgomery's *Lady in the Lake*. In *Dark Passage*, the first-person Parry point of view is intercut with shots of the protagonist in shadows, keeping his face a secret until his bandages come off.

Unfortunately, in a David Goodis world, there is little to no redemption. Even with help from the lovely Irene Jansen (Lauren Bacall), Parry remains plagued by the pesky Madge Rapf (Agnes Moorehead). Moreover, Parry is set upon by new foes, all the while living in paranoia.

The most faithful to both plot and tone, Delmer Daves's adaptation of Goodis's second novel is an overlooked gem in the film noir pantheon. Not as popular as other Bogart/Bacall vehicles such as *Key Largo*, *To Have and Have Not*, or *The Big Sleep*, *Dark Passage* is a terrific star vehicle for the classic Hollywood couple.

The Unfaithful *(Vincent Sherman, 1947)*

Adapted from the short story (and later play) by W. Somerset Maugham, *The Letter* has been popular fodder for films and television, appearing no fewer than six times on screen. The screenplay by Goodis and James Gunn (*Affair in Trinidad*) lacks both Maugham's name in the credits and the author's titular letter. Rather, it's a sculpture that busts Christine Hunter (Ann Sheridan) when she claims to have never met the dead man in her living room.

A dark melodrama with a wholly hollow happy ending, Vincent Sherman's film nevertheless provided a promising first foray in Goodis's brief screenwriting career.

Of Missing Persons/Seccion Desparaecidos *(Pierre Chenal, Argentina, 1956)*
Of Missing Persons *(Morrow, 1950)*

Originally an unproduced screenplay, Goodis turned his work into one of his oddest novels. *Of Missing Persons* takes place primarily in the Los Angeles Missing Persons Bureau, led by Captain Paul Ballard. Taking his job far too seriously, Ballard fights to save his department and his reputation, after becoming the target of smear journalists who question all of the unsolved missing persons cases, especially that of Myra Nichols. Convinced that her husband—reported dead by Ballard—is alive and well, Myra goes to the media to complain, setting off a series of events that include vicious office politics and the framing of Jean Landis, Myra's one-time nurse and the object of John Nichols's affection.

The majority of this book takes place in Ballard's office, which would make for a fairly dull film. Luckily, screenwriters Agustín Cuzzani, Domingo Di Núbila, and Pierre Chenal (who also directed) took the action out of the office and concentrated on the Nichols case.

Seccion Desparaecidos opens with Juan Milford in the arms of Diane "Dante" Lander. The only problem is that Juan is married to Mendy Milford, a controlling shrew who holds proof of Juan's past misdeeds. In order to escape, Juan seizes the opportune death of a drunk to fake his demise. Unfortunately for him, Diane isn't quite so keen to have her lover back. She's horrified to find that Juan plans to murder his wife, and Diane is determined to stop it. Here Chenal's film intersects with Goodis's book. Mrs. Milford is murdered and Lander is set up to take a fall. To the rescue comes the shrewd Commissioner Uribe to set the record straight.

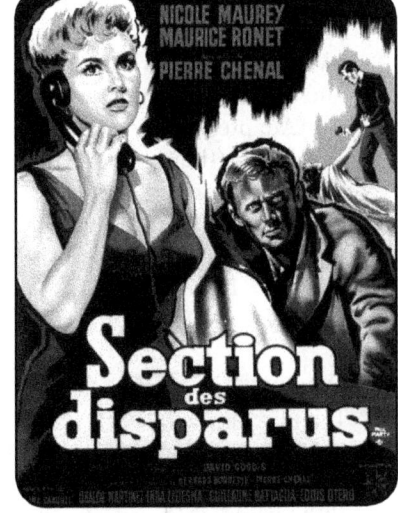

Juan Milford proves to be a troublesome character. While he neither murders his wife nor the drunk for whom he's mistaken, it wouldn't be out of character. Yet he's somehow redeemed at the end, getting his name cleared and resting in a hospital bed while Diane Lander dotes on him (much like the end of *Descent aux Enfers*). Improbable finale aside, Chenal's little movie is a tight, albeit trite, thriller.

Nightfall *(Jacques Tourneur, 1957)*
Nightfall *(Messner, 1947)*

Aldo Ray displays his infamously narrow acting range as James Vanning, a commercial artist on the run from the police for a crime he didn't commit and from the guys who actually did. They think that Vanning has the three hundred grand they liberated from a financial institution. Also on Vanning's case is insurance investigator Ben Fraser (James Gregory). He's made something of a career of following Vanning's every move and watching him from the apartment across the way. At the end of his days he goes home to his wife (Jocelyn Brando), where he tries to make sense of Vanning's "innocent act." Little does anyone know that Vanning isn't kidding around when he says he dropped the money and can't remember where it is.

In Goodis's book, Vanning's relationship with Marie Gardner (Anne Bancroft) is more fleshed out and slightly more nebulous, as Vanning is lead to believe on two occasions that Marie is actually an agent of the nefarious John (Brian Keith), rather than a truly virtuous girl who falls for Vanning almost at first sight. On the night that Vanning and Marie meet, they're happened upon by John and his partner, Red (Rudy Bond). They end the date by taking Vanning away and working him over. In Jacques Tourneur's film, they take Vanning to some incongruous oil fields and threaten to tear his head off with one of the giant pumps. This is just one of the odd locations of the film. Known more for his other noir work, *Out of the Past*, this Tourneur film, with its great swaths of Western winter snowfields, stands as one of the most sun-drenched and airy noirs around.

Adapted by Stirling Silliphant, *Nightfall* suffers from the miscasting of Ray and Keith (they would have been better off switching roles), the addition of Vanning's hunting buddy Doc (Frank Albertson), and the expansion of Marie's background to include her life as a fashion model. Too often this take on David Goodis's second book feels like a lukewarm television drama rather than a taut film noir. If anything, *Nightfall* is most notable for being one of the few Goodis books to have a happy ending.

The Burglar *(Paul Wendkos, 1957)*
The Burglar *(Lion, 1953)*

This ninth Goodis novel is similar to *Black Friday*, if only to show the stress of close quarters on career criminals. Most of *The Burglar* takes place in the Philadelphia hideout of Nat Harbin (Dan Duryea), the leader of a quartet of criminals. Two of these characters, Baylock (Peter Capell) and Dohmer (Mickey Shaughnessy), are direct progenitors of Mattone and Rizzio of *Black Friday*. Meanwhile, Nat acts as the younger version of Charley, schooled in the art of burglary by Gerald Gladden. The final member of the group is Gladden (Jayne Mansfield), the daughter of Gerald. Nat is torn between his love of and protectiveness for Gladden. On the one hand, he wants her to leave the life of crime from whence they came; on the other, he feels wrong loving this girl who he sees as something of a sister and daughter.

The Burglar film is highly faithful to the original text. Nat suffers from an almost maniacal pledge to his lost father figure while his compatriots stew in their hideout, waiting for the heat to cool off from a jewelry heist. Hot and bothered, Nat sends Gladden to Atlantic City so he can think straight. He doesn't have much time to get his thoughts together before he's got Della (Martha Vickers) picking him up in a bar. Meanwhile, Gladden is getting some attention of her own from a bloke named Charlie (Stewart Bradley). When Nat happens upon Della chatting with Charlie, he recognizes Gladden's new boyfriend as a cop who saw him the night of the jewelry robbery. The fix is in and now it's a race against the clock to save Gladden and, if possible, keep the jewels out of the hands of the corrupt cop and his treacherous moll.

The action climaxes in Atlantic City with an ending akin to *Lady from Shanghai* and *Strangers on a Train*. Though less nihilistic than the book, *The Burglar* stays true to Goodis's work throughout. This is in stark contrast to Vahé Katcha and Henri Verneuil's version of the same story in *Le Casse*.

Paul Wendkos's *The Burglar* was shot in Philadelphia in 1955, but went unreleased until 1957. The film may never have seen the light of day, if not for the newfound popularity of starlet Jayne Mansfield (*The Girl Can't Help It, Will Success Spoil Rock Hunter?*). Still unofficially released on home video, *The Burglar* can be counted among the highly stylized later entries in the film noir canon, including *House of Bamboo, Touch of Evil,* and *Blast of Silence.*

Shoot the Piano Player/Tirez Sur le Pianiste *(Francois Truffaut, 1960)*
Down There *(Gold Medal, 1956)*

One of the most popular films based on Goodis's work, *Shoot the Piano Player* is wedged nicely between Nouvelle Vague director Francois Truffaut's most noted works, *The 400 Blows* and *Jules and Jim*. Demonstrating an immense love for Goodis's prose, Truffaut and co-writer Marcel Moussy perfectly capture the tone and plot of *Down There*, the sixteenth Goodis novel. There's even a bit of dialogue cleverly lifted from *Nightfall*.

Charles Aznavour stars as Charlie Kohler, a slight man with a sardonic smile who ekes out his meek living banging the ivories at a beer hall. His lowbrow routine is disturbed by the unexpected appearance of Chico (Albert Rémy), his brother. In another life, Charlie was known as Edouard Saroyan—back then, he tinkled the keys in concert halls as a famous pianist. Chico and Charlie's other sibling, Richard (Jean-Jacques Aslanian), are bad seeds. As wild as Eduoard was refined, the reappearance of Chico brings with it bad memories—as well as two thugs, Ernest (Daniel Boulanger) and Momo (Claude Mansard).

Cut from the same cloth that would later be used to fashion Jules and Vincent from *Pulp Fiction*, Ernest and Momo bicker like a married couple when not discussing the finer points of women's undergarments. They add a wonderfully absurdist touch to the otherwise nihilistic proceedings. Charlie enters into a relationship with a waitress, Lena (Marie Dubois). Like the women from *Nightfall* and *Dark Passage*, Lena turns out to be a fan of Charlie's, and even has an old Eduoard Saroyan advertisement in her apartment. She knew him before his fall from grace and loves him, even as the man he is now.

We don't learn of Charlie's life as Edouard until a half hour into the film, when the audience is given a fifteen-minute flashback of his life with his wife, Therese (Nicole Berger), and his rise to fame. Rather than betraying Edouard, Therese ultimately betrays herself by sleeping with his manager in order to get her husband the access to concert halls he desperately deserves. After her defenestration, Edouard gave up his fame and became a shell of a man as Charlie. Just when it seems that Lena may be able to give him back his humanity, he accidentally murders a fellow employee and takes to the hills, back to his family's farm in the wilds of New Jersey (or the French equivalent thereof). Like *Nightfall*, the film culminates in the bleak whiteness of a snowy landscape, anticipating the blanc neo-noir of the Coen Brothers's *Fargo*.

Typical of French New Wave films, Truffaut employs a variety of filmic techniques meant to call attention to themselves, such as irising out of scenes, superimposed images, and even a bit of karaoke subtitling during a performance of "Framboise" by Boby Lapointe. The only bit that rings false in the film is the addition of another Saroyan; a younger sibling, Fido (Richard Kanayan). This superfluous character adds nothing of value to the storyline and merely gets in the way. Luckily, his small amount of screen time doesn't detract from the overall effectiveness of Truffaut's film.

The Burglars/Le Casse *(Henri Verneuil, France, 1971)*
The Burglar *(Lion, 1953)*

Directed by Henri Verneuil, this film pales in comparison to his previous work, *The Sicilian Clan*. Starting off promisingly with a long opening robbery that's nearly free of dialogue (similar to the robbery scene of Jules Dassin's *Rififi* [1955]), the movie quickly turns into a cat-and-mouse game between protagonist Azad (Jean-Paul Belmondo) and dirty cop Abel (Omar Sharif). Azad's crew is barely a blip on this film's radar, and the same can be said of Azad's femme fatale, Lena (Dyan Cannon). The rest of the film consists of a few spectacular set pieces (including a car chase that makes those in *Bullitt* and *Ronin* look tame) and countless setups by Abel to get millions of dollars worth of emeralds away from Azad.

The scenes between Belmondo and Sharif work terrifically well—especially when they have a showdown over Greek food—but they're too few and far between to redeem the movie as a whole. Even when set to a score by Ennio Morricone, *The Burglars* doesn't succeed as either an effective Goodis adaptation or heist film.

And Hope to Die/La Course du Lievre a Travers les Champs *(Rene Clement, France, 1972)*
Black Friday *(Lion, 1954)*

A loose adaptation, *And Hope to Die* merely follows a few touch points of Goodis's twelfth book, *Black Friday*. The original French title of Rene Clement's *La Course du Lievre a Travers les Champs* roughly translates as "Chasing a rabbit through the fields," recalling the pursuit of the white rabbit by Alice in Lewis Carroll's *Through the Looking Glass*. Clement begins the film with a quote from Carroll, "We are but older children dear, who fret to find our bedtime near," and often draws parallels between the film's gangsters and children (as Truffaut also did in *Shoot the Piano Player* in the scenes with Ernest, Momo, and Fido).

Jean-Louis Trintignant stars as Tony (referred to by the group as "Froggy," due to his French heritage), who runs from one band of thieves to another. He lies to the second group, telling them that he was running from the cops after shooting a police officer. After seeing one of the group killed and helping to off another of them, he still manages to ingratiate himself enough to earn the trust of their leader (and obvious father figure), Charley Ellis (Robert Ryan). Accompanied by the faithful Rizzio (Jean Gaven) and Mattone (Aldo Ray, in his second Goodis film), the group executes an elaborate kidnapping caper whose only flaw is the apparent suicide of its planned victim, the oddly named Toboggan.

In *Black Friday*, the caper is a botched robbery. Most of the book takes place at the gang's hideout and explores the relationships between the gangsters. Despite killing her brother, there's chemistry to be found between our main character (here named Hart) and the Pepper character. There's also a strange and strained triangle between Charley, Hart, and Sugar. Here Sugar is more than a handful—both in size and in sexual appetite. Charley is unable to provide what Sugar needs, and has always encouraged her to seek satisfaction outside of their relationship. It isn't until she meets Hart that she finally does.

Sugar is the only person who figures Hart for what he really is. He's not a murderer. He's on the lam because he killed his brother. Not for money, like the police think, but because his brother was suffering from multiple sclerosis. This exemplifies the complexity of the characters in *Black Friday*. Again, rather than flesh out these characters, screenwriter Sébastien Japrisot treats them as children. Meanwhile, Rene Clement directs them like a low-grade Sergio Leone (complete with pan flute on the soundtrack). This results in an unremarkable heist film.

The Moon in the Gutter/Lune Dans le Caniveau, La
(Jean-Jacques Beineix, France, 1983)
The Moon in the Gutter *(Gold Medal, 1953)*

Every night, Gerard Delmas (Gerard Depardieu) stands transfixed at the mouth of an alleyway. There, illuminated only by the moonlight, he can make out the accusing bloodstains left by his sister Catherine (Katya Berger), who took her own life with a rusty razor after being violated. Catherine was too good for the world into which she was born—a slum where the only means of escape seem to be via booze or death.

Gerard obsesses about his sister while keeping an eye on his drunken brother, Frank (Dominique Pinon), and fending off the advances of insanely jealous Bella (Victoria Abril). A billboard outside his hovel declares "TRY ANOTHER WORLD." The other world to which Gerard aspires is the elusive "uptown." His keys to the kingdom come in the form of Loretta Channing (Nastassja Kinski). Driving down to the slums in her MG, Loretta acts as guardian to her drunken brother, Newton (Vittorio Mezzogiorno).

Is Loretta just slumming, or does she love Gerard? Will Gerard ever fit in uptown? Is Newton responsible for Catherine's death, or is it her brother, Frank? *The Moon in the Gutter* is filled with these questions, while brimming with overwrought music and sensual images. Beineix and screenwriter Olivier Mergault succeed in capturing the tone of Goodis's tenth novel. However, *The Moon in the Gutter* doesn't have much plot. Rather than being a murder mystery about Catherine's rape, the film and book are more of a moody piece, wherein the slum in which Delmas lives is second only to Delmas himself.

This was the second time Beineix worked on a Goodis-based project. A decade before directing *The Moon in the Gutter*, he served as assistant director on Rene Clement's adaptation of *Black Friday*.

Savage Street/Rue Barbare *(Gilles Béhat, France, 1984)*
Street of the Lost *(Gold Medal, 1952)*

Both *The Moon in the Gutter* and *Street of the Lost* revolve around streets with a viselike grip on their slum-bound inhabitants. While Gerard of *The Moon in the Gutter* may attempt, albeit briefly, to escape the gutter and the memories of his sister's suicide, the main character of *Savage Street*, Chet (Bernard Giraudeau), simply wants to be left alone. "I stick my neck out for nobody," is his Rick Blaine-like philosophy. He works hard to be noncommittal, promising to never get involved in the problems of others. However, one night he finally heeds the cries of an innocent girl who has just been raped.

In this crime-riddled world, Chet makes himself a target of Hagen (Bernard-Pierre Donnadieu), the slimy underworld boss who victimized the girl. It was also Hagen and his gang of lowlifes who used to sexually abuse Edie (Corinne Dacla), Chet's wife. To say that Edie is unbalanced is an understatement. She fits right in with Chet's off-kilter family, which includes his sister-in-law, who appears to be bedding both her husband, Rocky (Jean-Pierre Kalfon), and Rocky's father (Michel Auclair). Rather than love, Chet feels obligated to Edie, playing the role of her protector. The real object of his affection (though he won't admit it), Manu (Christine Boisson), works at the factory club that doubles as Hagen's base of operations.

Chet hopes to keep the peace. "I got no intention to butt into anyone's business," he says. When he doesn't react to Hagen's gruesome description of how he raped the young girl Chet helped, Hagen beats him to a pulp. Chet takes the beating, begging Hagen for mercy. Yes, it takes quite a lot to get Chet's goat. It isn't until Hagen sends his knife-wielding lackey to knock him off that Chet finally gets mad enough to take Hagen down.

Despite the glossy neon-lit sets, Chet's blow-dried hair, terrible synthesizer score, and cheesy kickboxing finale, *Savage Street* is actually a fairly faithful

'80s rendition of Goodis's eighth novel. Adapted by director Gilles Béhat and Jean Herman, the film was released to DVD in France in 2006.

Descent into Hell/Descent aux Enfers *(Francis Girod, France, 1986)*
The Wounded and The Slain *(Gold Medal, 1955)*

One of the more faithful adaptations of Goodis's work—in spirit, if not in exactness—this French film has estranged couple Alan and Lola Colbert (Claude Brasseur and Sophie Marceau) on vacation in Haiti, hoping to escape their domestic strife. Stunningly beautiful but completely untouchable, Lola has been rendered frigid by the past that haunts her. Needless to say, this has put a considerable strain on their marriage and on Alan, who tries to drink his troubles away.

Distraught at seeing his bride flirting with another man (Hippolyte Girardot), Alan goes on a bender outside of the safety of his resort walls. Heading to the rougher area of Port-au-Prince, he finds nothing but trouble. When he's attacked for his thick wallet, Alan accidentally kills a man in self-defense. Just when it looks like he'll get away with it, he and Lola are approached by two blackmailers who have evidence of the event in their possession.

From here, things get even more complicated by innocent patsies, corrupt police officials, and double-crosses. Eventually, our couple (the wounded) is redeemed via the murder (the slain).

The tenth adaptation of Goodis's fourteenth novel, *Descent into Hell* cleverly makes the main character a writer in order to provide narration through his writing. Screenwriter Jean-Loup Dabadie also did well to move Lola's sexually scarring incident from her childhood to her teens/twenties, and to create a second blackmailer character. We see much more of Lola's character in the film, making her nearly equal to Alan. We also certainly see a lot of Sophie Marceau playing Lola, as the actress spends the majority of her screen time in the nude.

Street of No Return *(Samuel Fuller, France, 1989)*
Street of No Return *(Gold Medal, 1954)*

The pairing of Samuel Fuller and David Goodis—two American outsiders who found their appreciation in Europe—had its roots prior to Fuller's swan song. Fuller had met Goodis years before, and they discussed the race riots in New York that Fuller had covered during his days as a journalist. A similar set of riots becomes the backdrop against which Goodis's thirteenth novel is played. An effective precursor to *Down There*, *Street of No Return* begins with three drunks arguing about getting another bottle of booze on Philadelphia's skid row. When one of them, the quiet Whitey, goes off on his own, his pals assume he's off to get them some grog. Rather, Whitey embarks on a wild night during which he's accused of murdering a cop, sees his lost love, and unravels a plot involving guns, Puerto Ricans, and a criminal mastermind named Sharkey. At the end of the night, Whitey comes back to skid row to rejoin the ranks and fade back into obscurity.

Adapted by Fuller and Jacques Bral, *Street of No Return* shares the same neon-drenched aesthetic of *Savage Street* and *The Moon in the Gutter*. Here Keith Carradine stars as Michael (the Whitey character), in a dingy fright wig that makes him look like a more disheveled version of Fuller. Michael/Whitey is one of Goodis's "fall from grace" characters. He gained his fame via his golden voice. When he fell hard for Celia (Valentina Vargas), he was asked politely to leave her alone by her possessive beau, Eddie/Sharkey (Marc de Jonge). When Michael didn't back off, he was asked more persuasively by Eddie's pals Bertha (Rebecca Potok) and Meathead (Antonio Rosario). They cut his vocal cords, ending his career. He became a shell of his former self; a burned-out, desolate man. We get several flashbacks of Michael playing guitar and singing cheesy rock ballads that contrast his current state with his strained, almost comical, voice.

The Puerto Ricans of *Street of No Return* have been changed to African Americans, and Eddie's plot seems much more tenuous here, as the city politics on which he plays don't seem as heated. While Bill Duke gives a terrific performance as the frazzled Lieutenant Borel, the competition between and possible corruption of his underlings isn't at the fore, as it is in Goodis's book. The other damaging change to the Goodis work is the tacked-on happy ending.

Goodis on TV

Much more elusive than forgotten Argentinean crime melodramas, television shows can be as tangible as ether. A few Goodis TV adaptations remain unseen, including a pair for *Lux Video Theater* from 1952 ("Ceylon Treasure") and 1956 ("The Unfaithful").

Studio One *"Nightfall"* (1951)

Far more faithful in tone and plot to the Goodis book than the Jacques Tourneur film version, this hour-long drama perfectly portrays the summer heat and paranoia of "Nightfall." Sponsored by escalator manufacturer Westinghouse, this Summer Theater presentation was penned by Max Erlich and directed by John Peyser. Our hero, Vanning, is played by John McQuade, whose moody performance comes across as appropriate for a guy on the lam. His gal, Martha (Margaret Hayes), isn't an unquestioning dope but, rather, proves to be a spitfire. These two characters really take center stage, though Herbert Rudley holds his own as police Lieutenant Fraser.

The flashback of Vanning in Colorado is forgone in order to keep the story in the present-day New York. This also eliminates the rather bizarre way in which Vanning committed his accidental murder, and downplays the subsequent loss of the bank loot, which the menacing John (Norman Keats) hopes to regain. While the pace may be brusque, this three-act drama elegantly captures the essence of Goodis's original tale.

Nightfall had also been adapted for television the previous year on the CBS show *Sure as Fate*, with John McQuade as Vanning. This version has yet to be found.

False Identity *"Bourbon Street Beat" (1960)*
New Orleans shamus Cal Calhoun (Andrew Duggan) is hired by Alice Nichols (Irene Harvey) to investigate the disappearance of her husband, John (Tol Avery), a local shipping magnate. When Calhoun puts in a call to his policeman pal Sgt. Paul Ballard (Robert Colbert), he learns that the body of John Nichols was discovered just that morning. Or was it?

Adapted by W. Hermanos, this episode of the Warner Brothers-produced private eye show, *False Identity*, is based on *Of Missing Persons*. As with Goodis's book, John Nichols has faked his own death. He returns from the dead to scare his wife into a heart attack and sell his portion of his business to his partner, with the hopes of running away with his attractive secretary, Jane Landis (Lisa Gaye). She rejects the thickly bespectacled murderer, but he doesn't take no for an answer. When he tries to abduct her, Calhoun's partner, Rex Randolph (Richard Long)—a regular *deus Rex machina*—comes to the rescue.

The Alfred Hitchcock Hour *"An Out for Oscar" (1963)*
Based on the story "My Darlin' Evangeline" by Henry Kane, Goodis penned this teleplay for *The Alfred Hitchcock Hour*. Starring Larry Storch as the titular Oscar Blenny, our protagonist is a hapless banker who meets a beautiful gal, Eva Ashley (Linda Christian), at a resort casino. Oscar thinks he's her knight in shining armor, when he's actually a dope that becomes this treacherous dame's next mark. After helping Eva beat a murder rap through his earnest naïveté, Oscar thinks he's hit the jackpot when Eva requites his affection.

While Oscar makes his way up in the bank, Eva spends her days drinking. On the eve of his greatest triumph (a promotion to credit manager!), Eva's old flame and grifting partner, Bill Grant (Henry Silva), comes to call. Rather than be cuckolded, Oscar demands a divorce. Eva will grant his request in exchange for fifty grand. Here begins a series of double-crosses, a bank heist, and the eternal fall guy coming out on top.

With its shrewish female lead and eventual crime narrative, "An Out for Oscar" is closer to typical pulp noir than anything else in Goodis's oeuvre. This undoubtedly stems from the script's roots in Kane's tawdry tale. This episode of *The Alfred Hitchcock Hour* is neck deep in familiar television faces, with everyone from Larry Tate of *Bewitched* (David White) to Alfred Moneypenny from *Batman* (Alan Napier) appearing beside *F-Troop*'s bumbling Cpl. Randolph Agarn (Storch).

The Serious Moonlight: The Cinematic World of David Goodis

The Edge *"The Professional Man"* (1989)

Adapted and directed by Nicholas Kazan, this episode of the HBO series *The Edge* stars Christian Slater as a hitman-for-hire known only as "Kid." Bridget Fonda plays his strip joint waitress squeeze. When the big cheese, Paul (Dann Florek), tells him to lay off, he does—no questions asked. Slater's character knows that he doesn't deserve the love of anyone. He denies himself love and, when his gal rejects Paul, Kid's given the choice of either turning her heart or killing her. Kid chooses a third option.

Kid kills his victims intimately; he chokes them. "The strongest part of the body human body is the thumb," he says. He can crush a windpipe with his thumbs in less then eight seconds. Rather than rob the world of his lovely girl, he turns his powerful thumbs on himself. While many Goodis characters toy with the idea of suicide or simply choose to live in a hell they helped create, Kid redeems himself through his own death.

Slater plays his role with a quiet restraint unfamiliar to his other roles at the time (he'd be Jack Nicholson-ing it up in *Heathers* and *Pump up the Volume* shortly), while Florek gives one of the most balls-out performances of his career. The most awkward part of *The Edge* is Barry Sattels as "The Watcher," a kind of overdramatic Crypt Keeper for the episodes of this short-lived series. Goodis's short story "Black Pudding" was adapted for another episode of *The Edge* by *Night Moves* scribe Alan Sharp. Despite its '80s air date, no copies of this elusive show have been found.

Fallen Angels *"The Professional Man"* (1993)

Elevator operator by day, assassin by night. Brendan Fraser plays Johnny, the titular "professional man" who never misses. Adapted by Howard A. Rodman for the *Fallen Angels* Showtime series and directed by Steven Soderbergh, "The Professional Man" is a taut half-hour drama that beautifully builds its story through well-paced revelations. The story sticks close to Goodis's original short piece, with the interesting exception that the love interest, Pearl, has been changed to Paul (Bruce Ramsay).

This clever twist of exploring the Lavender Underworld turns a fine episode into a remarkable one. The original Goodis story line of Johnny's boss falling for his squeeze and, when his love isn't returned, ordering Johnny to kill his former flame takes on an entirely new level of complexity in the moon-drenched Los Angeles of the '50s.

Unbeknownst to each other, two major cable networks boasted adaptations of the same Goodis short story within four years. Later, Nicholas Kazan and Howard A. Rodman would learn that they had both adapted the same work for HBO and Showtime. A comparison of the two half-hour episodes provides a fascinating study of the creative process and how the same material can be adapted into such widely varying end results. The differences far outweigh the similarities, but the few intersections (white gloves, walks in the park, *Law and Order: Special Victims Unit* cast members) are fascinating.

Conclusion

There is still a lot of life left in Goodis's work. Shortly before this article initially went to print in 2007, Lou Boxer and Deen Kogan held the first Goodiscon in Philadelphia. The event subsequently became the broader appreciation of all things hardboiled as Noircon (noircon.com). A year later, the West Coast played host to a month of films based on Goodis's works with the Pacific Film Archive's "Streets of No Return" series, curated by gentleman scholar Steve Seid.

Edward Holub has been struggling to find funding to bring his dream project to light. An adaptation of *Cassidy's Girl*, this may move the action from Philadelphia to Holub's stomping grounds of New Orleans. Finally, Larry Withers delivers a proper documentary about the man himself with 2010's *David Goodis: To a Pulp*.

The original version of this article ran in *Cashiers du Cinemart* #15.

47年、

ロサンゼルス市内の空き地で、

頭から切断された

若い女の死体が発見された。

被害者は女優志望の女。

世界一有名な死体になった彼女を、

人はこう呼んだ——

ブライアン・デ・パルマ監督作品

ブラック・ダリア

ジェイムズ・エルロイ原作（文春文庫刊）

ジョシュ・ハートネット／スカーレット・ヨハンソン／アーロン・エッカート／ヒラリー・スワンク

配給：東宝東和株式会社　www.elgafan.com

THE BLACK DAHLIA

実話から生まれた、魂をえぐる衝撃。

Impossibly Funky

THE DARK PLACES OF JAMES ELLROY

By Mike White

I wouldn't want to find James Ellroy in my house sniffing my sister's underwear. Standing six feet, three inches tall, Ellroy's imposing stature must have made quite a sight when he broke into boudoirs for his felonious panty raids. Luckily, Ellroy gave up his life of crime after his literary career bloomed.

Born Lee Earle Ellroy in 1948, much of the writer's early life is chronicled in his autobiography *My Dark Places* (1996), as well as the documentary by Reinhard Jud, *James Ellroy: Demon Dog of American Crime Fiction* (1993). Haunted by the death of his mother, Gene, at age ten, Ellroy associated her unsolved murder with the brutal slaying of Elizabeth Short, "The Black Dahlia." Short's murder occurred on January 15, 1947—a year before Ellroy's birth—and haunted Los Angeles for decades afterwards. In Clara and Robert Kuperberg's *James Ellroy: American Dog* (2005), Ellroy says, "I did not choose to transmogrify my mother into Elizabeth Short. I simply read Jack Webb's book, *The Badge*, and Gene became Betty and Betty became Gene. I used Elizabeth Short as my narrative expositional device to feel all the horror and outrage and compassion that I did not feel on the occasion of my mother's death."

Illustration by Pat Lehrerer

The motherless lad grew up to be a drunk who graduated to speed. He'd masturbate to stroke books for hours, and even days, at a time. All the while, he claims to have harbored a dream to write novels.

Ellroy's luck began to change when he started caddying in 1975. A friend convinced him to dry out and start writing. Ellroy penned *Brown's Requiem* in 1978, and despite a rocky start, never looked back. Ellroy peppered his early works with autobiographical touches, most notably in *Brown's Requiem*, *Clandestine*, and *Silent Killer*.

These hardboiled tales demonstrated some of the themes that would become staples of Ellroy's writing. His tawdry tales are steeped in psychosexual obsession, and many of his characters have a dark secret (often incest). There's a crime that puts in motion an investigation that reveals a larger, deeper mystery. The author weaves fact, fiction, innuendo, and second-to-sixth-hand information into his tales. He directly contrasts real life, embellishes it, documents it, or omits it altogether. Ellroy introduces famous historical figures (usually Mickey Cohen, Howard Hughes, J. Edgar Hoover) to one another when they may not have ever met, or riffs about what might have gone down, throwing in his characters as witnesses.

The Dark Places of James Ellroy

After his initial novels, Ellroy began writing *L.A. Death Trip*, which was radically rewritten to create *Blood on the Moon* (1984), the first of three books to feature Detective Lloyd Hopkins. Along with *Because the Night* (1984) and *Suicide Hill* (1985), the Hopkins books have been repackaged as Ellroy's "L.A. Noir" series. "Noir" is a bit of a misnomer, as the Hopkins books are more contemporary and come off as rather staid, albeit twisted, crime novels. Ellroy continued to find his footing with *Killer on the Road* (1986—also known as *Silent Killer*), but wouldn't hit his stride until he went back to the world of post-WWII Los Angeles for *The Black Dahlia* (1987), the first entry in the "L.A. Quartet."

White Men Doing Bad Things: The Films of James Ellroy

Ellroy writes like a director: he cross-cuts the action as he builds his scenes. His descriptions are infused with cinematic quality, which makes them ripe for plundering by Tinsel Town. Early adaptations of Ellroy's work left something to be desired. The thriller *Cop* and TV adaptation for the Showtime series *Fallen Angels* were blips on the radar. It wasn't until 1997's *L.A. Confidential* that Ellroy's work was given a proper cinematic adaptation.

Most folks first heard of James Ellroy when *L.A. Confidential* came to theaters. The filmed adaptation of Ellroy's novel—his ninth book and the third entry in his "L.A. Quartet"—captivated audiences. Apart from this film, Ellroy hasn't had a great relationship with Hollywood. "I like hamburgers, but I don't take them seriously. Same goes for movies," Ellroy said about the adaptations of his work in *James Ellroy: Demon Dog of American Crime Fiction*.

After the success of *L.A. Confidential*, Hollywood clambered to cash in on the Ellroy name. Rights for Ellroy's previous works were snatched up left and right, promising something of a wet dream for fans of the hardboiled author. There was even a pilot for an *L.A. Confidential* television show.

For a while it looked like *White Jazz* (1992) would be made, based on a script by Ellroy and Chris Cleveland (*Glory Road*). Nick Nolte, John Cusack, and Uma Thurman were to go in front of cameras in 2002. Interlight, the film's production company, went so far as to release a lovely full-color prospectus, but the project has been mired in production troubles and has yet to see the light of day. Rumors started to surface a few years later that George Clooney would

The Black Dahlia

take the lead in this project, with a screenplay written by Joe and Mathew Michael Carnahan (with Joe directing).

At the time this article was written, only two additional Ellroy adaptations have successfully reached fruition: Jason Freeland's *Brown's Requiem* (1998) and Brian DePalma's *The Black Dahlia* (2006). There was also a short film from Mitch Brian called *Stay Clean* (2002), based on *Killer on the Road*, with a performance by the author. Between novels, Ellroy has penned several original screenplays, including *The Plague Season* (filmed as *Dark Blue* [2002]), *The Night Watchman* (filmed as *Street Kings* [2008]), *L.A. Sheriff's Homicide* (a pilot that airs as a TV movie in Belgium on occasion), *77*, and an adaptation of *White Heat*.

Cop *(James B. Harris, 1988)*

In mystery writing, a recurring character can be literary gold. Lloyd Hopkins was James Ellroy's attempt at mining this vein. The focus of three novels—*Blood on the Moon*, *Because the Night*, and *Suicide Hill*—Hopkins is a man on the edge; an unhinged cop on the outs with his department. Think of Hopkins as a predecessor to Bud White, down to his penchant for playing Russian roulette with suspects in the hopes of gleaning crucial information. Like White, Hopkins

James Woods in *Cop*

didn't have the greatest upbringing. Hopkins also has the same "wild hair up [his] ass about murdered women."

James Woods perfectly captures the "out-to-fucking-lunch" Hopkins, while Lesley Anne Warren wonderfully conveys the goofy romanticism of Kathy McCarthy. The narrative relies heavily on some odd coincidences, in that Hopkins happens upon the object of a killer's affection (Kathy), and that they all grew up in the same neighborhood. There's also a strong strain of homophobia that runs through the film, with any and all gay or bisexual characters being deceitful, if not completely murderous.

Written and directed by James B. Harris (*Fast Walking*), *Cop* stays faithful to the Hopkins narrative from the source material. The film's flaw stems from the absence of an antagonist. While there's a killer lurking in the shadows, he's unseen. The audience only knows as much as Hopkins, which plays as an interesting twist on the genre but ultimately fails. Viewers are never made privy to the killer's motivations or inner-workings. He's simply a faceless force leaving corpses in his wake. Moreover, the film ends abruptly, with no sense of closure.

The Dark Places of James Ellroy

L.A. Confidential *(Curtis Hanson, 1997)*

Writer/director Curtis Hanson and screenwriter Brian Helgeland fashioned a remarkable film that feels like great literature. Where too many films falter under the weight of two protagonists (even most modern ensemble pieces eventually focus on one character), *L.A. Confidential* skillfully balances three fully realized protagonists and several well-developed supporting characters.

Think of *L.A. Confidential* as the Rosetta Stone of Ellroy films. Detective Lieutenant Ed Exley (Guy Pearce), Detective Sergeant Jack Vincennes (Kevin Spacey), and Officer Wendell "Bud" White (Russell Crowe) are three Los Angeles police officers who become mired in the corruption that seethes under the surface of the City of Angels. Mobsters, prostitutes, scandals, sexual obsession, and murder loom as large as the Hollywood sign in the background of our protagonists' lives. The story mixes Hollywood fact with hardboiled fiction while exemplifying other staples of the author's work, such as the dark secret that haunts someone's past, along with two or more seemingly unrelated mysteries being incongruously linked. ("You help me with mine; I'll help you with yours. Deal?")

Exley and Vincennes have clouded visions of justice, which slowly come into focus as they unravel the details of the Nite Owl diner massacre. ("It's supposed to be about justice. Then somewhere along the way, I lost sight of that.") Meanwhile, Bud White has to reassess his own myopic version of right and wrong, adjusting his allegiances while maintaining a strict personal code. ("How's it going to look in your report?" "It'll look like justice. That's what the man got.")

Russell Crowe and Guy Pearce in *L.A. Confidential*

The adaptation of *L.A. Confidential* (1990) stands as one of those rare instances where there are major differences between a novel and film, but neither suffers due to this. Rather, novel and film are both triumphant works that stand on their own as mutually exclusive masterpieces.

Brown's Requiem *(Jason Freeland, 1998)*

This film defies you to pay attention to it. As boring as *L.A. Confidential* is riveting, *Brown's Requiem* is a languorous, laborious film that fails to entertain despite its remarkable cast, with everyone from Michael Rooker as protagonist Fritz Brown, to female lead Selma Blair, to a host of minor characters played by the likes of Brad Dourif, Brion James, and Tobin Bell.

Golf, sexual obsession, and dark family secrets are in abundance in *Brown's Requiem*. Writer/director Jason Freeland (*Garden Party*) sets the action in modern-day California, turning the Club Mecca firebombing of 1957 into a Molotov attack of a club owned by Sol Kupferman (Harold Gould). Against this late-nineties setting, the Ellroy dialogue (chunks of it taken verbatim) strikes a sour note. It's not too often that one hears "shitbird" thrown around, except in an Ellroy work. This "hardboiled dialogue in a modern setting" may (or may not) have played in Rian Johnson's *Brick* (2005), but it definitely fails here. While *Brown's Requiem* tries hard to be neo-noir, with its voiceover narration and winding plot, the film simply feels like an insincere aping of better works.

Dark Blue *(Ron Shelton, 2002)*

Originally set against the Watts Riots of 1965, *The Plague Season* was updated to play off the Los Angeles riots of 1992, at the behest of producer Caldecot Chubb. This contemporizing of Ellroy's original screenplay does little to make the dialogue feel realistic ("shitbird" is uttered again), but does well to telegraph the tense situation during the Rodney King trial. One good riot deserves another, and Ellroy enjoys dumping his characters into the middle of a full-scale urban war. The author did the same with his protagonists in *The Black Dahlia*, when he utilized the Zoot Suit Riots of 1943.

Rewritten by David Ayer, *Dark Blue* maintains a strong Ellroy feel in its tale of white men doing bad things. Kurt Russell stars as Eldon Perry, a strong-arming third generation policeman with a skewed morality and an unhealthy loyalty to his father's partner, Jack Van Meer (Brendan Gleeson). Through blackmail, intimidation, and murder, Van Meer uses his position in the L.A.P.D. to build his bank account and cement his position of power. When two of Van Meer's "pets" go awry and murder several innocent bystanders at the Jack O'Hearts convenience store, Perry and his young partner, Bobby Keough (Scott Speedman), are put on the case.

"Your job is not to think," Van Meer sneers at Perry after he and Keough get too close to solving the Jack O'Hearts case. Perry takes the hint and brings the heat down on two other criminals, rather than questioning Van Meer. "We're in the 'getting shit done' business," Perry tells Keough. This dynamic recalls Bud White (Russell Crowe) and his blind dedication to Dudley Smith (James Cromwell) while investigating the Nite Owl murders. *Dark Blue* feels like *L.A. Confidential*, if White and Exley had been partners and Exley was a completely weak, ineffective character.

On the outskirts of the proceedings is Arthur Holland (Ving Rhames), who aims to be the first black police chief of the L.A.P.D. He maneuvers through deadly political waters, hoping to bring credibility back to the force. Unfortunately, Holland comes across more as a conniving opportunist willing to "play the race card" than any kind of honest civil servant wanting to end the corruption that plagues his beloved Los Angeles. This makes for a troubling addition to a film where race is already a hot button and where blacks are portrayed as bloodthirsty animals during the post-Rodney King verdict riots.

Kurt Russell carries the film on his seasoned shoulders, playing a truly fascinating and dynamic character. He's like a sympathetic version of Alonzo (Denzel Washington) of *Training Day* or Jim Luther Davis (Christian Bale) of *Harsh Times* (both films also penned by David Ayer). If not for Russell, the movie would have been much more of a messy amalgamation of Ellroy and Ayer.

The Black Dahlia *(Brian De Palma, 2006)*

A milquetoast attempt at film noir, *The Black Dahlia* comes as yet another entry in the disappointing post-*Mission Impossible* career of Brian De Palma. This fast-and-loose adaptation of James Ellroy's first "L.A. Quartet" novel comes from Josh Friedman, the scribe who brought us the laughable *Chain Reaction* and ill-conceived *War of the Worlds* remake. The *Black Dahlia* consists of overwrought dialogue that would put any actor to the test. Alas, not only is the dialogue wrong, but so is every actor in De Palma's tepid film.

Horribly miscast with current Hollywood luminaries, the stinkiest performance of the film emanates from Hillary Swank who, as Madeleine Linscott, affects some kind of Katharine Hepburn accent while pretending to be prettier than she is. "Elizabeth [Short] and I made love once. I just did it to see what it would be like with someone who looked like me," she confesses to protagonist Dwight "Bucky" Bleichert (Josh Hartnett). This should tip him off that her character must be absolutely nuts: Elizabeth Short (the titular Black Dahlia) is feminine and lovely (as played by Mia Kirshner); Swank possesses neither of these qualities. Moreover, no bisexual character in an Ellroy work should ever be trusted.

While the film bears the title *The Black Dahlia*, the murder of Elizabeth Short is overshadowed by a handful of other plotlines, including Bucky Bleichert's partner, Leland "Lee" Blanchard (Aaron Eckhart) going crazy for reasons unexplained in the film. This creates a dangerous situation, as Blanchard might chew up too much scenery, leaving nothing for Ramona Linscott (Fiona Shaw) to feast on during her laughable climactic scene. There's also a major plotline wherein Bucky falls for Blanchard's live-in gal, Kay Lake (Scarlett Johansson). If we were to channel the amount of electricity between Bucky and Kay in this film, it couldn't power a pocket calculator.

Between the unbearable acting, wretched dialogue, and whacked-out camera work, *The Black Dahlia* feels like a home movie recording of a high-school play rehearsal. What made this torturous experience even more unbearable was the appearance of Ellis Loew (Patrick Fischler). His appearance kept reminding me of the other movie that Ellis Loew was in: *L.A. Confidential* (as played by Ron Rifkin). Wow, that was a great movie. What is Loew doing in a piece of shit like this?

Impossibly Funky

Street Kings *(David Ayer, 2008)*

Written by Ellroy as *The Night Watchman*, the story originally opened in October 1995, with the O.J. Simpson verdict rocking the Los Angeles Police Department. A burned-out cop, Tom Ludlow, becomes embroiled in an ever-widening case that begins with a convenience store robbery and spreads out like blood spatter: one smaller, bloody crime leading to the larger, more pervasive problem of corruption in the L.A.P.D.

This second draft of this script is dated September 2, 1997. It was since rewritten by Kurt Wimmer and Jamie Moss, retitled *Street Kings*, and directed by David Ayer (*Dark Blue*). With an updated present-day setting, it's ironic that much of the plot hinges on planted D.N.A. evidence, the same thing that allowed O.J. to go scot-free. How far we've come in thirteen years!

Keanu Reeves and his fellow officers in *Street Kings*

Street Kings suffered from a lousy title and deceptive marketing campaign. Previews and commercials paint a far different story than what was actually on screen, showing rappers-turned-actors Common and The Game to be far more present than they actually are (Common is portrayed as being a lead, rather than appearing in his *one* scene).

Despite being 43 years old when the film was released, his boyish good looks and surfer affectation undermine Keanu Reeves's ability to bring gravitas to the role of seasoned cop Tom Ludlow. He's surrounded by a capable supporting cast, with stand-out performances from Forest Whitaker as the corrupt Captain Wander and Hugh Laurie as the righteous Captain Biggs. Ludlow is caught between these two paradigms of police power and political players.

The long-running conspiracy of Ellroy's original draft makes a brief appearance, but is secondary to the investigation that Ludlow undertakes in which he could be seen as a suspect. He risks burning himself in his quest for justice and self-redemption. Without exception, the modifications made by Wimmer and Moss were great improvements. The dialogue cooks (" 'Phone Book Tom,' I heard you got your best confessions with the '91 directory") and the plot, though similar, plays out like a far better version of *Dark Blue*.

My Dark Places *(Unproduced)*

TV writer (*Cold Case*) and documentary director (*Thank You and Good Night*) Jan Oxenberg does a fair job of adapting Ellroy's autobiographical tome. The story switches cuts between a young Ellroy and the present day (1997, actually) author on the trail to uncover his mother's killer. An unsympathetic lead character may be possible in documentaries and even some docudramas, and apparently, Oxenberg was trying her darndest to test the limits of this. Her Ellroy "character" is an unrepentant bullshitter who's often described as being in "asshole mode."

There's no pretending that Ellroy's characters are anything other than substitutes for himself. Like Lee Blanchard and other detective protagonists, we see Ellroy creating a shrine to his mother using police photographs. During one of the few poignant scenes, he dances with a waitress while "the dance is intercut with the images flooding Ellroy's head. Murdered women. His mother, the Black Dahlia, the murdered women of his fiction, his imagination, of the pulp magazines he read as a kid." The direction here states, "This has to be done carefully, the images should not be titillating but they should be horrible—in the sense that we feel the horror the women victims feel, as Ellroy does in the movie he can't stop in his head."

For a while it looked as if David Duchovny would play the author, but the entire project seems to have gone offline.

77 *(Unproduced)*

As with the Zoot Suit Riots, Watts Riots, Bloody Christmas, O.J. Simpson trial, and Rodney King trial (to name a few), Ellroy sets the action of *77* against a famous historical event in Los Angeles history. This time, it's the shootout between the Symbionese Liberation Army and L.A.P.D. of May 17, 1974. Set shortly after the kidnapping of Patty Hearst (February 4, 1974), *77* plays off of the same racial and social environment that fueled the S.L.A. The screenplay also fictionalizes the unsolved murder of police officer Michael Lee Edwards, who was killed six days before the S.L.A. shootout. Here Edwards is "Donny Miller," and he's a real shitbird (a word strangely absent from this Ellroy work). Think of Miller as the Leland "Buzz" Meeks of *L.A. Confidential*, as he seems to have been involved with some seriously bad juju, and unlocking his death allows the rest of the narrative to unfold.

The script's title comes from the precinct where Edwards worked and where fictional officers Chuck Lynley and Billy S. Burdette are partnered. Lynley is a white peckerwood, while Burdette is a black lawyer slumming as a cop in some kind of protest against his upper-class family. Lynley appears to be a racist, sadistic bastard. He manages to kill five men—all black—in the line of duty during his first month at the 77th. Yet the salt-and-pepper partners inexplicably endear themselves to one another. Cruising the streets like Freebie and the Bean, the pair realizes that they both search for justice in a corrupt world. Meanwhile, like the triangular relationship of *The Black Dahlia* among Bucky, Lee, and Kay, *77* has Lynley falling for Burdette's sister, Jane, with the couple unable to escape his influence after his untimely demise.

While the S.L.A. skulks in the background of the story, an audience for *77* would likely be confused when Lynley unearths porn loops of prominent

S.L.A. members. Unseen through the rest of the film, the sudden appearance of Willie Wolf, Cinque Mtume, Mizmoon Soltysik, etc., would leave everyone except Patty Hearst scratching their head as to who these people are and why we should be shocked by their appearance.

The title page of *77* states that it was to be produced by television mucky mucks Dick Wolf and Tony Ganz. Dated October 14, 2003, this is the second draft of the script. The project dates back to 2001, but hasn't had much traction in the years since.

White Heat *(Unproduced)*

The screenplay for this adaptation of Raoul Walsh's 1949 classic *White Heat* doesn't bear a date. The best estimate is that this was written circa 2000. In Ellroy's update of the Ivan Goff and Ben Robert screen story, the author keeps the high points of the original film—a train robbery, an unbalanced crook who's close to his mother, and an undercover cop. Add some paternal conflict, latent homosexuality, police corruption, and a couple of shitbirds, and a new, as-yet-unfilmed version of *White Heat* is born.

Cody Jarrett and Hank Fallon are second-generation criminal and cop. Jarrett's daddy killed Fallon's daddy, and Fallon goes undercover as a criminal when Jarrett goes to jail. Far rawer than the 1949 film, prison in Ellroy's *White Heat* comes filled with racial violence and rape around every corner. Along with the paternal back story, Ellroy intensifies the blatant relationship between Jarrett's wife, Verna, and his criminal partner, Ed. Jarrett appears to be impotent and almost actively encourages Verna's liaisons with Ed, much to Ma Jarrett's chagrin.

Oddly, Ellroy doesn't play up the Oedipal overtones between Jarrett and his mother. This is surprising, as incest is a thematic staple for Ellroy. What's at the center of *White Heat* is the relationship between Jarrett and Fallon. In the Walsh film, Fallon (Edmund O'Brien) doesn't enter the picture until the second act. The protagonist of the first act is T-man Phillip Evans (John Archer). In the Ellroy script, the Evans character is combined with Daniel Winston, The Trader (Fred Clark), to provide requisite police corruption. In Ellroy's work, "Trader" doubles as "Traitor."

The thrilling conclusion of the 1949 film is omitted from Ellroy's work, making his work feel padded and laborious. No "Top of the world!" here, in any sense.

The Big Nowhere *(Unproduced)*

Penned by Kazan brothers Chris and Nick, this adaptation does justice to the most overlooked of the four entries in Ellroy's "L.A. Quartet." The story has two detectives from disparate backgrounds and widely varying motivations ultimately pursuing the same criminal. Deputy Danny Upshaw is the incorruptible younger officer whose dogged pursuit of police procedure alienates his girlfriend (though he may be shutting her out for other reasons). Chief Deputy Hash Reed acts as muscle for the mob to pad his bank account. While Hash plays lackey for mobster Mickey Cohen, Upshaw obsesses about a murder case even while working undercover, infiltrating a communist organization at the behest of District Attorney Ellis Loew.

Hash performs double duty in the Kazans' screenplay, as he was two characters in the Ellroy book: Leland "Buzz" Meeks and Mal Considine. Also missing from action is Lieutenant Dudley Smith. He's been replaced by a nefarious L.A.P.D. officer, Clyde. He and Loew are as crooked as a dog's hind leg and work as hard to gain and maintain power as Mickey Cohen. It's only Upshaw and Hash who pursue justice.

Further motivating Upshaw's sojourn into the Red and Lavender Underworlds (where communism and homosexuality collide) is his realization that he's gay. This makes his quest to solve the murder of homosexual Marin Goines personal. All signs point to bisexual Union man Reynolds Loftis (think Pierce Patchett from *L.A. Confidential*), which means that he's a red herring with frame around him. The true killer plays into some of Ellroy's favorite themes: murderous homosexuals, secret love affairs, and incest. Add in some killer wolverines and you've got a fairly twisted, albeit compelling, labyrinthine tale.

Dated September 25, 1997, there were rumblings in 1998 that Gregory Hoblit would direct, but this never came to fruition. James Crumley also did an adaptation of the work. He told Craig McDonald (hardluckstories.com), "That was a real chore. The guys who figured *L.A. Confidential* out, I thought were geniuses."

TV Death Trip: Ellroy on the Boob Tube
"Since I Don't Have You" (Jonathan Kaplan, 1993)
Adapted by Steven Katz, this episode of Showtime's *Fallen Angels* series based on a short story (found in *Hollywood Nocturnes*) brings together two of Ellroy's favorite characters: Ganster Mickey Cohen (James Woods) and industrialist Howard Hughes (Tim Matheson). Working for both men and playing them against each other is Turner "Buzz" Meeks (Gary Busey).

Both Cohen and Hughes are interested in bedding Gretchen Rae Shoftel (Aimee Graham). It's up to Meeks to find her, unraveling a mystery involving Milwaukee mobsters, accounting antics, and Gretchen Rae's old man (Dick Miller). Too much of the action gets wrapped via dialogue-heavy descriptions of things past, while current events are rather dull.

L.A. Sheriff's Homicide *(David Anspaugh, 2000)*
An attempt to redefine the police procedural, this television pilot came off as a little too cut and dry in Dick Wolf's *Law & Order* landscape. Boasting technical assistance from Ellroy's friend Detective William Stoner, the pilot aims for the terse tone of *Dragnet* while sharing cast dynamics of another 2000

premiere, *C.S.I.* As the Grissom character, Miguel Ferrer plays staid Sergeant Walter Drazin. He's bound to have a rocky relationship with the series' Sara Sidle: Elizabeth Lackey as Detective Anne Coates.

Also known as *L.A. County 187*, the pilot follows an arson case that follows a typical Ellroy trajectory, in that the one event is at the center of a vast web of misdeeds that include murder, illegal gambling, pedophilia, "weenie wagging," and more. Despite its abrupt ending, the show plays fairly well, though the knack for coincidental relationships may have quickly worn thin.

L.A. Confidential *(Eric Laneuville, 2000)*

The first part of a proposed thirteen-part series for HBO moves along lethargically, having the benefit of time to develop its story arcs. As a pilot, however, the forty-minute program doesn't do much to grab an audience's attention. The initial episode introduces the three main protagonists from Curtis Hanson's *L.A. Confidential* and two central antagonists, intertwining their stories so tightly as to contradict the events of Hanson's film.

A prequel to the events of *L.A. Confidential*, the series should have delved deeper into events covered in *The Black Dahlia* or *The Big Nowhere*, rather than trying to shoehorn Exley, Vincennes, and White into further conflicts with Pierce Patchett (Eric Roberts). Rather than exploring Exley's shady past (as explored in Ellroy's book), or giving Wendell "Bud" White more shading, the screenplay by Walon Green (who also penned the rejected *Zero Effect* pilot) merely illustrates backstory of which *L.A. Confidential* fans would be well aware.

The pilot gives Kiefer Sutherland the chance to shine in his role as Jack Vincennes, the most complex character in *L.A. Confidential*. Still, the decision to make the series a prequel was ill-advised. Instead, a re-teaming of Exley and White and recasting them as the prototypical cop duo, solving crimes around L.A., would have served the material far better and the fans far more.

The Demon Dog Barks: Documentaries of James Ellroy

There are almost as many movies about Ellroy as there are Ellroy adaptations. One of the most heavily documented living authors of the twentieth century, Ellroy is the subject of at least four full-length documentary films. Along with the aforementioned *James Ellroy: Demon Dog of American Crime Fiction* (1993) and Clara and Robert Kuperberg's *James Ellroy: American Dog* (2006), Ellroy was the main subject of Nicola Black's *White Jazz* (1995) and Vikram Jayanti's *Feast of Death* (2001).

James Ellroy: Demon Dog of American Crime Fiction *(Reinhard Jud, Austria, 1993)*

Director Reinhard Jud treats Los Angeles as a character in his documentary. Unfortunately, it's as underdeveloped a character as Ellroy. The city isn't given a voice, nor does Ellroy provide one for it. Rather, there are too many bits of Ellroy merely rehashing his books and discussing settings. Much of the film is comprised of shots of police cars and lulls in narrative. There are also embarrassing moments of Ellroy howling at the moon and using language like "hepcats" and "nowheresville" with an acute lack of irony. The author also displays an absence of humility as he rambles on about his "stupefyingly complex [...] spellbinding social documents." Surrounded by framed press clippings about his work, he says, "I wanted to give people crime fiction on an epic level."

Somewhere in this lousy 90-minute documentary hides a good 30-minute film. Viewers are introduced to James Ellroy: his past, his proclivities, and his body of work. His job is to make the nightmares of Los Angeles explicit. All of this makes for some fascinating material for Ellroy fans, but not for anyone else.

White Jazz *(Nicola Black, United Kingdom, 1996)*
Nicola Black's work should be considered a good balance of *Demon Dog* and *Feast of Death*.

Like *Demon Dog*, there's plenty of embarrassing poetry and howling from the "Demon Dog," along with background on the writer (provided by Ellroy himself). And similar to *Feast of Death*, there's a large portion of the film dedicated to Ellroy hanging out with Detective William Stoner, going over the case files of Geneva Ellroy. Luckily, the author doesn't come across an ingratiating cop groupie in Black's Channel Four documentary.

Feast of Death *(Vikram Jayanti, 2001)*
This rambling, rambunctious documentary displays the endless obsessing of James Ellroy over the death of his mother, Geneva. Most of the film is made up of diner conversations between Ellroy and police detectives. This makes for an intensely disinteresting documentary that makes viewers want to scream, "She's dead! Get over it!" Even to an Ellroy fan, this film is an complete bore.

James Ellroy: American Dog *(Clara and Robert Kuperberg, France, 2005)*
This documentary should be considered as the filmed adaptation of *My Dark Places*. Another hour of James Ellroy obsessing about the murder of his mother, this work by Clara and Robert Kuperberg gives some background on Ellroy before diving into voiceover readings from the author's maternally obsessed autobiography.

Shot on digital video with some nicely saturated colors (lots of deep red and blue filters), *James Ellroy: American Dog* chugs along the Dead Mother Highway, with some pit stops along the way. Exits include Film Noir Boulevard, Crime Photos Way, and Dana Delany Drive. The radio is tuned to

Overwrought Strings FM. Like Nicola Black's *White Jazz*, the Kuperbergs' work strikes a good balance between the oddball writer and quixotic investigator. Definitely the sharpest of the Ellroy documentaries, this French work—while not entirely riveting—is the best of the lot by default.

The original version of this article ran in *Cashiers du Cinemart* #15.

MADNESS IN THE 20TH CENTURY

By Mike White

"A boy who doesn't have a father around doesn't develop a superego."

"That's silly. Superego is only a jargon word for 'conscience,' and everybody's got a conscience."

"Have it your way, Bernice."

—*The Burnt Orange Heresy*

While I could bemoan the shabby treatment that Charles Willeford has received by his peers, lament the unavailability of his work in local bookstores, or herald the coming of a new era in which Willeford will attain the attention he deserves, I won't. That would be unfair and overly idealistic. The time has not yet arrived for Charles Willeford. I fear that it never will.

Charles Willeford's books are unpleasant ventures past the veneer of "modern life." The cop, the critic, the soldier, the writer, the director, the priest, the short-order cook, the artist, the cockfighter, the used-car salesman; he showed their dirty little secrets (and big ones too). He did so with even-handed, well-mannered, eloquent prose.

Reading about the gritty lives of his protagonists, it's hard not to be impressed by his polished love of language. His well-chosen words hit like a gut punch, unadorned by baroque turns of phrase. Along with the often hard-boiled narratives was an element of dark humor that made Willeford's works unique. Even when presenting rough-and-tumble narratives, there was a glimmer of crazed glee behind the Willeford poker face.

It's dubious that Charles Willeford will ever become a household name. Yet lovers of quirky, engrossing literature should continue to seek out Willeford's work and embrace it. His voice is true, steady, and unequivocally American.

"I parked and went into a bar. I ordered a straight gin with a dash of bitters. Sipping it, I looked over the customers. The man next to me was my size. I put my drink down, raised my elbow level with my shoulder and spun on my heel. My elbow caught him just below the eye. He raised a beer bottle over his head and my fist caught him flush on the jaw. He dropped to the floor and lay still. I threw a half-dollar on the bar and left. No one looked in my direction as I closed the door. I felt a little better but not enough."

—*High Priest of California*

Willeford's work is delightfully unsettling. Usually writing from a first-person point of view, Willeford has his readers identify with sociopaths like Russell Haxby, a used-car salesman obsessed with a married woman, in *High Priest of California*. More than bedding the object of his affection, Haxby is trying to determine "if she was really mysterious or just plain stupid." As evidenced by the quote above, Haxby also has a penchant for random acts of violence to soothe his savage soul.

Willeford challenges the reader to determine if the protagonist is clever or simply crazy. His characters are not murderous psychopaths who drool at the thought of spilling blood, nor are they petty thieves who cut corners in order to make a buck. No, they fit into society simply enough and function with relative ease. That's the scary part.

Often Willeford's protagonists don't even realize they're off-kilter. They take what's given to them with natural aplomb. For example, in Willeford's short story "Some Lucky License" (found in *Everybody's Metamorphosis*), police Sergeant Bill Hartigan finds himself penalized under Section 1277 of the Criminal Code, which states that "any police officer who fatally shoots six persons—in the line of duty or no—will be separated from the force, and will not be reinstated." This section is known unofficially among policemen as the "trigger happy" rule.

Charles Willeford signs a copy of *Miami Blues*

Instead of being tossed off the force, some political strings are pulled and Hartigan is reassigned as an unnecessary guard in a low security prison. Upon learning of an escape plot, Hartigan determines that apprehending the culprit will allow him to be reinstated on the force as a hero.

Waiting in the dark for the prisoner to make his way down the prison wall, Hartigan realizes that what he enjoys most about police work is having a shooting license. "I wanted to shoot and kill men," Hartigan thinks to himself. And why not? "Why should I wait for someone else at a later date? Sooner or later I was going to get a sixth victim anyway."

Willeford learned during his days in the Army that too many men gained an affinity towards cold-blooded murder. "Tankers I knew used to swap bottles of liquor in exchange for prisoners, and then just shoot 'em for fun... I used to wonder, 'What's gonna happen to these guys when they get back into civilian life?'" These men and their carefree attitude about killing helped populate Willeford's fiction.

Even when a Willefordian character doesn't have a penchant for bloodshed, they're not entirely stable. Take, for example, the Hoke Moseley books—named after the cantankerous police detective.

Willeford's early works often closed with a morality that felt forced. His protagonists were caught, killed, or institutionalized for their misdeeds. However, this changed in 1984 with the release of *Miami Blues*, wherein Willeford employed a third-person narration and two protagonists: the psychotic Freddy J. Frenger, Jr., and the man on his trail, Hoke Moseley. Willeford had used this technique a few years prior in his fictionalized recount of Son of Sam, *Off the Wall*.

Having written for over forty years, Willeford finally attained popular praise with *Miami Blues*. Suddenly there became a demand for another Willeford novel starring the ornery toothless detective, Moseley. Willeford didn't want to become beholden to maintaining a series, yet this prospect also presented an interesting challenge. Willeford knew "the rules" of the detective series from teaching them at the University of Miami, and here was an opportunity to break every one of them. This possibility and Willeford's popularity helped him relent—to a certain extent.

An early draft for the second book in the Moseley series, *New Hope for the Dead*, is commonly known as "The Grimhaven Manuscript." Herein we witness Hoke burned out from his job as a homicide detective. He begins a quest for "absolutely nothing" and determines that this may best be attained through killing off his ex-wife and two daughters. Needless to say, Willeford's publisher refused the draft. The second (and successful) stab at the sequel, *New Hope for the Dead*, stands as not only the best of the Moseley books, but of Willeford's oeuvre.

He stayed true to this idea of Hoke enjoying inner silence courtesy of synaptic misfires from the third Moseley book, *Sideswipe*, in which Hoke has a complete nervous breakdown by page thirteen. Balancing the story of the less-than-stable Hoke is the parallel tale of Troy Louden, which was reworked from Willeford's 1962 *No Experience Necessary*. Willeford would write a fourth Moseley book, *The Way We Die Now*, before his death in 1988.

> "Freddy unwrapped the bath sheet and dropped it on the floor. He probed her pregreased vagina with the first three fingers of his right hand. He shook his head and frowned.
>
> 'Not enough friction there for me,' he said. 'I'm used to boys, you see. Do you take it in the ass?'
>
> 'No, sir. I should, I know, but I tried it once and it hurt too much. I just can't do it.'
>
> 'You should learn to take it in the ass. You'll make more money.'"
>
> —*Miami Blues*

Willeford's world was not limited to historical events; his books weren't world-spanning epics. America was Willeford's playing field and his predominant theme was the madness that plagued the post-war nation. They were usually first-person accounts of men dealing with their private worlds and obsessions.

As ambitious a writer as Willeford was, when becoming familiar with his bibliography, one can't help but sense the uncanny recurrence of phrases, names, and themes. Wallets are made of ostrich skin. Men wear gabardine suits. Telephones are not hung up; they're "racked." Cigarettes are never lit, they're "lighted." Protagonists often bare the name Richard Hudson, Russell Haxby, or some variation of Jacob Blake. It's not unusual for a Willefordian protagonist to shower with the water as hot as they can stand it, as if trying to rid themselves of their dirty tendencies, or the filth of the world.

The music his characters move to was also born of the crazed twentieth century. The challenging compositions of Bela Bartok frequent the pages of Willeford's work. When Richard Hudson of *The Woman Chaser* finds his artistic calling, it's while exerting himself to Bartok's "Miraculous Mandarin." This is the same music to which Russell Haxby reads T.S. Eliot's "Burnt Norton" in *High Priest of California* (right before donning a blue gabardine suit). Additionally, it is Eliot who inspires Hudson before bedding his formerly chaste assistant in *The Woman Chaser*.

Along with this appreciation of a modern composer, Willeford's formal schooling in art was apparent in his works. Willeford often cited artists of this century's art movements, such as Chagall, Klee, and Kandinsky. From the dealer in *Wild Wives*, to the collector in *Sideswipe*, to the student in *Lust Is a Woman*, to the failed painters of *Pick-up* and *No Experience Necessary/Sideswipe*, art often played a major role in Willeford's work.

Art was the central theme of *The Burnt Orange Heresy*, wherein art critic Jamie Figueras (another popular Willeford moniker) scores a once-in-a-lifetime interview with the father of Nihilistic Surrealism. The price for the exclusive privilege is having to steal one of the elusive "great master's" paintings.

More than the occasional mention of waking up at 6 a.m. or an errant copy of *Heidi* laying around, of all Willeford's themes and motifs, the one that flourished late in his career—especially in his Hoke Moseley books—was the practice of anal sex. Willeford had a number of instances in the Moseley books of characters taking "the road less traveled." Along with Freddy Frenger putting a can of Crisco to good use in *Miami Blues* (see above), Hoke attempts to indulge in some assplay with a murderess in *New Hope for the Dead*, and has the sanctity of his own bunghole threatened in *The Way We Die Now*. This preoccupation with anal sex most likely sprang from Willeford's experiences during his years in the service with Filipina prostitutes who stayed "good catholic girls"—protecting their hymens by selling their keisters.

> "If a restaurant owner pays a cashier fifteen dollars a week and he, or she, sees that the owner is raking in two or three hundred dollars a day,

that cashier is going to supplement his income from the cash register. One is merely correcting the moral deficiency of the employer. Any employer who shortchanges his help gets the kind of worker he pays for."

—*Something about a Soldier*

Orphaned at eight, Charles Willeford was raised by his grandmother in Los Angeles. Growing up in the Great Depression, Willeford left home as a young teen and spent his youth as a hobo, riding the rails and wondering where his next meal was going to come from. He learned the art of storytelling in railroad jungles and Hoovervilles of the Southwest U.S., and found that a properly told tale could help him bum money and food. These days of living by his wits also aided in forming Willeford's unique work ethic.

Unable (or unwilling) to find proper work by the age of sixteen, Willeford lied about his age and entered the service. *I Was Looking for a Street* chronicles these days on the road, while Willeford's *Something about a Soldier* is an account of his days in the military. Throughout *Soldier*, Willeford jockeys for positions in the service that require the least work for the best pay. In other words, Willeford was an ideal slacker.

Even in his post-Armed Services life (beginning in 1956), Willeford was highly concerned about the number of hours he had to work. He enjoyed a post as the Associate Editor at *Alfred Hitchcock Mystery Magazine* and boasted about only having to work fifteen hours a week. Eventually, he was wooed away from this position to a job where he was promised a twelve-hour workweek: serving as a professor at the University of Miami.

This is not to say that Willeford was lazy. The less he had to work, the more time he had to write. Likewise, the commonalities in his oeuvre don't reflect a penchant for redundancy. Rather, Willeford is more of a perfectionist. He would retool his ideas, sometimes growing them from asides to short stories, lean books, or possibly magna opera. Willeford would take incidents from his life and either weave them into his fiction or use them as a jumping-off point for a story or book. For example, "Jake's Journal" (one of the stories found in *The Machine in Ward Eleven*) contains many passages that would later be found, nearly intact, in *Something about a Soldier*.

Some critics of Alfred Hitchcock contend that he was content to make the same "man on the run" film repeatedly throughout his career. And, likewise, some could say that Willeford tread familiar waters with his tales, often finding voice from a maladjusted male protagonist who might mention murder as casually as a tweed coat. Upon closer examination, however, there is no such animal as a "typical Charles Willeford novel." Even when dealing with protagonists of the same profession (writers, police officers, and used-car salesmen), Willeford placed them in disparate contexts.

Similarly, Willeford was not content to keep to fiction. In addition to the aforementioned autobiographies, Willeford recounted significant incidents in his life, such as the adaptation and filming of his novel, *Cockfighter*, in *Cockfighter Journal*, or his hemorrhoid operation in *A Guide for the Undehemorrhoided*.

Willeford also wrote nonfictional literary and social critiques, a good number of which are collected in *Writing and Other Blood Sports*. Willeford was a scholar of writing. In addition to his love of words and diction, he was a student of the writing process. Willeford has written about the importance of a proper photographer for one's dust jacket ("What Book Covers Tell You"), the merits and pitfalls of book dedications ("A Matter of Dedication"), and of the significance of how large one's name is in comparison to the title of one's book ("The Name Above the Title").

Willeford has frequently written ruminations about his strong opinions regarding book titles. The author penned "The Trouble with Titles" in a 1958 issue of *Writer's Digest*, in which he wrote, "I have always been fond of titles with a double meaning. For the first time in my life I had an idea for a private eye novel. I wrote it and I was proud of it, chiefly because I had never written anything like it before. The manuscript, however, remained on my desk while I racked my mind for the perfect title. After two weeks I finally got it. *Death Finds a Lover*! I typed a cover page and mailed the novel to my publisher. That's right, you guessed it. The title was changed by the publisher and issued as *Wild Wives*. No. I don't know why."

In "What Book Covers Tell You," Willeford discusses the profitability of longer titles: "Perhaps the only valid clue in the title as to the readability of a novel is the word count. A two-word title usually indicates that this will be a better book than a novel with one-word title, and a four-word title better than one with three words. But there are too many exceptions to make this rule infallible." Practicing what he preached, Willeford often aimed for four- to six-word titles: *The Machine in Ward Eleven*, *The Burnt Orange Heresy*, *Nothing Under the Sun* (released as *No Experience Necessary*), *The Black Mass of Brother Springer* (originally released as *Honey Gal*), *Until I Am Dead* (released as *Pick-up*), *Deliver Me from Dallas* (released as *The Whip Hand*), and *The Man Who Got Away* (which ended up being *The Woman Chaser*), to name a few.

Willeford was said to have bandied about the titles *Kiss Your Ass Good-bye* and *The Shark-Infested Custard* for a handful of his books until they finally found homes among Willeford's bibliography. *Kiss Your Ass Good-bye* and the short story "Strange" (found in *Everybody's Metamorphosis*) were recombined and expanded upon in *The Shark-Infested Custard*, posthumously published in 1993. Of course the one time Willeford desired a two-word title—*The Difference*—the book (published under the name Will Charles) bore the name *The Hombre from Sonora*.

> *"My eyes fell on a copy of* Newsweek *on the coffee table near the whitebrick fireplace. I read* Time! *A vocabulary of only 20,000 words is required to read* Newsweek, *but the* Time *reader needs a vocabulary of 25,000 words. A little thing, maybe. But on such minutiae rest the standards of culture in the United States, and in this one qualification, at least, Richard Hudson was a notch above THE MAN."*
>
> —*The Woman Chaser*

During his time in the service, Willeford found time to polish his abilities as a poet (among his first published works was a collection of poetry, *Proletarian Laughter*). Additionally, he began to hone his skills at writing dialogue and suspense by penning a story for Armed Forces Radio, "The Machine in Ward Eleven." He also wrote a weekly radio serial, *The Story of Mrs. Miller*, where Willeford began sharpening his acting chops by playing a doctor in the series. He was in several plays while with the occupation army in Japan. Back stateside, he was active in Community Theater in Santa Barbara and West Palm Beach throughout the '50s and '60s.

The show business in his blood became a frequent theme in his work. From opinions on script writing ("Why Write for Television" from *Writing and Other Blood Sports*), to acting ("An Actor Prepares" from *Everybody's Metamorphosis*) to directing ("The Machine in Ward Eleven" from the collection of the same name and *The Woman Chaser*), Willeford's apparent Hollywood ambition would culminate in Roger Corman's New World Pictures' purchase of the rights to his novel, *Cockfighter*.

Willeford agreed to sell the rights to his work with the stipulation that he could write the screenplay. "Not every novelist wants to adapt his novel for the screen, but I had wanted to write a screenplay for some time, just to see if I could do it. I had even considered the mad idea of writing an original screenplay, on speculation. But to write a screenplay on speculation, knowing in advance that it has such a very small chance of ever being produced, is a luxury for any writer who never has enough time to write anyway."

Directed by long-time *Cashiers du Cinemart* favorite Monte Hellman, *Cockfighter* saw Hellman directing his favorite actor, Warren Oates, in the role of Frank Mansfield. Stoic and determined, Oates gives a remarkable performance as Mansfield, who swore himself to silence and sobriety after an incident of drunken braggadocio, which left him without a bird and a chance at the Cockfighter of the Year Award. Uttering nary a word for the majority of the film, Oates still gives one of his best performances. Oates certainly was on a roll that year, as he did *Cockfighter* on the heels of *Bring Me the Head of Alfredo Garcia*.

According to Willeford, he loosely based Frank Mansfield's mute quest for the Cockfighter of the Year Award on Homer's *Odyssey*. It's a journey of self-discovery, aided by an amazing cast of characters, including Steve Railsback and Ed Begley Jr. (two men a little too fond of their chickens), as well as Oates' nemesis, Harry Dean Stanton. Also among the cast were Troy Donahue, Richard B. Shull, and a few other Hellman regulars, including Millie Perkins and Laurie Bird.

The most notable casting choice was Willeford as Ed Middleton, an ex-cocker who gives Frank a helping hand. "Charles became an actor in the film at the last minute, when I fired the actor set to play the role the night before shooting was to begin," says Hellman. Not only was Willeford able to experience the filmmaking process from behind the camera, but in front of it, as well. Willeford wrote that he hadn't "worked [as] hard since I left the horse cavalry in June, 1942."

Though *Cockfighter* was ultimately a commercial failure, Willeford was apparently not entirely soured on the filmmaking process. The author stayed in touch with Roger Corman, who asked Willeford to do some location scouting in the Florida Everglades and Marco Island for Corey Allen's *Thunder and Lightning*. "Charles read the script, drove across the [Tamaiami] Trail, spent a couple days looking around, made some notes, arranged for housing for the crew and the cast, and bought a few junk cars," says Charles's widow, Betsy Willeford.

Willeford plays a bartender who gives booze runner David Carradine the short end of the stick when competition (Roger C. Carmel, best known for playing Harcourt Fenton Mudd on *Star Trek*) moves in on Carradine's territory. Not much of the film is remarkable, except perhaps for the many ingenious uses of Kate Jackson's undergarments and the great line from Charles Napier: "Hey asshole, stop that kung-fu shit!" Otherwise, *Thunder and Lightning* boasts long-winded car chases and cornball set pieces.

Willeford wouldn't write for the screen again. He refused a chance to adapt *Miami Blues*, leaving that task up to the film's director, George Armitage—another Corman alum. *Miami Blues* was made under the impetus of Fred Ward, whose Passing Moon production company optioned the rights to Willeford's book in 1986.

Originally, Ward wanted to play the role of Freddy Frenger, while Gene Hackman agreed to play Detective Hoke Moseley. That idea was scrapped after Alec Baldwin tried out for the Frenger role, blowing everyone away with his performance. Hackman graciously accepted the decision of Baldwin to play Frenger, with Ward taking over as Moseley. Baldwin does an excellent job as the unstable Frenger, while Ward shines during his all-too-brief moments on screen as Moseley. With his unshaven face and dour expression, Ward often resembles Warren Oates and provides a performance worthy of the late actor.

For years rumors circulated about Fred Ward reprising his role as Moseley for film versions of the rest of the books in the series, though that's unlikely, as

Passing Moon doesn't own the options for the books. Instead, the film rights for those and *The Shark-Infested Custard* were once in the hands of Curtis Hanson, who had plans of producing a series of Moseley films for HBO. Additionally, the film rights for *The Burnt Orange Heresy* belonged to Eamonn Bowles of Shooting Gallery productions.

> "That was the beginning. It is also a flashback and narrative hook. This much about writing I have learned from the movies. Also, I don't want to fool anybody, including myself. Especially myself. I believe now that I should have remained Richard Hudson, Used-Car Dealer, and I should never have become Richard Hudson, Writer-Director-Producer."
>
> —*The Woman Chaser*

On the opposite end of the Willeford protagonist spectrum—far from the essentially noble characters of Mansfield and Moseley—is the disillusioned and delusional Richard Hudson of Robinson Devor's 1999 film adaptation of *The Woman Chaser*. Unsatisfied with his success as a used-car salesman, Hudson determines that his only path of redemption is through creating a work of art. Of course, Hudson realizes that becoming a true craftsman takes years of practice and perhaps an inherent ability. However, it's his opinion (which is ultimately proven true) that the one area remaining where a nobody can create a masterpiece is in Hollywood.

The Woman Chaser is the most cinematic—leastwise in its construction—of Willeford's works. Herein, the protagonist writes a recollection of his days as a movie director in quasi-screenplay style, preceding every transition in the novel with direction such as "CROSSFADE," "DISSOLVE," or "FADE TO BLACK." Throughout the novel, the reader is given insight not only regarding Hudson's life, but also in the method by which audience members react to the words on the page or the images on screen.

Like Hudson, *The Woman Chaser* is director Devor's first try at a full-length motion picture. And, like Hudson's film-within-the-film, *The Man Who Got Away*, Devor has created a masterpiece. Running six full reels, Devor's film is free from unnecessary padding and moves at a breakneck pace. Though low budget, *The Woman Chaser* has tremendous production values. Shot in color but presented in breathtaking black and white, *The Woman Chaser* is a beautiful-looking film. The screenplay (penned by Devor) is delightfully accurate in its adaptation of Willeford's work, not only in being faithful to the tone of the book, but in keeping ninety percent of the original dialogue.

Starring Patrick Warburton as Hudson, the actor doesn't "portray" Hudson so much as he "inhabits" the role. His deadpan narration holds true to Hudson's sociopathic outlook on life. Hudson is a bastard and makes no bones about it. His moral ambiguity frees him to be completely outrageous in his appraisals of the world and unapologetic in his heinous actions.

Warburton often comes off as flat as a flapjack. Contrasting this insouciance are wild turns of emotion. Hudson is passionate about his desire to create—to give meaning to his money-grubbing life. Unfortunately for him, he learns too late that Hollywood's studio system is far more ruthless than he could ever be. As Hudson, Warburton often wears a mask of indifference, slightly squinting at scenery as if trying to make sense of the way of Hollywood. It's only after he dons a conspicuous set of sunglasses that he can operate in this foreign place with all the autonomous command he had over his used-car lot.

Hudson's hardboiled demeanor, the employment of first-person voiceover narration, a flashback framing device, the use of the classic Milkos Rozsa theme from *The Asphalt Jungle*, and an inherent moral ambiguity might lead critics to assume that *The Woman Chaser* is a "modern-day film noir." Indeed, *The Woman Chaser* has an absurdity reminiscent of the work of Edgar G. Ulmer, but there is a modernity and self-reflexivity in Willeford's scenarios that puts *The Woman Chaser* head and shoulders above films that try to ape the classic noir traits.

> "[In the 11th Horse Calvary] I had trained my mount to piss into a Pepsi-Cola bottle. The way you do this is to put a case of 24 empty Pepsi bottles under the horse. Each day you remove one bottle, until only one is left. When there is only one bottle left, the horse is forced to pee in it."
>
> —*Cockfighter Journal*

By everyone's accounts, Don Herron is a nice guy. He's learned in fiction and can craft quite a story. Whether intentional or not, Herron's biography of Charles Willeford (simply called *Willeford*) comes off as an ingratiating, self-serving publicity piece wherein he touts his prowess as a writer and friend to the often cantankerous Willeford.

Herron's book is divided into three sections: "In Life," "In Conversation," and "In Print." The second section is undoubtedly the most infuriating for those readers who want to know more about Charles Willeford and not Don Herron, who dominates the transcription of (often inane) taped discussions. Rather than discovering/disclosing the source of Willeford's motifs, themes, and goofy "facts" (see above) that went unexplained by Willeford's body of autobiographical work, Herron merely states that he was never sure when Willeford was pulling his leg or not. Now that's investigative journalism!

While it might be nice to allow Willeford to keep some of his enigmatic qualities, Herron shirked the critical onus in his refusal to provide interpretation of the author's work. Apart from that, one would hope that a proper biographer would have *at least* included a more structured look at Willeford's life, including the years not covered by his autobiographical texts.

While still an invaluable volume of Willefordian lore, *Willeford* is ultimately more frustrating than informative.

> "Incentive, O disposed one.
> A dishwasher has no future.
> But if you, too, require incentive
> To equal my hard-earned success—
> I know where a dishwashing job is open..."
>
> —*Understudy for Love*

Not every Willeford novel is as delightful as the last. At times his work was marred by overzealous editors who demanded tawdry sex scenes (*Understudy of Love*), or felt themselves more qualified to write than the author (the first few chapters of *No Experience Necessary* were rewritten by one such editor). While Willeford's career progressed, his writing improved as he gained autonomy over his novels.

As mentioned earlier, Willeford was constantly improving on the stories and themes that fascinated him. His early works provide valuable insight into the greater themes present in his oeuvre. The following three books are undoubtedly the quirkiest entries in his bibliography—not only in their themes, but in their production.

Lust Is a Woman (1958) is a shoddy book—not necessarily in the quality of writing, but in the treatment of the material by publisher Beacon Books. Initially, one may presume that the stature of *Lust Is a Woman*, as a rarity among Willeford bibliographies, may stem from the cover sporting a byline of "Charles *Williford*." The text of the work contains instances of twice-printed sentences and paragraphs as well as a scattering of omitted letters.

Aside from the textual flaws of the book, *Lust Is a Woman* is a tawdry, compelling read. One of Willeford's first and few ventures into a third-person narrative, the novel is structured with the conceit he would employ in *Off the Wall*, *Miami Blues*, and *Sideswipe* of alternating the narrative between two central figures. In this case, the dual protagonists are Ralph Tone—an art student working as a bellboy for summer break—and Maria Dugan.

The cover states that Maria desperately wants "to become a movie star." This was an apparent ploy to paint the novel as a seedy tale of star-struck seduction. Yet Maria is on vacation in Miami Beach—hundreds of miles from both the footlights of her native New York and the alluring glare of Hollywood glamour. Escaping from the typing pool to the sandy beaches of Florida, Maria never expresses desire for anything other than money. Her single-minded ambition ensnares the beautiful gal in "an evil game" of white slavery.

Despite her apparent amorality, Maria is a more sympathetic character than the hapless Ralph. Though he only manages a solitary, aborted date, Ralph becomes hopelessly infatuated with the "big buxom woman" (whose breasts are under intense narrative scrutiny). Ralph's obsession is fueled by sleep deprivation, booze, uppers, and a lack of self-respect. Willeford highlights Ralph's underlying dementia in a familiar manner: "In less than an hour, Ralph was standing beneath the shower in the upstairs bathroom…completely sober, sick to both heart and stomach, as the hot water sluiced over his head he repeated to himself: 'I'll never be clean again. I'll never be clean again.'"

Lust Is a Woman was cleaned up and released as *Made in Miami* in 2008 by Point Blank Press.

The protagonist in *Understudy for Love* (1961) bears the name "Richard Hudson." However, there's little in common with the anti-hero of *The Woman Chaser*. Actually, the Hudson of *The Woman Chaser* is a direct descendant of used-car dealer (and all-around bastard) Russell Haxby of *High Priest of California*.

The Richard Hudson of *Understudy for Love* could be viewed as a primitive amalgam of the art critic (Jamie Figueras) and artist (Jacques Debierue) of *The Burnt Orange Heresy*. Like Figueras, Hudson is a writer for a periodical. In this case, Hudson churns out crappy copy for a daily newspaper in Lake Springs, Florida. Additionally, like Debierue, this Hudson is a frustrated artist.

Having some success at dramatic writing in college, Hudson had ambition of becoming a Broadway playwright. Instead, he spends his days ruminating over the handful of pages he's penned. His proposed play, *The Understudy*, is a tale of duplicity in which a gifted amateur actor, employed as a dishwasher, plots to steal the job of a well-educated theater director by aping the mannerisms and skills of the director. (Willeford's dishwasher-as-actor turns in an appearance in his story "An Actor Prepares" from *Everybody's Metamorphosis*.)

Hudson recognizes that he is both "director" and "dishwasher" by being the creator of the play, as well as being stuck. Like the dishwasher, Hudson sees his job at the newspaper as unbefitting his creative gifts. It takes a quixotic quest for "the unattainable" for Hudson to begin to glean that he is fortunate to have a job writing poignant items about a child bitten by a pet raccoon, a drunk throwing a bowl of chili through the window of Charlie's Chili Bowl, or an old boy of eighty exposing himself to some elderly ladies at the shuffleboard courts.

The impetus for Hudson's change of heart is derived from a feature assignment regarding the upswing trend of suicide in America. At the center of his research is the murder–suicide of Marion Huneker and her two children. Written from Hudson's point of view, the reader is repeatedly presented with Hudson's apathy about his task and his slipshod journalism. Hudson's self-centered personality helps foster an inability to observe his surroundings. Hudson makes little progress in finding any motivation for Mrs. Huneker murdering her children and taking her own life. While Hudson's busy chasing the skirt of Huneker's best friend, Gladys Chatham, he fails to realize that his wife has taken a role in the latest Community Theater production. By this, Hudson's wife becomes "director" to his "dishwasher."

The required sex scenes meant to sell the book as "adult reading" provide the novel with an overabundant amount of padding. A thoughtful character study and astute treatise on the creative process, *Understudy for Love* is flawed in its herky-jerky pacing and abrupt resolution.

The Whip Hand (1961) is undoubtedly the strangest entry in Willeford's bibliography. Published by Gold Medal (a major paperback publishing house that Willeford failed to crack), *The Whip Hand* bears the sole byline of W. Franklin Sanders. An old Army buddy, Sanders is said to have worked with Willeford on the original manuscript in 1946 (making it Willeford's first full-length book). Gold Medal rejected the book in 1946, accepting it fifteen years later after an extensive re-write by Sanders. By all accounts, *Deliver Me from Dallas* (the original title of the book) was released unbeknownst to Willeford. The amount of Sanders's input during the 1946 writing of *Deliver Me from Dallas* is questionable. *The Whip Hand* stands as the elusive Sanders's sole title.

Employing eight narrators—four of which speak in thick Okie vernacular—*The Whip Hand* follows Bill Brown, an ex-Los Angeles detective, through his misadventures in Dallas. Brown gets mixed up in a kidnapping-turned-murder performed by three yokels. The leader of the trio is Junior Knowles, a cold-blooded killer who seems to be a graduate of the John D. MacDonald School of Unexpectedly Shrewd Rednecks. The victim's family is the aristocratic Dixon clan, led by Galin Dixon and his firecracker of a daughter, Kay. Despite the implications of the cover art, Kay never gets to use her father's bullwhip.

However, Kay might like to have one used on her: "I leaned against the staircase and forced my right breast between two of the posts, under the top rail. The space between was a tight fit. The pressure felt nice against my flesh…I twisted my body as much as I could and the pain was nearly brutal. I flipped my skirt up to my waist and dug my nails in, all the while punishing my captive breast… In a few short minutes I felt better…I'd gotten some relief for my screaming nerves."

The use of so many narrators often proves tiresome, as events are unnecessarily explained from multiple points of view. Yet a few scenes benefit this conceit, especially those chapters narrated by characters that would otherwise remain minor without a narrative voice.

Like Willeford's subsequent work, *The Whip Hand* bears plenty of brutality, perversity, and a prominent mention of a gabardine suit. Publisher Dennis McMillan released the original Willeford version (as *Deliver Me from Dallas*) in 2001.

> "The collector's role is almost as important to the world of culture as the critic's. Without collectors there would be precious little art produced in this world, and without critics, collectors would wonder what to collect."
>
> —*The Burnt Orange Heresy*

Finding the books of Charles Willeford can be a challenge, but it's a quest that guarantees satisfaction.

While it's a shame that some of his early works are difficult to track down, the fruit of these seedlings can be plucked from Willeford's polished novels (such as *Cockfighter*, *The Woman Chaser*, *The Burnt Orange Heresy*, *The Collected Memoirs of Charles Willeford*, and the Hoke Moseley books).

On occasion, an odd novel will be republished without warning, such as Carroll & Graf's January 2000 release of *The Burnt Orange Heresy*. Meanwhile, 1999 saw Disc-Us Books publishing both of Willeford's primary memoirs (*I Was Looking for a Street* and *Something about a Soldier*) in one volume.

The true champion of bringing Willeford's work to print, especially the more rare titles, is Dennis McMillan. Publisher of a good number of Willeford's later, more challenging tomes (*Kiss Your Ass Good-bye*, *Everybody's Metamorphosis*, etc.), the last few years have seen McMillan releasing the aforementioned biography of Willeford, along with *The Difference* and *Writing and Other Blood Sports* (which contains *New Forms of Ugly*). McMillan even offers harder-to-find works via his website at DennisMcMillan.com.

The original version of this article ran in *Cashiers du Cinemart* #11.

TRAGICALLY OBSCURE: JOHN PAIZS'S (*THE BIG*) *CRIME WAVE*

By Skizz Cyzyk

Call it fate. In the summer of 1992, while sifting through a pile of used VHS tapes from a video store that had gone under, I stumbled upon a copy of a 1986 movie, *The Big Crime Wave*. While I rarely impulse shop and considering at that time I was in no position to be able to afford to, something about the box made it look too interesting to pass up. I'll never forget the first time I popped that tape into my VCR. Within the first 10 minutes, *The Big Crime Wave* had jumped onto my list of favorite films, eventually settling among the top three (the other two being *Brazil* and *The Forbidden Zone*).

Not only was I amazed at how cool the film was, I couldn't believe I had never heard of it before. Aside from being one the most original, unique, and unpredictable films I have ever seen, it is also one of the most undeservingly obscure films I know of. I can't help but think that if this film had gotten proper distribution, it would be a well-known cult classic by now, putting its filmmaker, John Paizs (pronounced "Pays") on the map of cool, inspirational indie filmmakers.

The film looks and sounds like a 1950s educational movie. Everything about it is done perfectly: the lighting, the sound design, the narration, the sets, the costumes, the music, the title cards, the color, the overall feeling. Whenever I show it to someone who's never seen it before, I like to have them play a little game, which is to simply try to predict what's going to happen next.

So far, no one has been able to.

There's so much to it despite its simple story line. The humor of the film is dry and deadpan, yet quirky in a way that probably kept it from finding any kind of mainstream acceptance. It was, perhaps, years ahead of its time, and might still be today.

John Paizs took much of his inspiration for *The Big Crime Wave* from 1950s B-crime melodramas, educational films, and from Fellini's *8 1/2*, which he considers "the ultimate (and possibly the only other?) 'blocked filmmaker' film."

"I lived in those days, to an alarming degree, in a fantasy world of old movies," he says, "and my own films had to be, as much as I could make them, old movies." Obviously, the "blocked-filmmaker"/"film-about-making-a-film" genre has taken off since then (*Barton Fink, Living in Oblivion, Man Bites Dog, An Alan Smithee Film, Mute Witness, The Pickle, Irma Vep*), but back in the mid-'80s it was still wide open for exploration. And explore he did, in a way that had never been done before and has never been done since.

The Story

The Big Crime Wave is the story of Steven Penny (played by Paizs), a quiet man. So quiet, in fact, that he never says a word throughout the entire film. Steven is a filmmaker who is trying to write the script for his next film, titled *Crime Wave*, which he hopes will be "the best color crime movie ever." Aside from the fact that he is only able to write by streetlight, Steven also suffers from a writer's block that allows him to write countless beginnings and endings to *Crime Wave*, but has trouble writing middles worth keeping.

Steven befriends Kim (Eva Kovacs), a young neighbor who wants to do whatever she can to help Steven complete the script to *Crime Wave*. Kim also narrates the film, making up for the lack of dialogue caused by Steven's "quietness."

The majority of the story focuses on the relationship between Steven and Kim, but it's tied together by the beginnings and endings to *Crime Wave* that Steven writes within the film, all of which seem to be the exact same story, with different characters in different situations. In one, Ronnie Boyles (Darrell Baran)—an Elvis impersonator—wants to be the world's greatest tribute artist, but his career is sidetracked and ultimately ended by an unintentional crime spree. In another version, Dawn (Tea Andrea Tanner) and Skip (Jeffrey Owen Madden) Holiday, a couple on the road to worldwide domination of the door-to-door sales racket, á la Amway, ends in a similar predicament. In all the versions, we are introduced to the competition before meeting the protagonists, and then we're thrust directly to the ending, which usually involves tragic deaths.

Later, Kim finds the middles that Steven throws away and as she reads them, we are treated to those, too. These wordless vignettes feature scenes of Ronny Boyles accidentally shooting a hunting partner; another shows him consoling a crying child whose pet he's just run over with a lawn mower. Meanwhile, one middle has Dawn and Skip stuck in a traffic jam, and examining the marks left on ankles by extension cords used for sexual bondage activities in another. The creativity is endless and these throw-away (literally) moments make for some of the funniest scenes in the film.

Eventually Steven gives up on *Crime Wave*, but then regains interest when Kim sets up a meeting between him and Dr. Jolly (Neal Lawrie), a script doctor who suggests that all Steven needs are "twists." Unfortunately, the good doctor goes psychotic before meeting Steven, which results in a freak accident that leaves Steven's head stuck inside a fallen streetlight—a series of events that allows Steven to finally overcome his writer's block, thus enabling him to write the final version of Crime Wave.

Throw in a costume party, a private club for imaginary friends, gay-bashing rednecks in pickup trucks, a quarantined city, and countless other brilliant yet insignificant ideas, and you just barely get the gist of Crime Wave. For those who have yet to see it, I've already given too much away.

The History

In March of 1984, then 26-year-old Canadian filmmaker John Paizs sat down for three weeks and wrote the screenplay for a movie called Crime Wave—a comedy about a filmmaker with writer's block. Turns out, Paizs was no stranger to writer's block himself. He was, in fact, hampered by self-doubt, much like his main character. The fact that he already had two unsuccessful feature screenplays under his belt did not make matters any better.

Yet before that period in his life, Paizs had managed to establish himself with a series of shorts. At the age of 22, he made The Obsession of Billy Botski, a film that seemed to jumpstart the "weird films from Winnipeg" movement epitomized by the likes of Guy Maddin, and also predating the current lounge music craze by more than a decade. He followed that up with three more shorts: The International Style (which he considers his worst film); Oak, Ivy, and Other Deadly Elms; and Springtime in Greenland, which he considers his best short. All three shorts were eventually packaged together as a feature called The Three Worlds of Nick.

From May of 1984 to June of 1985, Paizs and his small crew (usually consisting of no more than three people and sometimes as few as one—himself) spent their weekends shooting Crime Wave.

John Paizs deals with a cocky actor

The film was shot with a rented Arriflex BL 16mm camera, plus Paizs's own wind-up Bolex, and funded with about $60,000 worth of Canadian art council grants. Most of the cast consisted of friends, friends of friends, or relatives. Paizs employed several techniques to make Crime Wave look and sound like an old movie: the camera rarely moves (like in many silent films), and the film is lit with hard lighting and harsh sunlight to achieve a Technicolor look. All of the sound was replaced in post-production—a process Paizs called "Select-O-Sound," which gave the film a clean, controlled, retro-sounding soundtrack.

Tragically Obscure: John Paizs's *(The Big) Crime Wave*

In September of 1985, *Crime Wave* premiered at the Festival of Festivals in Toronto. Audience reaction was positive for the beginning and middle of the film, but Paizs decided the ending needed to be different. By the spring of 1986, slightly more than two years since its inception, the final version of *Crime Wave* was completed.

Though *Crime Wave* was picked up for distribution, it was buried by its distributors—most likely due to them getting cold feet over the film's quirky style of humor. To this day, it has never had a theatrical run outside of Winnipeg. The U.S. distributors of the film had an extra problem to contend with: *Crime Wave* was being released around the same time as the Sam Raimi/Coen Brothers film, *Crimewave*. "That my title is two words as opposed to one—*Crime Wave*—obviously wasn't a big enough distinguishing feature for them," Paizs says. The distributors solution was to essentially deface the beautiful *Crime Wave* title card with an overlapping video title, reading "*The Big*," thus changing the film's title to *The Big Crime Wave*.

Jon Coutts, Gerry Klym, Eva Kovacs, and John Paizs

The trouble didn't end there. All of the companies that released *The Big Crime Wave* on video went out of business by the early '90s. The video has been out of print for years and there has been no way to get a non-pirate copy of it ever since (unless you are one of the lucky ones to find a used copy at a video store). However, pirate copies have kept *The Big Crime Wave* alive, though only in obscure cult-film status.

After *The Big Crime Wave*, Paizs went on to direct music videos, commercials, and television shows (including episodes of *Maniac Mansion* and segments of *The Kids in the Hall*).

Then from the North…or, My Weekend with John Paizs

In late 1998, Jed Dietz founded the Maryland Film Festival and asked me to be on the advisory board. When asked for programming suggestions, I quickly piped up, "There's this great, but criminally obscure, Canadian film from 1986 called *Crime Wave* that really needs to be discovered by a new audience. I went on and on until I had Jed convinced it would be a good idea to get it for the festival.

I should mention that for five years previous, I had been trying to track down a print of *Crime Wave* and bring it to my hometown of Baltimore. Year after year I would hit brick walls while trying to find *Crime Wave*: it wasn't listed in any catalogues; every company ever associated with it had long since gone out of business; and web searches turned up very little. Attempting to write anything more than a review seemed hopeless, and I had no idea what to tell Jed as far as how to program a film I couldn't find.

Then, as luck would have it, I stumbled upon a website for Winnipeg filmmakers, and there was John Paizs's name. Not only that, but under his name were listed a few of his films besides *Crime Wave*. And that's not all—the films were available to rent.

With new contact info in sight, I had two concerns: how could I bring a print of *Crime Wave* to Baltimore, and how could I arrange an interview with John Paizs? Within minutes I had all the print traffic info I needed and had been granted an interview by Paizs himself. I quickly came up with all sorts of questions about *Crime Wave*, as well as his earlier films and his latest, *Top of the Food Chain*, and emailed them back to him.

To make this part of a long story a little shorter, by February I had finished the back-and-forth email interview, written the article, and forwarded the print traffic info to the Maryland Film Festival.

Imagine my shock when Maryland Film Festival Programming Consultant, Gabe Wardell, called to tell me that he had not only booked a print of *Crime Wave* for the festival, but he also managed to convince the distributors of *Top of the Food Chain* to book an April screening in Baltimore, five months before the film's scheduled premiere at the Toronto International Film Festival! And not only that—Paizs would be attending the Maryland Film Festival in person, and I would be introducing him before his films.

John Paizs conquers the world…slowly

After my article about *Crime Wave* ran in *Cashiers du Cinemart*, I began to receive a small but steady flood of fan mail from people who have loved *Crime Wave* but either couldn't find anyone else who had seen it, or couldn't get anyone else to like it. I described the film as "tragically obscure" without realizing how large, yet unorganized, the film's cult following really was.

Cut to April. I'm standing in the lobby of The Charles Theater during the packed Maryland Film Festival when I notice a man standing by himself, looking a little uncomfortable. Sure enough, he looks like *Crime Wave*'s silent star, Steven Penny, but a few years older. The first time I heard him speak I was shocked. There I was, standing in front of a character from a movie I've watched a hundred times, yet this was the first time I'd ever heard his voice. It never dawned on me that he had one.

Tragically Obscure: John Paizs's *(The Big) Crime Wave*

That night I introduced John Paizs to a very small audience who turned out to see *Crime Wave*. Despite my efforts to hype the screening, many people thought the $10 admission price too risky for an obscure film they had only heard of because of my incessant raving (in the meantime, the screening of the obscure Liz Taylor/Richard Burton flick, *Boom*, was standing room only because it came with John Waters's recommendation). Nevertheless, those who came to see it loved it, and stuck around afterwards for one of the longest Q&A sessions I've ever stood through. Paizs was charming and funny, with his modest views of his work and his quiet demeanor struggling through his strong Canadian accent. Most of the audience wanted to know why they had never heard of his film, when it so obviously deserved much more recognition. Paizs explained how his distribution deal was to pay him out of profits from the film's theatrical release, but how the distributors had no intention of releasing the film theatrically. He also told the crowd about how he left the theater during the film to slip into one of the other screenings to watch *Divine Trash*, Steve Yeager's documentary on John Waters's *Pink Flamingos*. Knowing that Paizs was a big John Waters fan, it was a real thrill for me to introduce him to Mary Vivian Pierce out in the lobby. He seemed almost as starstruck by her as I was by him.

I guess word of mouth about how cool *Crime Wave* was had spread around the festival, because the next night's screening of *Top of the Food Chain* was packed. Not only that, but the audience roared with laughter through the entire movie. Again, many people stayed for a long Q&A session afterwards. Originally Paizs seemed like he was shunning *Food Chain* as an example of his work simply because he didn't write it. But his touch is obvious throughout the film, and he seemed to reconsider his stance once he realized people liked it.

Top of the Food Chain

The Boston Review described John Paizs's previous feature, *Crime Wave*, as "the funniest Canadian movie ever made." Almost a decade and a half later, Paizs returned with a new comedy featuring a cast moviegoers may have heard of, and a script less likely to scare away general audiences. While being very different from *Crime Wave*, *Top of the Food Chain* still maintains Paizs's trademark touch of absurd humor set in a 1950s-looking setting.

Campbell Scott leads the charge in *Top of the Food Chain*

Welcome to the town of Exceptional Vista, once famous for producing "the finest damned nuts in the Western Central Northeast" (not the snack food but the kind you screw onto bolts—note the colloquialism is appropriate for the town's residents). Nowadays, Exceptional Vista is run down and filled with bored characters obsessed with TV, fishing, and weird sex. Though not entirely obvious at first, it turns out that when the nut factory closed, the town's more sane residents packed up and moved to the neighboring burgs of Right Hemisphere, Left Hemisphere, Bladdertown, Dunk, Walkadogathon, New Imbroglio, and Fetus. When a comet knocks out the town's TV transmitter tower, the remaining residents suddenly find themselves at risk of being eaten by aliens.

Meanwhile, Exceptional Vista is paid a visit by vacationing Dr. Karel Lamonte, a famous atomic scientist from the Atomic Institute, who speaks with amazing intelligence without saying anything intelligent (an amazing over-the-top performance by Campbell Scott). A romance immediately blooms between Dr. Karel Lamonte and motel keeper Sandy Fawkes (Fiona Loewi), a girlish femme fatale who puts her incestuous affair with her brother, Guy (Tom Everett Scott), on hold in order to pursue the doctor. When mutilated bodies begin turning up ("in the lumpy, bumpy part of town outside of town"), along with government agents and flesh-eating aliens, Dr. Karel Lamonte, Sandy, Guy, and the rest of the town are thrown into a battle to remain at the top of the food chain, plunging the audience into sophisticatedly twisted cornball territory.

John Paizs directing Campbell Scott in *Top of the Food Chain*

This is not just a very funny film, it's a tribute to classic sci-fi/horror films of the '50s and '60s (*War of the Worlds*, *Them*, *The Blob*, *Night of the Living Dead*) mixed in a setting that is equal parts David Lynch's *Twin Peaks* and any silly world created by the Abrahms/Zucker team. Paizs's directing is flawless, with help from a brilliant script by Phil Bedard and Larry Lalonde and amazing performances from the cast, each given very cartoonish characters to flesh out. Overall, the film serves as more of a tribute within a comedy setting than a flat-out parody, and as a result, comes off seeming familiar while remaining original. With pacing that never lets up, *Food Chain* delivers one gag after another—whether it's one of many absurd lines of dialogue uttered by Dr. Karel Lamonte, or ongoing references to fish (such as a table laid out with all sorts of food dishes, each with entire fish sticking out of them for either decoration or flavor).

Much like *Crime Wave*, *Top of the Food Chain* is laced with amusing, yet mostly insignificant, details. All of the male characters have women's names (Michel O'Shea, Dr. Karel Lamonte, Mayor Claire, Officer Gayle, Deputy Dana, Jan Bathgate)—excluding Guy, of course. Two different traveling salespersons arrive in town at the same time—one sells vacuums, the other sells banjos. A *Night of the Living Dead* homage consists of a country house being attacked by zombie-like aliens all wearing Polo shirts and khakis. A seemingly unrelated detail earlier in the film, involving women bringing a fish back to life and turning coal into gold, leads to a happy ending—much happier than any viewer could have expected.

The sci-fi/horror genre has often left a lot to be desired, and genre spoofs often take that which is lacking a step further by being funny only to those who love that particular genre. *Top of the Food Chain*, however, rates high on all counts. As a sci-fi/horror film, it contains some good suspense and special effects. As a spoof, it lovingly celebrates the genre it's spoofing. But overall, as a comedy, its humor is universal, not to mention gut-busting.

Top of the Food Chain was released on video in the US in November of 2000 as *Invasion!*

Conclusion

At the closing night party, I was genuinely sad that he would be heading back to Canada soon. I gave him a videotape of some of my work and a copy of *The Forbidden Zone*. Days later, he emailed to tell me how much he liked one of my films—even better than Richard Elfman's! What a compliment. What a relief that he was a cool guy and not some snooty film jerk. But he'd have to be cool to have made such unique and worthwhile films.

With my John Paizs Weekend behind me, I now spend frequent moments planning how to bring him back to Baltimore for a retrospective of his films, and how to get *Crime Wave* re-released so that it can get the recognition it deserves.

Portions of this article ran in *Cashiers du Cinemart* #9 and #10.

OEDIPAL KETCHUP

By Andrew Grant

A group of pre-pubescent children clad in military uniforms rebel against their parents and begin hunting adults. A choir of schoolgirls strip while singing "when I grow up to be a whore." A young man struggles in vain to break through his cousin's chastity belt. Images culled not from some drug-induced dream, but from visions of the revolutionary poet, playwright, and filmmaker Shuji Terayama. Virtually unknown in the United States, Terayama's work is extremely important in the history of Japanese experimental cinema, and he belongs in the ranks alongside Nagisa Oshima, Shohei Imamura, and Hiroshi Teshigahara. With the exception of 1981's *Fruits of Passion* (a quasi-sequel to *The Story of O*), none of Terayama's films have been available in the United States.

Born in 1936, Terayama was primarily raised by his mother after his father died of dysentery while in Indonesia. Unable to earn enough in their town, she would seek work in Kyushu at the American military base, leaving young Shuji in the care of his aunt and uncle, owners of the village movie theater that became a second home for him. At eighteen, Terayama was diagnosed with nephritis (the disease that would ultimately be responsible for his early death) and spent nearly four years in and out of hospitals. It was during one of his extended hospital stays that he began writing tanka poetry, which would win him the prestigious Chekhov Poetry prize in 1954. The hospital years also afforded Terayama the chance to become a voracious reader. He devoured Gide, Sartre, Freud, Malraux, Capote, McCullers, and Mayakovsky. He also discovered the French surrealists, particularly Lautreamont's *The Song Of Maldoror* (about which he would make a short film in 1977). This book, over any other, was to have a tremendous impact on his art. In the years that followed, Terayama continued to write poetry, but he also ventured on to compose novels, essays, plays, and screenplays.

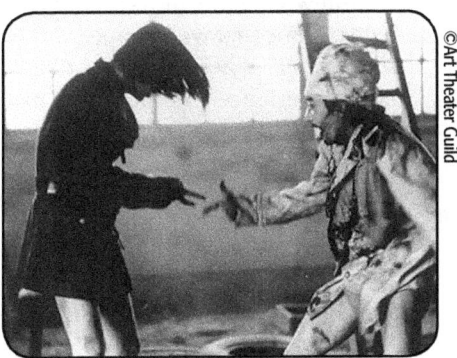
Roshambo in *Emperor Tomato Ketchup*

When Terayama was twenty-one, he wrote and produced a radio play (*Adult Hunting*) that was presented in the form of an emergency news broadcast, à la Orson Welles's take on *War of the Worlds*. The broadcast claimed that a revolution was taking place, and young children were rising up to claim Tokyo as their own. This theme would later be reworked into one of his earliest films, *Emperor Tomato Ketchup* (1970).

Oedipal Ketchup

With its cryptic title (more commonly recognized as an album by electronica band Stereolab), *Emperor Tomato Ketchup* is one of Terayama's most challenging works. Lacking a conventional narrative, the film's gritty, often over-exposed imagery at times resembles a home movie gone horribly wrong. Set in a Japan in which children have mysteriously gained control, its revolutionary gaze is as much sexual as it is political. Some of the rules that the young dictators establish include:

- Adults who upset children, use physical strength, or are too protective will have their civil status removed.
- Adults who steal children's snacks, who deprive them from freedom of speech or sex, or who try to impose their prejudice in matters of education will be given the death penalty.
- In the name of God, all children will enjoy their freedoms: freedom of conspiracy, freedom of treason, freedom to practice sodomy, and the freedom to use The Bible as toilet paper.

Terayama has referred to *Emperor Tomato Ketchup* as a joke, but not a comedy. Japan at this time was caught up in a wave of protests: the renewal of the Japan–U.S. Security Treaty, the corporate dominance of Osaka Expo 70, the Vietnam War, and corruption at the universities drew students to the streets by the thousands. Is the film a parody of these protests, or rather an exaggerated representation of the public's worst nightmare—that is, what if the revolutionaries won?

But what of the film's sexual politics? Here we find the earliest example of a major theme that will reappear in several of his later films—the Oedipal nature of a mother–son relationship tied with the boy's sexual initiation by an older, more experienced woman. It is in *Emperor Tomato Ketchup* that this idea is (literally and figuratively) at its most explicit. A young boy brandishing a rifle makes sexual advances on a nude woman. "I seduce my mommy and I become my daddy" appears as an inter-title on the screen. Later in the film, a boy is the sexual partner of three women described by film scholar Amos Vogel as "magical...yet protectively maternal."

Terayama has cited an Oedipal crisis as a key factor in the problems besetting Japan. At the same time, he was interested in a sexual revolution wherein women would take the active role in heterosexual relations. As film scholar Steven Clark puts it, "women should stop marrying ugly balding men with secure jobs for their money." By taking younger lovers, they will in effect breed such men out of existence, leaving a world where youth reigns supreme. Though highly exaggerated, this is one possibility of what he wished to express with *Emperor Tomato Ketchup*. Terayama would be far less vague in his follow-up, *Throw Away Your Books, Go Out Into the Streets*.

Originating as both an experimental theater piece and a book of the same name, *Throw Away Your Books, Go Out Into the Streets* (1971) is one of Terayama's greatest achievements. Voted one of the ten best films of the 1970s by the prestigious *Kinema Junpo* magazine, it vividly captures the youthful rebellious spirit that was sweeping Japan at this time. Once again eschewing narrative, Terayama's first feature still manages to tell the story of a decaying urban family as seen through the eyes of the teenage son, Eimei Kitamura. Entwined with the film are poems and stories written by teenagers recruited during the theatrical production as it toured Japan. On top of that, the film boasts several musical numbers that would fit nicely in a Japanese version of *Hair*.

The film's theatrical roots are made clear from the opening scene. Eimei breaks down the cinematic fourth wall and addresses the audience directly, mocking our passiveness and encouraging us to put our hand on the knee of the girl sitting next to us. After a brief introduction to the members of the dysfunctional Kitamura family, the film takes off in collage-like fashion. Intertwined with Kitamura's story are songs, confessions, dreamlike interludes, and bits of agitprop that on first impression appear unrelated to Eimei's story, but on subsequent viewings reveal them all to be part of his own experience.

Taking a cue from the titular command, much of the agitprop throughout the film occurs on the streets of Tokyo. Quotes from Malreaux, Fromm, and Mayakovsky are spray painted on walls. An American flag is burned, revealing a fornicating couple behind it. A young woman encourages people at a crowded intersection to release their anger by hitting a phallus-shaped punching bag. Another tries to discourage people from going into a cinema. Shot in vérité style, these scenes brilliantly capture the revolutionary energy that was present at this time.

The Kitamura family is a polar opposite to Terayama's own. Whereas Terayama was raised in the countryside without a father, motherless Eimei lives in a tiny Tokyo apartment with several family members who treat each other with disdain, aggression, and an overall lack of respect. Eimei's man-hating sister Setsuko spends all her waking moments with her pet rabbit. Their grandmother, thinking it best for Setsuko, has the rabbit killed and makes a stew out of

Director Shuji Terayama and friends from Pastoral: To Die in the Country

it. Eimei tries to help his chronic-masturbator father find a new job—not out of love, but out of a desire to stop taking care of him. In turn, the father secretly plans to have his mother sent away to an old folks home. It is only between Eimei and Setsuko that a semblance of compassion can be found, even though an incestuous relationship is hinted at.

Oedipal Ketchup

The film continually questions the hierarchy of the Japanese family. As one character puts it, "when the family fulfilled different functions it still had some meaning; economic, hierarchical, educational, recreational, protective, and religious. But now the state and society have taken over those functions. All that's left is affection. Blood ties are still at the heart of it all." The film implies that the family is a tyrannical, cruel unit whose destruction should not be mourned. Yet this change does not come without a price: the old traditions (now destroyed) have been replaced with cheap imitations of American culture. Eimei compares Japan to a lizard trapped in a Coca-Cola bottle—too big for its prison, but lacking the strength to break out.

Of great concern to nineteen-year-old Eimei is his virginity. Beyond base sexual desire, he wishes to destroy the greedy sexual bonds that (in fantasy) bind him to his dead mother. His initiation by a prostitute is far from romantic, and quite unpleasant. In one of the lengthiest sequences in the film, we watch as Eimei uncomfortably squirms and struggles to get away (writhing on sheets adorned with erotic poetry), but is ultimately overcome by the woman. Though not a positive experience, it will ultimately contribute to Eimei's evolution from the meek but curious introvert into the angry rebellious character he is at the end of the film.

The film ends much as it begins, with Eimei once again addressing the audience, though this time he is reflecting on the film's fantasies and his own experience, which in effect unwinds the illusion of cinema. Here is Terayama made real, and he will go on to play an even greater role in his next film, *Pastoral: To Die in the Country* (1974).

After a three-year hiatus from film, Terayama returned with his second feature, the introspective *Pastoral: To Die in the Country*. A personal exorcism of his past, the film is considered by many to be his masterpiece. Martin Scorsese has championed it on several occasions, and a proper release in the States is long overdue.

The film reveals its autobiographical foundation from the onset. The setting is a village at the foot of Mt. Osore in Aomori, where Terayama was raised. Renamed "Terror Mountain" in the film, Osorezan is famous for both its strong sulfur smell and for the existence of *itako*, female shamans who act as mediums to communicate with the dead. The village and its inhabitants are presented through the eyes of a fifteen-year-old boy raised alone by his mother. The boy (nameless, as are all the film's characters) suffers from typical adolescent angst, but finds little understanding from his overbearing mother. Desperate, the boy visits an *itako* to speak to his deceased father, but finds little solace.

The life of the villagers is dominated by the inherited weight of rural tradition, something Terayama considers dangerous. Superstition abounds in the village. A young unmarried woman giving birth has rules barked at her by a gaggle of black-clad old women peering in from the doorway; she suffers a miscarriage, and as a result is tormented by the women. Such superstitions are used as a metaphor for the burden of the past in present-day Japanese consciousness. Traditions are carried out, yet nobody can actually explain why. Conformity is critical to the point that every house in the village is governed by the time of the family clock.

Standing in opposition to this conformity is a traveling circus that has arrived in the village. The life of the circus members is equally as ritualistic, though unlike the obscure nature of those in the village, their lives are often about sex, violence, work, and play. The boy, peering through the tent flap, sees his first glimpse of hedonistic behavior in the form of an all-out orgy, which causes him to flee in terror.

Falling in love with the married woman next door, the boy asks her to elope, offering them the chance to escape the oppressiveness of their village lives. At their moment of escape, the narrative suddenly stops and we are in Tokyo, where the director has been showing this film to friends and colleagues. The director (clearly Terayama) worries that in choosing to make a film about his past, he might end up exploiting his childhood and creating little more than a cheap spectacle. At a smoke-filled bar, his art-critic friend assures him that he must go on with the film, adding, "if one isn't freed from one's own memory, then one isn't free." The director, still living with his mother, meets his teenage self and decides to return with him to correct the mistakes of his past.

This time around, things are slightly different in the village. Accompanying his younger self, the events this time are somewhat more akin to the truth. His mother now physically prevents him from eloping, and the woman he loved has run off with a lover. The young unmarried woman gives birth, but drowns her baby and runs off to the city. Witnessing this, the director convinces the boy that his mother is at the root of all these problems, and he must kill her. By doing so, he will be free to escape his own history. This odd twist on the Oedipal fantasy is further enhanced when, on his way to kill his mother, the boy meets the woman who had fled the village, now returned as a prostitute. Against his will, she takes his virginity in a lengthy scene that mirrors the one in *Throw Away Your Books*, though instead of a brothel the scene takes place in a temple. Whereas Eimei suffered from his mother's absence, here the boy is smothered by her overbearing presence.

In a 1977 interview, Terayama stated that "if we wish to free ourselves, wipe out the history of humanity inside of us and the history of society around us, we must begin by getting rid of our personal memories." That the boy berates his adult self by accusing him of distorting his youth shows how difficult it was for Terayama to reconcile his fantasies with reality. As the final shot of the film proves, the line between the two is often blurred.

After *Pastoral*, Terayama made his most commercial film, *The Boxer* (1977) for Toei Studios. Made after the success of *Rocky*, the film tells the story of a retired boxer who leaves his family in order to train an up-and-coming fighter. Terayama then contributed a segment to the erotic triptych *Collection Privées* in 1979. In 1981, he went on to create the aforementioned *Fruits of*

Oedipal Ketchup

Passion, his only non-Japanese produced feature. Though not a bad example of European "art-core," it is a far cry from Terayama's earlier, personal works. However, Terayama does tread on familiar ground—one of the characters tells of her incestuous past with her father.

Terayama's final film was *Farewell to the Ark* (1984), which he made while he was dying. Unfinished at the time of his death, members of his production team completed the film. Set once again in a village lost in time, the film is loosely based on Gabriel Garcia Marquez's *100 Years of Solitude*. As he did in *Pastoral*, Terayama presents a village ruled by traditions and superstitions even more confounding than the Aomori of his childhood. Whereas the villagers in *Pastoral* were slaves to the family clock, *Farewell to the Ark* begins with a mass burial of all but one clock. The family that owns the one clock now rules the village. At the film's core is a story of a young man who wants nothing more than to have sex with his cousin. Though the other villagers warn him of the danger of having a child with her, his desire continues. Frustrating the situation is the cousin's iron chastity belt that yields to no amount of attack. After stabbing the head of the ruling clan, the cousins flee to begin life anew. Those familiar with Marquez's book will recognize elements of the novel—the cockfight early on in the film, the warning about the offspring of their union, and the modern gadgetry that are scattered throughout.

Sadly, the film is only available without subtitles. Complicating matters is the strong Okinawa dialect that, with my limited understanding of Japanese, left me in the dark. However, the sheer beauty of the images was such that I could not pull myself away from the film. Terayama's grand swan song, the film is a summing up of his ideas, and it is brimming with the most extraordinary visions he could conjure up.

When Terayama died at the young age of 48, he left behind a staggering number of poems, stories, and plays, many of which are revived for new productions year after year. In 1984, there was a nationwide retrospective of his plays, and several of these were recorded for Japanese television. One of these, *Our Age Comes Riding in on a Circus Elephant*, is made of up of small vignettes and songs. First performed in 1969, the play is very critical of America, its policies, and the re-signing of the Japan–U.S. Security Treaty. While the energy of the 1969 performance might be absent, it is nonetheless a rare chance to see this odd little musical.

If there is any justice in the world, a complete retrospective of Terayama's films will be forthcoming, with new prints and subtitles. They certainly belong in the canon of post-war Japanese films, and their lack of availability leaves a gaping hole in our ability to fully understand and appreciate the independent Japanese cinema of the 1970s. Discovering Terayama was, for me, a major cinematic find. See these films at any cost.

The original version of this article ran in *Cashiers du Cinemart* #14.

ON THE ROAD TO MEIFUMADO

By Mike White

In darkness there is movement. It's difficult to determine what we're seeing until the object breaks in two. It's a door sliding apart. Behind it, there is dazzling white light.

Surrounded by the brilliance are a man and a child, nearly in silhouette. They enter, coming closer on a silent walkway. Slowly, we begin to hear men weeping. They kneel to the side of the walkway and bemoan the fate of the little boy, their Daimyo (Lord). How could the Shogun be so cruel as to sentence a boy to death?

Such is the way of the world in Japan at this time.

Our concern is not to befall upon *this* man and *this* child, but *another* man and *another* child.

The diminutive Daimyo is taken into the execution chamber and instructed on how to signal that he is ready to enter the next world. Another door opens. Out of the black steps the Kogi Kaishakunin, the official decapitator of the Shogun who aids the small samurai in his seppuku. He is expressionless: neither cruel nor caring. He does his job, and he does it well.

He is Ogami Itto. His post is well respected in the hierarchy of his time. So much that men would kill for it. And they do.

When he returns from his day at work, he is welcomed by his bride, Azami, and baby boy, Daigoro. While he prays in his temple for the souls of those he's helped execute on behalf of the Shogun, ninjas enter his household. They slaughter his wife and plant false evidence to support a conjured plot that Ogami Itto means to kill the Shogun—a plot conceived by Lord Yagyu Retsudo, head of the Ura Yagyu clan. The power of the Shogun is tied to the Yagyu clan, who act as official spies and assassins and who wish to control Ogami Itto's post, as well.

Confronted by the mechanisms of his undoing, Ogami Itto is quick to realize that he's a patsy. Soon he will be donning white death robes to plunge his short sword into his belly while Yagyu Retsudo stands behind him, waiting to help put the Ogami clan into the grave. Ogami Itto is no dummy, and he is not a man to be fucked with.

"I'll make you pay with rivers of blood. I will dedicate my life to wreak vengeance. From now on, my path will be littered with bodies soaked in blood.

I will be ruthless," he swears to Lord Retsudo after dispatching one of Retsudo's sons, Bizen, with Itto's renowned Seagull Style Horse Killing Slash.

Itto gives the infant Daigoro a choice between joining his father (as a merciless demon) or his mother (in the afterworld). His father places a ball and sword before him and, after much childish deliberation, Daigoro places his chubby fingers on his father's weapon. Thus, they become Kozure Okami, Lone Wolf and Cub, assassins for hire.

Yagyu Restudo pits another of his sons, Kurando, against Ogami Itto, with the proposal that Ogami will live in peace as long as he never steps foot inside Edo (Tokyo) should he win the battle. In a glorious duel, Kurando stands with his back to the sun, while Ogami stands with his son on his back. Kurando does not survive.

Of course, Yagyu Retsudo has no intention of keeping his word. He constantly plots to see the defiant Itto killed while Itto wanders Japan as a formidable killer, pushing Daigoro in a large, wooden, weapons-laden baby cart. They travel Meifumado, the path between heaven and hell, always prepared to die.

All of the above occurs within the first forty minutes of Kenji Misumi's *Lone Wolf & Cub: Sword of Vengeance* (*Kozure Akami: Kowokashi Udekashi Tsukamatsuru*), the first of a series of six films shot between 1972 and 1974, starring Wakayama Tomisaburo as Ogami Itto and Tomikawa Akihiro as Daigoro. The story's roots are in manga (comic books written by Kazuo Koike, who penned the scripts for the first five *Lone Wolf & Cub* films) and spawned not only these films but also a 1993 remake, a made-for-Japanese-TV movie, and two television series (so far).

If Wakayama Tomisaburo looks familiar, it could be that he's the brother of Katsu Shintaro, one of the most popular stars of the cinema in Japan (and producer of the *Lone Wolf & Cub* film series). Shintaro played Zatoichi, the blind masseur in over twenty films and on television. Or, it could be that you're recalling him as Coach Shimizu from *The Bad News Bears Go To Japan*, or Sugai in Ridley Scott's *Black Rain*.

The story was adapted by Max Allen Collins for the graphic novel (and subsequent film) *Road to Perdition*. It was also reworked as the culpable *Shogun Assassin*; a Roger Corman-produced splicing of *Lone Wolf & Cub* #1 with the second film of the series, *Baby Cart at the River Styx*. Even the bad dubbing, poor picture quality, and confused storyline are not enough to rob the films completely of their art, but they don't begin to represent the beauty of Kenji Misumi's work. Even when delving into incredible scenes of violence that border on Monty Pythonesque excess (Itto's vengeance does flow with, if not rivers, at least geysers of blood), the films are breathtakingly beautiful. Unfortunately, Kenji Misumi did not direct all six of the theatrically released Kozure Okami films. His presence is missed in the fourth and sixth entries in the series.

Figure 1. Babycart, exploded view

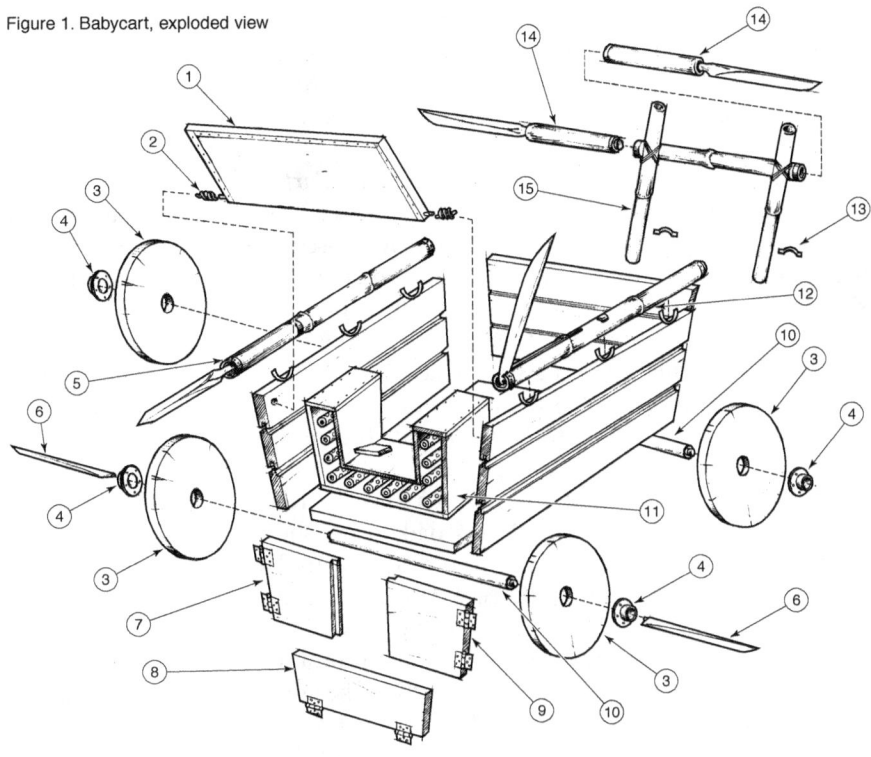

1.	Spring-loaded blast shield	9.	Left front gun door
2.	Blast shield spring	10.	Axle
3.	Wheel	11.	Machine gun unit
4.	Axle nut	12.	Single-edged swing-arm blade
5.	Double-edged retracting blade	13.	Bracket
6.	Front wheel, single-edged retracting blade	14.	Retracting short sword
7.	Right front gun door	15.	Handle assembly
8.	Bottom gun door		

©2008 Jonathan Higgins

Every shot is wonderfully composed and skillfully executed. Witness the death of Retsudo's son, Bizen, in which we see the skill of Ogami Itto as a swordsman and Kenji Misumi as a director. Standing in a river, his sword lowered beneath the surface, Itto's weapon emerges from the water; the action repeated via editing (similar to what would be done decades later in John Woo's *The Killer*). Silence emphasizes the gravity of the moment. The lack of the water's roar tells us that this story is far greater than Nature itself. Or, perhaps, Nature knows the importance of Itto's fate and silences itself in anticipation. Finally, the quiet is broken with the rough slash of Itto's sword as it cuts through Bizen.

On the Road to Meifumado

Despite the ever-present Yagyu threats and assassination contracts, no formulaic "typical Kozure Okami film" ever develops in the series. One never knows what one might get when viewing these films, except for the sleepy-eyed, low-voiced Ogami Itto, the cute-as-a-button Daigoro, and some unbelievable action scenes.

In the second film, *Lone Wolf & Cub: Baby Cart at the River Styx* (*Kozure Okami: Sanzu No Kawa Ubaguruma*), the Yagyu clan is hot on Ogami Itto's trail, sending Sayaka and her band of female assassins to kill him. The scene in which we first see Ozuno, leader of the Kurokawa clan, contact Sayaka is classic. He expresses doubt in her Kunoichi warriors. To this challenge, she asks for his best warrior to simply attempt to leave the room.

"With my ninja skill it's a simple task," the warrior blithely replies. Don't count on it, brother. One has to give the guy credit, though, for even as a limbless stump, he's still trying to crawl outside before the Kunoichi deliver their death blows.

When he's not dealing with Sayaka and her Kunoichi (who like to implement razor-sharp hats and deadly daikon radishes as weapons), Ogami is attempting to track down Makuya, the Awa clan's Headmaster of the blue-dyeing process who threatens to reveal his clan's indigo secret to the Shogun, thus ruining his clan's economy. In order to ensure his arrival, the Shogun has put Makayu under the protection of the Hidari brothers—Ben, Ten, and Rai—fearsome foes who fight with clawed hands, spiked gloves, and an iron bat. The desert showdown between the Brothers Hidari and Ogami Itto is truly breathtaking.

Ogami Itto (Tomisaburo Wakayama) and Daigoro (Tomikawa Akihiro)

The third film, *Lone Wolf & Cub: Baby Cart to Hades* (*Kozure Okami: Shinikazeni Mukau Ubaguruma*) was dubbed and released as *Lightning Swords of Death*, and can be found on video with the redundant title *Lupine Wolf*. More than previous entries, this film deals with human relationships.

Ogami Itto saves the life of a young girl who has been sold by the House of Koshio, a yakuza group. The girl bites off her betrothed's tongue as he wantonly molests her. Apparently, this surprises the lecherous fellow so much that he dies from his wound. In order to save the girl's life and her virtue, Ogami Itto strikes a bargain with the yakuza gang's boss, the lovely Torizo—he'll be tortured instead of the girl, and he'll also perform an assassination for Torizo.

The man to be killed is an underhanded governor, Sawatari Gemba. Scared stiff of the dreadful Ogami Itto, he calls for backup. Roughly three hundred men come to his aid, and Ogami Itto has to fight every last one of them. This is where those special modifications to Daigoro's baby cart really come in handy.

The third *Lone Wolf & Cub* film includes a subplot about Magomura Kanbei, the former Chief Palanquin Guard for the Maruoka Clan. Kanbei risked his life and saved his liege when his palanquin was attacked by marauders. Yet he's been reduced to a ronin, as he went against the word (but not necessarily the spirit) of Bushido (the Way of the Samurai).

After a strange turn of events, Bushido dictates that Ogami Itto and Magomura Kanbei must duel. With swords raised, Itto cancels the match in order to let a bushi (true) samurai live. You have to love how cocky Ogami Itto can be! Often, he's confident enough to put his sword away before the fools who challenged him fall dead to the ground. That is, when his sword isn't embedded in the skull of his last victim.

Kanbei meets up with Itto again on the battlefield as one of Gemba's army. Their final confrontation is astounding. The sequence ranks among the best in the series and shows Kenji Misumi as a master of his craft.

Until the fourth installment of the Kozure Okami films, subplots of Yagyu aggression, flashbacks of past treachery, and the main narrative thrust have been intricately intertwined. However, director Saito Buichi's *Lone Wolf & Cub: Baby Cart in Peril* (*Kozure Okami: Oya No Kokoro Ko No Kokoro*) feels episodic in its construction.

In this film, Ogami Itto almost plays the role of a private detective. He is hired, for reasons explained later, to kill Oyuki, an expert swordswoman with a torso riddled with tattoos: on her back, a sea hag; on her front, an imp that grasps her breast.

Daigoro plays a major role in the beginning of the film. He becomes separated from his father and wanders alone, searching for him at temples across Japan, accompanied by a maudlin tune with a refrain of "it freezes the poor child's heart, as he seeks, day after day, trying to find his father, the man people call assassin." Eventually Daigoro finds someone in the temples he frequents—none other than Yagyu Gumbei, son of Lord Retsudo Yagyu, who has been outcast from his clan and forced to live as a dead man.

It's here that we learn more of the origins of Lord Retsudo's plot against Ogami Itto. In a duel for the post of Kogi Kaishakunin, Gumbei faced off against Itto and quickly disarmed him. However, Ogami Itto was saved (and rewarded) for his knowledge of Bushido, for he quickly positioned himself, unarmed, between Gumbei's naked blade and the Shogun, as if he were protecting the Shogun with his life.

On the Road to Meifumado

After losing the match, Lord Retsudo (played by Tatsuo Endo this time around) determines that Gumbei must commit hara-kiri in order to prevent a loss of face for the clan. Instead of allowing his son to kill himself, Retsudo banishes his son and kills a double instead. By allowing his son to live and delivering the makeup artist's head to the Shogun, Retsudo shows his blatant disregard for Bushido.

Presently, the wandering Yagyu Gumbei takes stock of the strange child. He sees that Daigoro has the eyes of one who has killed hundreds of men. Just as Gumbei begins to test Daigoro's mettle, we hear the now-familiar horn section of composer Sakurai Hieoki, signaling Ogami Itto's triumphant return. Instead of taking care of unfinished business, Ogami determines that one cannot kill the "dead" for a second time and merely liberates Gumbei of his sword arm.

Oddly enough, we are never to see the one-armed Gumbei again. He is never to make good on his promise: "I will kill you. Not any other Yagyu or Kurokawa." This is just one of the unresolved items in *Lone Wolf & Cub* #4 that leaves audiences scratching their heads.

Eyes and fire are two of the major motifs of *Kozure Okami* #4. Oyuki uses her tattoos to distract the eyes of her opponents, Gumbei comments that Daigoro has the eyes of a master swordsman, and Goomune Jindayo (Oyuki's

father) is without the use of his eyes. His daughter's downfall (and subsequent need for revenge) comes from her being hypnotized by her former Daimyo's top man, Kozuka Enki. As Oyuki and Enki duel in a flashback (this film is rife with them), Enki commands her to look into his eyes. This is to distract her from the fire that surrounds his sword.

Flames are visible throughout the film. During Daigoro's little adventure, he is trapped in a field of fire. When the tattoo artist describes the process of marking Oyuki (where she wore a mask that only revealed her eyes), a candle appears on the left side of the screen. Later, when Oyuki has her flashback, another candle appears on the right side of the screen, burning brightly initially and shown smoldering after she has been beguiled by Enki's "flaming sword."

Instead of working behind the scenes, Lord Retsudo makes overt moves against Ogami Itto, enlisting the help of the Owari clan in order to throw another army at Ogami. This time the former Kogi Kaishakunin doesn't come away as unscathed—in fact, he looks a bit worse for wear at the end of the film—but does manage to give Lord Retsudo a wound he won't soon forget. The Yagyu lord is minus an eye after savagely battling Ogami Itto—punctuating the film's eye motif.

Lone Wolf & Cub: Baby Cart in the Land of Demons (*Kozure Okami: Meifumado*) saw the return of Kenji Misumi to the director's chair. It was to be his last *Kozure Okami* film, and the second-to-last film he directed before his death.

The film begins with an interesting conceit of Ogami Itto (alive and well, despite his condition after fighting Retsudo's army in the previous film) being tested by five men in his journeys. Each gives him 100 ryo, along with part of the reason they need him to fight for them.

Despite its strong beginning, lack of a musical number, brilliant set pieces, and copious bloodshed, Kenji Misumi's final effort in the Kozure Okami series, while still a good film, doesn't begin to compare to his previous entries.

The need for a seventh Kozure Okami film is obvious after watching the sixth, Kuroda Yoshiyuki's *Lone Wolf & Cub: White Heaven in Hell* (*Kozure Okami: Jigoku E Ikuzo! Daigoro*), the final theatrically released Kozure Okami film with Wakayama Tomisaburo as Ogami Itto.

Lord Retsudo finds himself in dire need to be rid of Ogami Itto, whose presence (after so many plots to eliminate him) has become a subject of ridicule among other Daimyo who demand an overt attack by Shogunate troops; such a move would mean a loss of face for the Yagyu clan. Retsudo makes reference to Ogami Itto being responsible for the deaths of his three sons, despite that the audience has seen only two perish (Gumbei is counted among the dead). Retsudo is thus forced to employ the skills of his daughter, the cute but creepy Kaori, whose "finishing move" is the planting of a short sword deep in her opponent's skull.

The pacing of the film is quite odd. Though we see Ogami Itto and Daigoro during the credit sequence, the beginning of the movie is primarily concerned with Retsudo and his daughter.

The film meanders. Characters appear and are quickly eliminated. After promptly killing Kurando, Retsudo rushes to the mountains to beg for help from Hyoé, his bastard son who, abandoned at five, lives as a sorcerer in the Tsujigumo clan. Having no allegiance to the Yagyu and knowing of his father's precarious position, Hyoé decides that the Tsujigumo clan will gain glory by disposing of Ogami Itto. He goes about this with a unique tact by resurrecting Mujo, Mugo, and Mumon, three of the Tsujigumo's best warriors who have been dead some forty-two years (but have funked-out hairdos that go well with the film's Curtis Mayfield-inspired score).

Will zombies be able to stop the man and child on the path of Meifumado? Will the threats of the undead to kill any innocents that Ogami Itto encounters slow our heroes' trip to Edo? Will the burrowing bugaboos bother the former official decapitator with their touting of the Tsujigumo Five Wheel Sword Style? Don't count on it.

On the Road to Meifumado

"The Tsujigumo style is pitiful," scoffs Ogami Itto.

The wintry wonderland of the film's conclusion provides Ogami Itto with an effective defense against Mujo, Mugo, and Mumon. Moreover, it feels like a poor counterpoint to the desert setting (and face-off against three killers) in the second film, and a good excuse to have an attack take place on skis and toboggans. Yet, after having seen Ogami Itto take care of two armies of warriors, a third feels tiresome.

After slicing, chopping, and hacking his way through Retsudo's forces, Ogami Itto (and the audience) are robbed of a final duel. Instead, Lord Yagyu sleds away, muttering, "I will kill you someday." Huh? When?

It was five years before Wakayama Tomisaburo returned to act in a *Kozure Okami* film. In the meantime, Japanese audiences were treated to seventy-eight episodes of the television series—two of which were cut together in order to produce *Fugitive Samurai*. Instead of being an incoherent hack job like *Shogun Assassin*, *Fugitive Samurai* is definitely worth a watch.

The backstory from the fourth *Kozure Okami* film, involving Gumbei and Itto's initial fateful duel for the post of Kogi Kaishakunin, provides the jumping-off plot point of *Fugitive Samurai*. This time around, the post of Kogi Kaishakunin is called "High Constable," and after Gumbei's seppuku is staged, Yagyu Retsudo calls for a rematch in order to prove whose school of swordplay is superior.

The Lord Retsudo of *Fugitive Samurai* is much sprier than any of the actors who have portrayed him before. This Lord Yagyu is also more cunning. During his match with Ogami Itto (Yorozuya Kinnosuke), Retsudo loses, but not before his blade "accidentally" takes out a member of the Shogunate—a member

who is aware of the Yagyu plot to create a shadow government greater than the Shogunate (this idea shows up in a different form in *Lone Wolf & Cub* #7).

After Ogami is rewarded the post of High Constable, the film continues linearly (while within a lengthy flashback), showing the destruction of the Ogami household. While the direction of *Fugitive Samurai* does not begin to compare with the panache of Kenji Misumi's interpretation, the events are filmed with enough difference to avoid being merely a rehash of the first *Kozure Okami* film.

Yorozuya Kinnosuke makes a good Ogami Itto, but lacks the heavy-lidded, wild-haired looks and deep, menacing voice of Wakayama Tomisaburo. Nishikawa Kazutaka plays an older, chubbier, and far less cute Daigoro. One very interesting casting choice is Lord Yagyu, played by a very Eurasian actor. It seems that something not explored in the *Kozure Okami* films is that Lord Yagyu is a "half-breed."

The *Kozure Okami* television series lasted three seasons. Wakayama Tomisaburo returned to "finish" the Kozure Okami film series in a made-for-TV production, *Lone Wolf & Cub: Baby Cart in Purgatory* (1979). This time around, however, he donned a long beard and thick mane of white hair to portray the evil Lord Retsudo Yagyu. Though his face is relatively discreet and his eyes are aflame with the mad thirst for power, it is rather disconcerting to see Tomisaburo playing the enemy of the character he made famous on the silver screen. He adopts the gravelly delivery of the first Retsudo from the early Kozure Okami films, but his voice is unmistakable when he says Daigoro's name. Of all the actors to play Ogami Itto, only Takahashi Hideki comes close to capturing the imposing form and dark features that Wakayama Tomisaburo made necessary for the character.

Baby Cart in Purgatory includes some familiar characters and situations, often putting a new spin on them. The action is neatly broken down into segments of length to not be harshly interrupted by commercial breaks. The lighting is often flat and the direction leaves much to be desired. *Baby Cart in Purgatory* is often painful to watch, especially when seeing shaky camera pans or faltering zooms.

"I'll make you pay with rivers of blood."

The film begins with the tests of five warriors from *Lone Wolf & Cub* #5. When Ogami Itto arrives (sans Daigoro) to dispose of his prey, he finds Gumbei and Bizen Yagyu waiting for him.

Eventually, the movie finds a central idea to wind the rest of the plot around. The Yagyu clan has perfected a secret code that allows them to pass innocuous-looking messages to one another across great distances. These missives are carried by shichiri (seven-league) messengers from Daimyos to the Shogunate. The shichiri had license to kill anyone who stood in their path—the mail must go through! Thus, people went to great lengths to avoid being anywhere near a shichiri as they hauled ass through town.

Leaving Ogami Itto at the side of the road for a while, the film concentrates on Otoshi, ex-wife of Jinza, a shichiri messenger to Kishuu. Otoshi now lives as a prostitute, as Jinza divorced her after her baby died. She now carries

On the Road to Meifumado

a blank memorial tablet, trying to get Jinza to give her baby a name so that it can rest in peace. After relating her sad tale to Ogami Itto, trying to get him to kill Jinza, the shichiri is attacked just at that moment by Yagyu agents attempting to steal away his message box. Realizing the importance that the missive must have to the Yagyu clan, Ogami takes it from them and begins his quest to crack the code. Upon news of Ogami Itto's possession of the Yagyu message, Kurokuwa agents are sent to find him.

Ogami Itto's path to Edo is littered with bodies. Word has gone out and he is a wanted man. After several Daimyos have failed, the Yagyus finally take matters into their own hands, attacking Ogami Itto with a small army, including Gumbei and Retsudo Yagyu (who gets a short sword in the eye).

In this movie, not only does Ogami Itto reach Edo, but he is also given a chance to duel Retsudo Yagyu. However, they pause in their fighting after Daigoro passes out from being in the sun. On his way to see if his son is alright, a shot rings out and Ogami falls wounded into a nearby river and floats away. Yagyu Bizen makes his way out of nearby undergrowth and excitedly runs to his father, overjoyed with his luck.

"Bizen, as of this moment you are disinherited," proclaims Retsudo. "Our duel just now was not out of personal hate. It was a duel between two samurai warriors."

Knowing his duty, Retsudo brings Daigoro to his home and takes care of him. The old tyrant acts as a kindly grandfather to Daigoro, even when telling

him that if his father dies, he will die, too. When Ogami Itto and Retsudo Yagyu meet again, the former Kogi Kaishakunin tears up the secret Yagyu message, and the two men agree that they are not fighting for personal reasons any longer, but to preserve Bushido. Their fight lasts for hours, perhaps days. As they duel on the beach, word reaches the Shogun who, along with vassals and Daimyo, visits the battle sight to witness the historic fight. They watch solemnly while the two men fight like elemental beasts, not mortals.

Though the filmmaking was wanting, the acting of Takashi Hideki and Wakayama Tomisaburo is superb and the ending is highly satisfying. This conclusion is echoed in the 1993 revisionist Kozure Okami tale, *Lone Wolf & Cub: Final Combat* (*Kozure Okami: Sono Chisaki Te Ni*, also known as *A Child's Hand Reaches Up*). This will be referred to *LW&C93* for the sake of brevity.

LW&C93 is a beautiful film. Each shot is wonderfully framed and if the camera moves at all, the beginning, middle, and end of each move reveal a beautifully composed mise en scene. Strangely, even Ogami Itto himself is pretty. The rich, soulful eyes of Tamura Masakuza don't befit his scorned, demonic character.

The film begins with Ogami and Azami living their idyllic life with their new son, Daigoro (Yushi Shoda), while Retsudo Yagyu plots to take the post of Kogi Kaishakunin. *LW&C93* is the first film where Azami has been given any significant screen time and where the audience witnesses to her death. She is butchered by a Yagyu warrior as she tries to defend her husband's honor, giving Ogami even more impetus to hate the Yagyu clan.

Ogami's nemesis is a much younger Retsudo Yagyu (Tatsuya Nakadai) than we've seen before—with no beard, he appears to be more of a brother to Gumbei, Kurando, and Bizen than a wizened patriarch. With his dark features, Nakadai would have made a better choice to play Ogami.

After Ogami bests Yagyu Kurando in a duel, he and Daigoro spend years outside of Edo. When we next see them, Daigoro is walking and talking. They appear to be living a life of tranquil contemplation briefly broken when news of Yagyu activity wakes Ogami from his somnambulistic existence.

You can't call this one a "Baby Cart" film. The iconic perambulator cum battle device isn't part of *LW&C93*. Ogami often gets around on horseback in this film, leaving Daigaro free to run away from home, only to be found by Lord Retsudo.

Of course, their paths finally cross. It's here Ogami kills Retsudo's wife. The two part and, after some more wandering, they meet again on a beach. As the waves crash around them, the men contemplate their losses. They privately duel on the secluded stretch of beach. However, despite the similar settings as *Baby Cart in Purgatory*, the outcome is vastly different in this battle.

Inoue Akira's *LW&C93* can be considered much more an "art film" than any interpretations that have come before it. While aesthetically pleasing, it satisfies neither the thirst for blood nor vengeance. Ogami Itto's struggle is infinitesimal, like a grain on sand upon the beach. Instead, he should be seen as one of Nature's elements, like blazing Fire surrounded by Air, Water, and Earth.

The original six *Kozure Okami* films are cinematic gems. Exploring universal themes of filial responsibility, honor, and duty, the films translate well to the American screen while giving audiences a fascinating look at the cinema of the samurai. The on-screen carnage in the films is at once audacious and aesthetic, presenting violence with a beauty that is unrivaled by filmmakers in the West. No amount of praise can suffice for Kenji Misumi's ability to paint such beautiful scenes, dappling his canvas with unnaturally bright red blood.

The original version of this article ran in *Cashiers du Cinemart* #10.

Paul Williams in the '70s

ALL THE GOOD GUYS AND THE BAD GUYS THAT I'VE BEEN

By Leon Chase

He's written songs for Barbra Streisand, Three Dog Night, and Kermit the Frog. He's been covered by Frank Sinatra, David Bowie, Diana Ross, Cracker, and Elvis, just to name a few. He's recorded more than twenty albums, acted in over thirty movies, composed fifteen scores, and made dozens of TV appearances. He has a Golden Globe Award, a star on Hollywood Boulevard, two Grammys, and an Oscar, and has been nominated for even more. Nevertheless, as Paul Williams himself has said, "I could find the cure for cancer and you know what I'd be remembered for? Writing the *Love Boat* theme and playing Little Enos in the *Smokey and the Bandit* movies."

You know who he is. Blonde shag. Amber porno glasses. Five-foot-two. For most of the '70s, Paul existed as a behind-the-scenes big shot who seemed to have a little hand in a whole lot of things. In a time when popular music was only just beginning to make way—for better or for worse—for the era of arena egos and album-length excess, he was a throwback to an earlier breed of star, the celebrity songwriter, a guy whose biggest commercial successes came consistently from other people's versions of his songs. And, for those of us born in the '70s, the man practically wrote the soundtrack to our childhoods, from *The Boy in the Plastic Bubble* to *Rocky IV*. And, of course, "The Rainbow Connection."

> *"My songwriting and my career in songwriting came when I was denied what I really wanted. I thought I wanted to be a leading man. I thought, 'You're so attractive, you're so handsome.'"*
>
> —Paul Williams, commencement speech at his son's high school

Born in Omaha, Nebraska in 1940, Paul spent most of his childhood traveling with his father's architecture business. Later, he lived with relatives in Long Beach, California, where as a teenager, he set his heart on becoming an actor. After stints as an apprentice jockey, stunt parachutist, and local-theater darling in New Mexico, Paul went to Los Angeles to become a movie star. The land of image-is-everything was less than kind to a short guy who once described his teenage appearance as "the Pillsbury doughboy made of cantaloupe." Aside from a major role in the 1965 satire *The Loved One*—in which, at age 24, he played a 13-year-old—he found himself facing a stream of bit parts and industry frustrations (including an audition for The Monkees). Not coincidentally, he also found himself turning more and more to songwriting. It had started as a hobby, but he showed a natural gift for it—particularly old-style, sentimental love songs—and he ended up with a job as a staff writer at A&M records. One of his first musical marks on the world came in 1968, with a song he co-wrote for Tiny Tim called "Fill Your Heart," recorded as the B-side to the smash novelty hit, "Tiptoe Through the Tulips." Subsequent projects included Paul's first solo album; a song called "Out in the Country," written with fellow A&M man Roger Nichols for Three Dog Night; and a short-lived psychedelic band called The Holy Mackerel.

It was a bank commercial, though, that would launch Paul into songwriting stardom. The Crocker Bank of California hired Williams and Nichols to pen a jingle for a TV commercial depicting a young couple's wedding. The result was "We've Only Just Begun," which soon after became a hit for the Carpenters, and a staple of wedding receptions for a generation to come. In a 1995 interview, Williams recalled: "We didn't think that there was very much chance that anyone would record it... The number one album at the time was *In-A-Gadda-Da-Vida*. So I suppose that in a sense, the Carpenters, Roger, and I were really alternative at the time."

More releases followed, including "Just an Old Fashioned Love Song" (again, for Three Dog Night), and two equally sentimental, yet more successful, solo albums. Royalty checks, nightclub gigs, and variety show appearances followed; so did an even deeper descent into drugs, drinking, and all the other eccentricities of body and mind that seemed de rigueur for L.A. celebrity in the early '70s.

> *"I never looked like the type of guy who wrote those songs. I wore round black glasses and had shoulder-length hair, a top hat with a feather in it, tie-dyed pants, and took a lot of psychedelics. I remember Bing Crosby driving off the lot at A&M, pointing at me and talking to his driver with great disgust. And I thought it was interesting because I was probably the only guy on the lot who wrote the kinds of songs he would sing."*
>
> —Paul Williams, *Songtalk* interview

For all of Paul's songwriting success, the movie star in him wouldn't go away. Fueled by his newfound celebrity status (and more than a few ego-boosting pick-me-ups of the day), he embarked on what would become a decade-long blitz of TV-trivia asides and bizarre character roles. There was his split-second appearance in Melvin Van Peeble's screwball race/laugh riot *The Watermelon Man*. Then, in 1973, two films came out that would define Paul's dual life in Hollywood. The first was *Cinderella Liberty*, a James Caan drama for which Paul, working with a pre-Star Wars John Williams (no relation), wrote and sang funky lyrics—and received his first Academy Award nomination. The second was *Battle for the Planet of the Apes*, in which Paul played an orangutan.

It's no secret that the *Planet of the Apes* movies have attained pop-cult status. It's also generally agreed upon by fans that the series gets lamer as it goes on, thanks largely to financial strangulation by 20th Century Fox. Whereas the first couple of films manage to maintain a certain gee-whiz camp and allegorical charm, *Battle for the Planet of the Apes*—the fifth and last of the originals—finds the series wobbling on its last, opposable-toed legs.

Williams, for his part as Virgil, the amiable orangutan companion, manages to look eerily like himself behind the makeup, and does a decent job of walking awkwardly and saying wise things at appropriate moments. He doesn't break any ground dramatically; then again, the *Apes* movies aren't exactly known for their understatement. More intriguing than the movie itself is the fact that, after one particularly long day of shooting, Paul was scheduled to make one of his many appearances on Johnny Carson's *Tonight Show*. Not wanting to miss it, and always up for a good laugh, Paul arranged to sing a surprise, romantically lit version of one of Johnny's favorite songs…in full ape makeup. [Video copy of this, anyone? —Ed.]

> *"One day I saw Paul Williams walking out of the room, and suddenly the image of this bizarre rock impresario—this Napoleon of rock—came to mind."*
>
> —Brian De Palma, *Filmmakers Newsletter*

The following year, an upstart director with a couple of thrillers to his credit approached Paul with the script for a rock musical. It was the story of a songwriter who sells his soul to a satanic record producer, is maimed and double-crossed, and exacts costumed revenge. It was part *Phantom of the Opera*, part *Faust*, part *The Picture of Dorian Gray*. And, in Paul's hands, it would become at once a hilariously weird parody of the music industry and a well-crafted nod to classic morality tales, the American musical, and the larger mythology of rock 'n' roll. The director was Brian De Palma. The movie was *Phantom of the Paradise*.

Williams as Swan in *Phantom of the Paradise*

Phantom of the Paradise is definitely a product of its time, a testament to that period, somewhere between *Easy Rider* and *Star Wars*, when youth culture was the wild card cash cow, rock was still the rage, and Hollywood execs could be convinced to dump serious money in some very unserious places. The worst casualties of the genre—*Tommy*, *Sergeant Pepper's Lonely Hearts Club Band*—show their age with all the grace and relevance of a coke binge. The best—such as *Phantom* or its more popular and subsequent cousin, *Rocky Horror Picture Show*—stand up both as memorials of a cultural moment and as self-conscious signposts in a larger B-grade legacy.

All the Good Guys and the Bad Guys That I've Been

That's not to say that pitching a satirical horror-rock musical was easy, even in 1974. De Palma's solution was to go to the music industry first, land a record deal for the soundtrack, then use that to convince the movie folks they had a hit on their hands. While making his pitch at A&M's offices, De Palma met Paul Williams and got the brainstorm to not only hire him to write the music, but to make him the star, as well.

The story is classically simple, the details unapologetically ludicrous. Paul is Swan, the mysterious head of the all-powerful Death Records, legendary for his ability to create—and eliminate—stars at will. A sincere, bumbling composer named Winslow Leach (William Finley) shows up with a cantata about Faust. Swan decides to use the music for the much-hyped opening of his new concert hall, The Paradise—sans Winslow. After instantly falling for a singer named Phoenix (Jessica Harper) and enduring a series of mishaps (including having his teeth replaced with silver and getting his face smashed in a record press), Winslow returns, in bird mask and leather costume, to haunt the Paradise and sabotage Swan's pop bastardizations of his music. Swan eventually cuts a blood-bound deal with the Phantom. The evil nature of Swan, the deal, and the music industry at large is revealed, highlighted by some great rock parodies, budding De Palma trademarks (a *Psycho* homage, lots of voyeurism, early attempts at split-screen), and crazy sets by a young Sissy Spacek.

Paul Williams—who is by all reports a nice, unassuming guy in person—is genuinely creepy as the egotistical Swan. Paul was originally offered the part of Winslow, but feared he couldn't be menacing enough and didn't want to be accused of portraying himself as a bitter songwriter with a grudge. As it worked out, casting him as the villain was a stroke of genius. He pokes fun at the "other side" of the business with obvious relish, and the visual irony of the soft-spoken and decidedly odd-looking Williams as ultimate power-monger and sex symbol is played to its fullest, right down to the shortened doorways.

As Swan himself would tell you, though, "listen to the music." Originally, De Palma had wanted to recruit a supergroup such as The Who or The Rolling Stones to star as the Paradise band. When that didn't work, Paul Williams convinced him that they should create their own band instead. The result is The Juicy Fruits (AKA The Beach Bums; AKA The Undead) who twist the original heartfelt cantata into a series of bubblegum hits, spoofing Sha Na Na, The Beach Boys, and Alice Cooper along the way. Paul has said that this project, while not his favorite music, allowed him the most creative control. And it shows. He drops absurd rock hits into the forms and structure of a classic musical, all the while bouncing effortlessly between "Stardust" sentiment and Spinal Tap-quality satire. Originally a bomb at the theaters, *Phantom of the Paradise* has gone on to become a cult hit that draws fans in with its kitsch value, but brings them back for its deadpan artistry in the face of overwhelming weirdness. There was talk a few years ago about a special-edition laser disc, but nothing seems to have come of it. At one point in the early '90s, Brian

De Palma approached Williams about revamping the show for Broadway, but sadly, the project never took off. Now it looks like *Rocky Horror* has beaten them to the spotlight.

The *Phantom* soundtrack brought Paul Williams nominations for both the Oscar and Golden Globe. 1976 would bring them both again, for his song score of *Bugsy Malone*, the bizarre all-children gangster musical starring a very small Scott Baio and Jodie Foster (looking a little too much like her Iris character in *Taxi Driver* to make this film seem altogether wholesome). That same year, Paul was also nominated for—and won—an Oscar, a Grammy, and two Golden Globes for his work on the remake of *A Star is Born*, including the song "Evergreen," written with Barbra Streisand. (In a testament to his growing ego and/or inebriation, he came in to help with one song, mistakenly showing up ready to score the whole movie. He ended up with a job as Music Supervisor.) Yet another important event occurred in 1976: Paul made his first appearance on *The Muppet Show*. He quickly befriended Jim Henson, who recruited him to write the songs for the TV special *Emmet Otter's Jugband Christmas*.

> "You look like an aerial photograph of a human being."
>
> —Pat McCormick, upon meeting Paul Williams

In 1977, with a fresh Oscar and what was then the bestselling soundtrack of all time under his belt, Paul returned to the shiny side of the big screen, this time as Little Enos in the quintessential outlaw car movie, *Smokey and the Bandit*. What bad things can one say, really, about a film that was shot mostly in a speeding Trans Am, spawned a nationwide CB craze (the chat rooms of the '70s), and whose entire plot centers around a truckload of beer? It was reputedly Burt Reynolds's idea to team Williams up with six-foot-five Pat McCormick as Little and Big Enos, the mustachioed, cowboy-suited millionaires who attempt to bamboozle Bandit with their outrageous beer-running dare. Next to Jackie Gleason's bitter last gasps at humor, anything looks pretty good, and the Enos duo were apparently appealing enough to show up in two sequels—the last of which is notable only for the chance to see Paul Williams in drag.

> "Jim [Henson] didn't even want to hear the songs before we went into the studio. That's how trusting he was."
>
> —Paul Williams, *Nashville Banner* interview

Ask any adult under 40 how they felt about Jim Henson, and you'll begin to get an idea of the effect he had. Armed with a pile of fabric and the radical idea that children's entertainment doesn't have to be stupid, the man single-handedly upped the ante for educational television by creating one of the most consistently amusing (and technically involved) network TV shows. In the process, Henson touched a generation. The pinnacle of this extensive feel-good empire came in 1979, with his first feature film, *The Muppet Movie*.

At once a surreal road movie, self-mocking yuk-fest, and uncompromising expression of Jim Henson's own spiritual vision, *The Muppet Movie* follows Kermit the Frog from his humble swamp roots to his Hollywood dream of making "millions of people happy," collecting a carload of Muppet cohorts, and avoiding a sellout to the deadly frog-leg franchiser Doc Hopper (Charles Durning).

The emotional effect of the movie is bigger than the sum of its parts, due in no small part to the songs, all written by Paul Williams (with composer Kenny Ascher). His ability to slip from screwball to sincerity is a perfect complement to the movie's high-minded message and lowbrow running gags. I've seen the most jaded of cynics—me, for instance—break down at the movie's big final number, and find me a hipster alive who doesn't take pause at the opening banjo notes of "The Rainbow Connection." Gonzo's tear-jerking campfire lament "I'm Going to Go Back There Someday" is prime Paul, and the oft-overlooked "Can You Picture That?" performed by Dr. Teeth and the Electric Mayhem recalls *Phantom* in its dead-on rock satire. Those who only remember this movie from childhood would do well to sit down with it again and marvel at its sincere craftiness and its barrage of sly, adult-slanted details, from Orson Welles as the all-powerful studio head to the saxophonist Zoot's zonked memory loss. And of course, watch for Paul Williams, trademark glasses and all, as Fozzie Bear's piano player in the El Sleezo Café.

"You know you're an alcoholic when you misplace things—like a decade."

—Paul Williams, *New York Daily News*

The end of the '70s found Paul in a comfortable place, artistically and financially. *The Muppet Movie* brought two more Oscar nominations, a Golden Globe nomination, and his second Grammy. Jack Jones was belting out Paul's "Love Boat Theme" every Saturday night. There was a steady flow of television appearances as well—most notably as the mime-building camp villain Dr. Miguelito Loveless, Jr., in the just-plain-weird television movie *Wild Wild West Revisited*.

Years of alcohol and cocaine abuse, however, were taking their toll. Under the pretense of the isolated creative type, Paul regularly spent long periods locked in the top floor of his five-acre estate, often with a loaded gun in his hand. For most of his career he had succumbed to the classic drugs-equals-creativity reliance, and liked to put impossible demands on himself—writing the entire score for *Phantom* in four weeks, for example, or *A Star is Born* in nine. Now, the creative binges were giving way to full-blown blackouts.

There's a certain Faustian touch to the fact that, Little Enos aside, Paul's only major project during the '80s was writing the intentionally corny songs for *Ishtar*—a job which, incidentally, he has called his toughest: since each "bad" song had to be approved by every cast member, over fifty were written. As his addiction deepened, Paul retreated entirely from public life. He has stories of his first wife and children walking out on him, of waking up next to suicide notes he didn't remember writing, and, at one particularly memorable low point, of sneaking out of the puppy door on his hands and knees to score drugs. His rock-bottom and/or saving moment came when, in 1989, he phoned his psychiatrist during a heavy blackout and asked for help. He doesn't remember making the call.

Successful recovery and a slow, sober return to entertainment followed in the early '90s. Rather than resign himself to the ranks of *Behind the Music*-style drug-casualty clichés, however, Paul has taken an active part in helping other addicts and addressing the problem of substance abuse in the music industry. Soon after his own recovery, Paul became a certified substance-abuse counselor, a job that he continues to this day. He has also gotten involved with the Musicians' Assistance Program, a group that helps provide drug and alcohol treatment to music-industry professionals.

> "The cartoon acting I did in so many of the films, well, I'm going to have to live with that. But I look at some of my sober acting and I see a difference."
>
> —Paul Williams, *New York Daily News*

Although he has yet to take on the show-biz omnipresence of his early years, Paul has spent the past decade working steadily. After easing himself back into songwriting in the mid-'90s, he has begun pitching himself in Nashville—long a haven for professional songwriters, and a place where his name, to his own self-effacing surprise, carries legendary weight. Tribute concerts have been held in his honor in New York and L.A., he makes regular speaking appearances across the nation, and his ninth solo album, *Back to Love Again*, has just been released. On screen, he has shown up as Andy Warhol's P.R. guy in *The Doors*, a recurring recovering alcoholic on *The Bold and the Beautiful*, and the voice of the Penguin on *Batman: The Animated Series*, just to name a few. While, sadly, there don't seem to be any leading roles in his near future, one recent film role does stand out: James Bruce's surreal 1995 indie psychodrama, *Headless Body in Topless Bar* (available from eclecticDVD.com).

Paul Williams in the '90s

Based very loosely on a real event (the title is lifted straight from the *New York Post* headline), *Headless Body* details a botched robbery of a quaint topless bar, where a sociopathic gunman keeps five patrons hostage and makes them answer personal questions, one by one. The theatrical convention of sticking a bunch of disparate oddballs in a room and having them confess is nothing new and—*The Breakfast Club* aside—a trick that usually falls flat on the big screen. Despite some decent efforts by the mostly anonymous cast, the dialogue has an overwhelmingly stagey feel; the victims' personal revelations are less than earth shattering (The stripper is a lesbian! The businessman is kinky!), and the bad guy seems a little too eager to drum up a group therapy session to ever really be believable.

Paul Williams, however, stands out as Carl, a crusty, wheelchair-bound old regular. Not only is he credible as a timid multiple sclerosis victim forced to confront his own deterioration, but his scenes bring a subtlety and emotional honesty not found in most of his earlier, more high-profile roles. It's the work of an actor, not a celebrity, and if nothing else, the movie stands as heartening evidence of what Paul is capable of in his later, more understated years.

> "I made a deal with myself when I got sober that I would return to writing when I got excited about it, if I ever did. And now it feels right again."
>
> —Paul Williams, *People*

On June 16, 2001, Paul Williams was inducted into the Songwriters Hall of Fame. The announcement came just after Paul's March election to the board of directors of the American Society of Composers, Authors and Publishers (ASCAP). As part of the Hall of Fame, Paul was officially recognized for over thirty years of musical accomplishment, and joined the ranks of James Brown, Bob Dylan, and a bevy of equally prolific—if more immediately familiar—names.

In response to the news, Paul told an Ohio newspaper: "You know, I went to the Oscars and the Grammys and the Golden Globes a lot, but this is probably the peak of it for a songwriter. The best part is, I'll be able to remember it all the next day."

The original version of this article ran in Cashiers du Cinemart *#13.*

THE FOUR AND A HALF WORLDS OF PARKER

By Mike White

"Why do you keep calling that movie '*Parker*'?" Andrea asked me. She had seen *Payback* before I did and knew that Mel Gibson's character's name was Porter, so where was I getting this "Parker" thing from?

Huh. I could have sworn that that movie was called *Parker* at one point. I seemed to remember an annoying teaser from ages ago. The tagline "Get Mad, Get Tough, Get Even" had left a bad taste in my mouth. I dreaded seeing another Mel Gibson flick, as the memory of *Conspiracy Theory* was fresh in my mind. What was he going to do, act like a tortured goof again? Was it going to be his famous *Lethal Weapon* mix of Three Stooges violence with a wink towards the camera followed by a quick quip? No, this time Mel was going to "break the mold."

Little did I know at the time, but *Payback* was the bastard kin of one of my favorite films, *Point Blank*. Parker is the name of the ruthless anti-hero (or non-hero) of Richard Stark's book *The Hunter*; the first in a series of novels to feature the character. Stark is a nom de plume of prolific author Donald Westlake, as well as an adjective for the stripped-down prose Westlake employs in his Parker series.

Parker has appeared in various guises in, to date, over twenty novels and seven films. Parker became "Walker" in John Boorman's 1967 *Point Blank*, tenaciously played by Lee Marvin. Meanwhile, Parker was to become "Porter" in Brian Helgeland's 1999 *Payback*.

Regardless, before reading *The Hunter*, I unconsciously insisted on calling Helgeland's film *Parker*. This re-

Mel Gibson as Porter in *Payback*

mained a mystery until I realized that the film had once been called *Parker*, not *Payback*. This was one of myriad changes the film was to undergo between the aforementioned teaser trailer and *Payback*'s delayed release.

A second look at a film's trailer while the movie is fresh in one's mine can often reveal a wealth of lost shots or scenes. This has never been truer than when one takes a second glance at the early trailer for *Payback*. Roughly half the shots in this ninety-second preview do not appear in the finished film. Even a look at the longer preview released just prior to the film's opening reveals a shot or two that remained unseen in *Payback*. More than different line readings or camera angles, entire characters and scenes disappeared between the times those trailers were released.

After completion of Brian Helgeland's *Parker* (as his version of the film will be known for the rest of this article), studio heads expressed displeasure and Mel flexed his Hollywood muscles, shooting scenes penned by Terry Hayes (*Road Warrior, Mad Max Beyond Thunderdome*) for the film that would become *Payback*. It was Gibson's film that audiences saw, and it was worlds apart from Brian Helgeland's, John Boorman's, or Richard Stark's vision of Parker.

The Hunter

Richard Stark's novel *The Hunter* begins with Parker crossing the George Washington Bridge into Manhattan. He's described as being "big and shaggy with flat, square shoulders [with] arms too long in sleeves too short." The working ends of those too-long arms soon become the focus of the reader's attention. Parker's hands swing "curve-fingered at his sides," looking like "they were molded of brown clay by a sculptor who thought big and liked veins." Though Parker knows how to use a gun, it is his hands he wants to use to exact his revenge. "He wanted Mal Resnick—he wanted him between his hands. Not the money back. Not Lynn back. Just Mal, between his hands."

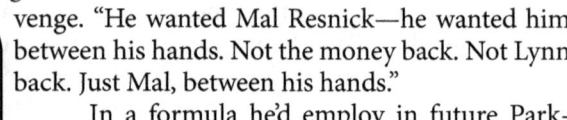

In a formula he'd employ in future Parker novels, Stark skillfully crafts a narrative that changes focus from Parker to his nemesis Mal, pausing often for extended flashbacks in order to explain their past. It isn't until the last chapter of the novel's second section that we learn the details of the island arms-deal heist where the tables were turned on Parker. Mal double-crossed him, took his wife, and killed the three other guys involved in the robbery. Mal and Lynn left Parker for dead, and by all rights, he should have stayed dead.

Crawling wounded from the building Mal set ablaze, Parker used those powerful hands to dig himself a makeshift grave where he stayed, like Christ, for three days before crawling out and being picked up for vagrancy—covered in blood, bruised and barefoot on the side of the road. He did six out of an eight-month sentence before breaking out and heading west to find Mal. He came into New York silently, like a ghost. "He didn't want Mal to know he was alive. He didn't want Mal spooked and on the run. He wanted him easy and content, a fat cat. He wanted him just sitting there, grinning, waiting for Parker's hands."

After following a trail from his wife, Lynn (who subsequently overdoses on sleeping pills), to a cab-stand operator, Stegman, he hits a dead end. At this point, Parker tries to get a bead on Mal from a former associate, Jimmy

Delgardo (remember this name), and a whore, Rosie. After some convincing, she gives him a lead to Mal's room at The Outfit's hotel.

Until getting word through Stegman, Mal had been relatively content. The money he took from Parker had let him buy his way back into The Outfit (often called "the organization," "the corporation," or "the syndicate," but never referred to as "the mob"). Now a mid-level executive, his only real complaint (before learning that Parker has returned for retribution) is that his girlfriend, a junkie named Pearl, just isn't a high-class enough piece of ass. Mal *is* ambitious, after all.

The news of Parker's resurrection startles Mal so much that he tries to get help from The Outfit. Doing this demonstrates Mal's weakness. His "manager," Mr. Carter, tells Mal that his problem has three possible solutions: 1) assist him, which would be protecting The Outfit's investment in Mal; 2) let Mal handle it himself, which would show The Outfit that he's self-reliant; or 3) replace him, thus removing the external danger Mal has brought with him.

Carter chooses the second option and boots Mal out of The Outfit's hotel. Left in the cold and more vulnerable to Parker and his eager, meaty hands, Mal rents a high-class hotel suite and orders a hundred-dollar blonde to spend the night with him. Little does he know what a favor he's doing for himself by springing for these luxuries. He's going out in style.

After finding Mal's Outfit hotel room empty, Parker returns to Rosie. It takes a few harsh words and some serious hair pulling before Rosie is motivated to locate Mal through alternate channels. Knowing Parker's intentions and that her nosing around for Mal will implicate her as an accomplice, Rosie begins packing after Parker leaves with an address. She's as good as dead. Her only comfort could be that her death is sure to be quicker and less painful than Mal's.

It's only after Parker has Mal between his hands for a while, choking the life out of him, that he realizes that Mal's death won't satisfy him. "For the first time he thought about the money. Killing Mal wasn't enough; it left a hole in the world afterward. Once he'd killed that bastard, what then? He had less than two thousand dollars to his name. He had to go on living; he had to get back into his old groove. The resort hotels and the occasional job, the easy comfortable life until this bastard had come along in his taxicab and told him about the job on the island. And to get back to that life, he needed money. Forty-five thousand dollars."

Thus begins the fourth and final section of the novel—Parker getting his money from The Outfit; going through the chain of command from Mr. Carter to Mr. Fairfax to Mr. Bronson, until Bronson agrees to pay "the mosquito" Parker. An agreement is made that Parker will receive his forty-five thousand dollars at a train station in Brooklyn. After disarming the goons that have been sent to eliminate him and sending them on their way, Parker finally gets his money. It takes some fancy footwork to make his way to safety back in his Manhattan hotel room.

Checking out with two suitcases—one holding his clothes and shaving kit, the other stuffed with cash—Parker is stopped by two police detectives wishing to question him about his relationship with Jimmy Delgardo. Suspicion had fallen on Parker after he had been asking around about Delgardo days before, as Delgardo had just been picked up for drug running. Using his wits and brutal hands again, Parker escapes.

It isn't until he's inside a cab speeding to Grand Central Station that Parker realizes that he's made a forty-five thousand dollar mistake—he grabbed the wrong suitcase as he made his way out the door. A marked man without a dime to his name, Parker knows that it'll take some doing before he can get back to a life of luxury. Naturally, the best target for getting some quick cash is the organization that wants him dead.

It wasn't until an editor at Pocket Books asked Richard Stark/Donald Westlake for a change in the ending and three Parker books a year that the unrepentant Parker managed to escape from the police. Until that point, when Parker was caught that was the end of him and, for all Westlake knew, the end of his writing career as Richard Stark. It appears that even from his earliest days in 1962, Parker exhibited his adaptability.

Point Blank

Parker first appeared on screen in Jean-Luc Godard's 1966 film *Made in U.S.A.*—loosely based on the sixth film in the Parker series, *The Jugger*. However, not only did Parker change names, but also his gender!

It wasn't until a year later that Parker's first adventure was brought to the big screen. John Boorman's *Point Blank* is often described as being an art film or a last gasp of the classic film noir genre. Certainly, Boorman's use of flashbacks, cutting, and sound is often avant-garde and quite unusual for what could be a typical robber/revenge genre film.

In it, Parker's name has been changed to "Walker," which could best be explained as a clue to the idea that Lee Marvin's character may not be quite alive. That is, he might very well be the walking dead. (Stark would later acknowledge this name in his *The Black Ice Score* by mentioning that Parker once operated under the pseudonym "Matthew Walker.")

The story's setting has been taken from New York to another classic backdrop of film noir stories, Los Angeles. Up the coast a bit, Alcatraz is utilized for the island drop of *The Hunter*. The film begins with Walker taking two bullets to the gut. Immediately we're shown how he found his way onto his back, bleeding, in a jail cell during a small, pre-credits flashback sequence. We see Mal Reese (John Vernon) talking Walker and his wife, Lynne (Sharon Acker), into helping out on a heist, and the subsequent betrayal.

Along with Parker's name change to Walker, Mal's last name has been Anglicized a bit. Why Lynn has an "e" on the end of her name perhaps ties her to the three vowels of Mal's new name.

Sometime after Walker performed the amazing feat of escaping from Alcatraz (if the bullet wounds don't get you, the swim just might), he returns for a tour and is confronted by Yost (Keenan Wynn). Yost is intimately familiar with Walker's plight and forces him into an uneasy partnership. "You want Reese, and I want the organization. I'm going to help you and you're going to help me." Yost then turns over Lynne's new address in Los Angeles.

The scene of Walker coming to see Lynne is amazing. Walker is shown traveling through a long corridor—his feet echoing—intercut with Lynne going about her day. The sound of his feet never ceases, even when he's shown driving to her apartment and waiting for her. On and on they go, marching back from the grave and into Lynne's nightmare world.

"Walker, I'm glad you're not dead," Lynne admits after he breaks into her apartment and shoots her mattress (expecting Mal to be there). Lynne soliloquizes as Walker sits silently on her couch, spent shells emptied across her plush pay-off apartment's coffee table. Lynne narrates the story of their meeting, along with the introduction of Mal into their relationship. She paints a long, idyllic past between the three of them; the scene is reminiscent of the "We'll always have Paris" flashback in *Casablanca*.

That night, Lynne overdoses on sleeping pills and Parker begins his long wait for Stegman's pay-off man to arrive. In *Point Blank*, we don't have a scene in which Walker disposes of Lynne's body, as we do in *The Hunter*. Instead, her body and even her sheets spookily disappear after Walker leaves the room and sees Yost staked out across the street.

In *Point Blank*, "Big John" Stegman (Michael Strong) personifies the stereotypical slimy used-car salesman. Walker takes Stegman for a test drive he won't soon forget and finds out that Mal has moved from sleeping with Lynne to courting her sister, Chris (Angie Dickinson).

Stegman reports his encounter with Walker directly to Mal, showing him the wrecked remains of Walker's test car. Mal assigns Stegman to find Walker and, amazingly, he does. Two goons try their best to get a piece of Walker in the back of Chris's nightclub. Amid the colored lights, screeching music and slides of women, Walker pounds the hell out of them before taking leave of their company and searching out his sister-in-law.

Reese comes to the fast-talking Mr. Carter (Lloyd Bochner) for help. The film's Carter is much more disapproving of Reese, saying that he was against taking Mal back into the organization because trouble seems to follow him like a lost dog. Carter admonishes Mal, but doesn't force his removal from The Outfit's hotel. By allowing him to stay, the film eliminates the work that Parker went through to get into Mal's empty room in *The Hunter* and, instead, tightens the flow of the narrative.

When Walker visits Chris, he tells her that he wants Reese and his money. Already inflation has driven up the stakes that Walker's out for—he wants his ninety-three thousand dollars. Walker decides to use Chris as bait, sending her up to Mal's penthouse room.

The Four and a Half Worlds of Parker

Walker brandishes a gun, not using his hands on Mal except when the cowardly Reese faints at the sight of him, forcing Walker to slap him around a few times to revive him. More than revenge, Walker is immediately concerned with his money, and gets the chain of command of The Outfit from Reese before the poor sap falls over the side of a building. Thus, Walker has been robbed of the satisfaction of killing his betrayers (Lynne and Mal).

After Walker finds him at a business conference, Mr. Carter sends Stegman to drop off Walker's cash. While Stegman drives to one of Los Angeles's famous storm drains (as seen in *Grease*, *The Junkman*, and *Terminator 2*), Walker breaks into Carter's office, informing him, "I want to be paid personally." Of course, Walker realizes that the drop is a setup and, by sending Carter out to Stegman, these two will both be eliminated (by sharpshooter James B. Sikking in an early role).

With Carter out of the way, Walker moves up the chain of command to Brewster. Oddly, there is no Bronson in *Point Blank*. Instead, Brewster is *The Hunter*'s Fairfax while Fairfax is a mere moneyman for the organization: an accountant.

Angie Dickinson and Lee Marvin in *Point Blank*

Walker consorts with Yost regarding the whereabouts of Brewster. As in *The Hunter*, this middleman is out of town, forced to return after the elimination of Carter. As Brewster, Carroll O'Connor is hilarious. After Walker knocks out his luggage-carrying bodyguard, Brewster admonishes him, saying, "You're a very bad man, Walker! A very destructive man! Why do you run around doing things like this? What do you want?"

Startled, Walker says, "I want my money."

"Ninety-three thousand dollars? You'd threaten a financial structure like this for ninety-three thousand dollars? No, Walker, I don't believe you. What do you really want?"

As if to convince himself, Walker has to repeat, "I want my money."

Confused and distraught by Brewster's assurances that no one is going to pay him, Walker shrugs and mutters, "Somebody's gotta pay."

When calling Fairfax, Brewster informs him that Walker has a gun pointed his way. Walker does not. Brewster is merely trying to prove that Fairfax isn't about to agree to extortion. The dialogue is similar to what Parker says to Bronson while he holds a gun on Carter in *The Hunter*, except that instead of shooting Brewster, Walker shoots the phone. Brewster appears to feel Walker's frustration and informs him that there's still one setup where large sums of money changes hands—the Alcatraz run.

Walker returns to the scene of his demise with Brewster. He waits in the shadows while Brewster retrieves the money and is promptly shot (hired gun Sikking strikes again). As he collapses, Brewster sees Yost entering the compound and shouts, "This is Fairfax, Walker! Kill him!" Walker remains hidden while Yost/Fairfax tells him, "Our deal's done." Yost/Fairfax tries to convince Walker to join him, as Fairfax has moved from being an accountant to the top spot in the organization.

Walker fades into darkness as Fairfax and his sharpshooter walk away, leaving Brewster and a wrapped bundle of paper (disguised as money) laying in the dim rays of the morning sun.

The sharp-witted Parker would never have allowed himself to be played the fool by Fairfax, as Walker had been. Though Walker is a brute (shoving around Lynne, putting a nail through Stegman's delivery boy, pistol-whipping some goons and using others' testicles as a punching bag), he's not nearly as malevolent as Parker is. His vengeance is more financially than personally or professionally motivated. When Brewster flatly refuses to pay Walker, he's defeated and has no real way of making The Outfit pay. Walker doesn't appear to belong to Parker's underworld of professional thieves. In contrast, his only ally is Chris…and Yost.

It's important to note that Walker never kills anyone. After his resurrection he becomes more of a catalyst, as if his presence alone were setting events in motion. Walker can be thought of as Yost's golem—being created and laid to rest on Alcatraz—and doing Yost's bidding. Remember that the two met on Walker's boat ride back to the island prison; why Walker would choose to return to the spot of his demise is never explained.

After *Point Blank*, Parker would become a semi-regular fixture on the silver screen, though never as "Parker," per se. He's been Macklin (*The Outfit*), Stone (*Playground*), McClain (*The Split*), Georges (*Mise à Sac*), Paula Nelson (*Made in U.S.A.*), and finally, Porter.

The name change to "Walker" makes sense when taking Lee Marvin's direct approach and unstoppable march through the film into account. Why Brian Helgeland changed Parker's name to "Porter" is a bigger mystery. Could this be a reference to William Sydney Porter, another author, like Donald Westlake, famous for his pen name, O. Henry? At one point in *The Hunter*, Stark describes Parker's trip from the prison farm where he spent six months to New York as "coming across the country like an O. Henry tramp." It's possible. Stranger things have happened. More likely, however, "Porter" came from a line in Stark's *The Green Eagle Score*, "Lynch was not of course the man's real name. One time when he had come with another man, the other had called him by a different name, which Berridge could no longer be sure he remembered. Porter, Walker, Archer…something like that."

The explanation for the Parker/Porter/Walker names gains clarity via a letter from author Westlake to *Cashiers du Cinemart*:

> "Lee Marvin refused to do sequels, under any circumstances, so it was agreed that we'd keep the name back and not squander it on somebody who wouldn't come out and play any more. Payback *began with Helgeland intending a small inexpensive sharp feature like* Red Rock West *or* The Last Seduction. *Gibson entered, and life changed. No one told me that the movie was to be made (the rights were owned by Warner, who had inherited* Point Blank*), so I first learned about it when the announcement was made to the trades that Gibson would appear in* Parker. *My agent called him and said, "You can do anything you want, you can fuck babies in wheelchairs, but you can't call him Parker. Look at the contract." They did their idea of negotiation, which went nowhere. Thus, Porter. Porter isn't Parker. Porter is what Ginger Rogers says, with her luggage, beside the ship: "Oh, Porter! Oh Porter!" Porter, as we see, is a mutt. Parker is not a mutt."*

Payback and *Parker*

Brian Helgeland's film took an odd journey from the time principal photography began in September of 1997 until its release in the commercial dead zone of February 1999. I refer to Helgeland's original version of the film as *Parker* for this article.

For all of the liberties Brian Helgeland took in adapting *The Hunter*, it remained faithful in the overall unapologetic tone of the book. First off, Porter is an enigmatic character—there is no voiceover in *Parker* in order to get inside Porter's head. True, the voiceover in *Payback* introduces a film noir convention, but without a voiceover the tone of the film is closer to the third-person omniscient point of view of Stark's novel. By hearing Porter, the audience is forced into identifying with him. The voiceover immediately sets Porter's goal at merely getting his paltry seventy thousand dollars. "Not many men know what their life's worth, but I do. Seventy grand. That's what they took from me, and that's what I was gonna get back."

Seventy thousand? Certainly it's more than forty-five, but it's less than the ninety-three that Walker wanted thirty-two years before! Porter would threaten a financial structure like The Outfit for seventy thousand dollars? Such a laughably small amount does make Porter's quest to take on The Outfit look more like an act of stupidity or blind bravado than a matter of honor. Even *Parker*/*Payback*'s Fairfax (James Coburn) cracks that his suits cost more than seventy thousand! Undertaking such a foolhardy quest for seventy thousand dollars could prevent an audience from sympathizing with Porter. Thus, by not presenting Porter's desire for his money as his primary goal, keeping it a matter of principle and not amount, Helgeland better captures the spirit of Stark's novel.

The first acts of both *Parker* and *Payback* are quite similar. *Parker* begins with Porter crossing a bridge on his way back into the city. The audience is never shown the moments between his betrayal and his return. Porter takes what he wants—when he sees a panhandler with a hat full of money, the green is fair game.

Helgeland updates the method by which Porter gets an initial bankroll by pickpocketing an easy mark on the street and charging up his Visa card, instead of grifting cash out of checking accounts, as Parker did in *The Hunter*. In the nineties, credit card fraud is the way to go. That's not to say that *Parker* is set in any particular age—the anachronistic rotary phones, references to President Nixon, and the vintage cars that Porter and Val (instead of Mal) drive set the film in more of a "timeless era." If Porter was stuck in a different era, then seventy thousand might seem like a good deal of money. Or maybe not...

Apart from the addition of a voiceover, Porter's character is softened and the narrative's impact is lessened in Mel Gibson's *Payback*. The film begins with Porter lying prone, two bullet holes in his back, while a less-than-reputable surgeon goes to work on him. Cut from that scene (Porter narrating all along) to him crossing the aforementioned bridge. Back in the city, Porter spies a panhandler begging for change. Now instead of just begging for change, the bum is heard saying, "Help a Vietnam vet walk again! Help a cripple!" Porter grabs the cash, and the mendicant ruins his ruse by standing up to confront the thieving Porter. Gibson's Porter has become an arbiter of social justice.

"You're cured," Porter glibly snarls and pushes the beggar to the street. Our first laughline has been introduced.

In *Parker*, When Porter confronts Lynn (Deborah Kara Unger), she asks if he's going to kill her. Porter doesn't react to this question, making the silence of his unresponsive visage even more menacing and keeping the audience on their toes.

His reaction is quite different in *Payback*. Instead of being a minacious blank slate upon which the audience can project their own fears of this silent figure, Porter now gives a sheepish look that indicates a bit of surprise and, gosh darn it, some bruised feelings.

Parker's Porter doesn't get bruised feelings. He bruises people. More often, he mashes people. He pounds people. He gives folks two quick jabs to the gut that leave them gasping for air. In contrast, Mel's showing us the kinder, gentler Porter. This one gets flustered when people misunderstand his want of a scant seventy grand. He sports a grin or even a smile at times and can crack jokes after he's been tortured.

At this point we still don't know what Porter's story is, or even the identity of this staggering bimbo. It isn't until Porter takes a shower while this woman overdoses on heroin that we're shown the two bullet holes in his back.

Parker and *Payback* have Porter find his dead wife and dissolve to the flashback in which we see the unfolding of the events that had come to pass. Like *Point Blank*, the heist that Porter commits is done in collaboration with only his wife and Val Resnick (Gregg Henry). In order to return to The Outfit,

Val is in need of both his and Porter's share of the profits of waylaying some Chinese Mafia bagmen.

As with *The Hunter* (but not *Point Blank*), Lynn pulls the trigger on Porter. Val has convinced her to do so by showing Lynn a picture of Porter and Rosie (Maria Bello). Though the photo shows nothing more than the two smiling, Lynn is not to be scorned.

Porter was employed as Rosie's driver—taking the expensive call girl from john to john—quite an emasculating position. Via Rosie and cab-stand operator Stegman (David Paymer), Porter tracks Val down at The Outfit's hotel. When Val wakes up to find Parker in his room, he doesn't find a whore or Porter's sister-in-law next to him, but Pearl (Lucy Liu). Her character has been changed from a junkie with no dialogue to an Asian dominatrix with a significant role. Pearl is in love with pain, both giving it and receiving it. She's instantly aroused by Porter's power. Also, Pearl has connections to the Chows, the gang that Parker and Val ripped off earlier.

Val doesn't fall over a balcony, nor does Porter choke the life out of him. Porter allows him to live, demanding payment. Val goes to see his boss, Mr. Carter (William Devane). This is the scene wherein *Parker* and *Payback* begin to diverge significantly.

In *Parker*, the scene is extended in the beginning. Entering Mr. Carter's office, Val meets up with Phillip (John Glover), who has pulled Val's file. It's huge! "Good read," Phillip tells him. "Nice art, too."

Mr. Carter menacingly tells Val, "When you go Outfit, you go Outfit all the way. You do not farm your work out to scavengers (Stegman)." Later Mr. Carter asks, "Phillip tells me you have a problem. Is it your problem that poked a man's eye out last night at the Oakwood?" In *Payback*, the scene begins approximately at this point, with the line changed to, "Is it your problem that breached security last night at the Oakwood?"

After Val leaves, Phillip and Mr. Carter exchange words. Phillip suggests that it might just be easier if Val disappeared. Carter counters, "I thought about that. I'm not worried about Resnick. He wouldn't last two minutes out on the street without us. It's that other mutt I'm thinking about. It takes a lot of moxie to walk into The Outfit and start whacking our guys around. Either that or he's shit nuts. Frankly, I don't understand it. I don't want Mr. Bronson hearing about this. He'll think I'm getting soft." This dialogue introduces Mr. Bronson and downplays the danger of Val.

Later, Porter returns to Rosie's apartment. She attempts to be affectionate with him, but his obsession with Val prevents him from conjoining with her, his phallic gun limp at his side as he leaves.

As Porter leaves, Val gets off the elevator, unseen by one another. Porter and Val's elevator switch juxtaposes their ability to interact with Rosie. While Porter has left her high and not necessarily dry, Val assures her that he's going to fuck her "six ways from Sunday." Val is impotent when not indulging in his

Impossibly Funky

propensity for violence. He's far more brutally psychotic than either Mal Reese or Mal Resnick.

The sexuality of Porter and Val is questioned in *Parker* and *Payback*. They act overly aggressive, as if to make up for their lacking. The cuckolded Porter has worked for Rosie, watching her interact with other men in the reflection of his rearview mirror, pining for her. (How Porter went from working for her to being married to Lynn is not explained—needless to say, their marriage was not ideal or without infidelity.)

Val proves what a nasty guy he is by putting a bullet in Rosie's dog and pushing her around. Just as Val threatens to relieve Rosie of her sexual frustration, Porter returns and immediately shoots his betrayer. This quick, brutal act is reminiscent of Stark's no-nonsense Parker. Remarkably, the violence of this scene is intact.

Payback's Finale

A dead dog? No way that's going to fly. The scene subsequent to Val's demise begins with Porter carrying the wounded dog into his fleabag apartment hideaway, with Rosie close behind. Almost immediately, his phone begins to ring. "Nobody knows I'm here," Porter says, confused.

"You're a very bad man, Walker!"

Porter discovers that the phone has been rigged to a bomb, and that the men calling him (including Phillip) are outside waiting in their car. It seems that they couldn't think of a more obtuse assassination method. Porter dispatches them and leaves the telephone-activated bomb undetonated. (Can you say foreshadowing?)

Porter's visit to Fairfax is more in line with *The Hunter* than Walker meeting Brewster in *Point Blank*. The majority of Porter and Fairfax's conversation remains the same between *Parker* and *Payback* (thought the scene had to be re-dubbed after Bronson's gender reassignment). *Payback* also includes additional moments of levity, such as Porter getting flustered by the constant error in sums—he only wants seventy thousand, darn it, not the full one hundred thirty that Val paid The Outfit. Also, Fairfax asks why Porter's going through such trouble for the small sum: "What is it, the principle of the matter?"

"Stop it, I'm getting misty," quips Porter in *Payback*. ("No, I just want my money," states Porter in *Parker*.)

In *Payback*, Carter's boss is Mr. Bronson (Kris Kristofferson). He painfully takes some time out of his conversation to dish some heavy exposition with his son, Johnny (Trevor St. John). Between the earlier introduction of a bomb and the exorbitant amount of information gathered by Porter's telephone call to Bronson, the course of events in *Payback* is fairly obvious. Porter uses Rosie (somewhat like Walker used Chris) to lure Johnny into a trap to kidnap him, to use as leverage against Bronson.

After yet another confrontation with the Chows, Bronson's goons capture Porter and begin the traditional torturing of Mel Gibson. Though not as gruesome as *Braveheart*, the hammering of Porter's toes surpasses *Lethal Weapon*'s torture scene, but at least has more substance than his dunking in *Conspiracy Theory*. Years later, Gibson would direct torture porn like *The Passion of the Christ*.

Porter gives up Johnny's location. Bronson, Fairfax, and the hammer-wielding thug throw Porter in the trunk of their car and make their way to Porter's apartment, where we begins the now-classic *Silence of the Lambs* cross-cutting between Porter trying to escape the trunk as the film's antagonists are making their way to the apartment door, and with Rosie and her dog watching over Johnny. Rosie and Johnny are nowhere near the apartment when Porter calls his old place, setting off the bomb under his bed. In fact, it's very unclear where Rosie is when Porter pulls up to retrieve her.

Porter sticks to the shadows

Porter, though a little worse for wear, gets the money (plus 50K above his 70K asking price) and the girl. "Just drive, baby," he says to her as they pull off. In contrast, *Parker* offers up an ending that is not only bleaker than the saccharine conclusion of *Payback*, but also far less hopeful than *The Hunter* and its exciting denouement.

Parker's Finale

In *Parker*, the film cuts from Val's death to Porter paying a visit to Mr. Carter. Carter is not as ready to talk as he is in *Payback*. After a while, he makes the offer to call his boss, Mrs. Bronson, played by the disembodied voice of Angie Dickinson. Instead of being merely businesslike, Dickinson's line readings are flat and unemotional.

After his third and final interaction with the Chows, Porter is not kidnapped by Mrs. Bronson. Rather, he runs off and gets in a panel truck that serves as a cold storage compartment for some of the goons he dispatches at the train station, while awaiting the arrival of a man with a blue, cash-laden backpack. Rosie (sans canine) helps Porter out a bit by watching over Mrs. Bronson's henchmen while they wait in the truck, as Porter locates the rest of the gun-toting group standing between him and his money.

The operation doesn't go nearly as smoothly as it does in *The Hunter*. Porter doesn't take notice of a very obvious assassin simply because she's a woman. As with his wife, he doesn't see this woman as a threat and pays dearly for this mistake.

After taking a slug to the chest, a gunfight breaks out and Porter narrowly escapes. It's this scene of Porter stumbling down the steps from the platform that became the image used in all of *Payback*'s promotional material. A look at the poster or video box reveals a flight of stairs behind Porter, who's squaring off to put a few bullets through the car that holds the very-much-still-alive Phillip (who met his demise earlier in *Payback*).

Porter slumps to the ground, his back against a parking meter as a bum wheels down the sidewalk and asks for the blue backpack, which may or may not hold seventy or more thousand dollars. Bleeding and semi-conscious, Porter begins thinking back on the events that have brought him to this point.

The camera tracks from left to right while simultaneously panning from right to left, creating an odd spatial effect. We cut from this single shot to images from earlier in the film, juxtaposed with sound bytes. Done with such a steady rhythm, it's not entirely obvious when these older shots become replaced with current action as Rosie pulls up and tries to wake Porter from his daze. This is a wonderful bit of filmmaking.

To the sound of sirens, Rosie gets Porter into her car and they drive off. Cut to Rosie driving while the wounded Porter sits next to her on the front seat of her car. "I've got to get you to a hospital," she says.

"No, I know a guy," Porter croaks.

"Is he a doctor?"

"No."

"Tell me where. Tell me where to go," she pleads.

This brings us back to the last spoken line in *Payback*, "Just drive, baby," he says and, despite his wounds, grins. Worse for wear, he doesn't have the money, but he's got the girl. The camera pulls back and we see that Rosie's driving Porter across the bridge he walked in on. Cue Dean Martin's "Ain't That a Kick in the Head" and fade in the end credits.

Straight Up, No Chaser

The dog was dead, the money taken, and Porter was on his last legs. Paramount head Sherry Lansing wasn't having any of it, and Brian Helgeland didn't feel like giving Paramount anything other than what he had originally done. Mel Gibson had no qualms about making the requested studio changes: "One cuts the cloth to suit the audience."

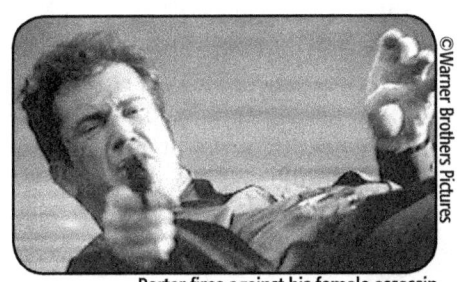

Porter fires against his female assassin

Fortunately, Porter's journey didn't end with the February 1999 release of *Payback* to theaters. Six years later, Helgeland was given an opportunity to revisit his work. He worked alongside editor Kevin Stitt, rebuilding the film from scratch. The result, *Payback: Straight Up*, reconsidered all the raw material from the original film.

Payback was originally edited on an Avid and the negative was treated to a bleaching process to give the film its unique bluish hue. Ironically, the *Straight Up* version was cut on a flatbed editor and color-treated on a computer, switching the analog and digital processes.

More than shifting the tone of the film back to the darker hue of *Parker*, *Straight Up* is even bleaker. It's also considerably tighter, running a few minutes shorter than *Parker*. Gone are scenes of Porter's plucking out a mobster's eye, the "he might bite back" line from Rosie to her dog, nearly all of Philip, and more. Added back to the film is a scene missing from any previous incarnation: Porter beating the hell out of Lynne upon his return home. Another significant addition is the cold-blooded murder of a thug in the back of the cold storage truck. As this is motivated by a remark about Rosie, this killing is the most romantic moment in the film.

The twisted relationships of *Payback*

Also of note is the new score by Scott Stambler and a new voice for Mrs. Bronson. Sally Kellerman rerecorded all of Angie Dickinson's lines (and more), instilling them with much more emotion than Dickinson's original delivery. All the way around, *Payback: Straight Up* has far more punch to it.

This incarnation of Porter is much more dangerous and far closer to Stark's vision. He's not the smarmy, smirking sociopath of Gibson's version. Oh, and in *Straight Up*, Porter keeps the money. Helgeland was willing to concede on that one.

Conclusion

Having four disparate takes on Stark's *The Hunter* begs the question: which one is better? Not to take the easy way out, but each of them has their merits. *Point Blank* is a highly enjoyable watch—the acting from Lee Marvin, John Vernon, Carroll O'Connor, and even Angie Dickinson is second-to-none. Boorman's mod, experimental filmmaking is appropriate for Stark's offbeat narrative and unusual protagonist. Though Walker's unflinching devotion to his money keeps his character at a distance from the audience, we still sympathize with him and revel in his violence towards those he sees as having wronged him. Crossing the best parts of his brutal thug and money-hungry gangster, Marvin's Walker stands as one of his best roles.

While Porter may share Walker's drive to regain his lost cash in *Payback*, he manages to snag much more. He is a winner. He's got Rosie (who is said to be giving up her life as a prostitute), the money, and has rid himself of the immediate threat of retribution by killing Fairfax and Bronson. He's in the clear. Yet Porter's intense search for monetary restitution overshadows any other need for retribution—personal or professional.

While seventy thousand dollars is a fair amount of money, it becomes a punch line for *Payback*. Everyone is incredulous of his desire for what is seen as a paltry sum—including the audience. Though I wouldn't mind an extra seventy grand, I'd not risk my neck taking on the mob for it, nor would I encourage anyone else to do so. Thus, identification with the rakish Porter is only gained through his glib retorts ("I got hammered") and winks to the camera, as if he were assuring the audience, "It's okay, it's really me, ol' lovable Mel!" Gibson certainly never got lost in his role. Or, if he did, he wanted to find his way out of it and throw an affable lacquer over Porter.

That is not to say that *Parker* and *Payback: Straight Up* are not without their flaws. When the stories depart from Stark's original work, the films falter. The use of Asian characters as villains and sexual deviants is inappropriate and offensive. While Helgeland may be indulging in a time-held film noir tradition of using Asians as "the other"—assigning characteristics of mystery and veiled perversity to this ethnic group—it's time this stereotype is laid to rest.

In Helgeland's *Parker* and *Payback: Straight Up*, the audience can better identify with Porter for being a man betrayed by his wife and partner, and not for his blind ambition to collect what he's due. Whether he's gotten the money (*Payback: Straight Up*) or not (*Parker*), he's regained a bit of his humanity, and that is what Val and Lynn took from him—they made him a dead man in a figurative sense. His wounds and his interaction with the world have helped resurrect his spirit—even if he's only got scant seconds left to live.

The original version of this article ran in *Cashiers du Cinemart* #11.

THE PRIZE IS YOUR LIFE

By Mike White

Man is a dangerous animal. For decades, audiences have delighted in films in which human beings are hunted. From *The Most Dangerous Game* to *Predator* to *Hard Target* to *Surviving the Game*, the list of man-hunting movies continues to grow a title or two every year. Taking the predatory pursuit out of the jungle (urban or verdant), we find that mano a mano confrontations feel "safer" to audiences when placed in gladiatorial arenas of Ancient Rome or in the distant future. In both of these cases, the recreational bloodletting takes on a more political subtext—the games find sponsorship with the state.

We find that the state-funded contests stem from a desire to placate citizenry with cathartic violence. The attendees, or viewers, of these confrontations convey dronish complacency when not frothing at the mouth, chanting "Jonathan" while watching the latest *Rollerball* contest, screaming dissatisfaction at the antics of Ben Richards in *The Running Man*, or throwing themselves into the road for the love of Frankenstein in *Deathrace 2000*.

While showing barbarism in the distant past or sometime in the future provides some comfort to an audience, the real challenge comes when this kind of event takes place here and now. Far more provocative than Ridley Scott's *Gladiator* (2000) or John McTiernan's remake of *Rollerball* (2002) were two 2001 films bereft of major marketing campaigns, but with a far more radical realization of mortal combat as sport.

Series 7: The Contenders

Employing an accomplished television parlance, Daniel Minahan's *Series 7: The Contenders* mixes the gritty vérité of *COPS* with a hyperbolized competition that dwarfs the contests of television shows like *Survivor*, *The Mole*, or *The Runner* (the latter ultimately deemed too sensitive for production). Shot on digital video, *Series 7* stars Brooke Smith as Dawn Logarto, an expectant mother and reigning champion of this horrific competition, wherein six randomly chosen civilians struggle to kill off their opponents. Their prize? Nothing more than staying alive and fighting in *Series 8*. Keeping the details of the contest sketchy keeps *Series 7* from becoming a science fiction story and, in turn, gives it more of a punch.

Brooke Smith as Dawn Logarto in *Series 7: The Contenders*

The Prize Is Your Life

Director Minahan presents *Series 7* as a full season of a program boiled down to a tight 87-minute running time. As with actual television programs of its ilk, *Series 7* creates drama in its presentation. The contestants come from vastly different backgrounds—from the "Angel of Death" nurse, Connie (Marylouise Burke) to the blowhard loser, Tony (Michael Kaycheck). Minahan drives further into television faux-reality by placing *Series 7* in Dawn's hometown and making one of the contestants an old high school flame—Jeffrey Norman (Glenn Fitzgerald), a terminally ill artist with a long-suffering, manipulative wife (Angelina Phillips).

The film presents characters in rapid-fire shorthand, though remarkably, none of them come off as stereotypes. Rather, they're infectiously enjoyable and become so familiar so fast that the audience can invest in nearly all of them.

By consciously employing the clichés of television reality shows, Minahan brings to fore commentary about the desires of today's audiences, while not overpowering the film's narrative. Indeed, audiences have found *Series 7* disturbing in the film's ability to minister to and underscore the undeniable bloodlust that prevails in today's "enlightened" society.

Series 7: The Contenders succeeds in every milieu it invades. Unfortunately, the same cannot be said about its distributor, USA Films. *Series 7* played in few U.S. venues—USA hoped to shirk any potential controversy that this insightfully violent film could incur. After avoiding several major film festivals, USA dumped the film onto video and DVD in late 2001—not bothering to make the film available to several major retailers or to update the film's website with this information.

Perhaps USA Films took its low-profile cue from the problems faced by Kinji Fukasaku's *Battle Royale*. Embroiled in controversy, Battle Royale hasn't come under fire because it pits forty-two contestants against one another in a similar life-or-death game. Rather, the dilemma stems from the fact that the players are all high school students.

Battle Royale

The sixty-first film of 70-year-old director Kinji Fukasaku, *Battle Royale* begins with a prologue:

> "At the dawn of the millennium the nation collapsed. At 15% unemployment, 10 million were out of work. 800,000 students boycotted school. The adults lost confidence and, fearing the youth, eventually passed the Millennium Educational Reform Act, AKA the BR Act."

While the logic of instating the BR Act due to the downturn of the Japanese economy is tenuous at best, *Battle Royale* screams into action and doesn't allow time to ponder such issues. After a few scenes setting up core characters—Shuya (Tatsuya Fujiwara) and Noriko (Aki Maeda)—they and forty other high schoolers are trapped on a remote island, where they're reintroduced to their seventh grade teacher, Kitano (brilliantly played by "Beat" Takeshi Kitano).

"This country's become no good," Kitano says. "The bigwigs got together and passed [the BR Act]. So today's lesson is…you kill each other off. 'Til there's only one left. There's nothing against the rules."

Armed with a random weapon (some get semi-automatic guns, some get less lethal implements like frying pans), each student has three days to dispatch their classmates in hope of being the last one standing. Again, there is little time for logic and no room for pacifism. *Battle Royale* finds fuel in the heightened melodrama of adolescence. As these kids struggle to stay alive, classroom rivalries skyrocket, and doe-eyed crushes become heavyweight love affairs.

Shuya, whose father abandoned him by taking his own life, becomes the stand-in for the audience, as well as the prototypical Japanese. Struggling in this microcosm of Japan, Shuya is a young man without a father, as Japan is a country without a strong leader. Meanwhile, the only male role model for Shuya appears to be Kitano, the slump-shouldered former teacher plagued with family problems of his own.

Battle Royale

Shot as a movie rather than a TV show, *Battle Royale* has its moments of "score-keeping," via graphics that appear that tally the names of those who have died, as well as how many students are left. Though not a public spectacle, the competition of *Battle Royale* sucks an audience into its world. As the body count goes higher, director Fukasaku keeps raising the stakes, never relenting in this dogged contest. Cleverly, Battle Royale doesn't appear as an outright parody, but it takes melodrama to the nth degree. The film's score booms with riveting classical pieces, giving the proceedings an operatic tinge.

The controversy surrounding *Battle Royale* is to be expected. People feel they should be outraged at the idea of teenagers forced to kill one another. There is a conception that a film such as this would encourage teen violence across the country. At some level, there is a realization that countless Columbine powder kegs exist. Rather than looking at the problem from a preventative perspective and diffusing the issues that cause such combustible situations to exist, these brave little moralistic firefighters take the tack of rushing around madly, throwing water, and heaping accusations on provocative elements such as songs, television shows, and films.

Sadly, *Battle Royale* seems destined to never find widespread distribution in the United States. Rather, the premise of the film will keep it, and any discussions surrounding it, to a limited audience.

Punishment Park

Shamefully suffered a similar fate in 1971 that *Battle Royale* endures today, *Punishment Park* played a mere four days upon its U.S. release to some violently negative reviews. The film quickly disappeared from public view, leaving the film and its director, Peter Watkins, largely unknown to younger cinephiles. Until 2002, the only version of *Punishment Park* available on video was a French-subtitled copy whose muddy picture quality only further emphasized the subversive subject matter of the film.

Like Minahan with *Series 7: The Contenders*, Watkins employs a set of stylistic conventions to give his film more weight. As with the lion's share of Watkins's oeuvre, he shot *Punishment Park* as a documentary "for European television" (years before faux documentaries were in vogue).

Like *Battle Royale*, *Punishment Park* begins with a prologue that explains the basis for the film. "Under the provisions of Title 2 of the 1950 Internal Security Act, also known as the McCarran Act, the President of the United States of America is still authorized—without further approval by Congress—to determine an event of insurrection within the United States and to declare the existence of an 'Internal Security Emergency.' The President is then authorized to apprehend and detain each person as to whom there is reasonable ground to believe probably will engage in certain future acts of sabotage. Persons apprehended shall be given a hearing, without right of bail, without the necessity of evidence, and shall then be confined to places of detention."

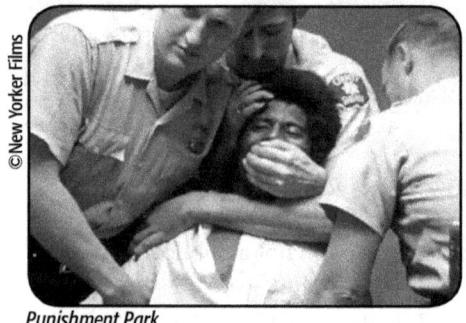
Punishment Park

If this sounds familiar, that is probably because several of these tenets made their way into the Patriot Act, which Congress hastily passed after 9/11/2001. The detention camps of *Punishment Park* don't openly reside on the U.S. mainland but, rather, at Guantánamo Bay, Cuba, and other parts unknown.

Those accused of insurgency have the option of serving out their sentence in a federal penitentiary, or taking their chances in Punishment Park. The "Park" is a sun-baked, rocky landscape where participants have three days to complete a fifty-three-mile trek to a U.S. flag. Additionally, the detainees must evade capture by pursuing law enforcement officers who have transportation, guns, and water; the detainees do not.

Punishment Park follows the trial of a group of alleged dissidents. Having been held for two months without ever hearing the charges against them, they're given a chance to speak—to a certain extent—at this tribunal. The kangaroo courtroom setting, with the comments of those on trial and of their uptight, white, bourgeoisie jurors, are intercut with scenes of the previous group of troublemakers making their arduous journey through Punishment Park.

Watkins doesn't skimp on ironic juxtapositions of actions and sentiment between any of those involved, yet he spares viewers from ham-fisted theatrics or preachy sentimentalism. *Punishment Park* is thoroughly convincing. The "acting" never feels theatrical. Instead, the performances in *Punishment Park* feel frighteningly real, helping audiences to invest in the story. From there, the editing and pacing are truly hypnotic.

If *Punishment Park* feels shocking and relevant today, how disturbing must it have been for audiences in 1971, when the Vietnam War was still in high gear?

The Heirs of Count Zaroff

Along with Richard Connell's *The Most Dangerous Game*, the roots of the human hunting human films are firmly entrenched in the works of Robert Sheckley, who frequently explored this theme in short stories ("The People Trap") and books (*Hunter/Victim*).

Based on Sheckley's "The Seventh Victim," Elio Petri's 1965 Italian film *La Decima Vittima* (*The Tenth Victim*) contains the kernel of a good idea but ultimately folds under the weight of its gynophobia. The film's protagonist, Marcello Polletti (Marcello Mastroianni, sporting an unlikely head of flaxen hair), plays in the state-run contest wherein participants alternate roles from hunter to victim, until they either perish or retire after ten games. Polletti closes in on the end of his career, becoming the final prey to Caroline Meredith (Ursula Andress). More dangerous than this assassin (with her bullet-shooting bra) are Polletti's wife and mistress, who vie for his attention and income. Despite terrific pop art cinematography, *La Decima Vittima* doesn't know when to call it a day, having a series of false endings that only serve to help wear out its tired presence.

A stronger satire of sensationalism and mass media, Sheckley's short story "The Prize of Peril" anticipated the reality television that *Series 7* and *The Condemned* would satirize. Adapted by Wolfgang Menge and director Tom Toelle, *Das Millionenspiel* (*The Millions Game*) plays as a two-hour block of crazed German television, complete with commercials from corporate behemoth Stabilelite Trust. These slick spots sell everything from birth control injections that last 90 days (Deproprovera, anyone?) to the perfect knife for murdering chatty women. They also appear to have influenced Paul Verhoven's *Robocop* and *Starship Troopers*.

Jörg Pleva stars as Bernhard Lotz, a poor schlub who's moved from one TETV show to another. He won *Godspeed*, a racing show, despite not being a good driver. He survived *The Real Thing* despite not ever having flown an airplane (waking up behind the stick with ten minutes worth of fuel) and he seems destined to win *The Millions Game*, even with three trained killers trailing him all the way. A ratings sensation, the show plays out like a variety spectacular, with frequent breaks for "The Millions Dancers" to strut their stuff while Thilo Uhlenhorst (Dieter Thomas Heck) keeps things lively as the show's host.

Das Millionenspiel aired once in 1970, not appearing again until 2002.

In 1983, "The Prize of Peril" came to the silver screen in France. Starring Gérard Lanvin as an ex-con turned TV sensation, Yves Boisset's *Le Prix du Danger* takes far too long to get started. Likewise, the scenes of six average citizens hunting Lanvin bear little excitement. The finale of Lanvin's confrontation of TV host Michel Piccoli should be viewed as an unsuccessful dry run for Arnold Schwarzenegger taking on Richard Dawson four years later in *The Running Man*. Paul Michael Glaser's 1987 film often appears closer to *Le Prix du Danger* than to the Stephen King story on which it was based.

Modern-Day Gladiators

The idea of violence as public spectacle—especially for mass consumption—becomes less farfetched with each coming television season. Boris Paval Conen's 1998 Dutch film, *Temmink: The Ultimate Fight*, questions the plausibility of modern-day gladiator games as popular entertainment. Taking a cue from the frighteningly popular "Ultimate Fighting Championship" series, Temmink pushes the envelope and gives a bloodthirsty audience what they're afraid to admit they want. The fighters of "The Arena" don't merely beat each other to a bloody pulp; they battle to the death!

As with nearly all participants in filmic "experimental programs," the contestants of "The Arena" consist of convicted murderers. Jack Wouterse plays the titular fighter, finding that his uncontrollable bouts of rage come in handy during these death matches. When his face isn't flaming crimson with anger, Temmink seems to be a fairly nice guy. Occasionally, Conen's film feels as though it might stray into more science fiction territory, but the director does well to stay his hand, providing a credible world in which "The Arena" might exist.

With the Iraq War (Gulf War 2) and Afghanistan conflict underway, 9/11/2001 six years past, and reality television a staple of popular culture, where else could human hunting go, other than the World Wide Web?

A co-production of Lion's Gate Entertainment and WWE Films, *The Condemned* stars retired wrestler "Stone Cold" Steve Austin and former soccer hooligan Vinnie Jones. Written and directed by Scott Wiper, the 2007 film plays like *Battle Royale* (2000) meets *Con Air* (1997) by way of *No Escape* (1994).

A group of ten convicts are taken from their death row cells to a remote island, where they're set against each other in a fight to the finish. The last person standing will regain their freedom (and some phat cash). Brainchild of entertainment pioneer Ian "Breck" Breckel (Robert Mammone), he hopes his webcast will be "bigger than Live Aid meets 'We Are the World.'" He's aided by a typical crew of morally ambiguous geeks.

As Jack Riley, Steve Austin is the Nicolas Cage character from *Con Air*: a Delta Force soldier who was in the wrong place at the wrong time. Sarah Cavanaugh (Madeleine West) is his long-suffering girlfriend back in Texas, working with Agent Wilkins (Sullivan Stapleton), an intrepid F.B.I. agent and the most slovenly government employee ever. The Cavanaugh and Wilkins subplot feels shoehorned in to add emotional resonance and overbearing morality. That these characters aren't seen until thirty-six minutes into the film adds to this tacked-on feeling.

Sarah and her coworkers watch Riley's progress at the bar where she slings drinks. That Sarah continues to go to work while she's worried about her boyfriend seems disingenuous. And that her coworkers scream and cheer for the action is particularly rude. As soon as the webcast of *The Condemned* ends, the bar's televisions cut to a reporter who rallies against Ian Breckel's brand of exploitive entertainment and harshes everyone's good time. What a downer, man.

The bar crowd is probably meant to be a microcosm of society, showing how far reaching Breckel's webcast can be. However, it feels that—despite myriad subscribers—only Wilkins and the patrons are watching. There isn't even an obligatory evening news teaser segment ("Millions of people are logging in to see people dying off! Story at eleven.") In these kinds of films, that is what invariably telegraphs what's on the nation's mind.

Back on the island, a few of the convicts form alliances, with Riley showing his nice side by helping out a pair of lovebird murderers. On the other side of the coin, government mercenary Ewan McStarley (Vinnie Jones) teams up with convict Saiga (Masa Yamaguchi). Cutting a swatch of rape and murder across the island, the pair makes Breck's team squeamish (and increases click-thru rates on the_condemned.com astronomically). One has to hand it to Breckel; he's got one heck of a server environment that can handle so many hits and live streaming video (despite the invalid URL).

Too much of *The Condemned* is shown via slick cinematography (there's always an extra zoom or pan at the end of each shot) rather than via the webcast milieu (à la *My Little Eye*). If Wiper had wanted the audience to identify as a voyeur rather than an active participant, he would have presented more of the film through the "television" lens, rather than the film lens. That said, the few snatches of webcast seen (usually via shots of monitors rather than direct feed) display a lack of production value. *The Condemned* webcast (and film) should have had a countdown clock and an up-to-the-moment death toll (taking a tip from *Battle Royale*).

The Prize Is Your Life

As to be expected, Riley and McStarley survive, and the fight is taken to Breckel. The resolution will not being televised, undoubtedly causing a flurry of emails to Breck's website for a refund. Austin makes a pretty good "speak softly and pack a wallop" protagonist, and *The Condemned* proves entertaining, albeit scattered, though it's nowhere near as subversive or disturbing as the aforementioned films.

The dearth of creativity in the Hollywood filmmaking machine churned out the 2002 *Rollerball*, as well as the 2008 *Death Race* remakes. An "in name only" remake, *Death Race* scaled back the science fiction and nationalism of Ib Melchior's original short story ("The Racer"), and fuel injected a product placement vehicle for Ford Mustang. Like *Temmink*, *The Running Man*, and *The Condemned*, *Death Race* participants are criminals pit against one another for national sport. It's all about ratings, and warden Joan Allen is out to get them no matter what it takes, even if that means setting up an innocent man (Jason Stratham) as a ringer for the race.

Director Paul W.S. Anderson plays up the gimmicks and gadgets in his version of *Death Race*, eliminating the points system of the Paul Bartel film and making it more like the central race in the Wachowski siblings' justly maligned *Speed Racer*. Think of Anderson's version as a pacing lap for his *Spy Hunter* film.

As the twenty-first century progresses, movie manhunts display a strong influence by the popularity of video games. "First-person shooter" games have crossed over to the silver screen directly with film versions such as *House of the Dead*, *Resident Evil*, and *Doom*. In order to avoid censorship, these games and movies replace living human targets with the living dead, aiding the popularity of zombie films in the late '90s/early '00s. The directing team Mark Neveldine and Brian Taylor have managed to successfully breach the gap between the two media with their *Crank* films. They pushed the envelope with *Gamer*, wherein the plot had characters serving as living video game avatars for remote players. While one character lived out her life as a living sex toy in a *Second Life* environment, the protagonist, Kable (Gerard Butler), spent much of his waking hours as a human killing machine in Slayers, a shoot 'em up similar to *Call of Duty*. The humanity (or lack thereof) of serving as a pawn in a real life video game never gets its due. Similar to two other 2009 releases, *Avatar* and *The Surrogates*, *Gamer* had an interesting premise albeit an ultimately unsuccessful execution.

While *Gamer* came and went quickly to theaters, Scott Mann's *The Tournament* had its premiere on DVD, never garnering a theatrical release. A direct descendant of *La Decima Vittima* with its public arena and *The Condemned* with its shady conclave of betting, *The Tournament* proves surprisingly entertaining. When drunk, desperate priest Joseph MacAvoy (Robert Carlyle) gets a little something extra in his coffee—a tracking device—he becomes an unwitting player in the latest round of the yearly contest in which the world's best assassins are pitted against one another. How this game can last more than one year is never addressed but, apparently, there are a lot of good assassins around including flawed beauty Lai Lai Zhen (Kelly Hu), parkour practitioner Anton Bogart (Sebastien Foucan), batshit crazy Miles Slade (Ian Somerhalder), and the former champ Joshua Harlow (Ving Rhames). The story may feel familiar with its redemption through violence, but *The Tournament* transcends its pulpy plot to become an exercise in excess and fun-filled bloodshed.

On the road from Roman and futuristic bloodletting to the reality-rooted, state-funded killing films, a handful of works reside between spectacle and scathing social satire. Too often only the lack of sheer audacity has pushed these films into the fringes. *Punishment Park, Battle Royale,* and *Series 7: The Contenders* bear backbone in abundance. By setting themselves in the now and by appropriating or playing off stylistic conventions, these films provide concurrent catharsis and caricature.

The original version of this article ran in *Cashiers du Cinemart* #13.

Impossibly Funky

A DYNAMITE DOUBLE FEATURE

By Rich Osmond

I don't know if just two movies make up a subgenre, but I do know the concept of pissed-off southern women blowing shit up with dynamite is good enough for a dozen movies, if not a 24-hour specialty cable channel!

In Lee Frost's 1975 *Dixie Dynamite*, sisters Dixie (Jane Anne Johnstone) and Patsy (Kathy McHaley) live an idyllic existence in backwoods Georgia, helping their daddy brew moonshine and hanging out with their motocross-racing buddy Warren Oates. But things turn grim when crooked fat millionaire Dade (Stanley Adams) comes to town and tries to steal everyone's land for the natural gas deposits. Daddy is killed during a high-speed chase with the corrupt local cops, the bank auctions off Dixie and Patsy's house to Dade, and Patsy is raped by evil Deputy Frank (co-writer/co-producer Wes Bishop). The only thing left for the sisters to do is steal motorcycles, shotguns, and a truck full of dynamite and start kicking the ass of everyone who has wronged them, becoming the saviors of their little town in the process.

Dixie Dynamite is rated PG, not a typical seventies-style PG (which would usually be an R today) but a nudity, gore, and basically profanity-free PG. This is about as tame as a drive-in movie could be and still be considered exploitation. Warren Oates is the only real name in the cast, and his presence always raises a movie up another level. Add to Warren the likable heroines and a nicely twisted escape plan during the climax, and you've got a decent rural time killer—one with the greatest exploding toilet scene in movie history. Would you expect anything less from the creators of the classic *The Thing with Two Heads*?

Michael Pressman's *The Great Texas Dynamite Chase* (also from '75) may not have had Warren Oates, but it boasts its own brand of star power in Claudia Jennings, *Playboy*'s 1970 Playmate of the Year and the ass-kickingest white woman in drive-in history. Jennings plays Candy, a recent prison escapee who robs a bank by threatening the employees with a lit stick of dynamite, all to save her daddy's farm. During the heist she meets teller Ellie Jo

A Dynamite Double Feature

(Jocelyn Jones, the hitchhiking terrorist from the opening of *The Enforcer*). Since Ellie Jo's being fired at the moment, she has no problem helping Candy with the robbery. After replacing Candy's dud "honkey dynamite" with the good stuff, the duo embark on a hell-raising crime spree through Texas, blowing safes, engaging in high-speed chases, and seducing the stunned (but always willing) dudes they stumble across.

For most of its running time, *The Great Texas Dynamite Chase* plays more like a softcore sex comedy than an action movie. Not a complaint, believe me, but it does make the gory violence in the last act a bit jarring. Jocelyn Jones is great (check her out in the seventies horror obscurity *Tourist Trap*), but Claudia Jennings is the undisputed star, just as she was in every other movie she made. One problem, though: Jennings was at her high-energy best when her character had some edge, like the sneaky white-trash daughter in *Truck Stop Women* or the crazed roller derby queen in *Unholy Rollers*. *Dynamite Chase*'s Candy is a sweet, honorable gal (except for robbing banks, I guess), but I get the feeling Jennings was a bit bored with this character, as she never cuts loose like she did in the aforementioned movies. But that's a minor criticism; anything with Claudia Jennings in it is worth a look, even the infamous "Johnny Bravo" episode of *The Brady Bunch*, featuring Jennings as the hippie talent scout.

The original version of this article ran in *Cashiers du Cinemart* #10.

DOUBLE IMPACT: THE DUPLICITY OF JEAN-CLAUDE VAN DAMME

By Mike White

In *Cashiers du Cinemart* #13, Pat Bishow explored the multifaceted personality of action hero Arnold Schwarzenegger. Even more splintered is the Belgian beefcake, Jean-Claude Van Damme. Studying the oeuvre of the "muscles from Brussels" reveals a filmography beset with duplicity.

For Sheldon Lettich's *Double Impact* (1991), Van Damme co-wrote the screenplay wherein he portrayed Alex and Chad Wagner, twins separated at an early age and raised in Paris and Hong Kong, respectively. That they share the same accent isn't addressed in the film. Despite their differing tastes in undergarments ("You, of all people, should know I would never in my life wear black silk underwear!"), the two team up to kill the men who murdered their family.

The following year, Van Damme's Luc Deveraux was remade as super soldier GR44 in Roland Emmerich's *Universal Soldier* (1992). Here, Van Damme was much more than two sides of the very same coin. He was the virtuous side of the vicious soldier Andrew Scott/GR13 (Dolph Lundgren).

In 1993, Van Damme would have his first experience with a recently expatriated Hong Kong director in John Woo's *Hard Target*. Two other Hong Kong directors cut their American teeth on Van Damme: Ringo Lam and Tsui Hark. The two had worked together in Hong Kong on several occasions, most notably as co-directors on *Shuang Long Hui/Twin Dragons* (1992), in which Jackie Chan plays twins—one a concert pianist, the other a thug—separated at birth.

Ringo Lam's initial American venture was *Maximum Risk* (1996). The film plays like a neo-noir, with Van Damme as French Inspector Alain Moreau. He takes the place of a dead man in order to find a killer. This is made easier as the victim, Mikhail Suverov, was Moreau's long-lost twin brother. That Moreau speaks with a French accent (and not a Russian one) is, again, not addressed in the film.

To date, Lam and Van Damme would team up twice more. Their second outing, *Replicant* (2001), was a minimal science fiction thriller. This boasted a rare appearance of Van Damme as a villain. He plays Edward Garrotte, a firebug who's working out childhood issues. He kills women he sees as "bad mothers," and he's relentlessly pursued by Detective Jake Riley (Michael Rooker). The investigation is aided (for murky reasons) by a government cloning program, which creates a Garrotte "replicant" in the hopes that his DNA might be encoded with memories and motives for criminal behavior. That the replicant speaks with Garotte's same accent is, as you may have guessed by now, not addressed in this film (that must be in his genes, as well).

Double Impact: The Duplicity of Jean-Claude Van Damme

Replicant co-writer Les Weldon teamed up with Van Damme later in 2001 to pen Sheldon Lettich's *The Order*, a thriller heavily inspired by *Indiana Jones and the Last Crusade*. Set primarily in Israel, the film opens with Van Damme portraying a French crusader, Charles Le Vaillant, who founds the titular religious sect. Centuries later, art thief Rudy Cafmeyer (Van Damme) follows his religious scholar father to the Holy Land in search of the lost scroll of Le Vaillant's writing. Any relationship between Le Vaillant and Cafmeyer goes unexplored, though Cafmeyer manages to purge The Order of its bad elements, save his father, bed an Israeli policewoman, and rehabilitate himself.

In Simon Fellows's *Until Death* (2007), Van Damme is a man renewed by a life-altering coma, going from dirty cop to nice guy. Like his *Universal Soldier* character, this is an opportunity to witness one Van Damme playing different aspects of the same person. Typical of the majority of the aforementioned films, Van Damme's secondary character represents a chance at redemption.

In Mabrouk El Mechri's *JCVD* (2008), the two sides of Van Damme collide. Here the actor plays a close approximation to himself in a metafictional tale of JCVD, a burned out action star struggling for artistic credibility, cash, and his daughter (she's embarrassed by her dad and would rather live with her mother). Returning to Brussels, he gets caught in the crossfire of a bank robbery, suddenly plunging him into some all-too-familiar action film territory.

A highly engaging experiment in self-reflexivity, this film continues to prove that Van Damme has a keen sense of humor about his screen persona. In the film, he's credited twice as "the man who brought John Woo to America." It's apparent that Van Damme's subsequent films have been multinational lower-tier efforts with nothing approaching the promise the actor expressed in the early '90s.

Told via a fractured time structure that continually shatters into smaller pieces, the film works as a cohesive whole. *JCVD* boasts a washed-out, dirty color palette which helps reflect our hero's drab mood. Those surprised by Van Damme's acting chops in El Mechri's film must not be familiar with Peter Hyams's *Time Cop* (1994). Indeed, *JCVD* allows Van Damme to flex his inner thespian and kick some emotional butt.

In *Time Cop*, two equally evil Ron Silvers can not occupy the same space. Even touching each other will lead to their utter destruction. More than a movie rule of temporal physics, this speaks to the larger issue that Van Damme duality always holds one member of the pair striving for goodness. Whether righting wrongs from Vietnam (*Universal Soldier*), outing agents in the pocket of the Russian mob (*Maximum Risk*), living a good life despite a bad childhood (*Replicant*), or feeling free and comfortable enough with one's sexuality to wear alternative undergarments (*Double Impact*), the knot-headed Belgian sees these doppelgangers as a way to show the goodness that lies in everyone's heart, even his own.

Portions of this article ran on impossiblefunky.blogspot.com.

THE *HIGHLANDER* RETURNS!

By Mike Thompson

It has come to my attention that there is a film that is being overlooked by film schools, scholars, and critics in this country and around the world. A film that stands out in a crowd and is so unlike anything else we've even seen that people fail to notice it.

That movie is *Highlander 2: The Quickening*.

I know what you've heard. Hell, you may have even seen the damn thing and just not known what to make of it. We fear change and tend to reject such revolutionary ideas. That's why I'm here: to guide you down the path of righteousness, allowing you to experience the quickening yourself.

Let's start with the plot, or rather the Plot Hole. The writers had to know they were up a tree when they were asked to write a sequel to a film whose story was wrapped up in a neat little package. No room for an evil twin or a forgotten immortal; Connor McLeod (Christopher Lambert) was the only one left and he had gotten his prize (as lame as it was).

So what do the writers do? They elect to throw out every aspect of the first film and create what has to be the most ridiculous idea since the Ewoks in *Return of the Jedi*.

"See, they aren't just immortal, they're aliens, too!"
"Yeah, that's great! But why are they here?"
"Hmmm…that's a problem."

And so the great Plot Hole opened. Just a tiny crack in the earth into which a seed was planted. The seed was hungry and the writers were more than happy to feed the Hole.

"We'll say they were banished from their planet for being rebels and they all have to fight until there is only one, and that guy can choose to live out his life or go back to their home planet…uh… Zeist."
"But how come nobody knew about that in the first movie?"
"Hmmm…I got it! Their memories were blanked out. That way they won't have any trouble killing each other, because they won't remember if they were friends or not."
"Well, I… No! You're right, it's great, let's go."

Now that's a pretty big Hole you've got there. You can see how they were just piling one thing onto another. But this is just to get the movie started. Next comes the girl.

"Now we've got to have a chick. And it can't be the girl from the first one, 'cause she's old."
"Okay, we'll introduce a new chick."
"Fine, but she's got to be more than just a chick."
"Why?"
"People just don't dig chicks being chicks anymore."
"Fine, let's give her a cause."

And at that moment, the eyes of one of the writers, or perhaps both at the same time, glanced at the newspaper with a little article about the ozone layer and its hole. The light bulb went on over each head, and they just added the ozone hole to their own Hole.

"Great, but this is the future. Won't they have solved it?"
"Yeah. Hey! We can have McLeod solve it! That will give them something in common."

What happened next is pretty hard to foresee. How these two Ed Wood protégés came up with putting a giant shield around the earth that would keep out the sun, keep in the humidity, and somehow cause everything on earth to go back to the old days (old cars, planes with propellers, etc.) is beyond even this theorist.

Regardless, they did it. At this point, the Plot Hole in *Highlander 2* is so big it's talking to these two, making its own demands.

It's pretty difficult for me to think in the same way the Hole must have. The Hole is just beyond me, beyond us all. And, damn, it was hungry for more!

Maybe it was the writers or the Hole or some contractual obligation thing, but somehow Ramirez (Sean Connery) arrives on the scene. Now anyone who has seen the first film knows that Connery was decapitated and that means it's all over-right? The Hole had no other ideas and Connery returned, but not right to McLeod—no, that would be too easy. Instead, Connery's soul bounces off the shield that McLeod invented. (See how this film starts to take on symmetry? It's fascinating.) Connery being lost paved the way for a bizarre Shakespeare scene and the funniest part of the whole (Hole?) movie—the safety film on the airplane. We're talking high comedy here, ladies and gentlemen.

The Hole was pretty big by now. Okay, it was huge. All that was missing was a bad guy. Enter Michael Ironside, generic antagonist, doing his best impersonation of the Joker. He's hated McLeod for almost a millennium and yet doesn't look a day over 35. How? That question has no meaning in the face of the Hole.

The rest is really a sight to see. It's too much to go into unless I were to write a book. But that doesn't mean I don't have more to say. This article has turned into a Hole itself, demanding to be written, demanding to move beyond plot summary and to a new level-the level of criticism.

When *Highlander 2* came out, fellow critic Roger Ebert put it as his number-one worst film of the year. He was right. And he was wrong. Most people seem to think that being the worst is a bad thing, and most of the time it is—but not this time. *Highlander 2* really is one of the worst films of all time, but in the best way; the film is perfectly imperfect, and wears it as a badge of honor.

Every aspect of the film is wrong. Every rule of good storytelling, film making, acting, and even common sense are thrown out the window. It takes a lot of courage to do something like this. Few people have. *Highlander 2* finds its home among the works of Godard and Hudson Hawk. *Highlander 2* pulls out all the stops and what happens is an explosion of just plain wrongness. And therein lies the greatness.

Most films just have a few holes here and there, but this film went for something more and succeeded—it actually became the Hole. The tragedy of *Highlander 2* is that few people can appreciate it. They blow it off as trivial or even stupid.

Fools.

I guess it's just too obvious. Maybe it's because the film never ceases to take itself seriously. Maybe it's because people just don't buy "I'm Connor McLeod of the clan McLeod. I was banished from the planet Ziest nine hundred years ago and I cannot die" as a pick-up line. But, folks, I'm here to tell you that for my friend Brian, it almost worked!

Renegade

Now with the director's cut (the Renegade Version, which includes fifteen more minutes of Hole), perhaps *Highlander 2* will find a new life. With the title "Renegade Version" boldly written in *Star Trek* font, I was ready for an ungodly revelation.

It would seem that the real hero of *Highlander 2* was not Conner McLeod or Ramirez or the writers, or even director Russell Mulcahy. No, the true hero was the person who edited *H2* into its theatrical-release form. But again, *Highlander 2* proves itself to be a truly ground-breaking film, in that this is one of the best cases of a "director's cut" of a film being worse, and I mean a lot worse, than the original.

Sure, critics may debate about the merit of a *Blade Runner* voiceover, dream sequence and ending, but let's look some of the big differences between *Highlander 2*'s theatrical release and the Renegade Version.

Remember when Conner McLeod becomes immortal again, tells Virginia Madsen's character this, and they kiss? That may be hard to believe in the original, but the *Renegade* goes one further (rebelling against good taste and not the movie studio, perhaps?) by having them do the wild thing right there up against a Dumpster.

I can think of nothing more sexy, except maybe the subplot wherein our heroes climb a mountain that peaks above the atmospheric shield to see if the ozone has really repaired itself. As *The Lost Continent* showed us, there's nothing that causes deep hurting more than rock climbing. Ten solid minutes of rock climbing. And when they reach the top, guess what? The ozone's fixed. I guess we really needed to see this, even after the earlier scene where Virginia Madsen broke into the high security facility to run a check on their computers. In any other movie this would be called excessive padding, but here it's "exclusive footage."

What's better than pushing the running time of a movie into triple digits with rock climbing? An unnecessary and poorly edited fight scene, of course! In the Renegade Version, Michael Ironside and Christopher Lambert duke it out on a moving truck! Of course, the truck looks like it's going a total of ten miles per hour and is so choppy that I thought Lambert fell off the truck, when it was actually Ironside. But hey, at least it's a fight scene, and those are always fun.

And "fun" doesn't even come close to being an adequate word for describing *Highlander 3*.

You know, since the original *Highlander* left so many unanswered questions, a sequel had to be made—and, boy, that *Highlander 2* was quite a cliff-hanger too, now wasn't it?

Highlander 3: **The Search for a Subtitle**

Coming in number one on my list of unneeded sequels is *Highlander 3*, with subtitles *The Magician*, *The Sorcerer*, or *The Final Dimension*. Take your pick; it went through three title changes before it ever was released.

It's not as much a sequel to *Highlander* as it is a prequel to *Highlander 2*. It takes place between the two films, but I don't know where to rank it in terms of its awfulness.

We begin with Conner McLeod hanging out in India with a kid. It's not his kid, of course, since immortals are sterile. Now, all I kept thinking was, "this kid had better die, because there's no trace of him in *Highlander 2*." But does he die? Of course not! He's a kid, fer chrissakes! Are you some kind of an animal?

"There can be only one." Was Conner talking about the number of immortals or the number of villains a film should have? *Highlander 2* undid all the logic the first movie employed, and this keeps right on unraveling that big mess. Because even though McLeod could only claim the "prize" after he killed all of his fellow immortals (at least those on Earth, I gather), three—count 'em, three—more bad guys show up. Apparently, you can get the prize if you think you're the only immortal left, because McLeod assumed they were killed four hundred years before in a cave in. Nope, they were just hanging out, biding their time for the right sequel to rear their ugly heads.

Also making an appearance is one of the most wasted characters I've seen in years, and probably the only cop on the NYPD with an English accent. He's trying to connect McLeod with some beheadings that went on a few years back. In case you missed those (and the film makers sure do hope you did), there's even a little rap by McLeod in the beginning of the film where he tries to sum up the first movie. Fuck that—I want to see him try to explain the second movie, and, for that matter, the third!

If I seem angry, it's because I am. At least in *Highlander 2*, the filmmakers attained some sort of Zen state where their movie became a void. That, to me, is an admirable achievement. But this rehashed mess just doesn't even come close. And dig this tag line: "When there can be only one, you've already lost." No shit.

The Special Edition

And years passed, giving us *Highlander: Endgame* (part 4 if you're counting) and *Highlander: The Source* (part 5) as well as *Highlander* the TV series. But more significantly (to this critic, anyway), it also gave us *Highlander 2: The Special Edition*. When I first heard about this new version, I thought that perhaps after so many years the Plot Hole had awoken and was hungry for more. Sadly, this was not the case.

This time around the producers or studio heads or whoever it was who currently owns the rights decided that they needed to fix up the special effects. And by fix up I mean change the color of the shield from red to blue. Yes, I'm sure there were a few more highlights here and there (more lightening to represent the Quickening—no, wait, we removed that subtitle), but none of them stand out as much as the color change. Of course the logical question isn't why would they do this, because why never matters in a *Highlander* film. No, the question is does this change help. No. It doesn't. At all. The crappy red coloring they originally used was one of the few (probably the only) effects that actually went along with the plot. People hated the shield. Ramirez called it a monstrosity. And it was. Now it's this pleasant shade of blue, beautifully undercutting the already awful dialogue between McLeod and Louise (Virginia Madsen) as she talks about how just once before she dies she wants to look up and see a blue sky. Just look out the window, jackass.

The only other major difference is the removal of a short scene toward the end, in which Louise and MacLeod hold off a bunch of guards at the Shield facility. Apparently it made more sense for Louise to have even less to do. Instead, we get only the first shot of this scene: Louise peeking around a corner. That's it. And that, for me, was the only moment that the Hole really appeared again in the Special Edition. Something had happened to it over the years. I'd always believed that its power had been damaged by the bloated Renegade Version from years before. But then I watched the deleted scenes and found, what I believe, is the moment that the Hole was truly hurt.

The *Highlander* Returns!

The Fairytale Ending

Originally only shown in the European cut, the "Fairytale Ending" of *Highlander 2* has McLeod, once again the only living Immortal, choosing a different prize: returning to the planet Zeist. And he does so by, well, basically floating up in the air and becoming translucent. He beckons Louise to come with him, but she says, "I can't and you know it." But this is *Highlander*. And the Hole will not be denied. He reaches out for her and she also becomes translucent. The two of them kiss and then turn into crudely animated comets that fly off into space toward Zeist.

Or did they? Perhaps they were actually just swallowed up by the void of space. Void? No, not a void. A hole. The Hole. This fairytale ending is the true ending of *Highlander 2*. The Hole, having consumed every plot point, every bit of sense and reason now, finally consumes the main character and his love interest. It's the ultimate triumph: a perfectly senseless conclusion to a movie that has completely defied reason. But this ending wasn't released in the States. And even now it's not part of the actual movie presented in the Special Edition or Renegade Version. In fact, the version in the Special Edition presents Lambert's scenes unfinished, with him suspended on wires in front of a blue screen (amazingly making the sequence even more hilarious). A more finished version does exist; it's what they used for the European cut, but here it's gone (check YouTube). A final insult to injury that may have closed the Hole forever. Or has it? Who knows, Highlander? Who knows?

Portions of this article ran in *Cashiers du Cinemart* #4 & #6.

PSYCHO VIXENS

By Rich Osmond

Slobbering old dudes harassing nubile teenyboppers…there's laws against it, you know. But what about the flipside social ill nobody likes to talk about: psychotic teenage girls terrorizing hapless middle-aged men? In Douglas Hayes's *Kitten with a Whip* (1964), David Stratton (John Forsythe), a millionaire separated from his wife, wakes up one morning to find Judy Dvorak (Ann-Margret in *Viva Las Vegas* sex-bomb mode) curled up like Goldilocks in his daughter's bed with a stuffed monkey. Being a political candidate, Stratton's first thought is that young Judy is part of a blackmail setup. But Judy tries several other stories before she finds one Stratton will buy, that she is a runaway fleeing the advances of her mother's new "gentleman caller," Barney the Slob.

Determined to do right by this scrappy kid, Stratton buys her new clothes and a bus ticket to her aunt in L.A. But when he gets home, he finds Judy has beaten him back. He learns the truth—that Judy Dvorak is actually a violent beatnik reform school escapee, and she torched the place and stabbed a matron during her breakout. Now the cops are after her and she needs a place to lay low, and if Stratton doesn't cooperate, things will get ugly. "You poke your finger at that dial, Mister, and that's when I start screaming 'rape.'" And if he does help out, well… "We're alone; we have the whole house to ourselves. You be Daddy, I'll be Mommy."

Unbelievably, Stratton fights off Judy's advances (may I remind you this is Ann-Margret we're talking about), but before we can ponder that for very long, Judy's delinquent friends show up at the Stratton mansion, ready to party. Mayhem soon erupts, and Stratton and the kids take a joyride to Tijuana for a night of black market medical treatment, strippers, car chases, and mindless cruelty.

Based on a novel by the Wade Miller paperback writing team, *Kitten with a Whip* was strong stuff for the early sixties, with a not-too-subtle S&M subtext that's truly shocking for a major studio job of the time. Ann-Margret says the movie was originally even tougher before Universal watered it down.

This is Ann-Margret's show. She digs deep into Judy Dvorak's psyche, peeling back alternating layers of confused kid and sadistic hellion until Judy herself isn't sure which is the real her. John Forsythe is smart enough to stay out of her way, perfectly playing the noble stooge and giving some great reaction shots as he's busted again and again by Judy's schemes.

At least John Forsythe's David Stratton didn't have the sexual revolution to deal with. In Peter Traynor's *Death Game* (1976), asshole suburbanite George Manning (Seymour Cassell) tries to do the right thing when his wife is out of town and vixens Donna (Colleen Camp) and Jackson (Sondra Locke) show up one rainy night asking for directions. He lets them use the phone, loans them warm towels, and impresses Donna with his extensive collection of elevator music. And, sure, he tries to put up a fight when they strip down and come on to him. ("No thank you. I'm a happily married man.") But then the Love Unlimited sound-alikes kick in on the soundtrack, and it's time for some three-way hot-tub humping, seventies style!

George wakes up the next morning primed to write that letter to *Penthouse Forum*, only to find the girls have decided to stick around and cook him breakfast…and play with his stereo…and try on his wife's nightgowns. Pissed (though he didn't mind their company the night before), George drives these troublemakers to the bus station. However, when he gets back, he finds Donna and Jackson have pulled the old Judy Dvorak number and have beaten him home.

Upon his return, they mace him and tie him to the bed. From there things get seriously evil as Donna and Jackson launch into a movie-long psycho spree/temper tantrum that includes putting on scary makeup, throwing George's cat through a window, jumping on the bed topless, drowning a delivery boy in an aquarium ("You can't do that! That's murder!" George cries), and sloppy snack breaks. All of that happens before the girls' private "trial" of George for statutory rape and subsequent breaking out of a handy meat cleaver.

Meeee-ouch: Ann-Margret in all her glory

These kinds of movies are only as good as the leading lady in the psycho role, and in *Death Game* we find two great actresses rocking out in scary fashion. Sondra Locke had a few pages of stuff to say about *Death Game* in her autobiography, *The Good, The Bad, and The Very Ugly*. She said the only direction she got from Peter Traynor was when in doubt, break something or eat something. This explains a lot! Locke reports leading man Seymour Cassell was so disgusted by the lack of behind-the-scenes professionalism he refused to return for post-production looping, so Traynor had a crewmember dub Cassell's entire performance.

Despite everything that's inept and laughable about *Death Game*, it pulls off some genuinely creepy moments in the second half—Donna and Jackson are not only complete maniacs, they're also having so much fun.

The original version of this article ran in *Cashiers du Cinemart* #9.

scripts

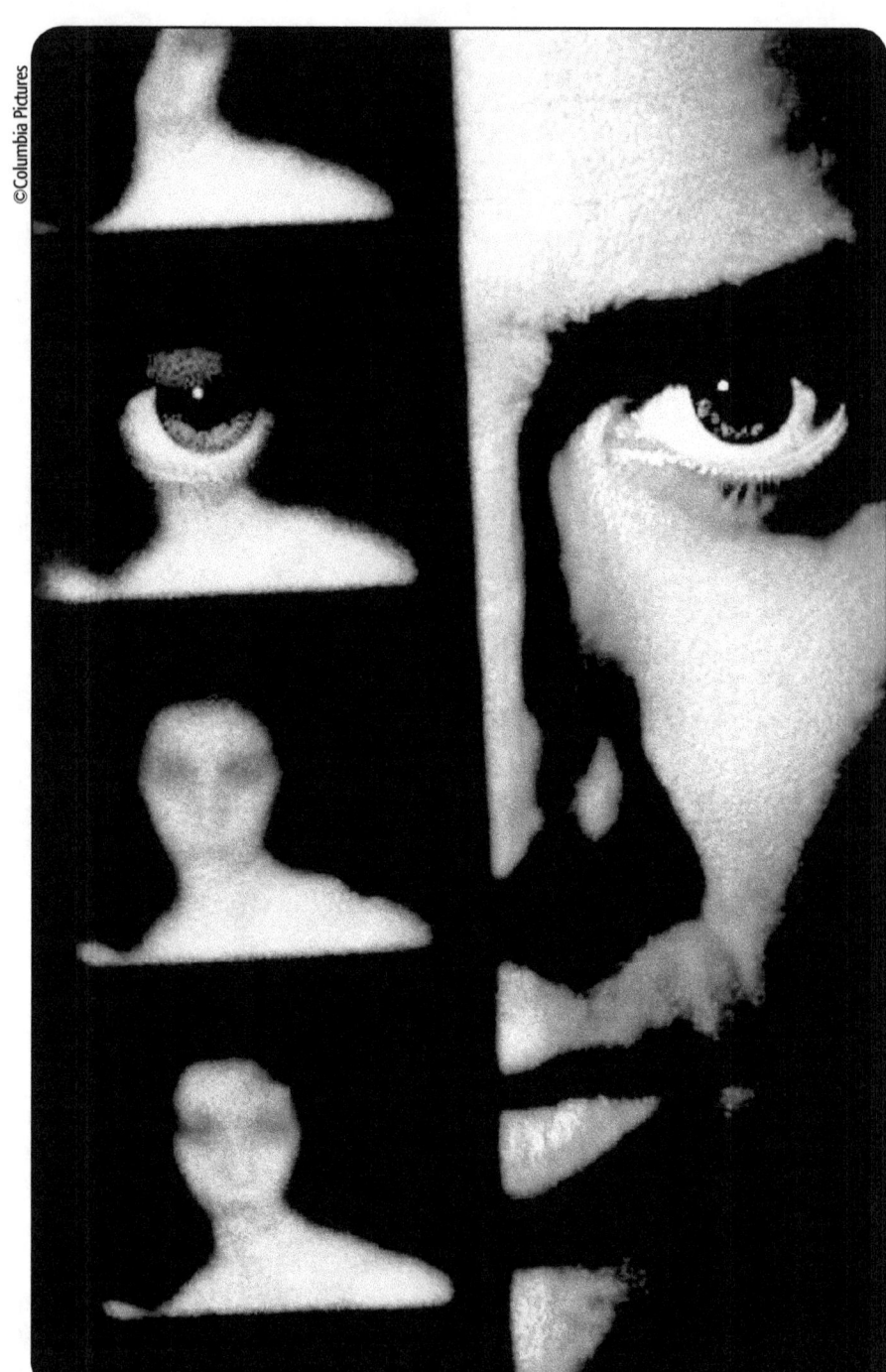

NOT SO SUPER...*8mm*

By Mike Thompson

Joel Schumacher. Easily the two most horrify words you can associate with any film. For years he's been torturing audiences. *St. Elmo's Fire, Dying Young, Flatliners, Falling Down,* and what most people feel is the ultimate cinematic travesty, *Batman and Robin*—the crescendo of his career has built to a level of almost unbearable pain caused by the mere mention of his name.

However, *Batman and Robin* is a walk in the park, a fine example of "entertainment" compared to Schumacher's brutal rape of what was once a fine screenplay. I'm talking about *Eight Millimeter*, or, as Schumacher would have us know it, *8mm*.

I had the pleasure of reading Andrew Kevin Walker's original script for *Eight Millimeter*, a gut-wrenching trip into the worst aspects of human behavior. For the guy who wrote *Se7en*, it's not exactly new territory. Andrew Kevin Walker is a master at exploring human frailty. He isn't afraid to show people as they are. In his work, heroes are often created by accident, rarely profiting from their actions. More often they're punished for them. The script was powerful, uncompromising, and poignant. As fellow staff writer Rich Osmond assured me, it would never be made. And, for all intents and purposes, it never was.

Walker's script tells the story of Detective Tom Welles, who is called in to find the men responsible for killing a woman and filming it. To find them, Welles goes on a bizarre odyssey into the disgusting world of illegal porn. The journey changes him, and not necessarily for the better.

Now, I understand that the above description isn't too different from the film released to theaters. The main narrative thrust is the same, but it's the subtle differences in character and reaction that turn a strong work into a pointless movie made by a director getting off on the world he is showing.

One of the general tenets of screenwriting is to never tell the director how to move the camera or what to show. The reason for this is that nine times out of ten the director will purposefully do something else (usually just to show that he or she is the boss). Screenwriters break this rule sometimes because either (a) they really want to direct the movie, or (b) they know how a particular part should be shown because the way it's presented is critical to the story. In the script, Walker specifically states that the actual murder shown on the eight-millimeter film is not seen and never will be seen. The reason for this is obvious: what's happening on the film is so horrible, there's no way to show it without undermining it. Schumacher, master filmmaker that he thinks he is, decides he can show at least part of the murder, and what comes out looks like a grade-Z horror movie made in somebody's house one afternoon—Herschell Gordon Lewis would scoff at it. Maybe Schumacher did this so the audience would wonder if the film was indeed real, but then why is Welles so distraught at what he's seeing? I think Schumacher just couldn't resist the idea of showing this kind of brutality on the screen. His rational, I'm sure, is that he didn't want to walk away from it—that it took courage to show the brutality. Or, it could just be that he just gets off on it.

As the film continues, Welles manages to discover the name of the girl in the snuff film (requiring considerably less work in the film than in the script). From there he is able reach her mother, and searches her house for clues. After some digging, he finds the young girl's diary. In the film it's in the toilet (which is a powerful statement in and of itself), while in the script it's in a velvet box underneath an old silverware tray. In the film, he skims through it briefly and then leaves it for the mother to find. The film Welles isn't interested in finding out who this girl was, just where she went.

In the script, Welles sneaks the diary out of the house, photocopies the entire thing, and reads it to discover who this person was. As he continues his search the audience hears voiceovers from the diary, so we know about the girl, too. She becomes a character to us, giving her murder weight and relevance.

While some might make the case that this omission was merely to save time, it's a critical blow to the success of this story. We need to know the victim. We need to care about her and be angry over the fact that she died. But Schumacher isn't interested in her, only in her death. For Schumacher, this girl was just another victim. Like his penchant for putting style well over substance, it's the act of murder, and not the person, that he cares about.

Nicolas Cage emotes

As the story pushes on, Welles meets a porno store clerk, Max California. Max is Welles's guide into the illegal side of porn. When Welles first meets him, Max is sitting behind the counter reading a copy of *Anal Secretary*, highlighting certain passages. Welles asks him what he's really reading. In the film, Max pulls the cover back to reveal Truman Capote's *In Cold Blood* underneath. In the script, however, Max is reading Capote's *Music for Chameleons*.

Now what could possibly be the point of changing the books? Both of them have the same effect: we know Max California is obviously smarter than the average porn store clerk. The only reason I can think of is that Schumacher figured that no one had heard of *Music for Chameleons*, and everybody knows *In Cold Blood*. You have to keep it simple for your audience, right down to the smallest detail, apparently.

After agreeing to help Welles, Max takes him to an underground porn dealership, which features all sorts of different horrors. In the film, as they walk through the door, the bouncer asks Max if he is a police officer. Max responds, "Fuck you, Larry." When the bouncer asks Welles, he responds, "Fuck

Impossibly Funky

you, Larry." It's a light laugh, but fairly meaningless. In the script, however, Welles's response is "No." The character that Walker is painting is a man who is serious about his job and serious about the situation. He doesn't want to make light of where he is or what has happened. Schumacher, however, seems to want to lighten the mood a little. Just because it's a movie about illegal porn doesn't mean it can't be funny, right?

In terms of this particular line of dialogue, I'm not sure if Schumacher or Nicolas Cage (playing Welles) is to blame. It should be stated that Cage does a particularly awful job in this film, moving through scenes like a mindless automaton, displaying little emotion or purpose until the end (at which point it comes off as almost comical).

Inside the porn bargain basement, Welles flips through some plastic packets holding pictures. In the film, the packets have the word "KIDS" written on the front. Granted, it's a horrible idea. In the script, however, the packs are separated, with the numbers 16 and 5 written on them. The idea of kiddie porn is horrible, but by assigning age Walker gives a much stronger image for the audience to deal with.

The pictures are a perfect example of the main problem with the film, and with Schumacher's approach. He doesn't know how to balance the subject he's dealing with. Walker understands that this world is horrible, and there are parts of it we have to face and other parts best left to the imagination. Schumacher, however, works to throw certain things in our faces (the actual murder), while shielding us from other aspects (kiddie porn). It's as if the director has taken it upon himself to reveal this dark side of human nature while protecting us from it all along.

The script features a long speech from Max California about the insidious nature of pornography:

Max
You've got Penthouse, Playboy, Hustler, etc. Nobody even considers them pornography anymore. Then, there's mainstream hardcore. Triple X. The difference is penetration. That's hardcore. That whole industry's up in the valley. Writers, directors, porn stars. They're celebrities, or they think they are. They pump out 150 videos a week. A week. They've even got a porno Academy Awards. America loves pornography. Anybody tells you they never use pornography, they're lying. Somebody's buying those videos. Somebody's out there spending 900 million dollars a year on phone sex. Know what else? It's only gonna get worse. More

and more you'll see perverse hardcore coming into the mainstream, because that's evolution. Desensitization.

Oh my God, Elvis Presley's wiggling his hips, how offensive! Nowadays, MTV's showing girls dancing around in thong bikinis with their asses hanging out. Know what I mean? For the porn addict, big tits aren't big enough after a while. They have to be the biggest tits ever. Some porn chicks are putting in breast implants bigger than your head, literally. Soon, Playboy's gonna be Penthouse, Penthouse'll be Hustler, Hustler'll be hardcore and hardcore films'll be jerking off to women lying around with open wounds. There's nowhere else for it to go.

Walker is not into softening the blow. Schumacher apparently doesn't feel the speech is necessary. Maybe he thought it was too long, or heavy-handed. A shot of two prostitutes in front of acres and acres of dead cattle is apparently much more effective in the oh-so-subtle world of Joel Schumacher.

After a brief skirmish, Welles captures one of the killers. He drags the man, Eddie, to an abandoned house and tries to find out why they killed this poor girl. In both the script and the movie, Eddie isn't afraid of Welles and stands up to him, even taunting him. Welles knows he's out of his league. He hasn't reached a point where he can take revenge on these men. He wrestles with this idea internally and then places a call to the mother of the victim. In the script he tells the mother what happened to her daughter. The mother is terrified, wanting to know why he's telling her this, why he's doing this to her. And Welles doesn't know why. He's lost. He's gone further than he thought and now he's in a new place emotionally. He's looking for an anchor, but can't find it.

In the film, however, Welles wants the mother's permission to kill these men. Schumacher wants Welles, and the audience, to know that it's okay to kill people if they really, really deserve it. And if the victim's mother tells you to. In both script and film, Welles does go in and kill Eddie, but in the film he comes across like John Wayne, out to deal some American-style justice (we even get the cliché shot of our hero walking toward the camera, with burning chaos behind him), rather than a tortured soul about to forever damn himself, as he's presented in the script. Cage does try a little to show that Welles is having a hard time with this, but Schumacher gives us no reason to doubt or question Welles's actions.

As the film stumbles along, Schumacher's heavy, protective hand destroys another of the most effective aspects of the script. In both the film and the script, one of the evil characters is named Machine. Machine is the man who killed the girl on the eight-millimeter film. In the script he wears a wrestling mask, and never takes it off. In the film, he wears a leather mask. And when it comes off, what little the movie had going for it really falls apart.

In the script, Machine is the personification of evil—a faceless creature with no soul or compassion, able to kill anything. At the script's climax, Welles finds Machine living with his grandmother. After she leaves, Welles enters the house and struggles with Machine, eventually strangling him to death. After his death, Welles pulls the mask off, but we never see his face. Why? Because there's no reason to. Machine was the mask on his face. There isn't anything underneath that mask that will explain to us what or why he was.

Schumacher, however, cannot live with that. In the film, Welles finds Machine living with his grandmother, as in the script, only this time Machine's room has Danzig posters on the wall, which, of course, mean he's evil, right? Welles and Machine fight for what feels like an hour, and then Welles forces him to take of his mask. Machine stands there and puts his glasses on (which were somehow not destroyed during a fight in which he fell from the second story window of a house), making him look even more like a child molester. He looks at Welles, accusingly. "What did you expect?" he asks. "A monster?" Machine goes on to explain himself. He tells Welles that there's nothing wrong with him. Machine didn't have a bad childhood, his father didn't rape him; he just likes to kill and hurt people.

In Walker's script, there is no explanation because there can't be one. Evil is evil. It's not explainable or understandable. And when you cross evil, it doesn't help you deal with it.

As the script draws to a close, Welles character is torn apart by his actions. He has found the killers and he has killed them. But rather than feeling as if he has served justice, Welles is feeling tremendous guilt. He is a moral man, and in his world, murder—even of people who are evil—is wrong. Walker was quoted on the Mr. Showbiz site as saying "[he] certainly never intended [Welles] 'to be let off the hook,' as he is at the end. There's no attempt to justify [the murder of those guys] in my script," says Walker. "In my opinion, if you feel kind of horrified by someone being murdered in cold blood, that's the way it should be."

But not Joel Schumacher. After Welles kills all of the men, he receives a letter from the mother of the murder victim, telling him she's glad the men are dead. It's a moment reminiscent of the letters from Iris's parents in *Taxi Driver*, except that Schumacher presents the letter without irony. So now, he's done the right thing and even though it wasn't the best way to do it, he's been forgiven. And that is just bullshit. But it's Joel Schumacher, who gave us the revenge-promoting movie *A Time to Kill*. Murder's okay when the people are really bad, isn't it? And aren't we all lucky that we've got Joel Schumacher to show us who the bad people really are?

Not So Super…*8mm*

In the months following the completion of this article, the gods of screenwriting publishing have seen fit to release Andrew Kevin Walker's scripts for both *Se7en* and *8mm* in a single volume (titled, surprisingly enough, *Seven and 8mm*). The scripts inside are the original first drafts. The script for *Se7en* is similar to the movie, although the ending is a little different (actually darker, if you can believe that). The script for *8mm* is the same one addressed in this article. There is also an interview with Walker at the beginning where he talks about what went wrong with *8mm*. Many of his comments echo what you've just read, although Walker doesn't come across as disgusted with Schumacher as I have. The interview and original script make fine examples of what can happen when a good screenplay falls into the hands of an idiotic, shallow egomaniac. At least now, you can know what might have been, and maybe more importantly, who to blame.

The original version of this article ran in *Cashiers du Cinemart* #10.

THE MOUSE THAT ROARED: AN EVOLUTION OF CATWOMAN

By Mike Thompson

The *Spider-Man* and *X-Men* franchises proved that comic book movies don't always have to suck (*Spider-Man 3* notwithstanding), prompting a flurry of comic book movie development. 2004 alone saw heroes and antiheroes like the Punisher, John Constantine, and even Man-Thing come to theaters (albeit briefly). And, in the middle of it all, we finally got a Catwoman movie, too.

Warner Brothers has been developing a Catwoman project since *Batman Returns* in 1992. In the interim twelve years the script has gone through multiple drafts, changing everything from the storyline to the location to the main character's alter ego. Long before the awful new costume made the scene, two different drafts were written. One of them is a surreal exercise in trying to do something new, while the other feels like just an exercise in trying to get the job done.

In the DC comic book, Catwoman is no longer just a cat burglar who bothers Batman every now and again. She's a real person with real problems, not just dilemmas that stem from her life as a crime fighter. Writer Ed Brubaker took the character to new depths, trying to explore her as a person rather than a sexy outfit. The screen incarnation of Catwoman, however, is far more concerned with aesthetics than character. Halle Berry sure does look sexy in her ripped up leather pants, tank top, cat mask, and whip. Oh, did I say sexy? I meant stupid.

Waters Runs Deep

Daniel Waters's draft of *Catwoman* picks up after the events of *Batman Returns*. Dropping the Gotham City setting, Waters has moved Selina Kyle to Oasisburg, a neo-Vegas hellhole where people drive golf carts instead of cars and the city has more tourists than residents. Selina lives with her mother, working as a wage slave at Frank's Fun Palace, the tackiest of the city's casinos. Most significantly, though, Selina has no memory of her life as Catwoman.

When we first see Selina, she's in a "self-help" meeting conducted by Penelope Snuggle, a "post-feminist" and author of *The Catwoman Complex*. It's Snuggle's conviction that women in power are the most dangerous people in the world, and they all need to embrace the typical subservient role that society has set down for them. Before Selina can escape, Oasisburg's protective superteam, the Cult of Good, interrupts the meeting. Led by Captain God, the Cult of Good is a collection of superhero clichés that make fighting crime a spectator sport. The women in the support group fawn like little girls over the superheroes, while Selina tries desperately to ignore it all.

The Mouse That Roared: An Evolution of Catwoman

Yet Selina can't run away from her surroundings, or her past. A lone black cat follows her, and a strange old hag sets up a hut outside Selina's mother's house. When the cat leads Selina to the Cult of Good's hideout and she learns they're actually evil, it isn't long before Catwoman is reborn.

And while all of this may seem a little typical (if somewhat bizarre), that's merely the first act in one of the weirdest scripts (comic book adaptation or otherwise) ever written. Before the script is even halfway through, the idea of Catwoman has infected almost the entire female population of Oasisburg, causing them to create their own Catwoman costumes and storm out in the streets, creating mayhem as they rail against their male-dominated society.

Screenwriter Waters worked hard in *Batman Returns* to make Catwoman more dynamic than just another antagonist for Batman to knock around.

Michelle Pfeiffer inspires fetishists as Catwoman

By starting her off as a timid, almost self-loathing woman, Waters turned her into the proverbial mouse that roared when she donned the cat ears and picked up the whip. And here he takes the idea of her as the ultimate symbol of female empowerment to the nth degree. Rather than just stop with Catwoman as a symbol, Waters goes on to show the danger of an unfocused revolution. As the reluctant cause of the uprising, Catwoman has to come to grips in the end that she has a responsibility as a role model.

Through all the layers, Waters keeps the story moving. In addition to having to deal with the not-so-good Cult of Good, Selina also has two love interests: Brock Leviathan and Lewis Lane, one of whom is almost certainly Captain God. There are several funny and self-reflexive moments where Selina tries to play detective when talking to the men, only to end up more confused than she was before.

The script continues to build to the inevitable conclusion between the Cult of Good and Catwoman and her army of Catwomen. When it's time, Waters's doesn't skimp on the action, but he never lets it get in the way of the characters.

While Waters's draft of *Catwoman* breaks the cardinal rule of following the comic book, it does respect the continuity created by *Batman Returns*. But even more, the script shrewdly uses the idea of the character as a springboard to bigger concepts. What ends up being so impressive is how much Waters goes for and actually achieves. The script celebrates and criticizes the male ego, the feminist movement, superheroes, and the clichés of most typical action films. It's no surprise that the studio passed on this draft. It's too cerebral, surreal, and smart to spend $100 million on. I mean, this is just supposed to be about a chick in a patent leather outfit, right?

Patience Has No Virtue

With the Waters draft out of the picture, the studio went back to the drawing board. The November 27, 2000 draft by Theresa Rebeck, with revisions by Kate Kondell, appears to have been written after Michelle Pfeiffer left the project and Ashley Judd had expressed interest. Aside from the title *Catwoman*, this script bears little resemblance to Waters's draft. Selina Kyle doesn't even make an appearance, although there is mention of the fact that the original Catwoman was killed.

This time around our heroine is Patience Price. We open with Patience, age 12, in a tree with her cat, Spooky. Patience's mother, Constance, is getting ready to confront her boss, Simon Greenaway, about royalties she feels she's owed due to a computer chip she created, but that he is taking credit for. Constance heads off to her meeting and never returns. We learn that she "apparently committed suicide" by breathing in carbon monoxide.

Flash forward twelve years and now Patience is grown up and working—where else?—at a pet grooming store. Patience's life outside of work is a mess. She never goes out, has no self-confidence, and while she's sure her mother was killed, she can't convince anyone. Simon Greenaway, however, has used the computer chip Patience's mother created to build an industrial empire.

As you already guessed, the story goes that Patience sets out to prove that her mother really created the chip. She's killed, resurrected by cats (in a scene similar to Selina's resurrection in *Batman Returns*) and turns into Catwoman. From there the story plays out like you would expect: an action sequence here, some witty banter there, the truth is revealed, and the bad guys are punished.

Halle Berry tries to hang on in *Catwoman*

It's not that this draft of Catwoman is particularly bad; it's just not particularly anything. Again the theme of a woman rallying against a male-dominated society is present, but it only rings hollow when stuffed inside such a typical storyline. Much of the time the script feels like it was written with very specific guidelines from the studio ("Get her in a sexy outfit, ASAP"; "Give her a snappy talking, slutty friend"), and if what they wanted was a story everybody has seen before, then they got what they wanted.

Into the Litter Box

It took twelve years for Catwoman to return to theaters. Her anticlimactic arrival resembled the by-the-numbers Rebeck/Kondell script, rather than the subversive Waters take on the character. Rebeck managed to snag a story credit on the 2004 movie, though only a few faint whispers of her draft remain in the

The Mouse That Roared: An Evolution of Catwoman

finished film. Directed by French special-effects maven Pitof, the weaknesses of *Catwoman* are exacerbated by the less-than-seamless CGI and Catwoman's ridiculous costume (she goes from a very cute outfit on her first night out to a simply skimpy ensemble for the rest of the film).

The final screenplay, credited to John Brancato & Michael Ferris and John Rogers, has our heroine now named Patience Phillips (perhaps to just barely avoid yet another cloying alliterative superhero name). According to the script, Patience is one of hundreds of "cat women" from throughout the ages. This tidbit helps explain away the Selina Kyle catwoman (if you look carefully, you can see a picture of Pfeiffer in her feline couture).

The remnants of Rebeck's script include the snappy-talking girlfriend (Alex Borstein), along with the resurrection scene. Otherwise, this Catwoman (Halle Barry) goes from meek to sleek without much railing against the patriarchy. Her few male foes include a couple thugs, her boyfriend (Benjamin Bratt), and her boss (Lambert Wilson). However, her real antagonist is Laurel Hedare (Sharon Stone), her boss's wife, former fashion model, and woman scorned. While her methods may be unsound, Hedare strives to regain youth and the power she had as a younger woman. Hedare usurps the society that cherishes youth by producing a cosmetic product that counteracts the effects of time. If Laurel Hedare is guilty of anything, it's a lack of patience (pun intended), as more testing might have overcome her product's nasty side effects.

Pitting the vivacious Catwoman against the aging magnate signifies that *Catwoman* isn't a tale of female empowerment, but rather, an anti-feminist statement. While Patience Phillips may not be the meek frump she was before her feline resuscitation, she's no role model for modern feminism. She is unable to reconcile her feline and feminine sides, remaining schizophrenic until she has dethroned Hedare, a woman who has managed to hold onto both power and femininity.

The Catwoman character can be seen as a barometer for female liberation. That said, it's sad to think that the last dozen years have brought about the neutering of such a powerful symbol. While I've given up hope that Daniel Waters's *Catwoman* will ever come to pass, I can only hope that the tide will turn, and we might again live in a world that can tolerate such a powerful character.

The original version of this article ran in Cashiers du Cinemart #14.

THE UNCREDIBLE HULK

By Mike Thompson

Comic book movies, in general, suck. The movie is either too stupid or doesn't follow the character's history enough. There are exceptions, of course (*Spider-Man 2*, *Batman Begins*, *Superman*). But all too often, the result is a bunch of people dressed up like idiots stuck in a moronic plot (*Batman and Robin*, *Supergirl*, and *Superman Returns*).

After a successful TV series, it only seems reasonable to put the big green Goliath on film. On the surface, the Hulk seems like a simple character: guy gets mad, guy turns big and green, guy breaks stuff. However, the original Marvel comic book character was always more than that. It was about a man struggling with his own demons in a world that rejects him as both man and "monster."

As a television show, *The Incredible Hulk* kept things as formulaic as possible. Every week, "David" Bruce Banner would travel to a new locale where he'd stop some sort of wrongdoing as The Hulk. Along the line he'd often say, "You wouldn't like me when I'm angry." Meanwhile, the comic book went to far greater lengths to examine the Hulk's psyche, making him a more interesting and complex character.

During his initial run with the Hulk, creator Stan Lee ran out of ideas after only a few issues. Luckily, other writers have stepped in and found new ways to keep Hulk interesting and dynamic. Peter David brought the Hulk character to a new level over his twelve-year run. No longer was it just Bruce Banner and his alter ego; David explored the idea that Banner had multiple personalities that came out in varying Hulk forms. Soon there was a green rampaging Hulk, a green "smart" Hulk (nicknamed "The Professor"), and even a return to the original gray Hulk, who became powerful gangster Joe Fixit.

David showed readers that the Hulk was more than what they saw on the TV show. Not every problem was going to be solved by Banner finally getting pissed off enough so that he could let his superego give in to his id, tear out of yet another set of clothes, and kick everybody's asses.

The question then becomes how much of those ideas are going to make it into the script. Most of David's concepts are too complex for a two-hour movie, but that doesn't mean that the whole internal struggle of good versus evil has to be jettisoned. Of the two drafts I've read, one strives for a genuine comic book movie, while the other seems to be interested in special effects and poor characterization.

Hensleigh's *Hulk*

Jonathon Hensleigh has been responsible for such epics as *Armageddon*, *Jumanji*, and *The Punisher* (2004). Sometimes he hits the mark, and other times he screws up so badly it hurts for days after watching the movie. Hensleigh came aboard *Hulk* with the intention of not only writing, but also directing the project. Fortunately, that didn't happen.

Hensleigh's draft begins with three death row prisoners gaining the chance to participate in a radical medical experiment instead of going right to the chair. Of course, the three cons (Hector, Deacon, and Novack) accept. They're taken to a secret facility where Dr. Bruce Banner is working on a way to colonize Mars. Banner's idea is that he can manipulate human genes and DNA so a person can survive on the red planet's harsh surface. These altered humans will begin the necessary steps to terraform Mars so it will be fit for regular humans to live there.

Soon Banner and his crew are working on the three convicts. Deacon has the DNA of a carpenter ant spliced into his genes to give him increased strength. Novack has pigeon DNA injected to increase his temperature so he'll survive the harsh Mars winter. And finally, Hector has hummingbird DNA (yes, hummingbird) mixed in to give him a high metabolism and eliminate the need to sleep.

All of the fillings are removed from the convicts' mouths before they can be irradiated by gamma rays as part of the experiment. If any metal is present during this step, it will cause an explosion. Seizing the opportunity for escape, Novack slips an aluminum gum wrapper into the gamma chamber with him. When the dust settles we find that Novack and his felonious compatriots have miraculously (and moronically) survived. Meanwhile, the destruction of the gamma chamber irradiates Dr. Banner, turning him into The Hulk.

From here, Hensleigh's script becomes a meaningless chase, with Banner trying to capture the three convicts and periodically changing into Hulk. These moments carry little dramatic weight, as only Banner's appearance alters. This Hulk is neither mindless nor raging, just the familiar doctor in a bigger, greener body.

As the story progresses, the three convicts metamorphose as well. Novack's temperature is so high that he leaves melted footprints in the ground (yet his clothes remain unharmed). Deacon slowly turns into a carpenter ant. And, embarrassingly, Hector's "arms flutter at an inhuman rate…like a hummingbird's." Later, Hensleigh seems to realize that maybe a hummingbird isn't threatening enough, but he won't let the idea go: "Hector is becoming a hummingbird, but he's real strong and real mean…and—" That's not a typo; that's where the sentence and scene end.

The script continues to spiral into a sillier mess as it progresses. Hensleigh hints briefly at Banner's incompetence when dealing with women, but it's a far cry from the bookish weakling from the comic book. And in the middle of it all, Hensleigh has the balls to introduce a kid. While serving no real purpose in the story, the kid, Ralph, does provide what might be one of the worst moments of dialogue…ever.

As Banner is about to leave to battle Deacon (who is now even more like a carpenter ant), Ralph offers this brilliant advice: "Hey Bruce. Better take this (holds up a can of RAID)... Just kidding." Never before have I been so dumbfounded by bad dialogue. The first line is horrible, but the addition of "just kidding" is like a swift kick to the balls after you've just thrown up. A line like this is more than just awful; it's humiliating.

Fortunately, Hensleigh's draft was rejected. The script is so bad that it begs the question of whether or not he wrote it that way on purpose. Maybe Hensleigh really thought this story was good, or maybe he thought comic books were so sophomoric that a movie based on one should be the same way. It's bad enough that Hensleigh disrespected the original story and concept of The Hulk so much that he changed the character's origin. But it's even worse that he left all the character, joy, and pain of the comic by the wayside, as well.

Turman's *Hulk*

For as much as Hensleigh tried to throw out the elements of the comic book, John Turman crams as many as he can into his draft. Turman manages to make room for Bruce Banner, Betty Ross, Rick Jones, General "Thunderbolt" Ross, The Leader, and even Doc Samson and Marlo (currently Rick Jones's ex-wife in the comic, but just the girl he desperately wants in the script). All of these characters are straight from the original comic, many of them present from the first issue.

Turman's draft begins with the gamma bomb project losing its funding. Bruce Banner, here presented as a meek genius, is on the verge of perfecting the bomb when a lack of results causes the government to cut him off. Banner's assistant, Leder, is a wannabe genius, currently wrapped up in a shady deal with two criminals to sell them Gamadium-282—the element that makes the gamma bomb possible.

As the bomb's set to be dismantled, Leder arms the weapon, making it look like Banner did it in a desperate act to prove that he really was worth the funding. Just as it went in the comic, Rick Jones turns up on ground zero, and Banner races to help him. The bomb goes off and Rick Jones is safe inside an old bunker while Banner is belted by gamma rays. While all of this is happening, Leder is trying to steal the Gamadium-282. Of course, Leder has an accident and becomes smeared with Gamadium. It's only a matter of time before the effects take their toll on both Banner and Leder.

We don't get to see Banner change into The Hulk until after page 40, and even that is kept mostly in the dark. Turman is smart to create a slow build before eventually revealing The Hulk in all his raging glory. He also cleverly cuts back and forth between Banner and Leder experiencing, analyzing, and sometimes even enjoying their very different transformations. Banner gets dumber when he changes into The Hulk, while Leder gets smarter as he gradually turns into The Leader. One of the Hulk's more interesting nemeses, The Leader's genius plays perfect counterpoint to the Hulk's (usual) mindless rage.

Turman works hard to keep all the elements and characters intact and relevant and for the most part, he pulls it off. He even gets the love story aspect right, with Banner and Betty Ross slowly realizing that they have always been in love. In the comic, Betty Ross is the one true love of Banner's life. Their relationship was always complicated by the fact that her father, General Thunderbolt Ross, is determined to kill The Hulk. Turman keeps the father–daughter relationship, and then adds in the further complication that Betty is a FBI agent whose investigation isn't always in line with her father's wishes.

The action in Turman's draft is always at a reasonable level. It's never absent for too long, but it's never allowed to become the focus of the story.

That's not to say that Turman's draft isn't without problems. For all the character balancing Turman does, there are times when it almost feels like The Leader is the main character instead of Banner/Hulk. Also, the inclusion of Rick Jones, while faithful to the comic, is sometimes painfully annoying. Jones's dialogue ranges from the dopey ("I saw a shortcut on the map and figured I'd do a Jim Morrison; you know, camp under the stars") to the downright lame ("Uh oh. Ladies and gentlemen, let's get ready to r-r-r-u-mble…").

Even with its flaws, Turman's draft of *The Hulk* is pumped full of pure respect and love of the characters and original stories. Turman even contrives a way to show Doc Samson changed from his normal human self to the gamma-irradiated, green-haired superhero all the comic fans know. At another point, Turman gives his opinion of the current state of comics (mind you, this was 1994), with the description: "CAMERA PICKS UP THE TV IN THE B.G. A DRAWING OF THE HULK. A really crappy, overmuscled artist's rendering of the Hulk by Rob Liefeld or one of the guys at Image." A little nod like that would probably go over a studio head's head, but for a comic book geek, it's pure truth.

Turman drives the script to a surprising conclusion, choosing to focus more on Banner's character flaws than straightforward action. "All my life I was afraid to care about anything…or anyone. If I didn't care, it couldn't be taken away from me…" In disarming The Leader's new gamma bomb, Banner is turned into The Hulk—permanently. The ending is so non-mainstream that it's not surprising that the studio passed on this draft.

It's too bad that Turman's draft was rejected. His love of the character is apparent on every page. He even goes so far as to use a different font for The Hulk's dialogue. With a little work and someone to punch up the dialogue, this script really could capture the appeal of Hulk.

Don't Make Me Ang Lee…

With both Hensleigh's and Turman's drafts rejected, hotshot screenwriter David Hayter (credited with writing *X-Men*) reworked a draft of *The Hulk* that

Impossibly Funky

appealed enough for Ang Lee to sign on. After the success of *Crouching Tiger, Hidden Dragon*, which perfectly blended real human drama with superhuman action sequences, it only made sense for Hollywood to come knocking on Lee's door, offering him a number of different action projects. While he passed on *Terminator 3*, Lee was intrigued by the idea of a man struggling with his inner demons. Watching Chow Yun-Fat and Michelle Yeoh leap over rooftops and across lily pads, it's not difficult to imagine Hulk bounding across the screen. And so Lee and his long-time writing partner, James Shamus, began putting together their own version, called simply *Hulk* (2004).

This time around, Lee and Shamus (Michael France and John Turman are also credited, although I see almost none of Turman's draft here) begin not with Bruce Banner, but rather David Banner, Bruce's father! A military scientist, David is working with starfish and other animals, attempting to replicate their healing abilities in humans. Of course, David realizes the best way to get the most immediate results is to experiment on himself, but to no effect. Then, however, David's wife becomes pregnant. At first the child seems fine, but as he gets older he begins to exhibit strange qualities (his skin turns green when he becomes upset). David, torn between his desire to cure his son and his own curiosity about what his son's altered genetics may have to offer, becomes more and more unhinged. When his supervisor, General Thunderbolt Ross (Sam Elliott), terminates his funding and forces him to shut down his experiments, David cracks, accidentally killing his wife while also destroying many of his experiments.

Flash forward some twenty years later. Bruce Krenzler (Eric Bana), now a scientist himself, has no idea that he is actually Bruce Banner. He's repressed the traumatic childhood memories, and has also been told that both of his parents are dead. Helping him with his experiments is Betty Ross (Jennifer Connelly), daughter of Thunderbolt. She and Bruce were once a happy young couple, but that time seems to have passed. Bruce's current experiments are very similar to his father's, which peaks the interest of Major Talbot (Josh Lucas), a corporate investor and former flame of Betty's, who's sold out and looking for the next big genetic paycheck. It isn't long before there's an accident during one of Bruce's experiments and he's exposed to "nanomeds," which, along with his altered DNA (thanks, Dad), will eventually turn him into The Hulk.

But before that can happen, a mysterious janitor (with a lot of dogs) shows up, telling Bruce that his last name isn't really Krenzler, but Banner. Who is this mystery man? Why it's

Eric Bana sulks in *Hulk*

The Uncredible Hulk

David Banner, Bruce's father. And he's even nuttier now than when we last saw him (punctuated perfectly by casting Nick Nolte). He's back to finish his original experiment, and he's going to use his son's DNA to do it.

And now we finally have the theme of the movie: the relationship between parent and child. How much of a person truly comes from his or her parents? Are we ever truly our own individual selves, or are we simply parts of the people that created us? And all of this really raises the even more immediate question: isn't this is a movie about The Hulk?

That it is, so it's time for The Hulk to do some fighting. But all we've got is a crazy dad and a corporate jerk, so just who is The Hulk going to fight it out with? Why, those crazy dogs that were hanging around with David. Having stolen a bunch of Bruce's equipment, David has created Hulk dogs. Yes, Hulk dogs (one of them is a poodle). "Let nothing stand in your way," he howls as he sends them after Betty. Fortunately, Bruce is with her, and he turns into the big green meanie and beats up all those pesky dogs.

From here the movie stumbles around with its parent–child theme, trying to make it work both with David and Bruce, as well as Betty and Thunderbolt. Talbot quickly devolves into caricature that exists only to aggravate Bruce and turn him into The Hulk. By the time he's finally extinguished, he's more of a prop than a person.

In the final third the parent–child theme is finally smashed into the plot by making David himself into a monster (a nod to the original comic's Absorbing Man). Father and son literally fight it out, and in true art house movie form, the only way the hero can win is to surrender to what he really is (even though we the audience aren't really clear on what or who that is).

Mr. Green (The Hulk) meets Mr. Orange (Tim Roth)

In the end, *Hulk* is a noble failure. Lee and Shamus attempted to make a superhero movie that was about more than special effects and violence. Unfortunately, they were never able to fully bridge the two, leaving us with a movie called *Hulk*, but with no sign of the character we were all waiting for.

I Am Jack's Undeniable Rage…

Realizing that the audience for The Hulk was still out there waiting for the movie they deserved, Hollywood decided to go as much the other way with the next version as possible. They hired Louis Leterrier (*Transporter 2*) to direct and Zak Penn (*X2*) to write the screenplay. All of the main characters were recast, and it was stated that Ang Lee's *Hulk* would not be incorporated into this version, causing people to create a new film term: the "re-quel."

Impossibly Funky

In the 2008 *The Incredible Hulk*, we breeze through Hulk's origin story with the opening credit sequence. Borrowing from the TV show, Bruce Banner (Edward Norton) is working with the government to create superior soldiers. He experiments on himself and turns immediately into The Hulk, destroying his lab, and wounding Betty Ross (Liv Tyler) in the process. Bruce is now on the run from the government, specifically General Thunderbolt Ross (William Hurt), who's not out for revenge, but rather the blood inside Banner: Ross wants more Hulks, lots more.

Cut to Brazil, where Bruce is working in a bottling factory. Taking elements from Bruce Jones's Return of the Monster arc from the *Hulk* comic, Bruce is using meditation techniques to keep his anger in check while also communicating online with a mystery man named Mr. Blue (Bruce's handle, of course, is Mr. Green). Mr. Blue is trying to help Bruce find a cure.

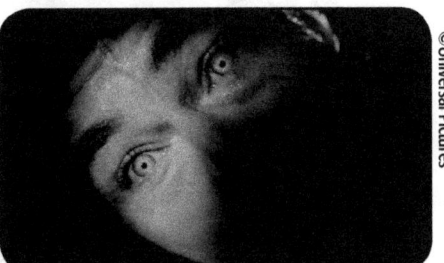

Edward Norton channels Bill Bixby in *The Incredible Hulk*

Unfortunately for him (but fortunately for us), it doesn't take the military long to figure out where he is, and we have a great action set piece where Hulk gets to punish some bullies while also knocking the military around. At this point we're also introduced to Emil Blonsky (Tim Roth). Updated from the Cold War stereotype Russian bad guy he was in the comic, Blonsky is now a career military man whose glory days are behind him. But he still wants a fight, and Ross is more than happy to provide him with one.

Bruce is now forced to return to America, where he once again finds Betty. And here is the film's biggest weakness. In *Armageddon*, Liv Tyler showed us that she can bring real life to characters that almost have no business even existing, but here all she's allowed to do is emote the name "Bruce" a lot. While very easy on the eyes, Betty too often feels more like a plot device than a person.

As Bruce and Betty determine their next move, Ross goes into the archives and pulls out some of the old supersoldier serum (a nice nod to Captain America). Blonsky is juiced up and we get another solid action moment where The Hulk and the military give each other all kinds of hell before the Green Goliath triumphs. And it's also in this scene that director Leterrier gives us some of the Hulk action we've been waiting for. There is a key moment where The Hulk looks like he's down, but his rage gives him the strength to overcome all of the obstacles. And that's followed up by Hulk rescuing Betty, which rings truer to the character than any screen version we've seen before.

The Hulk escapes with Betty (but not before nearly killing Blonsky), and once he transforms back to Bruce they head off to New York to find Mr. Blue. Blonsky miraculously recovers (thanks to the supersoldier serum) and is looking for payback. In New York, Bruce and Betty find Blue, who is actually

The Uncredible Hulk

Professor Samuel Sterns. Comic fans know that Sterns is the real name of The Leader.

As Sterns works to cure Bruce, Ross and Blonsky arrive. Blonsky, now almost completely insane, forces Sterns to expose him to Banner's blood. Once again the movie delivers what we've been waiting for: Blonsky's transformation into The Abomination—and also teases us with the start of Sterns change into The Leader.

A rare action moment from *Hulk*

The climactic battle royale between Hulk and The Abomination in the streets of Toronto—er, Harlem—begins with Bruce falling out of a helicopter (another nice comic nod, this time to Brian Azzarello's Banner), which forces him to change into The Hulk. From here we have more signature moments, including the best part of the entire film, where our hero finally says those two words: "HULK…SMASH!" Just as it is in the comic, The Abomination is clearly the stronger of the two, but just as it is in the comic, it doesn't matter. Hulk's rage, coupled with his love for Betty, help him defeat, but (in a surprising decision by the filmmakers) not kill, The Abomination.

We close with Bruce again on the run, this time hiding in a cabin. As he practices his meditation, this time it's different. He opens his eyes, which are green and he's smiling—yet another nod to Bruce Jones's run on the comic.

The Incredible Hulk does have its problems, the presentation of Betty being the biggest. There are also plot points that feel forced together. Rumor has it than an early cut of the movie driven mostly by Ed Norton (who had rewritten the script at one point, although now sole credit is given to Zak Penn) was three hours long, and cutting that down to under two hours has taken some toll. But all of that aside, comic fans can rejoice that The Hulk has finally come to big screen.

Portions of this article ran in *Cashiers du Cinemart* #13.

Impossibly Funky

THE *GREMLINS* THAT COULD HAVE BEEN

By Chris Cummins

Joe Dante's *Gremlins* is one of the most consistently entertaining films of the 1980s. It's a perfect blend of horror and comedy, with the added bonus of countless in-jokes for movie fans. However, what most people don't realize is that *Gremlins* was originally intended to be a straight-out horror film. *Gremlins'* screenwriter, Chris Columbus, was urged by Dante, along with executive producer Steven Spielberg, to eliminate some of the darker aspects of the film and punch up the too-subtle humor in early drafts of the script. It took Columbus *eight drafts* until he presented a script upon which all parties agreed. The result was the *Gremlins* that audiences are familiar with today.

Gizmo in *Gremlins*

But what of its precursors? There is a second draft of *Gremlins*, and it offers a view of a much different, and ultimately much less entertaining, film.

This screenplay opens with Rand Peltzer (here a businessman instead of the Ron Popeil, gone-wrong inventor from the finished film) looking for a gift for his son Billy. A wizened Asian shopkeeper sells him an intriguing pet called "mogwai." The man instructs Peltzer to be sure to keep the mogwai out of bright light, as it would kill the animal. On the return flight to his town of Kingston Falls, PA, Peltzer asks an Asian stewardess if she knows what "mogwai" means. She informs him that the word translates as "devil."

Roll credits.

Meet Billy Peltzer. In this early draft, Peltzer is the stereotypical geek, right down to the wire-framed glasses. Billy is an aspiring writer working a dead-end job at the local bank, who dreams of penning tales about King Arthur. Here Billy pines for his co-worker, Tracy Allen (name changed to Kate Beringer in the completed film). Unfortunately, the security guard of the bank is Gary Lucia—Tracy's semi-boyfriend and all-around jackass.

Billy is pals with Pete Fountane, a local teen who shares many of the same interests. The two often visit with Dorry Dougal, a local antiques proprietor who has custommade a sword for Billy. Back at the Peltzer household, we discover that Billy's mom, Lynn, is the extremely nervous type who enjoys popping Valium every two minutes. With the characters set up and exposition out of the way, the story begins.

Rand returns from his trip and gives Billy the unusual gift of the mogwai (at no point in the film is it referred to by any other name). Billy instantly dislikes the cute creature, and he'd rather not be bothered with it. After the mogwai knocks over Billy's precious new sword and damages it, Billy is so

The *Gremlins* That Could Have Been

enraged that he actually considers killing the creature. Instead, he inexplicably becomes sympathetic to it.

Soon enough water is spilled on the mogwai and it spawns several more creatures. Pete expresses a great interest in adopting one of the new mogwai and Rand immediately sees them as a great money-making idea. There's only one problem: the mogwai hate to be separated.

Enter Roy Hanson—Billy's biology teacher—to examine the creatures. Hanson discovers that the creatures are drawn to water and if one is separated from the group, the others will follow. (Can you smell the foreshadowing?) Later that night, while the Peltzers sleep, the mogwai move downstairs and eat Billy's dog. Rand grabs all the mogwai and locks them in the sealed attic, planning to release them into the morning daylight to destroy them. When the Peltzers awaken, they discover that the mogwai have undergone a transformation and are in cocoons. Rand has to go away on a business trip, and the family unrealistically decides to wait until he returns to remove the cocoons from the house.

Stripe in *Gremlins*

As Billy heads for work, his mother stays at home preparing for Christmas. At the bank, Billy receives a panicked phone call from his mother. The cocoons have hatched! By the time Billy gets home, however, Lynn Peltzer has been fatally attacked by the mogwai, who have now transformed into the monstrous gremlins we all know and love. Billy grabs his sword and proceeds to behead, blend, and microwave the creatures. He is wounded in the attack and when he tries to call the sheriff, a gremlin pulls the phone wire from the wall. Billy pierces the creature's arm with his sword. When the gremlin escapes, Billy pursues.

Meanwhile, Billy's friend Pete is Christmas caroling with a group of teens. Pete stands at the back of the line of singers and is pulled away and killed by a gremlin—his cries aren't heard over the festive singing. A pissed-off Billy chases the gremlin into the local YMCA, where a battle ensues. During the scuffle, Billy and the creature stumble and fall into the pool. The water instantly causes the gremlin to multiply. Billy flees the scene and runs to the sheriff's office.

Billy tells his story to Sheriff Frank Lucia and Officer Brent. They don't believe a word of it, but eventually the sheriff relents. At the Y, Officer Brent leaves Billy handcuffed in the police cruiser before going in to investigate.

Officer Brent is soon overcome by gremlins. The creatures spy the cuffed Billy who, luckily, has his sword with him. He cuts himself free from his cuffs and rushes to Tracy's home, which is under siege by the murderous gremlins.

After they escape, they discover Gary Lucia in an overturned police car. Gary had gone with his dad, Sheriff Lucia, when Frank was attacked by a gremlin and lost control of the vehicle. Billy rescues Gary from the car, but it's too late for Frank. By now, the gremlins are taking over the town, eating everyone in sight. Tracy, Billy, and Gary drive to Dorry's antiques store on the outskirts of the town. Billy predicts that the creatures will head to the nearby water tower. "If they get to the water tower…they could spread all over the state… maybe the country. They're like inhuman divining rods," Billy surmises.

Gary irrationally blames Billy for the death of the entire town, and they fight until Tracy breaks it up. Billy, Tracy, Gary, and Dorry (sounds like a troupe of Mouseketeers) hide in Dorry's antiques shop, hatching an ill-conceived plan to call the authorities to stop the gremlins from reaching the water tower. As dawn approaches, the gremlins leave, fearing the impending sunlight.

Now daylight, the group heads outside in search of rations. In a ringing endorsement for McDonald's, the group discovers that all the customers at the popular fast food joint have been eaten, while the food remains untouched. This is perhaps the cleverest scene in this draft, and it would have been nice to see it in the completed film.

Tracy realizes the gremlins are hiding in the town's old movie theater. As in the completed film, the group tries to blow up the theater. Tracy turns on the projector, which shows *Snow White*, to distract the creatures. When the reel ends, the gremlins hear the four do-gooders and begin to chase after them. Gary panics and leaves the others behind. The rampaging gang of gremlins kills Dorry, but Billy and Tracy are able to get outside just before the building explodes. Unfortunately, the sprinkler system comes on soon afterwards.

Billy and Tracy find Gary, and Billy and Gary start fighting over Gary's cowardice. Gary goes nuts and grabs Billy's sword, but before he can impale the geeky protagonist, Gary is fortuitously attacked by gremlins. Billy and Tracy get into the police car and escape, only to discover a gremlin on the back seat. Driving away, the creature begins screeching due to separation anxiety. Low on fuel, Billy stops at a gas station, where the gremlin escapes. It climbs into the engine and renders the car useless. Tracy and Billy eventually find the pesky critter and lock him in a toolbox. As the pack of angry gremlins approaches, Billy and Tracy decide to hide in a nearby greenhouse.

Billy puts the imprisoned gremlin on a table and sees the group of monsters right outside. Billy and Tracy climb a high tree, where Billy fights the oncoming gremlins with his sword. The creatures surround the tree, eating away at the trunk until it's knocked to the ground. Billy and Tracy are nearly killed by the impending mass of former mogwai when the sun comes up and melts all the creatures into nothing. After Billy and Tracy make their way out of the greenhouse, "they look out over Kingston Falls. Now a ghost town."

The *Gremlins* That Could Have Been

Exhausted, Billy collapses and wakes up in the hospital. Rand Peltzer has returned from his business trip and sits at Billy's side. Tracy is in the hospital as well. They will both survive. Billy suddenly remembers about the gremlin locked in the toolbox at the greenhouse.

Cut to a worker cleaning up the sticky mess at the greenhouse. As he leaves, he picks up the toolbox and takes it in his truck. Driving away, the toolbox starts shaking, and noises come from within. The worker throws it out his window, and it lands in a lake. As it sinks to the bottom of the lake, the sound of giggling gremlin can be heard as the credits roll.

Had this earlier draft been made, it wouldn't have been much more than just another standard horror film. While reading this draft, I recalled all of the post-*Gremlins* knockoffs, such as *Ghoulies* and *Critters*. The script is rife with pat action scenes and characters lacking clear definition. Rand is simply after money, Lynn loves her Valium, Gary is an asshole, etc. Furthermore, Billy never comes off as a sympathetic character. One doesn't feel an attachment to anyone, and therefore it doesn't really mean anything when characters die. Furthermore, when Gary becomes murderous towards Billy, it seems especially forced and unnecessary. The script follows a simple formula of Billy repeatedly making narrow escapes from the gremlins. This was beginning to tire me upon reading the script, and I'm sure that if it were filmed it would have been the same way.

The most important aspect missing from the early draft is the offbeat humor that the completed film provides. For example, take the characters of Mr. and Mrs. Futterman, as portrayed by the incredible Dick Miller and Jackie Joseph (who first worked together on the original *Little Shop of Horrors*). The Futtermans are the perfect comic relief after the film's scenes of surprisingly intense violence. Also sadly missed are the great invention gags from the completed film. (I would love to own a Rand Peltzer Bathroom Buddy!)

Likewise, in the bar scene where Kate Beringer (Phoebe Cates) is forced to serve drinks for the gremlins, there was only a brief description of that scene in the finished script. During production, Joe Dante and his crew created a list of visual gags resulting in a barrage of strange and hysterical images—gremlins playing poker, a breakdancing gremlin, a mugger gremlin, a flasher gremlin, etc. It is a testament to the genius of Dante to take written lines and expand on them in such an interesting way for the screen.

One of the most interesting subtexts in *Gremlins* is how deceiving appearances can be. Gizmo is just about the most lovable creature ever conceived, but he is essentially responsible for the destruction of a town. He may look harmless, but the terror he can cause is unimaginable. I was always fascinated about how *Gremlins* was marketed towards kids. However, in an unexpected twist, it is an incredibly dark comic film. While it is always interesting to compare a rough draft to a completed film, in the case of *Gremlins*, the rewrites drastically aided in helping to strengthen it into a contemporary classic.

The original version of this article ran in *Cashiers du Cinemart* #11.

DIGGING UP THE BONES OF INDY JONES

By Mike White

"How much of human life is lost in waiting?" asks Professor Harold Oxley (John Hurt) in *Indiana Jones and the Kingdom of the Crystal Skull*. In the case of the fourth Indiana Jones installment, nearly 20 years were lost since the action hero graced the silver screen.

Indiana Jones has lived a peculiar life. The scholarly archeologist first appeared in 1981's *Raiders of the Lost Ark* (a title since appended with his name to better fit in with the Indy oeuvre), where he battled Nazis for possession of Biblical treasure.

The subsequent Indy film left much to be desired. Though marketed toward the adolescent crowd, *Indiana Jones and the Temple of Doom* (1984) was a gruesome Indian adventure rife with human sacrifices, racism, and cheap laughs. Decried by concerned parents, *Temple of Doom* paved the way for the MPAA's PG-13 rating.

Raiders of the Lost Ark

The most offensive feature of this Indy prequel was the addition of a screaming female companion, Willie (director Steven Spielberg's wife, Kate Capshaw), and cute kid sidekick Short Round (Jonathan Ke Quan). The addition of the cute kid usually signals any series jumping the shark. In India, sharks are in short supply but alligators are plentiful; they jumped those instead.

With no Short Round in sight, *Indiana Jones and the Last Crusade* (1989) was hailed as a triumph. In retrospect, the film is an uneven mess that only satisfies because the pendulum swung so far from the mistakes in *Temple of Doom*. Rather than the juvenile cavorting that Steven Spielberg brought to *Temple of Doom*, *The Last Crusade* feels like a dry run for the damage producer George Lucas would inflict upon the world with his *Star Wars* prequels.

The third film in the series, *The Last Crusade*, was reminiscent of the third entry (chronologically) in the *Star Wars* series. If the Death Star worked so well in the first movie, let's bring it back in the third. Likewise, the Nazis and Biblical treasures from *Raiders of the Lost Ark* were trotted back to *The Last Crusade*. They may not have been Ewoks around to defeat these dastardly villains, but Marcus Brody (Denholm Elliot) and Sallah (John Rhys-Davies) were given lobotomies and set upon the Nazis, bumbling their way to victory.

The Last Crusade starts promisingly enough, with River Phoenix capturing the mannerisms Harrison Ford had brought to his Indiana Jones role. This quickly degrades into a series of events that explains away the entire Indiana Jones mythos within a matter of minutes. The hat! The snakes! The whip! The scar! It's all there! Like over-explaining everything that went into making Anakin Skywalker become Darth Vadar, these events effectively rob Indiana Jones of his mystery. (It's reminiscent of Rankin & Bass's *Santa Claus Is Comin' to Town* the way the mythos gets reduced.)

After *The Last Crusade*, Indiana Jones didn't have much luck as a television character. He was transformed from swashbuckler to tutor, incredibly interacting with more historical figures than *Zelig*. Indiana Jones is only passing through history—he shouldn't be making history. Characters that appear at crucial turning points in history fit better in sci-fi television shows like *Voyagers!* or *Quantum Leap*.

At the 1994 Venice Film Festival, actor Harrison Ford professed that he would don Indiana Jones's fedora one more time if a compelling script was available.

Two viable scripts saw the light in 1995; *Indiana Jones 4* by Chris Columbus and *Indiana Jones and the Saucer Men from Mars* by Jeb Stuart. The scripts by Stuart and Columbus are dated ten days apart, supporting the idea that George Lucas commissioned several writers to work on scripts at the same time, with the idea to choose the best ideas later. Eight years later, Frank Darabont (*The Shawshank Redemption*) took the reigns (and dictation) for his screenplay, *Indiana Jones and the City of the Gods*.

Harrison Ford as the iconic Indiana Jones

George Lucas doesn't like to give up his ideas. Back in 1973 he wrote an outline for what would later become *Star Wars*. It was called "The Journal of the Whills," and was all about "Mace Windy." It took 26 years before Samuel L. Jackson would portray the similarly named Mace Windu in *The Phantom Menace*. Likewise, the seeds of *Kingdom of the Crystal Skull* were sown 14 years before they finally saw the light of day.

Indiana Jones and the Monkey King

Called *Indiana Jones 4*, Chris Columbus's script has since gotten two snappier titles: *Indiana Jones and the Monkey King* and *Indiana Jones and the Garden of Life*. Columbus's script exemplifies nearly everything wrong with the Indiana Jones series.

Similar to his father's quest for the Holy Grail, Indiana has long been searching for the remains of Sun Wu-Kung, the Stone Monkey God: the half-man/

half-monkey guardian of the Garden of Immortal Peaches. Eat a peach, live forever! Marcus Brody shows Indiana a film of anthropologist Clare Clarke and her latest discovery, Tyki, a 200-year-old pygmy with a peach-pit necklace.

Indiana wastes no time in heading to Africa, where he hooks up with Scraggy, an old friend who speaks in platitudes that he must have stolen from a bag of fortune cookies. Matters get complicated when Indiana learns he didn't travel alone. His teaching assistant—the love-struck, low-class Brooklyn babe Betsy—has stowed away, determined to win the love of her paternal professor. Betsy is a constant source of embarrassment to Indiana, and to herself. Her presence doesn't do anything to win Clare's admiration, nor does it do much for the story other than provide some cheap laughs.

Monkey King pits Indiana against Nazis one more time. They're furious about his theft of the Ark of the Covenant. After fits and starts, the narrative becomes a ho-hum chase through the jungle with our heroes on the run from a battalion of Nazis armed with a tricked-out supertank and teaming up with a group of bloodthirsty pirates. As if it couldn't get any worse, the trail to Tyki's home leads to the "Land of City in Clouds," guarded by hyper-intelligent killer apes. The story spirals further into the realms of the ridiculous when head Nazi, Gutterbuhg—sporting a machine gun arm—takes control of the city. Indy is briefly dead before Sun Wu-King resurrects our hero with a mystical Golden Hooped Rod.

Getting through *Monkey King* was a challenge. Not only was the story outlandish, but it was poorly written. Columbus's script was packed full of description that did nothing to either enrich the narrative or move it along. In order to denote that a scene was exciting, Columbus writes the cue, "SOUNDTRACK MUSIC SWELLS." The ongoing recurrence of this is tiring and often contradictory, as the story lacked any real thrills.

Indiana Jones and the Saucer Men from Mars

Set in 1949, Jeb Stuart's script shows Jones feeling the aches and pains of his rough and tumble life. Rather than Nazis, he employs Cold War paranoia, pitting Indiana Jones against the Soviet Union. Stuart does a fine job of keeping the story moving, while avoiding action scenes for the sake of action scenes.
The beginning of Stuart's *Saucer Men from Mars* is similar to *Temple of Doom* with its revelation of the film's love interest, Elaine McGregor. Armed with the fighting spirit of Marion Ravenwood (unlike girly-girl Willie), Elaine also bears the archeological expertise of Indiana Jones. By the end of the first act, she and Jones are about to make their way down the wedding aisle.

Poor Indiana is left waiting at the altar as his bride-to-be is driven away from the church just minutes before the ceremony. Is it cold feet, or did Indiana's whirlwind romance leave a few stones unturned about his betrothed's past?

Elaine's trail takes him to New Mexico, where he finds her working for the U.S. government, using her linguistic skills to translate a stone cylinder that's been found in the desert, clasped in the hand of a dead alien.

The cylinder is something of a Rosetta stone, marked with Egyptian, Mayan, Sanskrit and Chinese pictographs. It's also a limitless source of power that the U.S. government aims to harness. Indiana and Elaine work to translate the cylinder, but before they can finish, Russian spies maneuver to steal it. The rest of the film consists of Indiana and Elaine chasing after the dirty commies to recapture the cylinder and avert Armageddon.

Stuart keeps his villains adequately ominous and plentiful. Aliens, though well-intended, are singular of purpose to fulfill their cosmic obligation by retrieving their cylinder, regardless of who stands in their way. Meanwhile, neither the U.S. Army nor the Russians wish to give up a powerful item, despite the consequences.

Indiana Jones and the City of the Gods

The creation of *Raiders of the Lost Ark* is the stuff of legends. The story goes that George Lucas and Steven Spielberg sat down with screenwriter Lawrence Kasdan and started throwing out ideas of what they'd always wanted to do or see in a movie: "I want a guy running away from a huge boulder," "I want him jumping off a horse onto a moving truck," and so on. Regardless of this tale's veracity, George Lucas apparently had a short list for what he required in the fourth Indiana Jones film.

"It's not the mileage, it's the years."

The plot follows a roadmap from Roswell, NM to Marshall University to Peru in pursuit of an alien artifact—a crystal skull. Bringing more light to the Lucas ingredient list, Frank Darabont's *Indiana Jones and the City of the Gods* bridges the gap between Jeb Stuart's script and David Koepp's *The Kingdom of the Crystal Skull*.

Both Stuart and Darabont include appearances of an "Atomic Café," the scene of Indy visiting a bombing test town, a rocket sled, waterfalls, giant ants, and other scenarios that came to life in the 2008 film. Though neither writer gets screen credit, the names of both screenplays do, when Indy scoffs about "Saucer men from Mars" and a "City of the Gods."

So much of Darabont's screenplay found life in *The Kingdom of the Crystal Skull* that it's easier to highlight the differences rather than the similarities between his work and the finished film. Most importantly, there is no Mutt Williams in *City of the Gods* (though there are vine ropes employed). Marion Ravenwood still makes an appearance, though here she's married to a duplicitous archeologist, Baron Peter Belasko. It's no surprise when he's revealed to be in league with Russian forces who strive to unleash untold power with the "skull of destiny."

Also added to the mix is Peruvian dictator Escalante who finds great pleasure in killing communists to keep his powerbase secure. There's also turncoat Von Grauen and his band of Hovitos. All of these folks provide fodder for the oversized creatures that populate the "lost world" surrounding the City of the Gods. These are the re-envisioning of the incongruous pirates from Chris Columbus's script.

While Darabont revisits some of the dialogue from *Raiders of the Lost Ark* (changing the "it's not the years, it's the mileage" line to "it's not the mileage, it's the years"), he also seems captivated by the advertising campaign for *Temple of Doom*, twice referencing the "if adventure has a name, it must be Indiana Jones" slogan. Apart from that, Darabont doesn't seem to realize that he's writing dialogue for Indiana Jones rather than Han Solo. Playing off of Marion's new status as a Baroness, Jones refers to her as "your worshipfulness," one page after saying the standard *Star Wars* line, "I have a bad feeling about this."

The Man in the Hat Is Back

With expectations leveled by these screenplays and audiences still raw from being ass-fucked by the *Star Wars* prequels, *The Kingdom of the Crystal Skull* initially appears to avoid the pitfalls and tiger traps of previous post-Raiders Jones adventures. George Lucas hasn't necessarily pissed all over another cherished series. Shia LaBeouf's Mutt Williams may not be the second coming of Short Round or Jar Jar Binks, but the film is still not free of comic relief (prairie dogs), extraneous characters (Mac), hollow promises (psychic abilities), and cutesy references that stop the story in its tracks ("Oh, look, the Ark of the Covenant!")

Some things that work in *The Kingdom of the Crystal Skull* include the fistfights, high adventure, and scenes of Indiana Jones exploring ancient ruins. If *Temple of Doom* and *The Last Crusade* were lacking any one thing, it was Jones doing what he did best: fighting through layers of cobwebs in search of items lost to antiquity.

Time hasn't been kind to Indiana Jones—and I'm not referring to his age. In the nearly two decades since Indiana Jones rode off into the sunset in *The Last Crusade*, several imitators to the throne have managed to usurp the whip-wielding archeologist, from Lara Croft raiding tombs to Rick O'Connell fighting mummies. The finale of *The Kingdom of the Crystal Skull* may have been fresh had it come in 1995, but by 2008, it seems an imitation of *The Mummy Returns*.

The fourth Indy film has stewed for nearly twenty years. Not free from flaws, *City of the Gods* ultimately played more successfully than the final product. The five years since Frank Darabont penned his script resulted in the once cohesive thread fraying at the edges, unraveling completely in parts.

These were the roads not traveled. The potential sequels took the Indiana Jones legend along completely different paths—though with familiar scenery.

Portions of this article ran in *Cashiers du Cinemart* #9 and the *Metro Times*.

TRAVIS MCGEE AND THE LONELY SILVER SCREEN

By Mike White

Hollywood culture vultures hunt for accomplished works to pour into standard molds rather than create something from scratch. Apart from revamping popular television shows, the modus operandi of too many shortsighted visionaries is to capitalize on a popular novel: the characters are there, the audience built in, and there's even a plot to go with all of this! Who could ask for a tastier morsel?

Author John D. MacDonald presents a feast for the scavengers of stories. MacDonald's prolific pen produced hundreds of short stories and over sixty novels in his lifetime. Several of MacDonald's tales made their way to the screen—large and small. The best-known MacDonald adaptations remain the two *Cape Fear* films, based on *The Executioners*. J. Lee Thompson's *Cape Fear* left MacDonald unimpressed, referring to it as a "dreary moving, I mean *unmoving* picture."

Six years after *The Executioners*, MacDonald introduced the character for which he would become best know, Travis McGee. Over two decades, MacDonald's character starred in twenty-one novels. Here, even more than a good bit of fiction to plunder, was the Hollywood dream: a franchise. McGee's adventures could last for decades on screen.

Author John D. MacDonald

Who Is Travis McGee?

Taking his retirement in chunks from monies earned doing "salvage consultation," Travis McGee is the Robin Hood of the Florida peninsula. Tanned, toned, and virile, McGee makes his living by retrieving ill-gotten gains and splitting them with the rightful owners when going through legal channels isn't an option. McGee's credo for his work: "half is better than none."

These daring quests provide the plotlines for the McGee books. However, the real pleasure of McGee's colorful world comes from his inner monologue. Over the span of his adventures, McGee observes and comments on nearly every aspect of an ever-changing America. He also provides insight on the wonderfully fleshed-out characters he meets. More than simply finding the key to a mystery, McGee takes readers on a journey of human emotion and interaction. And, more than his ability to bed down women or beat down foes, the pleasure in reading a McGee tale stems from his pilgrimage of self-awareness.

McGee's faithful companion on this sojourn is his neighbor at the Bahia Mar, Meyer. A swarthy, larger-than-life economist, Meyer acts as McGee's counsel, sounding board, confidant, and dearest friend. Most often, the appearance of Meyer framed McGee's crusades, though several times Meyer accompanied McGee and would put himself in harm's way.

As with all long-running characters, McGee comes with an assortment of accoutrements. Like better recurring characters, McGee amounts to more than his trappings. As it takes more than a cigar, raincoat, bloodhound, and Peugeot to be Columbo, it takes more than a houseboat (*The Busted Flush*), a converted Rolls Royce (*Miss Agnes*), and a glass of Plymouth gin over ice to be McGee. When trying to bring McGee to Hollywood, screenwriters have yet to capture, or notice, the complexity of McGee as the modern-day white knight.

One Percent

It took three rewrites of *The Deep Blue Good-by* for MacDonald to accept Travis McGee. To be sure that this character had what it took to stick around; the author had his publisher hold off on releasing the first McGee book until he penned two more. Confident that he and McGee would get along, MacDonald gave the go-ahead for the three novels to be released in a six-month span.

The disparity between the "novel McGee" and "screen McGee" wasn't for lack of trying. Almost immediately after the series began, the scribe started receiving offers to transport the character from books to television. In 1965, MacDonald had his first meeting with a quartet of Hollywood types who wanted to buy the television rights. They were so confident about the match between McGee and TV that they had began scripting episodes, signing contracts with sponsors, and casting Chuck Connors in the lead role. The chaps found that "it was extraordinarily difficult to find the right approach to a writer who doesn't believe in television," MacDonald wrote to friend Dan Rowan. "[They were] wrong. I believe in it. One percent of it is very very good… and 99 percent of everything is and always has been schlock. I don't want Trav to [be simplified as] the series tube requires, nor do I want the angle of approach wrenched this way and that when the ratings don't move and everybody…starts trying this and trying that."

Eventually, MacDonald signed with Jack Reeves and Walter Seltzer of independent production company Major Pictures. They intended to have McGee appear in a new motion picture every eighteen months, à la James Bond. Naturally, *The Deep Blue Good-by* would be a good place to start a McGee movie series, yet the first film slated for the screen was the seventh McGee book, *Darker than Amber*. MacDonald received the script on June 14, 1968, and was unimpressed to say the least. In a letter to Jack Reeves, MacDonald prophetically stated, "I am as sure of the sun rising tomorrow that you will make just one McGee movie… Aside from basic structure and some good visuals, you have a dog. It has a coarse and amateurish stamp, with less class and taste and insight than many a good television script… You have got something for the third feature at Kentucky drive-ins during the mating season… If you bomb with this, you are going to put me out of business insofar as the cinematic McGee is concerned. If you go with what you sent me, you bomb. It is that easy. I did not think that you would manage to lose McGee in the very first script, and turn him into some kind of hunk of dull, swinging, ass-chasing brutality, with no humor, no lift, and no awareness."

Reeves took MacDonald's comments and rewrites of the first 40 pages of the script in stride. He responded to the exasperated author, writing, "My enthusiasm, based on the script we have, still runs high and my judgment was reassured by the professionals who have read—some of whom run the studio and are committing the company's money into the making of the film. The consensus is we have an outstanding script which will transform into a hell of a good, commercially successful picture."

It took a few weeks for MacDonald to cool down. When he wrote back to Reeves, he expressed concern about the effort in remaining true to his work. "I recommend that the script be scrapped, and that a new script be prepared which would use many of the action ingredients, but would provide more room for meaningful character development and adult entertainment." MacDonald also provided a six-page outline of an alternate take on *Darker than Amber*.

In the weeks after that, MacDonald's letters became less frequent and less pressing, as if he knew that his battle had been lost. He managed to throw a good "I told you so" barb at Reeves with a letter dated September 5, 1968, in which he gloats about Reeves losing Robert Culp for the lead due to the incompetence of screenwriter Ed Waters.

In retrospect, Reeves should have taken MacDonald's advice. The 1970 release of Robert Clouse's *Darker than Amber* did nothing to kick off a McGee film series. Rather, it sounded the death knell of a film franchise.

"Travis McGee Is Rod Taylor"

As unfathomable as it may sound, the final version of *Darker than Amber* that hit theaters was even more dismal than Ed Waters's justly derided screenplay. If Waters had taken the flesh from McGee, the miscast Rod Taylor and unskilled Robert Clouse succeeded in sucking the marrow out of his bones.

One of the bleaker McGee tales, the opening of *Darker than Amber* undoubtedly captured the imagination of the Hollywood honchos involved. The pitch probably went something like this: "We open on a bridge. It's night and two fishermen are under the bridge—McGee (Rod Taylor) and Meyer (Theodore Bikel). Suddenly, a body falls into the water right by their skiff. It's a girl! She's been thrown over by two former associates who are ending their partnership. Of course, McGee jumps in and saves her from drowning, as she's been weighed down and has sunk like a stone—a very attractive stone."

"The girl is Vangie (Suzy Kendall); a con artist call girl who captures McGee's heart. She's been mixed up in some bad business involving bilking rich men out of their life savings and throwing them overboard on luxury cruises. After Vangie is killed (again), McGee makes it his business to avenge her death and bring down the ring of killer cons. Now, get this, McGee does that in part via the work of an actress, Merrimay (Suzy Kendall again), who dresses up just like Vangie to throw off the bad guys. She, McGee, and Meyer go aboard the ship where tough guy Terry (a blonde William Smith) and deadly dame Del (Ahna Capri) are putting their hooks into their next victim. When Terry sees Vangie/Merrimay, all hell breaks loose!"

Of course, the characters have been re-sculpted to a much more morally polar mold. Vangie's only been party to one murder (rather than over a dozen) before she's killed, and her partner in crime is so mean that he kicks a dog. There's little grey area in these characters—just black or white. The fallen woman's punishment could even be considered deserved in this clean-cut world where McGee appears to be the lone source of justice.

Darker than Amber suffers from a horrible score by John Parker, overacting by Taylor, and cornball dialogue that leaves viewers dumbfounded. The film showcases McGee as a swaggering lothario (with a wee bit of Irish brogue) who's only a hair smarter than his muscle-bound antagonist, Ans Terry (here named Terry Bartell).

Nearly all of the promotional material for *Amber* features images of McGee's knockdown dragout fight with Terry, properly reducing the film to its most base element of brutality. McGee may know how to throw a punch, but more often, he relies on his wits. An expert in chicanery, there are few situations that McGee can't talk himself into or out of. By contrast, Taylor's McGee appears to think only with his fists. While MacDonald's *Darker than Amber* may have been the dreariest McGee tale (at the time), the film adaptation boils away any of the adventure, leaving only a grisly murder mystery punctuated with fisticuffs and looking like a rejected pilot for a TV detective show.

The Deep Blue Good-By

Undeterred by MacDonald's augury, Seltzer and Reeves commissioned another adaptation of McGee's adventures. Ed Waters would go on to bigger and better things, like penning a few *Jake and The Fat Man* episodes. For this second attempt, Seltzer and Reeves tapped *Wojeck* writer Sandy Stern for the job.

Stern's adaptation of *The Deep Blue Good-by* proved to be both engrossing and faithful. Following the more tested and true McGee formula, *Blue* pits McGee against the dangerous, animalistic Junior Allen. Along the way, McGee nurses a damaged woman, Lois Atkinson, back to health while aiding and saving two other women of different stripes.

It wasn't until the later McGee adventures and on rare occasions (such as *Darker than Amber*) that Meyer would play an integral part of the story. Meyer doesn't even make an appearance in *Blue*, and Stern does well to not force him into the narrative. McGee acts as his own counsel, aided by his long-time female friend Chookie McCall.

With proper casting and direction, this could have been the movie that put McGee on the map. It would be another thirteen years until Travis McGee tried to come ashore again, and once again, he would founder.

The Bloodshot Rainbow

Rather than being the new James Bond, McGee would have been lucky to be the new Banacek. Transplanted to California and robbed of his houseboat ("The Busted Flush" here is a sailboat), McGee was downsized for the ABC TV movie of the week on May 18, 1983.

Directed by Andrew V. McLaglen, two writers took a crack at adapting *The Empty Copper Sea* with Sterling Silliphant's version winning out. Alan Sharp also penned a version which he titled *The Bloodshot Rainbow*—"A Travis McGee Adventure starring Sam Elliott." It's dated November 10, 1981 while Silliphant's initial draft—"a pilot script for Travis McGee"—bears the date April 9, 1981.

Published in 1978, *The Empty Copper Sea*—the seventeenth McGee tale—signaled a shift in the McGee series in that each book from then on depended heavily on the one before (where previous novels could be read out of order). The choice of utilizing this book would help bring an air of continuity to the storyline that random McGee adaptations may have lacked.

Sam Elliott as Travis McGee

Without the mustache (and southern accent), Sam Elliot would have made a great Travis McGee—almost a dead ringer for the sketch of the character that adorned the early Gold Medal-published paperbacks. Elliot was well cast in *Travis McGee*. Unfortunately, the same cannot be said for Meyer. Looking old enough to be Elliot's grandfather, Gene Evans does his best Lionel Stander impersonation as the intrepid economist. Luckily, the rest of the star-studded cast was a better fit.

Sticking well to MacDonald's story, *Travis McGee* stands out as one of the better TV mysteries. Surprisingly, it didn't spawn a follow-up, though that doesn't mean that such a plan wasn't in the works.

Back to *Amber*

A second Warner Brothers Television script by Kenneth Johnson had its first draft completed on January 5, 1982. Despite the conjecture of any second TV movie/series jumping off from *The Empty Copper Sea* and diving into *The Green Ripper*, Johnson's work was yet another adaptation of *Darker than Amber*. Sadly, Johnson's script never made it to production, as this version of the same material Waters covered was far superior to the 1970 film.

Also named *Travis McGee*, Johnson's script appears to be something of a sequel to Silliphant's script, except that Travis's love interest, Gretel, has been renamed Shannon. Keeping a woman in the picture at all is a break from *Darker than Amber* and more of a nod to *The Green Ripper*, especially when Shannon's demise on page 46 gives Travis a "now it's personal" gravitas that was missing from *Darker than Amber*, but was such a strong motivator in *The Green Ripper*.

The McGee in Johnson's script should be considered diametrically opposed to Waters's. This isn't a swaggering mass packing a pistol and looking for a fight. Johnson allows McGee to keep his wit during his repartee with Meyer, and even has him confess his distaste for firearms. Meanwhile, Johnson explores McGee's independent streak via his identification with the gulls of his (California) marina. Though there is an embarrassing bit of sappiness in the "mental songs" being sung by Travis and Shannon as they frolic together—"She's like breathing mountain air, so clean and fresh and rarified"—one would hope that these cloying bits would be eliminated in subsequent drafts.

Like Stern's earlier take on *The Deep Blue Good-by*, Johnson's work was doomed to obscurity, most likely due to the perceived lack of success of their predecessors.

A Letter Etched in Black

Along the path from MacDonald's colorful collection of McGee tales were strewn several unspectacular screenplays for other proposed McGee adaptations. None of these hit the mark, with the exception of the elusive *Bright Orange for the Shroud* by Terry Rossio and Ted Elliot.

Based on the sixth book of the McGee series, the script is dated March 10, 1989—a few short months before Rossio and Elliot found their earlier work, *Little Monsters*, on the big screen. When considering the string of kids' movies that the writing team has had a hand in—from *Aladdin* to *Treasure Planet*—the maturity of *Bright Orange for the Shroud* comes as a pleasant surprise. Based on one of the core McGee tales, the screenplay follows the knight errant and his trusted friend on one of their quests to right the wrongs done to good-hearted people by sinister forces. Not only does McGee vex two businessmen who sought to swindle one of his oldest friends out of his land, but he also squares off against the prototypical MacDonald foe, Boone Waxwell. Like Max Cady from *The Executioners* and Junior Allen from *The Deep Blue Good-by*, Waxwell acts like a backwards, backwoods buffoon to cover for his keen, albeit malevolent, intellect and unrepentant brutality.

Along the way, Travis helps out a pair of damaged women—one a recent widow and the other with a terminal illness. McGee's brand of common sense and emotional respect gives him the additional chivalrous quality that makes him an endearing and enduring character. The judicious use of occasional voiceover narration from McGee also increases our identification with his complex character.

With proper casting and direction, *Bright Orange for the Shroud* could have been the proper introduction to the silver screen for Travis McGee. However, this version foundered. On his website (wordplayer.com), Rossio wrote, "Our script hit all the key elements of the series-and when we turned it in, it was received with a gut-wrenching thud… We probably tried to do too much. Given that we were working from an entire series of novels, we weren't willing enough to pare it all back, and lose some key elements. With too many elements, we failed in fashioning them into a proper movie experience. Maybe, given time, those elements we chose could have been re-worked into something quite effective, but Amblin wasn't willing to wait. Key elements must be refined into film language in order to be effective."

In 2005, rumors surfaced of yet another attempt at a McGee screenplay. Dated May 13, 2005, Dana Stevens's *The Deep Blue Good-bye* (sic) portrays updates MacDonald's story to the twenty-first century. She toughens the rough and tumble "salvage consultant," taking away his qualms about firearms and giving him a snappy repartee. Stevens keeps McGee at arm's length by removing his inner monologue and sounding board. True to MacDonald's original book, there's no Meyer in *The Deep Blue Good-bye*. Travis shares a few scenes with his neighbor at the Bahia Mar, the Alabama Tiger, but theirs is a friendship more of convenience (Travis needs his speed boat).

Stevens remains fairly faithful to MacDonald's work though without McGee's narration and observations she's robbed him of charm. By giving Junior Allen a few pithy pop culture lines ("One of you bitches is getting voted off the island…") Stevens runs the risk of making the villain more interesting to viewers. The screenplay opens with a clever inversion of expectations. Stevens introduces two men; a clean cut observer and rough-hewn surfer. The latter man becomes our unlikely protagonist, Travis McGee, while the former, Barclay, puts McGee on the case. Tellingly, we first see McGee stopping traffic to help a hapless turtle cross a Fort Lauderdale highway, foreshadowing the man's habit of aiding those in need.

After the success of *Iron Man*, actor Robert Downey Jr. expressed interest in slipping into McGee's docksiders. He opted instead to play another detective, some schlub named Sherlock Holmes. By the end of 2008, Leonardo DiCaprio said he'd try his luck on a boat again.

McGee's relationship with Hollywood has been more of a one-night stand than a long marriage. Afterwards, both parties came to their senses and went their separate ways, appropriately ashamed of themselves and each other for such behavior. McGee may have seemed a natural match for Tinsel Town, but his real home was 2,700 miles away, safely nestled in Slip 18 of the Bahia Mar marina in Fort Lauderdale, Florida.

For every known adaptation of MacDonald's McGee books, there are doubtless countless others moldering somewhere in Hollywood. Having had two disappointing adaptations already, there's hope that these mistakes can provide guidance for future attempts at bringing McGee to the lonely silver screen. Only time will tell if McGee will ever successfully sail into theaters this century.

Portions of this article originally ran in *Cashiers du Cinemart* #14 & #15.

THE METAMORPHOSES OF *ALIEN III*

By Mike White

No one expected *Aliens*. Released in 1986, seven years after Ridley Scott's original *Alien*, the sequel took audiences by surprise—not merely in its timing but, moreover, in its story. To where could the tense amalgam of horror and sci-fi of *Alien* go? Would the sequel follow the pattern of earthbound slasher films and simply transplant a new batch of victims to within claw's reach of the terrifying Alien villain?

No. Instead of creeping along dimly lit corridors with a pathetic lack of weaponry, *Aliens* raised the stakes. Director James Cameron added generic aspects of the war film to the mix, played things smart by allowing *Aliens* to simmer for a while before bringing the action to a boil—all the while building tension and character.

The protagonists of *Aliens* may have been heavily armed, but there wasn't just one creature to deal with—there were *hundreds*, if not *thousands* of them. In addition, taking a cue from the insectival appearance of the H.R. Giger-designed Alien, Cameron imposed onto the Aliens a social order and breeding pattern based on colonial insects (like bees or ants). A new type of creature entered the fray: the Queen Alien.

It didn't take long before boffo box office returns made honchos at 20th Century Fox sit up and take notice. One word loomed large in the moneymen's heads: Franchise. Before they could hungrily tally the box office take, an edict came from the top. We need another *Alien* movie! This demand didn't fall on deaf ears. Rather, it landed squarely on the shoulders of the fellows who oversaw the first two *Alien* movies: producers Walter Hill and David Giler.

Hoping to push the creative boundaries of the *Alien* series even further, Hill & Giler sought the talent of cyberpunk author William Gibson for *Alien III*. The two saddled Gibson with a fifteen-page treatment from which the author felt he shouldn't stray. From there, Hill & Giler turned to the scribe who blessed audiences with scripts for *Blue Steel* and *Bad Moon*, Eric Red. The script Red turned in was an abomination, and slated director Renny Harlin left the project in disgust. Afterwards, Hill & Giler got lucky with D.T. Twohy. While Twohy's script fell victim to a change in directors, it paved the way for *Alien: Resurrection*.

The tale of *Alien III* grew dark. Instead of a tense psychological thriller or whiz-bang shoot 'em up, *Alien III* mutated into a muddled medieval mess under the direction of Vincent Ward. Displeased with the path *Alien III* traveled, producers Hill & Giler banged out a few drafts that borrowed liberally from the earlier scripts. Unfortunately, they didn't have much to work with, or didn't know what to do with what they had.

The Metamorphoses of *Alien III*

The story of *Alien III* doesn't end with Hill & Giler. When the project's third director, David Fincher, completed shooting, studio brass at Twentieth Century Fox gutted the film, leaving it a pale version of its former self.

Far from the shadow of Hollywood, Dark Horse Comics produced a long-running series of comic books that continued the story of *Aliens*, taking the tale worlds away from the troubled film project. Yet in order to maintain consistency, these books were subjected to a rewrite after the release of *Alien³*. The original books, along with the available early drafts and workprint of *Alien³*, provide us with an insight to the darkest spot in the *Alien* franchise.

The Last Visage of the Cold War
William Gibson (No Date)

Cold War politics permeate William Gibson's draft of *Alien III*. Gibson's screenplay pits humans against Aliens, and "The Company" against The Union of Progressive Peoples. The members of the UPP that readers encounter sport Russian monikers and/or Asian features. At the heart of the screenplay is political pussyfooting involving an "international incident" in which the Sulaco (the vessel from *Aliens*) passes through UPP space.

> To put it in diplomatic terms, they've got our ass in a sling. If they want to regard the Sulaco incident as a hostile act -- and let me assure you that they will, eventually -- they can compromise our position in the current round of arms reduction talks. We're talking serious ramifications here.

During this border indiscretion, UPP agents board the Sulaco and abduct the android Bishop. Details and reasons are left sketchy, as if Gibson is attempting to build suspense, but a good deal of the logic behind the actions in his screenplay is either left up to the audience to infer, or is missing altogether. Apparently, the UPP are interested in Bishop due to an Alien egg found in his cryochamber. Why they let the craft and rest of the crew float away into Company space is unknown.

When the Sulaco is intercepted a short time later by Company forces, a pair of Aliens on the ship (who apparently didn't bother with the UPP folks) takes out a few residents of the Anchorpoint space station. During the skirmish, an overzealous marine roasts Ripley's cryochamber. For the rest of the screenplay, Ripley remains in a coma—evidence of the doubt over Sigourney Weaver's return to the franchise.

As opposed to the final version of *Alien III*, Hicks and Newt remain unharmed. By page 17, Newt is off to her grandparents' place in Oregon, leaving Hicks to carry the picture. This would have been a terrific opportunity for

Impossibly Funky

actor Michael Beihn to take the reins in an action film that may have really put him on the map.

The UPP and The Company race for mastery of the Alien for bioweaponry, despite possible violations of treaty. Extensive DNA tampering results in two separate strains of Alien. Derived from Bishop, the UPP's Alien is hinted at being more biomechanical. However, the creature never makes an appearance! Meanwhile, The Company's Alien appears to be fungal, reproducing and infecting via airborne spores. This inexplicable method of inception results in people (and other organisms) suddenly "shedding" their skins and emerging as Aliens.

Illustration by Dean Stahl

The reasoning behind the ease of creating these different strains of Alien is apparently inherent to their origins. A Company scientist conjectures that "the readiness with which [Alien DNA] lends itself to genetic manipulation...the speed with which its cells multiply as though the gene structure has been designed for ease of manipulation. And this apparently universal compatibility with other plasms [is] perhaps the fruit of some ancient experiment... A living artifact, the product of genetic engineering A weapon. Perhaps we are looking at the end result of yet another arms race..."

Eventually, Bishop (repaired from his *Aliens* injuries) reunites with Hicks at Anchorpoint—a "gift" from the UPP and a diplomatic move to ease political tension. The return of Bishop also provides the reader with another familiar character, which is fortunate as all of the other characters—whether they be members of The Company or the UPP—are utterly interchangeable.

Another flaw is Gibson's attempts to make the struggle between the ultracapitalist Company and the socialist UPP a metaphor for the free-willed humans versus the Alien drones. The Company and the UPP are too similar in their impersonal corporate attitudes. Gibson should have pitched a rewrite of this draft to the producers of *Star Trek: The Next Generation*, with the free-willed crew of the Enterprise fighting Borg drones. Bishop's role as possible pre-programmed saboteur would have been ideal for Data (one scene with Bishop in Gibson's screenplay is similar to Data's takeover of the Enterprise in the episode "Brothers").

Once the elements are in place, Gibson's screenplay runs its course as expected. Members of the Anchorpoint crew transform into Aliens at inopportune moments, while survivors fight or run around willy-nilly. Someone gets the bright idea to set the station to self-destruct; the expected "race against time" ensues. The uninspired action doesn't pause for long. When Gibson isn't mining *Aliens* for material, he's aping other "creatures on the loose" films, such as George Romero's *Dawn of the Dead* (major portions of the screenplay take place in the Anchorpoint shopping mall).

Feeling like an afterthought, Hicks jettisons Ripley's comatose body into space. It's unclear whether this act is an attempt at euthanasia—death in cold space instead of being consumed by the Alien DNA—or if Hicks perhaps hopes she'll be rescued. Regardless, Gibson keeps the possibility of a sequel more than alive—not only does he end the script with Alien DNA being transported towards the space station just outside of Earth's orbit, but Bishop issues a mandate for a future Alien encounter.

> The source, Hicks. You'll have to trace them back, find the point of origin. The first source. And destroy it. This goes far beyond mere interspecies competition. These creatures are to biological life what antimatter is to matter. There isn't room for the both of you, Hicks, not in this universe. [...] This is a Darwinian universe, Hicks. Will the Alien be the ultimate survivor?

Gibson's draft was doomed to failure. Treading little new ground, the only fresh (albeit ridiculous) idea is that the Alien DNA is as much of a threat as the fully grown creature. Gibson's contributions to the final version of *Alien III* are negligible, save for the barcode tattooed on a UPP commando's arm that would find its way onto the prisoners of D.T. Twohy's Moloch Island and Hill & Giler's Fury 161.

Sam Smith Returns to Smallville
Eric Red (2/7/89)

Reading Red's screenplay, one gets the impression that he wasn't entirely confident in his abilities. Or, rather, that he had the sneaking suspicion that his work would undergo such serious reworking that he needn't put his all into his version of *Alien III*. Red's script is sloppy, silly, and forgettable.

Our hero, Sam Smith, is a military brat born and raised on North Star—a space station that resembles Midwestern farmland on its surface and the Death Star at its core. Sam is one of the unfortunate members of a rescue party sent to reclaim the survivors of the Sulaco.

When Sam and his crew arrive, they're met with:

> Alien eggs, three feet high and slimy with muck, resting in the chambers where the bodies of people were. Cocoon substance, like iron cobweb strings from floor to ceiling.

> Bones and shreds of uniforms are quickly glimpsed on the floor in the flashlight beams. Sam picks up a shorn off nametag with the word 'Ripley' on it.

A fully grown Alien attacks Sam and his compatriots. "Smash cut to: Sam Smith awakens in his parents' farmhouse on North Star. But, wait…something's not right here. Sam has a new bionic arm (which never comes into play again) and all of his former crewmates' families have packed up and moved away."

Sam has no memory of the attack, and his parents, John and Mary (very creative names) avoid speaking about his last mission. This version of *Alien III* might initially appear as a nod to *Invasion of the Body Snatchers*, with a thin façade of normalcy covering the dread within. However, that would be giving Red too much credit. Rather, this is the writer's foil to lull the audience into a false sense of complacency, then shock them with the page 28 revelation of Sam's attack caught on holographic video. Red doesn't appear to realize that this tape isn't much of a surprise to anyone but Sam, as the audience has already been made privy to his attack on page 4. Moreover, the reader *still* doesn't know—nor will they ever find out—how Sam survived the attack.

The choice of Sam Smith as a protagonist is a faulty one. Sure, he may have access to the underground military base, but he still has to sneak around in order to discover the experiments being conducted (yup, the military's trying to breed and control the Aliens!). And, though Sam's father is a General, his old man is a tight-lipped bastard. A better choice for a hero would be one of the hapless Terra Farmers of the surface of North Star. This disgruntled group has been kept in the dark as much as Sam. Additionally, the military constantly confiscates their livestock.

The full extent of the military's experiments become known to Sam as he stows away on a truck full of pigs and finds himself dumped into a breeding room.

> The air is ripped with the horrifying din of hundreds of shrieking animals. And the sounds of ripping flesh. Sam reaches into his pocket and brings out his lighter. He flicks a flame. In the light of the flame, a foot around him, a pig with a Face Hugger on it, its hooves shaking spasmodically on the ground… There are animals in cages everywhere… The floor is covered with straw and guts. Near him, the belly of a pig ruptures and [a] Chest Burster smashes out in a sickening spray of intestines. The Pig Alien has the wide torso, tiny head, and little legs of a pig… A Pit Bull dog struggling on the ground as its ribs explode out its stomach and a Dog Alien tugs itself out… Within, the Dog Aliens, and Cat Aliens, and Chicken Aliens scramble about, hissing and biting in

fury. The pigs move about in a raw panic as Face Huggers leap out of dark corners...

It's a barnyard from hell.

The ability for Aliens to adapt to these non-human hosts is explained on page 34 by evil scientist lady Dr. (Ayn?) Rand:

> This organism, on a cellular, even molecular level, is purely and totally predatory. We have never encountered an organism that had its characteristics...or its potential. To survive, this cell attacks and assimilates the cells of whatever it encounters. In this manner, it takes on the form of what it kills. But this is most interesting... Gentlemen, I put to you that this organism, this cell, can assimilate not only with organic matter but inorganic matter... The DNA structure doesn't screw around. Gentlemen, do you realize what we have here? Do you realize the potential we can use it for? Imagine a living, organic jet fighter, or an Alien tank.

The potential is that more than the ever-present spores of Gibson's *Alien III*, now even inanimate objects can become Alien. Red crosses the line from the epidemic to the ridiculous.

Red hasn't the faintest idea about dramatic tension. On page 36, Sam infiltrates a military meeting wherein Dr. Rand demonstrates that she's tamed the Alien. In a scene reminiscent of the demonstration of ED-209 in *Robocop*, Red shows absolutely no skill in building suspense within the scene. The reader knows that an Alien can't be tamed and that Dr. Rand will meet with a gory fate. Yet before the reader can even take in a breath in anticipation of the carnage to come, Rand has been brained and the Alien has begun its rampage.

In addition to the nightmare world of Old MacDonald, there's another strain of Alien present with a markedly different lifecycle. After cocooning its mutilated victims, the Alien passes away. From the cocoons spring new life. "A six foot tall, humanoid Alien is tearing its way out of the cocoons. Its armored, slimy snout snaps at the air as it tries to extricate itself from the thick, tendril-y cocoon substance... More cocoons are opening and fully formed Aliens are struggling their way out." So much for eggs, Face Huggers, and Chest Bursters—until later in the script, when they begin appearing again.

It doesn't take much imagination to figure out the rest of the screenplay. Sam, John, and some nameless soldiers run around the military complex fighting the Aliens. The creatures eventually make it to the surface, treading upon

Impossibly Funky

the heartland of, as Red frequently writes, "Main Street U.S.A. in space." Soon Red's script plays like an irony-impaired version of *Gremlins*, with rednecks versus Aliens.

The screenplay progresses with the action proving more tiresome than exciting. For some sort of attempt at a "statement," Red seems to riff off *Aliens'* theme of maternity and leans on the distrust of patriarchy. Sam's father represents the military—the organization that brought the dangerous creature to the quiet corner of space where wheat fields blow in the breeze. The Alien threatens the sanctity of the American family, just as John Smith threatens his own family's safety.

As an attempt at a surprise twist, on page 82 John Smith admits that he's been injected with Alien DNA. Despite the speedy process with which the Alien DNA works earlier in the script, it's taken all of the screenplay's second act for anything to happen to him. Suddenly, "blood pours out of John's eyes. Under his skin, his bones are reshaping, his muscles straining, his skin becoming hard and slimy. John's head jerks back. His mouth cracks open and the jackhammer-fanged jaws punch out of his mouth, taking his real teeth with them in sprays of bloody gums as the Alien jaws snap an inch from Sam's fingers."

It's on this same page that Sam's sister, Karen, finds that the family cow, Bessie (even the cow's name is unoriginal), has been transformed into a Cow Alien (that "emits an Alien, insectile moo") thanks to a bite from a Mosquito Alien. Within pages, the Mosquito Alien has created a Rooster Alien that falls into the North Star reservoir, tainting the water supply. Just when it couldn't get any worse…

Mary, Sam, Karen, and little brother Mark (who frequently has his name changed to "John Junior," just as North Star becomes the "Sulaco Space Station") escape Alien John and their Cow Alien and head into town. There they find "Fifty humans…fused together into one…thing. It is a two-story, moving, murderous mass of armor and flesh, eyeballs, and tongues, screaming mouths and jackhammer jaws in a huge anamorphous blob of arms, legs, talons, hooks, snouts, and teeth." Within two pages, this "Alien Thing" begins to assimilate/infect the entire North Star complex. Metal beams and all morph into one gigantic Alien creature, visible from the window of the Smith family escape ship.

Illustration by Dean Stahl

Yadda yadda yadda, missles are fired and the big Alien Thing blows up.

Red's screenplay is one of the worst things ever written. Red is inept at pacing, plotting, and spelling (all quotes from his screenplay have been corrected for mistakes). He's unable to describe action concisely or vividly. He immoderately relies on onomatopoeic phrases in an attempt to describe actions: PAPAPAPAKAKAKAKAKAKAKAKAKA-PPPPPPPPPPPPPP-POW-WWWW!!!! and RRRRRRRRrrrrriiiiiIIIIIIIiiiiiPPPPpp are two of dozens of examples.

It's a cinch to see why Red's script landed on the scrap heap without a second thought. The script sent director Renny Harlen running to the safety and comfort of a good project, *The Adventures of Ford Fairlane*. *Alien III* foundered without a director. Sadly, within eight months a far superior script would come down the pike to a lukewarm reception.

An Adumbration of Resurrection
D.T. Twohy (October 1989)

With the memory of Eric Red's horrendous draft of *Alien III* fresh in mind, D.T. Twohy's screenplay was a welcomed change. Twohy's writing is fresh and his script's pacing is fast. He avoids the now-typical recovery of the Sulaco and, instead, begins with a mining ship discovering a Face Hugger preserved in amber (shades of *Jurassic Park*). From there, Twohy introduces the foundry/prison colony idea that would morph and resurface in the later versions of *Alien*[3].

Welcome to Moloch Island, orbiting Earth thousands of feet above the South China Sea. Within a few pages, we meet half a dozen prisoners who serve as the audience's counterparts while they learn the ropes of their new surroundings.

Twohy balances the weight of these criminals—giving the reader insight on their characters before finally settling on one as the main protagonist: Scott Taylor Styles, serving ten years for fraud with thirteen more added for his two escapes. "You know, son, I've just got the feeling you're gonna give us snags," says the Captain of the guards upon Styles's arrival.

"Oh, no sir. I've learned my lesson. Well, *lessons*," says Styles, with all the unflappability of Cool Hand Luke.

Apart from the Face Hugger of the opening scene, the hint of any Aliens isn't given until page 18, with some inexplicable scratching heard under the new prisoners' cells. It isn't until page 22 that the first Alien is even introduced. This occurs after a prisoner is "executed," only to awake later and find himself trapped in a room with an Alien. He has unknowingly volunteered in a military operation.

If this is beginning to sound somewhat familiar, that's probably because Twohy's script was the apparent basis for Joss Whedon's draft of *Alien: Resurrection*. The similarities don't stop at the mere chance of six seedy characters trapped on an installation where top secret military experiments are taking place. Several action scenes mirror events of Whedon's script, along with the idea of an Alien born out of a womb. There's even this scene with Packard—a female doctor:

> Packard forces calm on herself. Now she heads back for a closer look. The room is a gallery of Aliens. An army of Aliens. All behind glass. Dreading it, Packard activates more case lights. Each Alien is slightly different: One is silvery instead of black, a chameleon that blends with its background... Another is a Siamese fused to a partner... Another is a complete abomination, as if mutated with thalidomide. There are more. But Packard doesn't have more nerve.

Twohy's script was a good compromise between a Ripley-centered script and a Ripley-less one. It would have been easy to place Ripley as one of the prisoners on Moloch Island. She could easily be incarcerated for all the damage she's done to Company property (destroying the Nostromo and vaporizing the complex on LV426). Twohy sets his *Alien III* apart from the series, only giving mention of Ripley once on page 74, when Packard sees her picture in a classified bioweapons file.

The script handles the characters effectively. Just about the time that the reader realizes that Styles is the protagonist, he discovers inconsistencies in the story of an inmate's death. From there, Styles begins planning to lead his five fellow prisoners on a prison break. This keeps the action going, and provides a shocking end to Styles's compatriots when they discover they're not alone in the ducts under the cellblock. The rogue Alien that took out their fellow inmates does away with Styles's partners.

Ironically, a squad of prison guards saves Styles. Knowing too much to return to the general population, Styles is placed in solitary confinement where he meets the man responsible for the Alien experiments, Mr. Lone. He's described as "an Amerasian" with "bottomless black eyes." One begins to wonder if the apparent xenophobia of Gibson's script was the product of a Hill & Giler mandate. This anti-Asian sentiment would rear its ugly head again in the Hill & Giler script.

After Packard and Styles team up and try to escape Lone, guards attack them. During the firefight, an explosion breaches the hull of Moloch Island. Debris from the station strikes an approaching supply ship that careens out of control and crashes against the prison colony. "In a vast cosmic abortion, we see a thousand bodies hurtling past view and into space." Of course, this becomes the most opportune moment for the Newborn Alien to claw its way out of its womb.

If there is one flaw to Twohy's screenplay, it's his lack of description for the Newborn Alien. Perhaps he knew that it'd be something designed later (hopefully by H.R. Giger). Regardless, Twohy doesn't even *attempt* a description.

Luckily, his screenplay delivers so well in other areas that this complaint is negligible.

The Aliens are unseen for most of Twohy's screenplay. Instead of being open threats, they're more effectively used as a looming menace. It isn't until the breakneck third act of the script that Aliens become a visible presence.

On page 93, Twohy states:

> NOTE: This final act unfolds in real time. Every move, every word, every look is made as if it were someone's last --
> which it may well be. Emergency lights whirl like capering demons, and wind sings through corridors like a choir of maniacs. Staring now, we push hard and never let up.

Twohy holds true to this bold statement. Air escapes from the installation. The Newborn Alien stalks the halls. Styles plays on Lone's desire for this source of Alien DNA in order to do away with the corporate executive. Meanwhile, Packard and the only remaining guard, Daggs, are left in the lurch, wondering about Styles's loyalty. Of course, they're not disappointed. The three have to jettison themselves into space and hope to rendezvous with their escape ship.

The Newborn Alien is hot on their trail in the cold void of space. "Doesn't it breathe? For Chrissake, doesn't it need any fuckin' air?" exclaims Daggs before Styles turns the needle nose of the ship directly at the creature's heart, impacting, and splitting it into two halves that "tumble for different corners of the universe." A rescue ship soon intercepts the trio. Styles is identified as a med-tech, his freedom restored.

A minor but consistent theme becomes obvious when reading these early drafts of *Alien III*. In Hill & Giler's original outline for *Alien III*, there must have been a scene wherein the protagonists have to put on space suits and traverse the outside of whatever station they're on. This occurs in Gibson's, Red's, and Twohy's drafts. Only Twohy uses this device effectively, instead of making it feel like an obligation to the film's producers.

Return to Dark Ages
John Fasano (Story and Screenplay) & Vincent Ward (Story) (3/29/90)

In the later part of 1989 and early 1990, director Vincent Ward came aboard the *Alien III* project. Ward's previous film, *The Navigator*, begins in the plague-infested fourteenth century England before introducing the element of time travel to beget a convoluted "fish out of water" tale similar to the 1993 French farce *Les Visiteurs*. Ward foisted his odd predilection of the medieval onto Twohy's *Alien III* prison environment. With its interstellar monastery and bookish protagonist, Ward and Fasano appear to have been inspired more by Walter Miller's *A Canticle For Liebowitz* than the previous *Alien* films. Oddly enough, this draft had the greatest impact on the final version of *Alien III*—from Ripley's introduction, the climax of the film, the colony's glassworks, and even a character's myopia.

Though she's a major character, Ripley is not the true protagonist of this *Alien III*. Rather, the audience follows Brother John, a diffident medic among a multitude of monks on the orbiter Arceon (as opposed to "Archeron," another name for "Hell" that Cameron used in his script for *Aliens*). The writers describe the planetoid as "a shell of lightweight foamed steel, five miles in diameter, constructed by The Company with habitable levels within, finished in whatever material suites its end user. This orbiter, for reasons to be discovered later, has been sheathed in wood."

"The reasons to be discovered later" are rather silly, or at least highly contrived. Arceon is home to a cadre of political exiles:

> We were sentenced as political dissidents. This orbiter is our gulag... Ten thousand men... When we left planet Earth seventy years ago, it was on the brink of a New Dark Age. Technology was on the verge of destroying the planet's environment... [Now] it gets colder all the time here...[the] wood-burning fires throw soot into the atmosphere... The Greenhouse effect... This planet is the supreme triumph of planned obsolescence. A certain amount of primitive materials with an atmosphere processing system as fragile as a real environment but not replenishable... Poetic justice for the anti-technologists.
>
> A computer virus was threatening to wipe away all recorded knowledge... Like the Monks who guarded Monastery Libraries on remote islands off England during the First Plague... Some of these books survived the burning of the Libraries of Alexandria. They contain knowledge that exists in no other record. Their value is inestimable.

Poor Ripley lands smack dab in the middle of all the Luddite claptrap.

Streaking from the sky like an unholy omen, Ripley and Newt come in one of the Sulaco's escape pods. Upon her arrival, the reader learns that an overlooked Alien egg killed Hicks and Bishop. How one kills an android lacks explanation. Additional Alien life forms were present, evidenced by the breach in Newt's cryotube (her body never surfaces).

Discovering that Newt hasn't survived, Ripley tries to warn her companions of the evil they have inadvertently unleashed. "The Abbot looks at her the way you look at that guy on the corner of Santa Monica and 3rd who's babbling about Judgment Day. The guy with his pants down around his knees." Of course, Ripley had already had to fight this battle in *Aliens*, when members of The Company refused to believe her wild tales of the Alien. To play the part of Cassandra again is tiresome.

Within pages of her recovery by Brother John, one of the scripts many dream/hallucination sequences implies that Ripley is host to an Alien embryo. "Without a mother, one cannot love. Without a mother, one cannot die." This quote from Hesse opens the Ward/Fasano script and continues the study of maternity in the *Alien* films—an issue heightened by the monastic setting of the film. Among these men, Ripley is a double threat. She is a female, and she is the bearer of the plague. She is the heretical, hysterical woman.

However, there is suspiciously no sexual threat to Ripley from the scads of faceless men of Arceon. This makes Ripley's second Alien dream even more disturbing. "The Alien's tail is coming up between her legs. She turns. Right into its grasp... The Alien spins her—pushes her over the sleep tube—like it's taking her from behind! The Alien wraps his arms around Ripley. Thin lips pull back for a kiss." In other words, the Alien has raped Ripley to impregnate her.

Ripley is a woman literally possessed with evil. The Alien bides its time, waiting to burst out of her chest like some terrible phallus. Even the Alien's methods of attack carry a phallic overtone—spewing acid, impaling with its "stinger," or thrusting its second set of jaws into its victim. It's no coincidence that the men of the subsequent drafts of *Alien III* would bear two Y chromosomes—as if they're even more masculine.

While Ward/Fasano's *Alien III* may be long on explanations of greenhouse gases and technophobia, it's light on plot. No one believes Ripley until monks start buying it courtesy of an Alien that gestated in a local sheep. In the meantime, Ripley's locked up in the depths of Arceon next to Brother Anthony, an android who appears more human than human, with his empathy for Ripley and bizarre delusions of bird-headed demons.

Eventually, Brother John realizes that the Abbot may have been wrong to incarcerate Ripley. After freeing her and Brother Anthony, the trio begins the typical running around with some vague notion of rescue, defense, and/or escape in mind. It's only a matter of time before the Abbot joins their little group—following his dynamic character arc. Instead of the Abbot making the typical heroic last act to save his companions, however, he soon falls victim to a new type of Alien. In previous films there have been Chest Bursters; in this script, there are Head Bursters.

> A horrible Alien Head Burster...is all that sits atop the blood spurting neck of the Abbot. It keeps its hold on the Abbot's spinal cord...The Abbot's body continues to stagger around, arms jerking mechanically as lack of fresh nerve impulses from the brain work their way through the system.

Impossibly Funky

This description quickly brings to mind a scene from *Eraserhead*, wherein the main character's "baby" springs forth from his shoulders, displacing his head.

How this secondary Alien came to be without a Queen to lay eggs is unknown. But in this draft, characters occasionally have their heads split open like ripe melons. As mentioned earlier, the Alien that terrorizes the group (the Head Bursters seem inconsequential to the action after they pop) gestated in a sheep. Anthony and Ripley hypothesize about the Alien's recombinant DNA on page 46. "Maybe they are from some sort of aggressive soldier race-warring parties drop the eggs on opposing planets… And the Alien takes on the form of the creature that finds it, assuming that animal is the dominant life form on the planet. So when it gestates in a man…it's a biped. In a sheep or cow: a quadruped." In this manner Ward and Fasano echo Gibson, and seem to be providing an explanation for the derelict ship full of Alien eggs in Scott's *Alien*—that it was on a mission of war. Likewise, they're giving enough leeway to account for these strange new Alien breeds.

Illustration by Dean Stahl

Yet gestating in a sheep doesn't necessarily give merit to the Alien's ability to take on a wooden appearance, or shine golden like the field of wheat in which it hides. The Alien of Ward/Fasano's script shares the chameleonic traits of one mentioned briefly in Twohy's draft.

In *Aliens*, James Cameron explored the notion that, despite fantastic technology, sheer numbers and instinctive aggressiveness of the Aliens reigned supreme. Taking away the technology and pitting even one Alien against a league of unarmed men is a step or two backward. This mistake is apparent in the third chapter of another popular film series—*Return of the Jedi* and its pre-industrial Ewoks. Yet logs and rocks are outside the realm of the Arceon monks, who ineffectually battle with good intentions. It's only through dumb luck that the Alien happens to fall into the Arceon glass works, located directly underneath the all-important library (surely some kind of fire code violation). Ripley then dispatches the foul creature by dousing its febrile exoskeleton with a cooling blast of water.

With its dreary hallways and lone antagonist, the *Alien III* of Ward and Fasano was closer to a pale imitation of Ridley Scott's *Alien* than a sequel to James Cameron's *Aliens*. Ward and Fasano take cues from Scott's film, inferring that food helps trigger Alien nascence. When Kane (John Hurt) began to eat in *Alien*, he fell victim to the Chest Burster inside him. In the Ward/Fasano script, Ripley remains famished throughout her stay on Arceon. "It hasn't come out yet because I haven't eaten. It's still dormant. So either I eat and it kills me or I don't and I starve to death. Either way I die."

In the final act, she passes the gestating creature inside of her after Brother John administers an ipecac. When Ripley begins to choke on the creature, the monk performs CPR and allows the beast to swim down his gullet. This idea of the monk accepting the evil inside Ripley is more than slightly reminiscent of *The Exorcist*—especially when he sacrifices himself to save her.

Another subtle nod to Scott's *Alien* comes at the conclusion of the Ward/Fasano script, when the audience realizes that only other living survivor of the Alien attack is Mattias, Brother John's dog. As with Jones the cat, Ripley secures her canine companion in a cryotube before laying herself down to rest.

Knowing now that the Alien doesn't require a human host, the script shows its only moment of humor in an aside after cueing the end credits. "Teenager in the back of the movie theater shouts, 'It's in the dog!'" Little did the writers know how prophetic this line would become.

Flight of the Navigator

To say that 20th Century Fox and the other folks involved in the *Alien* franchise weren't pleased with Ward's Dark Ages vision of *Alien III* is something of an understatement.

There are conflicting reports about the chronology of the events occurred around the departure of Vincent Ward as director. Fasano jumped ship for a while. During Fasano's absence, Ward worked with screenwriter Greg Pruss. Eventually Ward received his walking papers, flush with a healthy payoff to fund *Map of the Human Heart*. Fasano returned to hash out another draft, without success.

With the signing of first-time film director David Fincher to direct, the writing chores fell on Larry Ferguson. Instead of starting fresh with a new director and writer, the two had to rely on the Ward/Fasano draft. It's unclear how much impact Ferguson had on the project; suffice to say that his name appeared in the screen credits for the final film.

Trying to Make Due
Walter Hill & David Giler (12/18/90)

It was a recipe for disaster. Keep the religious zealots of the Ward/Fasano script, but add in the hardened criminal aspects of Twohy's draft. Follow the same framework of Ripley's arrival to this prison colony (now dubbed Fury 161) and the quick dispatch of the remaining Sulaco survivors. Instead of a sheep, an ox falls victim to a stowaway Face Hugger. Also, Ripley will change tactics once she's revived: she'll keep the presence of an Alien secret for as long as it dramatically suits the film. This story shift occurs when Hill & Giler take *Alien III* from the odd Twohy/Ward/Fasano hybrid into familiar running around dank hallways territory.

As illogical as an interstellar monastery might be, Ward and Fasano felt that the audience knew all there is to know about Ellen Ripley. They knew that the *Alien* franchise needed to shift its attention to a different protagonist. Ripley was present to provide the audience with comfort and stability (though Twohy proved that she needn't be there) and ensure a bigger box office draw.

Brother John served as the true protagonist of the Ward/Fasano script. Hill & Giler kept Brother John, rechristening him Clemens. They provide Clemens a background that he reveals slowly (albeit only through dialogue). He bucks the system as much as he can (given his status as Chief Medical Officer), but he's not without past events that keep him firmly grounded on Fury 161. He's an outsider from the pair of bureaucrats that run the prison complex, as well as the two dozen religious inmates.

The Hill/Giler draft of *Alien III* begins in the Sulaco's cryochamber, where Newt is under attack by a Face Hugger while she sleeps. Cutting between the helpless Newt, the restless Ripley, and the void of Space, the credits roll. By page three, the distressed Emergency Exit Vehicle of the Sulaco is hurtling through space at the planet Fiorina. Upon its crash landing, an "infected" Newt drowns, a support beam impales Lieutenant Hicks, and the artificial person, Bishop is smashed beyond repair. Remarkably, Ripley survives intact, save some minor scrapes and bruises.

Clemens witnesses the crash and takes Ripley to safety. When she awakens, he serves as Ripley's protector and guide, dishing out exposition like it was going out of style.

> Originally the whole place was a mineral ore refinery -- fifty years ago it was recycled into a toxic dump. The prisoners make lead sheets to seal off any leakage in the shafts -- we don't really get many shipments -- Weyland-Yutani's got the facility on hold...This used to be a thousand man operation but we're down to just twenty-five -- The Company just keeps the operation on pilot light...[the prisoners] got religion, so to speak, about five years ago... some sort of millenarian apocalyptic Christian fundamentalist brew... When The Company wanted to close down the place...the zealots stayed as custodians with two minders and a medical officer.

Concerned over the possibility that Newt might have been carrying an Alien, Ripley convinces Clemens to autopsy the little girl and, later, to cremate the bodies of Newt and Hicks. At a service held for Ripley's fallen companions, prisoner Dillon speaks a few words on their behalf. Dillon—leader of the prisoners' spiritual movement—is the direct descendant of Brother Kyle in the Ward/Fasano script, complete with eyeglasses.

The funeral service is intercut with a scene of Babe—the ox used to pull Ripley's EEV from the water. "A Chest Burster explodes from the ox's thorax, rockets out of the carcass and tumbles to the floor. This thing has four legs. Alien head and drooling mouth. Like a horrifying fawn, it struggles to get legs under it. Wobbles around the room. Struggling upright, the baby creature gurgles…clatters across the floor and disappears into an air duct."

Yes, it appears that the Alien has taken on some ox characteristics. In fact, the ability to spit acid has been unseen in earlier incarnations of the Alien as well. However, on page 25 (just in time for the second act to begin), that's precisely what the Ox Alien does: "Spits acid in Murphy's eyes. Clawing at his face, flesh peeling away from his cheeks. Murphy reels backwards. Smoke pours through his fingers. Screaming, he slams into a wall and staggers backwards into the fan, which rips him to pieces."

When Clemens confronts Ripley later regarding a similar "burn" found near Murphy's remains and on Newt's cryotube, Ripley stays mum. Perhaps Ripley's trying not to jump to conclusions. Instead of divulging her past, Ripley seeks the help of Bishop's remains and the EEV's flight recorder.

RIPLEY
Is it still on the Sulaco or did it come with us on the EEV?

BISHOP
It was with us all the way.

RIPLEY
Does The Company know?

BISHOP
The Company knows everything that happened on the ship. It all goes back into the computer and gets sent back to the network.

Ripley is more afraid of The Company than she is of the Alien, showing that Weyland-Yutani is the true villain of the screenplay. The knowledge of The Company's awareness prompts Ripley to reveal the presence of the Alien to Dillon, Clemens, and the overseer of Fury 161, Andrews.

Impossibly Funky

In the Hill/Giler draft, the twenty-five prisoners are all named, but only a handful are fleshed out. One of the other few "important" prisoners is Golic, an oversized lummox with a penchant for gluttony who survives an Alien attack for reasons unknown. Golic suddenly finds himself in touch with his spirituality, having faced and survived a living embodiment of Death. When the Alien attacks again on page 49, Golic survives a second time. He now feels that the Alien needs him. Bound in a straight jacket in the medical center he shouts at it, "Hey you! Get over here. Lemme loose. I can help you. We can kill all these assholes."

Instead, the Alien kills Clemens—leaving Golic and Ripley alive. This is the major dramatic gaffe of the Hill/Giler draft. The writer/producer duo does not seem to realize that Clemens (like Brother John) was the focus of the script; his death robs the film of its soul. Ripley is merely a cipher. Only the audience familiar with *Alien* and *Aliens* knows her past and invests anything into her character.

With Clemens gone, more weight is cast upon the shoulders of Dillon (instead of Ripley). She stays in the background as the prisoners work up a plan to find and trap the Alien in a toxic waste disposal unit. "You get something in there and close the door; no way can it get out."

This leads to page upon page of cat-and-mouse games with the Alien. This costs serious time and several lives. Two pages after the Alien is trapped, prisoner Morse lets Golic free. "Golic swings his arms—gets his circulation back… 'I got to see it again. It's the dragon of God. It's in the book.'…Smack! Golic hammers down with a fire extinguisher. Morse is down and out."

Quickly, Golic finds his way to the storage area where the Alien now resides. Feeling he's a pawn of the creature—like Renfield to Dracula—he slashes the throat of the prisoner guarding the door and releases the Alien back into the general population. Again, the Alien pays no attention to Golic as it slithers back into the shadows (perhaps he was meant to be seen as being "infected," too).

Ripley finally figures out that her constant nausea might not be from coming out of hypersleep too quickly. Either not realizing (or not caring) about The Company having access to the results, Ripley subjects herself to a full scan of her bio-functions. And, lo, Ripley learns that she is carrying a baby Queen Alien. "It has to be a queen, otherwise it would have come out by now. I've seen how they work. It's not pretty. So it's going to be a queen. An egg layer. Millions of eggs. It's not like the one that's out there running around loose. I don't know how long this thing takes to gestate."

After an exchange in which Ripley begs Dillon to kill her (he refuses, saying he's a changed man), there are several inconsequential scenes. Golic hunts his fellow prisoners. Dillon finds a cocoon in the Assembly Hall, sets it ablaze and pays for his action in blood as the Alien tears him apart on page 84. Meanwhile, Ripley realizes that the Alien won't attack her as long as the Queen resides in her body. It isn't until page 86 that the story begins to gain momentum again.

Nauseatingly similar to the earlier burn and bag mission that took up so many pages of act two, the screenplay's third act has the prisoners running around in an attempt to lure the Alien into the lead works. They succeed (at the cost of nearly everyone's lives), and dispatch the creature in a climax nearly verbatim to the Ward/Fasano script.

This denouement of the Hill/Giler *Alien III* introduces the audience to Bishop II—the allegedly human prototype for the Bishop android. Golic greets Bishop II and his Weyland-Yutani compatriots, leading them to the leadworks in time to witness the Alien's demise. As Bishop II attempts to persuade Ripley to join him, Golic mutters about his dislike for droids. Without warning or reason, Golic grabs a handy axe and uses the working end on Bishop II's head.

The Company men shoot Golic and continue to plead with Ripley to be reasonable. Within seconds:

> the Baby Queen bursts out... She catches it... Ripley holds it, the tiny beast kicking in her hands... extends is above her head... Choking it-fighting it -- killing it... Still shaking the Baby Queen...she steps backwards off the platform and disappears into the raging inferno... Down into the pure white flame... A moment of ecstasy... A moment of triumph.

The lone prisoner, Morse, suddenly waxes poetic over the molten pool of lead before he's escorted away by the Company men. A hollow victory for mankind.

Stoking the Animosity

Between completion of the Hill & Giler "final" draft of 12/18/90 and the shooting of *Alien III*, the script went through almost a dozen rewrites. Upon completion of the 12/18/90 script, Rex Pickett quickly turned in a revised version dated 1/5/91. The Pickett draft appears to sport updated dialogue that comes off as pithy rather than hip—the tone for which he was going.

Perhaps Pickett's greatest contribution to the *Alien* saga was throwing gasoline on the smoldering feud between writer/producer team Hill & Giler and director David Fincher. In the preface to his draft of the script, Pickett mocks the "broken paragraph prose style of Hill/Giler" and admits: "this was a 'crunch time' rewrite" and "not a true reflection of my own prose style."

Pickett changes few major issues, but his draft expounds upon items such as why the prisoners frequent the dark corridors of their prison (they're salvaging equipment and goods from the former miner occupants). These items would appear in Alan Dean Foster's novelization of the *Alien III* script.

You Can't Polish a Turd
Walter Hill & David Giler (4/10/91)
Nine drafts and four months later, Hill & Giler had left the major hindrances to *Alien III* intact. The changes included the paring down of dialogue, the elimination of Golic's apparent immunity to the Alien (he's killed when releasing the creature from the disposal unit), additional playing down of prisoner Junior, and the elimination of the padding in the script's second act.

Additions to the 4/10/91 draft included Ripley directly confronting the Alien in a quasi-suicide attempt on page 74. Also included are several specified instances of shots from the Alien's point of view. Apparently, Hill & Giler forgot their Film Theory 101. Otherwise, they desire the audience to sympathize with the Alien as it runs through the dark halls of the prison complex. More likely, they knew that the audience would be tired of a second, similar sequence, so they interjected POV shots in an attempt to spice up the action—relying more on style over substance. In this way, Hill & Giler appear to be striving for an *Alien III* that would share the vacuous traits of Ridley Scott's work.

A twisted take on *Snow White* in *Alien³*

The April draft gave more weight to Dillon and to the prison colony's second-in-command, Aaron—keeping both alive much longer. Aaron is given a bit more character as a well-meaning lackey who's constantly ribbed by the prisoners for his 85 I.Q. (Those in glass houses... There is a high predisposition to mental retardation among XYY males.) Meanwhile, there is no discovery of any Alien cocoons on Fury 161, and thus, Dillon is given longer to live. Hill & Giler cut several of Dillon's prayers and allow him to be more heroic—sacrificing himself to allow Ripley to leave the lead works before molten metal covers the Alien.

The only difference of note in the end of the 4/10/91 draft is Morse's increased role, aiding Ripley in her suicide. Additionally, Hill & Giler attempt to wrap up the franchise by including a voiceover of Ripley's last transmission from the Nostromo during the final shots of the third film—a haunting message from beyond the grave as the last survivor of the Nostromo signs off.

David Fincher's *Alien³*
"What are you listening to him for, he's a shoe salesman!" said co-writer/producer David Giler of director David Fincher. The set of *Alien³* wasn't a happy place between firings of writers, re-writers, line producers, etc.; arguments over script content, budget, and time management, peppered with barbs tossed freely by all the disgruntled parties.

The Metamorphoses of *Alien III*

Fincher was caught between a rock and two hard heads. With Hill & Giler acting as both writers and producers, Fincher had nowhere to turn when he found himself frustrated with the script. Saddled with the draft given to him, Fincher did a remarkable job of breathing life into the staid Hill & Giler script.

The duo of Hill & Giler was a perfect marriage with Ridley Scott—if not in personality, at least in emotional investment. Ridley Scott's best work to date remains *Blade Runner*. Dealing with a cast of androids with empathy impairment, Scott could devote himself solely to creating atmosphere and damning characterization. "Turn on the neon, blow in some smoke, and the actors will take care of themselves," might well be Scott's credo. The same holds true for Hill, who could be considered the poor man's director. Spending his early years as the poor man's Peckinpah, he's since moved on to being the poor man's Oliver Stone. Hill is much more involved with his look than his characters, making good films by accident (*The Warriors*, *The Driver*, *Trespass*). Note that both Peckinpah and Stone are severely estrogen impaired—the two (along with Hill) share a lack of well-written female characters. It was only James Cameron, with his track record of strong female leads, who managed to flesh out Ripley.

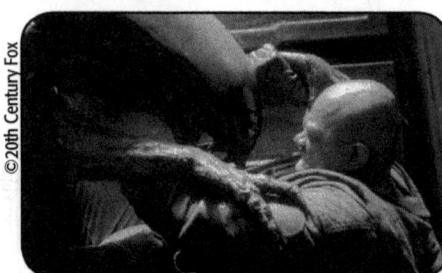
Charles S. Dutton fights off an Alien

While Ridley Scott did a wonderful job of creating an atmospheric film, at no time does the viewer have reason to care for anyone in *Alien*. Even when the character of Ellen Ripley takes charge of the film's one-note situation, the audience knows nothing more about her than at any point earlier or later in the film. More than providing an audience with thrills and a few hundred Aliens, writer/director James Cameron gave Ripley a personality and the *Alien* franchise a soul.

Armed with a cast of capable actors and a strong visual style, Fincher tried his best to keep the soul of the Alien films alive. Even when Fincher followed the inherently flawed Hill & Giler script, he still found himself thwarted by the powers that be.

Twentieth Century Fox's *Alien³*

David Fincher's *Alien³* was no masterpiece. It had a good look, fine acting, and a nice pace, yet Hill & Giler's ludicrous plot held it captive. Adding untold insult to injury, the cut Fincher presented to Twentieth Century Fox was marred beyond recognition before release to a studio audience high on hype and expecting another action-fest like *Aliens*.

Admittedly, David Fincher's *Alien³* would have received an overabundant amount of negative response from audiences and critics alike, but it would have made cohesive narrative sense. For as bad as Hill & Giler's script may be, it does manage to find its way from Point A to Point B and, subsequently, even bumps into Point C. What audiences witnessed instead was a jumbled mess that went directly from A to C, and had some sort of schwa in the middle.

A comparison between a rough work print and the final cut that Twentieth Century Fox firmly stood behind reveals well over two dozen changes, from trimming lines to hacking out corpulent sections of narrative. A ten-minute chunk is nowhere to be found in the Fox cut. That's like a projectionist losing an entire reel of the film. To make matters worse, this massive edit occurs during the initial "running around chasing the Alien scene," robbing it of its payoff. Instead of capturing the Alien, the action simply peters out without resolution.

In between these cuts were no less than seven separate scenes. During the burn and bag sequence there's a moment wherein Junior (Holt McCallany) makes amends with Ripley for his earlier attempt to rape her, sacrificing himself to capture the Alien and leading the beast into the storage tank. Afterward, while Dillon (Charles Dutton) bemoans the loss of his comrades, Aaron/85 (Ralph Brown) reveals that he's received a message from Weyland-Yutani, denoting Ripley as "top priority." Here Ripley realizes that The Company doesn't give a damn about her. They want the Alien gestating inside her.

The Alien is subsequently released by Golic (Paul McGann), who knocks Morse (Daniel Webb) cold and slits the throat of Arthur (Dhobi Oparei), the prisoner guarding the Alien's cell. Here, though, the Alien kills Golic—as if having no further use for him. Meanwhile, Ripley and Aaron/85 send a message to The Company, asking permission to terminate the Alien. "Permission to terminate Xenomorph denied," is the response. There's additional dialogue after this scene between Dillon, Aaron/85, Ripley, and Morse, in which they discuss Golic's unleashing of the Alien. Once the topic of their conversation turns to their new options, the Fox cut returns to the motion picture.

The removal of the Alien's capture prevents some redundancy between this and the later scene, but it makes Ripley and her cohorts appear completely ineffectual. There's no explanation given for why they couldn't succeed in their attempts. Rather, the action merely stalls, leaving little time before the subsequent endeavor to capture the elusive beast. Fox continued to ruin the pacing of the film by dropping shots willy-nilly in the second chase scene. Fox's sacrifice of suspense and clarity lacks clear motivation.

In addition to the changes noted above, there are scenes not present in either the Fox or workprint that exist. These include Clemens (Charles Dance) witnessing the crash of the EEV and finding Ripley washed up on shore. They are evidenced by the *Alien³* trading cards, as well as the full-length trailer released by Fox before the film's release.

The only piece of footage noticeably absent from the workprint of *Alien³* comes during Ripley's demise. In the workprint, Ripley simply propels herself from the scaffolding on which she stands, falling into the leadworks below. In the Fox cut, Ripley attains martyrdom. She's shown in close-up as she plummets, arms outstretched in a Christ-like pose. Suddenly the Alien that's been growing inside her expels itself. Shrieking with new life, the Alien writhes from Ripley's chest. She catches the beast and pulls it to her breast, keeping it with her as she is incinerated.

A scene that was not included until the later Hill & Giler drafts of *Alien³* showed the Baby Queen actually changing hosts—escaping from the drowning Newt and entering Ripley's mouth. It's not known if this scene was shot, but the event found its way into the Dark Horse Comics adaptation of the film.

Much of the missing footage finally saw the light of day in 2003, with the release of the *Alien* Quadrilogy. A documentary, directed by Charles de Lauzirika, accompanying the disc provides a bevy of information, though key players Fincher and Hill are missing from the proceedings. Giler's appearance further cements his reputation as being an unconscionable ballbuster.

A Hero's Death

Ripley dies a hero, sacrificing herself to prevent The Company from obtaining the Alien and saving countless lives. At least, that's what audiences may have thought before *Alien: Resurrection*.

But what of Hicks and Newt? Their deaths were ignominious, making the struggles of *Aliens* for naught. James Cameron spent the entire *Aliens* film creating a "family" with Hicks as father, Ripley as mother, and Newt as child. There is no reason why Hicks and Newt had to die, other than that the *Alien III* writers couldn't handle one significant character—Ripley—much less three.

The excuse most often given regarding Newt's untimely demise is that the actress who played her, Carrie Henn, had grown noticeably since her performance in *Aliens*. Skilled writers can concede to problems such as this and write around them. Was there any reason why *Alien³* had to continue on the heels of *Aliens*? Even if this was mandatory to the story, couldn't there be an error in the cryotubes that didn't keep Newt young? Hadn't any of these writers watched *Planet of the Apes* and saw Dr. Stewart (Dianne Stanley) dead in her tube from old age? Taken to a less significant extreme, this could have explained away Newt's age difference.

More than the redundant plot and reliance on atmosphere over action, the killing of Hicks and Newt stood as the insurmountable blunder of *Alien³*.

Baby Alien on Board

> "One of them managed to board the Sulaco, Hicks. Ripley killed it. She called it 'the queen.' It was larger than the others. Very large. Somehow it deposited some genetic material on the ship."
> —Bishop to Hicks in Gibson's *Alien III*

Apart from Twohy's draft of *Alien III*, every writer who hacked away at the script relied on the remaining crew of the Sulaco being incredibly stupid. After surviving the terror of Aliens, the notion that they would have left the orbit of LV426 with any Alien material onboard is fatuous. Sure, the Aliens don't show up on infrared, but there must be a way to detect and destroy any Alien eggs lying about.

The Company Gains a Name

In *Aliens*, Ellen Ripley (Sigourney Weaver) rallied against hard-headed bureaucrats who appeared more concerned about the price her former craft, the Nostromo, than her deceased colleagues. In the proceedings of *Alien*, audiences were introduced to a nemesis more sinister than the Alien itself: The Company. The bureaucracy proves far more insidious than the cold logic of the Aliens. As Ripley would say, "You don't see [the Aliens] fucking each other for a god damn percentage."

Other than Burke (Paul Reiser) in *Aliens* and somewhat through Ash (Ian Holm) in *Alien*, The Company remained faceless. It was a looming presence with a reach far beyond its earthly origins. As corporate conglomerates became more commonplace in the late 1980s, the insidious idea of an omnipotent—and omniscient—Company encroached the economic territory of the United States where multiple mergers and acquisitions were everyday occurrences.

In an expurgated scene from *Aliens* that The Company has its name revealed. During a brief exchange between workers on LV426, the name, logo, and slogan of the Weyland-Yutani Corporation appear. In the next scene (which appeared theatrically), Burke makes an offhanded reference to the Weyland-Yutani motto, "Building Better Worlds." Otherwise, it isn't until *Aliens III* that The Company establishes its brand.

Weyland-Yutani plays upon the love/hate relationship with Asia that has plagued Walter Hill for years. His attempt to remake John Woo's *The Killer* resulted in a script that was steeped more in Asian symbolism than the Hong Kong original. The Asian half of Weyland-Yutani consists of faceless salarymen who seem to admire the insectile emotionlessness of the Aliens.

All Creatures Great and Small

ANTHONY
I'm confused. Before you said it came out of the torso, not the head --

RIPLEY
I don't feel like a discussion of Alien biology.

Dog Aliens, Cat Aliens, Cow Aliens, Sheep Aliens, Chicken Aliens... When did this idea of the Alien possessing the ability to take on host characteristics or, moreover, the incredible malleability of their DNA, make their lifecycle and means of breeding so open to interpretation?

The Metamorphoses of *Alien III*

The introduction of a Queen Alien beset the Aliens with an insectile life-cycle, meaning that without an egg, there can be no Alien. Meanwhile, a few drafts of the *Aliens III* script have Aliens breeding seemingly at will, asexually.

There are no hard and fast rules in science fiction, but it helps to lay some groundwork in a story architecture and then either follow them, play with them, or play against them. It also helps to have some kind of jackass explanation for the fantastic.

The idea that gestation in another life form leads to an Alien that shares its host's physical characteristics is "neat." From a practical standpoint a species could breed itself out of existence if its new DNA was flawed or if the host was inferior. Hampster Alien? Rhino Alien? Ox Alien? It would make more sense for the Alien DNA to be rock solid, so that the fearsome soldier Aliens seen in *Alien* and *Aliens* could use "inferior" beasts to produce their sturdy stock. We already know from *Alien* that their eggs have a tremendously viable shelf life, showing the importance of continuing their ideal strain.

This obsession with Alien physiology recurs again in force in *Alien vs. Predator: Requiem*. This wretched film features a hybrid of the Alien and Predator creatures. The Aliens in the film don't seem interested in populating Earth with their progeny. Only the PredAlien hybrid seems capable of laying eggs, and does so in a way completely different than we're used to seeing Aliens reproduce. Yet the PredAlien's progeny are lacking the creature's outward Predator characteristics (the four-pronged jaws), and seem to be normal Aliens after their rapid growth. This is just one of many things that doesn't make sense in the film.

If an Alien ever encountered a superior life form, only then, perhaps, their DNA might change—those strong enough to survive this superior force would breed and continue. This is all basic Darwinism, of course, and perhaps it's not hip to apply science to science fiction. However, keep in mind that the best sci-fi, while appearing to fly in the face of logic begs either acceptance on its own terms or shakily stands on its pseudoscience.

It's poor science fiction that contradicts itself or portrays itself as logical while being too fantastic to be acceptable. Overall, it all goes back to the notion of simplicity. Keep the Aliens as killing machines and scrap the notion/fascination with them as gene recycling machines.

The Scariest Place of All

After Twentieth Century Fox released *Aliens*, upstart comic book company Dark Horse Comics secured the rights to print a comic adaptation of Cameron's film, as well as began a series of comic books based on the films. Without special effects budgetary constraints, contractual obligations from actors, or overbearing producers, and with a rabid audience of loyal fans, Dark Horse proceeded to produce one of the finest comic tales based on a film series.

Following the *Aliens* adaptation, Dark Horse produced dozens of *Aliens* titles, placing the beasts in a wide variety of settings and introducing possibilities far more fantastic than anything created by the writers mentioned in this piece. Moreover, Dark Horse continued the storyline of *Aliens*, essentially creating a comic sequel to the film. In early drafts of Dark Horse's *Aliens* stories—written by Mark Verheiden—the main characters were named Newt and Hicks. After a request from Twentieth Century Fox, their names were changed to Billie and Wilks (in an attempt to restore a sense of consistency between the comics and *Alien³*). The *Aliens* comic book series charted lands undreamed of by pointy-headed writer/producers. Verheiden's comic explored the Alien homeworld, and even had the guts to send the Aliens to Earth.

An early teaser trailer for *Alien³* returns to the egg motif of the *Alien* preview. The narrator states, "In 1979, we discovered [that] in space, no one can hear you scream. In 1992, we will discover [that] on Earth, everyone can hear you scream." Here, the egg breaks above the atmosphere of Earth. This misconception that the Aliens would make an appearance on terra firma was increased with the film's early tagline, "This time it's hiding in the scariest place of all."

Ellen Ripley's belly is sexy, not scary. Aliens hiding on Earth, on the other hand... Now that's a wild idea, and a natural continuance of the *Alien* series. Astronomical casualties and amazing action sequences would surely follow. However, that idea was too much for the limited scope of David Giler and Walter Hill. "Drop the Alien in Death Valley and you drop a nuke on him. End of story," claimed writer/producer David Giler. That shows his limited imagination.

Dark Horse collected Verheiden's tales into three books: *Aliens: Book One*, *Aliens: Book Two*, and *Aliens: Earth War*. (Upon changing the names of Hicks and Newt, they were re-released as *Aliens: Outbreak*, *Aliens: Nightmare Asylum*, and *Aliens: Female War*.)

Hicks volunteers to visit the Alien homeworld, stowing Newt aboard his ship. The two seek retribution, while Hicks's commanders want specimens.

Along with Hicks, a crack commando squadron mans the mission. Newt falls in love with one of the commandos, Private Butler, only to discover in the heat of battle that Butler and the rest of the crew are androids who have been existing under the delusion that they were human. Back on Earth things aren't going so well, either, between a new religious cult that worships the Alien and the poor schlubs the military has incubating newborn Aliens.

After near decimation, the crew on the Alien homeworld discovers an unlikely savior: a comrade of the derelict ship's pilot that crashed into Archeron (LV426)—the same ship where a Face Hugger attacked Kane and Newt's father. The creature, which they dub The Other, helps them to escape back to Earth, where they find the military packing its bags and getting ready to leave. Will the last humans please turn the light out?

The Metamorphoses of *Alien III*

The military ascertains that the Alien plague merely exacerbated an already bleak worldview. "The Alien attack isn't evil. It's opportunity. It's a chance to clean the slate—a chance to start again. After a few years, when it's over, the survivors can return and terraform Earth into something beautiful. The Aliens have given us a chance to rediscover ourselves." And with this, the Aliens swarm the base, forcing Newt and Hicks (with a functioning upper torso of Private Butler) to hijack a ship and get the fuck out of Dodge.

Aliens: Book One is riveting. While it functions as a fully formed three-act narrative, complete with suspenseful subplots, it leaves the Aliens in charge of Earth. *Aliens: Book Two* does little to change this fact. Instead, this book plays like a diversionary subplot to a larger story—one that gives the reader pleasure seeing, but does little to advance the narrative. *Aliens: Book Two* only successes in providing for the next chapter of the story are the introduction of a refugee family trapped on Earth and the re-introduction of Ripley.

Aliens: Earth War explains that Ripley had been shanghaied into active duty when a military ship intercepted the Sulaco. Complete with a crack squad of her own, Ripley descends back to the surface of LV-426 to visit the derelict ship. Here she makes contact with the apparent Mother of all Aliens. "We assumed the Alien infestations were sporadic—arbitrary—that they bred

wherever convenient, like some horrible cancers. We were wrong. They move with purpose. The pilot of the derelict ship had discovered the Aliens' genesis—the source of their power. She's calling her children back to her."

Returning to the "Alien as insect" idea, *Aliens: Earth War* focuses on the pheremonal link between a Queen Alien and her brood. Is it merely a glandular response, or do the Aliens communicate on a more telepathic level? As Ripley and her new crew blast off on some damn fool idealistic crusade, she says, "The drones are only vassals, guided by a superior external intelligence. Many of us have felt this Alien presence—the tortured empathetic bond it shares with its children—the hunger to be whole again."

Ripley plans to use this desire to be whole again to destroy the Mother Alien. The crew travels yet again to the Alien homeworld, finds this elusive Alien, and seals her up in a gift box for Earth. Meanwhile, Newt begins to get antsy about the little Earth girl whose transmissions she still watches. Ripley and Newt head to Earth's surface, where Newt saves the girl and Ripley lures all of the Aliens to their Mother before blowing them all to kingdom come. Then, in an attempt to wrap up the story with a reference to *Aliens: Book One*, we learn that The Other has been acting as puppet master in this whole ordeal. Apparently, The Other telepathically led Ripley back to Earth so that it could terraform Earth for itself. D'oh!

Essentially, this three-book tale is far better in its dullest spots than any of the scripts for *Alien III*. Yet, when it's all said and done, it may have been better to stop after *Alien: Book One* as the follow-ups to this book—like *Alien³* compared to *Aliens*—didn't deliver the excitement of the previous installment.

The Alien Home

The multiple trips to the Alien homeworld in the Dark Horse books bring to fruition an idea that, according to Renny Harlin, had been contemplated for *Alien III*. After jumping ship on the project, Harlin complained, "I specifically worked with two writers who sold me on their very ambitious plans to develop a story about the future of mankind and what kind of intelligence was really behind the Aliens' evolution. But what they turned in was nothing more than a rehash of the two previous movies."

The forces behind *Alien³* not only failed Harlin—they failed audiences, as well. More than involving three directors and over a half dozen writers, Twentieth Century Fox appeared determined to subvert the project, second-guessing audiences and shooting themselves in the foot. Rather than a blockbuster, *Alien³* is the definition of a lackluster sequel.

Ripley has yet to return to the Alien home. Subsequent *Alien* films have all taken the beast to Earth—from an encounter with the atmosphere in *Alien: Resurrection* to the two *Alien vs. Predator* films. With the trajectory that these films have taken, it's doubtful that they'll ever get off the ground again, much less make it to the homeworld of the Aliens.

The original version of this article ran in *Cashiers du Cinemart* #12.

We love you, Dr. Zaius (Maurice Evans)

RETURN TO THE *PLANET OF THE APES*

By Mike White

Word floated around Hollywood for years about a remake of *Planet of the Apes*, and screenplays by Sam Hamm and Terry Hayes substantiate these rumors. However, neither of these writers' visions of a new *Apes* film appears to be on the horizon. That's probably for the best.

Franklin J. Schaffner's *Planet of the Apes* left an indelible impression on American popular culture. Based on *La Planète Des Singes*, the 1963 novel by Pierre Boulle, the original *Apes* film spawned—among other things—a series of films, a television show, comic books, action figures, and an animated series.

In his novel, Boulle spins a tale of Ulysse Mérou, an Earthling journalist serving as part of a crew on an experimental journey to a planet orbiting Betelgeuse. Accompanying Professor Antelle are his assistant, Arthur Levain, and their chimpanzee, Hector. The crew travel two years at nearly the speed of light while three and a half centuries pass on their home planet.

After landing without a hitch, they dub this new land Soror (Latin for "sister"), as it is indeed terra familiaris. Here they find mute and primitive humans who take their clothes and kill their chimp. It is with great distress that they discover that the planet's ruling species are anthropomorphic Apes.

Helena Bonham Carter makes a case for bestiality in *Planet of the Apes*

Our protagonist, Ulysse, is modeled after Homer's Odysseus, conqueror of Troy and conceiver of the Trojan horse. Meanwhile, the chimp Hector recalls the Trojan warrior slain by Achilles. In Boulle's tale, Nova—the first primitive human the Earthmen encounter—strangles poor Hector with animal intensity. Boulle employs subtlety in his symbolism as well as he does in his social commentary.

The culture of the Apes is such that there are three tiers of social classes to which each of the three species of Apes belong. Gorillas are the hunters, warriors, and police—the proletariat exploited for their muscle. Chimpanzees make up the intellectual and bullied middle class, while orangutans occupy positions of pomp and power as the bourgeoisie.

A Planet Where Apes Evolved from Men

Amazingly, Michael Wilson and Rod Serling's screen adaptation is faithful, if often only in spirit, to the original source material. It's true that Boulle's Apes

Return to the *Planet of the Apes*

are far more advanced than those of the final film, driving cars and flying airplanes instead of riding horseback and walking unpaved streets, as if to show them more as a society on the verge of industrialization. The state of Ape advancement can also be attributed to their origins: they have had to rebuild an entire world after its former civilization was lost.

The lone surviving astronaut in the film is Taylor (Charlton Heston) who, like Ulysse, is captured by gorillas out on a hunt. However, Taylor loses his ability to speak after being shot in the throat. Stripped of his clothes and voice, he has lost all outward symbols of difference between himself and the savage *Homo sapiens*.

The moment in which Taylor speaks is a revelation on par with Ulysse's stirring speech to attendees of a scientific congress. By speaking, both protagonists reveal their intelligence and ability to communicate. Yet for this Taylor is condemned, while Ulysse is given a new lease on life.

Ulysse's acceptance into Ape society, along with Nova's pregnancy (and the danger her loquacious baby represents) would later be cleverly used in the third *Apes* film, *Escape from the Planet of the Apes*, but with chimpanzees Cornelius and Zira in the perilous limelight. *Escape* also holds a tale of the Apes' ascent into power that's markedly dissimilar to that of either the first *Apes* film or Boulle's book.

Like Ulysse's home planet, Soror was once dominated by human beings. In an odd, Jungian scene, Ulysse joins Cornelius in a laboratory, where cerebral experiments conducted on human subjects have produced a means of tapping into the collective unconscious of the human race. In this way, Ulysse hears snippets of memories about the Apes' ascension.

Apparently, Apes were trained as servants (as found in *Conquest of the Planet of the Apes*) and, eventually, became dissatisfied with their role in society, wanting something better. As time went on, the Apes' ability to mimic their human masters grew until some gained the power of speech. The first use they made of speech was to protest when they were given orders. Coupled with this surge of learning, a bout of "cerebral laziness" befell the human race, making the conquering of this feeble species all the easier.

Michael Clarke Duncan and his gorilla soldiers

The most noticeable disparity between the two works is their final ironic twists. The book's surprise ending comes when, after being jettisoned into space with Nova and his child, Ulysse returns to Earth seven hundred years after he departed, only to be greeted by a gorilla in full military regalia.

The film's ending is a moment that had to have been conceived by Rod Serling. A typical *Twilight Zone* moment: Taylor discovers that he and his now-dead fellow astronauts traveled only in time, not location. Yes, Taylor is on Earth, some hundreds of years after he departed. And, god damn it, the fools who ran the planet must have blown it up for there, along the beach, is the half-buried symbol of American freedom, the Statue of Liberty.

A Trip Down Memory Lane
The names of four writers were linked with a new *Planet of the Apes* script. The first of these is Terry Hayes.

Babies around the globe are being delivered stillborn, threatening the future of the human race. Led by Billie Ray Diamond (a moniker better suited for a rhinestone-encrusted country and western singer than a brilliant woman scientist), the Centers for Disease Control are aflutter with activity, trying to determine the cause. They're looking for a viral answer—little do they know that the origins of the problem reside in a mutation of human DNA.

The man who figures it all out is but a lowly janitor, Will Robinson (an acknowledged *Lost in Space* reference). Of course, that's not his real name. He's actually Dr. Robert Plant (an unacknowledged Led Zeppelin reference), an expert on mitochondrial DNA, in hiding after his career was ruined during a past experiment that went awry and left his fiancée dead.

It hurts to write this paragraph. The conceit of the film is so precarious that suspending disbelief long enough to even relate it is a arduous task. The "logic" of the film dictates that if you can unlock the secret of mitochondrial DNA, "you could physically travel back down it. Through evolution—like a time machine." By submerging himself in a sensory deprivation flotation tank (think *Altered States* or *Simon*), time travelling is exactly what Plant does, going back twenty-one hundred years in order to determine where the mutation occurred.

Once he's in our primitive past, Plant discovers some savage humans who speak fairly good English. The only difference between Plant and his fellow humans is his better posture and blue eyes. Within moments, there is a deafening thunder of hooves as they're attacked. The Apes have arrived!

Not quite advanced enough for guns or airplanes, these Apes prefer crossbows and pulley-driven battering rams. Plant is captured by Drak—one mean gorilla. Drak does such a good job of bashing Plant that when the human is taken back to Ape City, he's put under the immediate care of Dr. Zora.

Under the command of Ma-Gog, the Apes have a policy of ethnic cleansing to rid the planet of the scourge of man.

In Hayes's Ape-ruled world, there are only gorillas—no chimps or orangutans, and thus no class conflict. Subsequently the story has less social commentary and is far less interesting. After quickly escaping captivity, Plant interacts with his human brethren, including Aragorn, the Ranger of the

Easterlings, and Kip, leader of the Tiger Clan. We may have left the *planet* Earth and wandered somewhere into Tolkien's *Middle* Earth.

Reunited with a time-traveling Diamond (who hopes to save the unborn child in her womb), the two *Homo sapiens* search for the girl to whom the Apes will give the future world-threatening mutagen. Indeed, this is yet another ridiculous plot point, in that the Apes can somehow infect a human female with something that will mutate our DNA thousands of years hence.

I'm not a religious man by any stretch of the imagination, but even *I* was vaguely offended by the Apes' quoting of scripture and that the female "missing link" whom Plant and Diamond discover around page ninety is named Aiv (pronounced "Eve").

From here the script digresses even further as the humans fight the Apes, run from the Apes, and hide from the Apes, stopping briefly for inane dialogue. Of course, Plant and Diamond put a stop to Ma-Gog's attempt to corrupt Aiv's DNA, and humanity is saved.

Having never found a method in which he could climb back up the evolutionary ladder and travel back to his own age, Plant and Diamond are stuck in the past. After Diamond's successful birth, they know that the human race will survive. Then the viewer is presented with a completely ridiculous scene:

OUTSIDE THE CAVE:
Will and Aiv help Diamond. She comes out of the cave, still holding the baby. It's magic hour -- they stand on a rock ledge, looking at the ocean washed with color from the setting sun.

We see what Will was building. It's sort of like a sculpture -- just the head and crown of the Statue of Liberty.

Diamond smiles. She looks at him, wondering why --

WILL
It's to make sure we never forget where we came from.

The baby starts to cry. Will puts one arm each around Diamond and Aiv.

We pull back from them -- high up into the stars. The baby's cry carries over. We see Earth rise. In all this nothingness -- life.

Hayes just had to find a way to fit that Statue of Liberty thing in somehow, and as such, he picked a completely asinine way of doing it!

Another Deadly Plague

According to *Apes* lore, Apes moved into pet/servant positions after a plague killed the world's dogs and cats. With deadly viruses being in vogue in the late nineties, it's no wonder that this idea was used in Sam Hamm's script. Yet this time, mankind is in danger of being wiped out by a pathogen (as opposed to a rogue protein) brought to us courtesy of Planet Ape.

Again, babies are inflicted, living a maximum of three days once outside the womb. Enter Centers for Disease Control hotshot, Dr. Susan Landis. As fast as she's introduced, she's secreted away to a hidden army base where she's introduced to Dodge, Astor, Stewart, and her eventual love interest, Alexander Troy (a roundabout nod to Ulysses). She's shown a spaceship and the dead orangutan pilot that brought our planet this virus. The orangutan's goal: to poison humankind. Mission accomplished!

It's up to the scientists to save us. They pilot the ship back to the Ape's home planet, orbiting Alpha Centauri. The journey takes six years for the crew, while thirty-four years have passed on Earth. They hope to complete their mission and send back a cure before Earth is bereft of fertile females.

Upon arrival, the story begins to feel familiar. Stewart is found dead in his cryogenic tube (not to worry—the poor chap only had two lines up to this point) and our heroes' ship begins to sink. With the film's accelerated pace, the Earthmen soon encounter primitive, speechless humans and are subsequently attacked by Apes. These simians are quite advanced, sporting bazookas and traveling around in helicopters as they round up their prey.

Separated from their comrades, Susan and Troy find themselves placed in a zoo in Ape City. Here they meet the kindly chimpanzee zookeeper, Zira, and the lecherous orangutan Lord Zaius (described as "the Gordon Gekko of Apes"). Outside the Zoological Research Institute, daily protests against animal cruelty are led by the rabble-rousing chimp, Cornelius. He and Zira are secretly in cahoots, and the two of them have a hidden colony on the edge of the Forbidden Zone where they keep humans that exhibit better-than-average intelligence—selectively breeding them. The morality (or lack thereof) of this is never explored.

When they learn of Susan and Troy's remarkable abilities, Zira and Cornelius plot to move them to their colony. Their plans run afoul when Troy is kidnapped by his gorilla handlers and placed in a gladiatorial ring to fight his old friend Dodge (who's been turned into a savage courtesy of some Ape brain surgery). Making a daring escape, Troy is picked up by Caius, a circus trainer. Meanwhile, safely hidden, Susan learns that she's pregnant. Though Susan is our apparent protagonist, she drops out of the story for a while, given a role insultingly similar to Nova.

Apparently, the circus is a big event to Apes, for it's during an incredibly popular broadcast of his performance that Troy gives the same speech Ulysse presented to the scientific congress on Soror. Enjoying his stint as a popular

Return to the *Planet of the Apes*

freak, Troy and Lord Zaius engage in what Earthlings might call a pissing contest; both of them trying to push the others' buttons and find their weak spots. Susan's life is threatened, Cornelius captured, and Zaius shows Troy the marvels of the Forbidden Zone, including the multimedia center in which signals from Earth are intercepted by satellite receivers and translated into simian memes. Thus, orangutans are seen as progenitors of culture.

Tim Roth about to sink his teeth into some scenery

In order to expedite their return home, Susan creates a disease that affects only the orangutans of Planet Ape. This is ironic, as we have learned that it was humans who created the virus that affects Susan and Troy's brethren on Earth. Likewise, this disease rids Planet Ape of the majority of its high-tech human populace who traveled to Earth some ten to twenty thousand years ago. Unaffected were only those with a chromosomal aberration that robs them of all "higher functions," such as speech.

To make a long story short—Hamm fills out the last act with a couple of useless action scenes—when Troy, Susan, and their child make their way back home on the aptly named ship, *Bellerophon*, they are greeted by Apes in military regalia and find:

> ...Our old friend the Statue of Liberty, standing watch on her island pedestal. In the years since we last saw her, she's undergone radical plastic surgery. For, as we can now see, her once-proud porcelain features have been crudely chiseled into the grotesque likeness of a great grinning Ape.

With these convoluted tales of time and space travel, viruses, and birth defects, Hayes and Hamm have taken the easy route of making their Apes tale more of a revisionist retelling of the first *Apes* film. Neither of these writers has had the courage, the creativity, the intelligence, or the wherewithal to follow the story arc of the first five films, wherein Taylor would return to a much different Earth than the one in which he first arrived (as predicted by *Battle for...*).

In the years after Hamm submitted his script to 20th Century Fox, occasional rumors of progress sprung up and were quickly squashed. Chronicling the stalled project often uncovers James Cameron's name. It's said that Cameron would make a new film as the sixth in the series, playing into his penchant for circular time patterns from *Terminator*.

Ape Man's Burden

At the time this piece was originally written, a third screenplay by William Broyles was floating around, with Michael "Me Make Big Boom!" Bay attached as a director. Broyles's script went through several rewrites before he would share screen credit with Lawrence Konner and Mark D. Rosenthal. Broyles's original draft remains elusive, with the closest version available in the novelization by William T. Quick.

Broyles's script seems something of a hybrid of Hayes's and Hamm's work. The new *Planet of the Apes* (referred to as *POTA* 2001 for the remainder of this article) remains saddled with the convoluted concepts of time travel and DNA tampering.

POTA 2001 begins in 2021 A.D., with the crew of the spaceship Oberon, an apparent Ape training vessel, falling victim to a powerful "space storm" that catapults two of its crew into the future: Pericles and Captain Leo Davidson (Mark Wahlberg). The Oberon and the rest of its crew crash land on a handy planet where, three thousand years later, Davidson rejoins them. He finds scads of loincloth-clad tribespeople (descendants of the crew) and culturally superior Apes (descendants of the Ape trainees).

Unlike the other beasts of the jungle, the humans of *POTA* 2001 have kept their ability to speak. Ultimately, the presence of verbose humans severely hinders the development of the film. Speech is viewed as an anthropological gateway to culture. Yet humans lack a cohesive society, having de-evolved into wandering bands of primitives. The Ape sentiment that human culture takes place below the waist doesn't appear far from the truth.

The tribal humans Davidson encounters on the Planet of the Apes resemble unkempt androids. They share Davidson's interminable lack of personality. With both primitives and Davidson speaking fluent English, there is no difference to set Davidson apart from his fellow humans and position him in a place of heretical similarity to the Apes.

Davidson looks quite human but, as a leading man, he's a retail store mannequin. Mark Walberg, while a good actor, is not the cultural icon that Charleton Heston was before he zipped into the flight suit of Colonel Taylor. With such a milquetoast protagonist, the choice of Wahlberg becomes questionable. Who would be better to represent *Homo sapiens*? In the multicultural future, will white males still be the best suited to stand in for humanity?

Wahlberg struggles to give his character any character at all. Our only glimpse into his inner motivation is the contempt he holds for his simian "coworkers." He is propelled into the film as he attempts to prove that his superiors should "never send a monkey to do a man's job." Perhaps Davidson left Earth as a protest to some kind of simian Affirmative Action.

The crew of the Oberon apparently numbered enough to provide the necessary genetic diversity for thousands of years without serious inbreeding. Yet either the non-white progenitors have retreated far into the "Forbidden Area," they've been hunted hardest by the Apes, or they've been wiped out by their fellow humans. Regardless, they are in short supply.

In Quick's novelization, the only minorities mentioned are human servants: "Tival...a middle-aged black man [and] Bon, a tiny Chinese woman." In the final film, the Bon character (Freda Foh Shen) remains Asian, while Erick Avari—an actor often cast as a Middle Easterner—plays Tival. One of Daena's fellow tribesmen is black, but his race remains conspicuously not at issue. In the original *Planet of the Apes*, tribesmen were strictly white, with the only black person—Taylor's fellow astronaut, Dodge (Jeff Burton)—shot, stuffed, and stuck in a museum.

Rather than lacking depth, the Ape population lacks breadth. The main Apes represent singular notions of animosity, piety, and avarice in General Thade (Tim Roth), Attar (Michael Clarke Duncan), and Limbo (Paul Giamatti). As Thade, Roth spends every second on screen spewing and stewing; his enmity so uncontained and unexplained that he can't even function in simple social settings. Playing Thade to the hilt, Roth's performance becomes unintentionally comical, especially as he bounces around like an errant ping pong ball.

Thade, Attar, and Limbo represent the three species of Apes in *POTA* 2001: chimpanzee, gorilla, and orangutan. In early drafts of the script, Limbo was a chimpanzee. Making him an orangutan removes orangutans from the patrician role of the original *Planet of the Apes*. Limbo, a slave trader, is the most reviled Ape we see. Orangutans seem something of an endangered species; there are only two orangutans of note in the film, yet there are legions of chimpanzees and gorillas.

With the positioning of orangutans as a senator and a slave trader, it might appear that the social stratum of the original *Apes* film has been discarded. A closer look reveals chimpanzees clearly in a superior position to gorillas. More than distinguishing themselves with different armor while serving in the same army, every gorilla answers to a chimp, while no chimps do the same for a gorilla.

The chimpanzees in *POTA* 2001 enjoy positions of power, as well as a characteristic shared with the more civilized Apes of the original *Apes* series: British accents. Like Maurice Evans (Dr. Zaius) and Cornelius/Caesar (Roddy McDowall), three prominent members of society, General Thade, Ari (Helena Bonham Carter), and her father, Senator Sandar (David Warner), are played by Brits. Meanwhile, actors of color portray the two prominent gorillas in *POTA* 2001.

Ari is the only character of potential interest in *POTA* 2001. Unfortunately, her inner motivations remain cloaked behind her didactic pleas for human equality when she's with Apes. When she's with humans, she fades into the background. She's the poor little rich chimp, complete with her gorilla protector, Krull (Cary-Hiroyuki Tagawa), and social cause for which to fight.

It is only the occasional dispirited reaction shots of Daena (Estella Warren), leader of a human tribe, that could lead viewers to the assumption that Ari poses a threat to the humans. In early drafts of the film's script, Ari is not a physical danger, but rather a romantic rival to Daena.

Quick writes Davidson's inner monologue thusly: "If Ari had been a human woman, he would have understood it, known how to deal with it. But she was an Ape, and to him, no matter how smart or literate or compassionate, that meant she was an animal. And humans just didn't have that kind of relationship with beasts..." Ari's love goes unrequited, despite her having mounds more personality than Daena. The poor Ape woman falls so close to the mark, but her genes prevent Davidson from having feelings for her.

In mainstream American cinema, there is still reluctance to accept "race mixing." Heaven forbid that audiences consider species mixing! Bereft of this love triangle, Davidson seems doomed to a relationship with Daena—who, while being a wilderness-bound savage, nevertheless sports flawless hair and makeup. However, while Ari and Davidson may share a love that dare not speak its name, species mixing goes on between Apes. Witness the orangutan Senator Nado (Glenn Shadix) and his trophy wife, Nova (Lisa Marie), a chimpanzee.

Monkey Messiah

As a simple science fiction romp, *POTA 2001* quickly discards the more interesting aspects of the story. The one-dimensional characters populate a flat narrative: a simple trip from Point A to Point B with no sharp turns between. Even the so-called "Forbidden Area" gives pause to neither the humans or Apes who traipse about there. Davidson leads the expedition with single-minded determination. He's looking for his ship, and neither finds nor seeks anything else along the way. He doesn't come to grasp human/Ape interpersonal relationships, nor does any of his motley band. The Apes remain as ideologically separate from the humans from beginning to end.

Whenever there's a chance of the film getting interesting, it veers back to safe, dull territory. For example, rather than exploring the inner workings of Ape City, Davidson escapes with ease the first evening he's there. Likewise, the audience never becomes privy to the humans in their tribal elements. And, just when it appears that Davidson and his band of tribal humans are doomed... voila! They're miraculously saved by the arrival of Pericles, Davidson's simian pilot-in-training.

Ape religion focuses on the return of Semos—the Ape progenitor—as a messiah. Yet the overthrow of humans by Apes remains a shadowy mystery. Missing is the revelation of speech among the Apes and the motivation for Semos's rebellion. *POTA 2001* even lacks the irony to make Semos a recognizable Ape crewmate of its human protagonist.

The religion of the Apes is simplistic compared to the co-opted Christianity of the original *Planet of the Apes*. The Apes justify their superior attitude by classifying humans as soulless beasts, straddling the line between religious dogmatism and fascist rhetoric. Ironically, judging by the blank stares of the humans in *POTA* 2001, one would be hard-pressed to argue against this assertion.

It's not every day that simians fall from the sky, descending in a brilliant ball of white light. Yet mistaking Pericles for Semos is another gaping hole in the film's logic. (Imagine a Judeo-Christian messiah somewhere a few steps down the evolutionary ladder; that would be a bit of a letdown, wouldn't it?) Even more astonishing than adopting the as-yet-evolved chimpanzee as savior, with the appearance of this fortuitous *deus ex machina*, three thousand years of discord immediately dissolve. Let the healing begin! At least we're spared a slow-motion shot of Ape and human children playing together in harmony. However, the finale of *POTA* 2001 is just as cheesy and far more illogical.

According to actor Michael Clarke Duncan, director Tim Burton shot five separate endings to *POTA* 2001. The one chosen echoes the ending of Pierre Boulle's novel and Sam Hamm's *Planet of the Apes* script (as well as a Kevin Smith comic); the "big twist" ending of *POTA* 2001 has Davidson returning to Earth, only to find that Apes have conquered it. Certainly, the same genetically mutated Apes reside in Earth-bound labs. Perhaps they evolved and overthrew their numerous human captors. The real head-scratcher comes when we see that the Lincoln Memorial has been transformed into a monument to General Thade. How Thade managed to travel through time and space (and escape from his fate back on the Planet of the Apes) will forever remain a stupid mystery.

Separate but Equal

In his book, *Planet of the Apes as American Myth: Race, Politics, and Popular Culture*, Eric Greene notes, "Culture may…function as an ideological tar baby: the harder we struggle against it, the more entangled in it we may become. Therefore, even in the act of rebelling against the sins of the past, we may replicate them. Even in the midst of radical gestures, there may be reactionary counterstrokes." Broyles and Burton have gotten stuck in that tar baby. By rebelling against rampant political correctness, *POTA* 2001 is a reactionary counterstroke, demonstrating an attitude toward racial equality that falls somewhere prior to Brown vs. the Board of Education, Topeka, KS.

In the original *Apes* films, parodied racist phrases ("all men look alike to most Apes") serve to signal audiences that human culture is being critiqued. In Quick's novelization, when the orangutan Limbo finds himself at the mercy of his former captives, he "frantically tried to remember what sort of blasphemous, moronic drivel he'd heard." He begins spouting very familiar phrases, such as "separate but equal," and "to each his own!" In Burton's film, Limbo rounds out his insincere speech with "can't we all just get along?" This farcical use of Rodney King's plea to end the violence during the Los Angeles riots is appalling.

Greene writes, "An *Apes* story geared to the challenges and struggles of the nineties and early twenty-first century will look both like and unlike the Apes stories used to address the sixties and seventies… Both consistency and innovation will be required for the Apes mythology to register and respond to the way things have changed and the way they have stayed the same. This is the way mythology stays fresh and relevant."

POTA 2001 is not fresh. The only relevancy present springs from its ultra-conservative attitude. There may be some irony in casting Charleton Heston as Thade's father and giving the outspoken National Rifle Association representative a few lines of anti-gun dialogue (why the Oberon crew had twentieth-century pistols remains unknown). Far more striking is that a crucial plot point of *POTA* 2001 comes from the inability of the Apes to swim. Regardless of the ape's nautical abilities, this feels like an open play upon a widely held stereotype that African Americans cannot tread water.

Discussing the as-yet-unmade *POTA* 2001, Greene prophetically states, "Regardless of who eventually creates the new *Apes* project, or projects, the filmmakers will inherit a mythology that, if used imaginatively and intelligently, provides an open field upon which they may play with a variety of artistic, thematic, and political possibilities… The confluence of the political and cultural trends of the last several years has made the time right for a new Apes film. Our public mythologies, no less than our personal ones, are developed to address deep problems and concerns."

There was no intelligence and little imagination in the creation of *POTA* 2001. Rather, there was an overly strong reliance on special effects and cinematic advances in makeup. Knowing full well the ramifications of the original *Planet of the Apes* films makes the transgressions of those behind *POTA* 2001 all the more abhorrent.

Portions of this article ran in *Cashiers du Cinemart* #10 & #13.

Brandon Routh in dingy Superman duds

SUPERMAN: GROUNDED

By Mike White

Until 2006, Krypton's most famous son, Superman, hadn't officially graced the silver screen since the dismal *Superman IV: The Quest for Peace* in 1987. This fourth chapter seemed to successfully hammer home the final nail in the coffin of the doomed film series.

Superman's greatest enemy, it appears, was neither Lex Luthor nor any of the other superfoes he's faced over the years. Rather, Superman suffered most at the hands of his producers. Even from the first *Superman* film in 1978, *Superman: The Movie*, there were problems. In an effort to cut costs, director Richard Donner shot the first film and its sequel at the same time. In fact, the film's famous ending—in which Superman reverses time—was supposed to be his way of defeating the villains from *Superman II*.

While I used to think that *Superman II* was the best of the bunch, a re-appraisal of this work proves that it's a mess. More than the loss of Marlon Brando (whose legal wranglings kept his completed footage, and voice, from being in the sequel at the time), *Superman II* suffered from needless rewrites, a tinny re-orchestration of the John Williams theme by Ken Thorne, and embarrassing scenes starring Gene Hackman's body double (and poorly imitated voice).

Father-and-son team Alexander and Ilya Salkind drove the *Superman* story into the ground with the horrific third chapter of the series. Kicking a franchise when it was down, even more damage was done by schlockmeister cousins Menahem Golan and Yoram Globus, when they purchased the rights to *Superman* in 1987 to produce *Superman IV: The Quest for Peace*. Allegedly, Golan and Globus used less than half of their budget on *Superman IV*, reinvesting the rest into other film projects. The duo removed such costly items as plot and special effects, leaving a hollow shell of a film. There's no guarantee that *Superman IV* could be any better, but the original running time is said to have been closer to 140 minutes, not the 90 minutes most audiences saw in theaters. More likely, a longer running time would have just prolonged the agony.

Not content with the destruction they had wrought, Golan/Globus were prepared to unleash a fifth *Superman* film with hack-for-hire Albert Pyun at the helm, until financial troubles left them bereft of the rights. When the rights reverted to the Salkinds, they continued to strip-mine Superman with the *Superboy* television show. The Salkinds commissioned *Superboy* writing partners Mark Jones and Cary Bates to write a prequel. *Superman V: The New Movie* had Superman doing battle in the bottled city of Kandor against his rival Brainiac. While researching the article, I contacted Mark Jones in hopes of reviewing this script. He told me that Cary Bates was the only person with access to the *Superman V* script, but that Bates had fallen off the face of the Earth in recent years.

With the Salkinds' spotty Superman track record, it's probably for the best that *Superman V* died on the vine. *Superman V* and *Superboy* became casualties of the 1993 buyout of the Superman rights by Warner Brothers Studio. This event was to usher in a new era of *Superman* films…or so everyone thought.

The Life and Death of Superman

In the comic books, Superman died in 1993 at the hands of the 250,000-year-old creature Doomsday. It's easy to guess that Superman may have been down, but not out—he was quickly resurrected. This entire death and renewal story arc garnered massive media coverage and would have been perfect fodder for an immediate cinematic adaptation. Warner Brothers tapped producer Jon Peters to bring this to fruition. Rather than concentrating on the "renewal" aspect, it seems that Peters has worked hard at killing Superman ever since.

Horror stories about Jon Peters abound in *Hit and Run: How Jon Peters and Peter Guber took Sony for a Ride in Hollywood*, by Nancy Griffin and Kim Masters. The authors paint Peters as a man who speaks with his fists and various things below the waist (usually either his dick or his pocketbook). A hairdresser-cum-Lothario, Peters used to claim that *Shampoo* was based on his life. He went from styling hair to producing hits when he met and bedded Barbra Streisand. Making his mark with *A Star Is Born* (1976), Peters quickly climbed through the Hollywood ranks with his unique blend of bravado and bullying.

Though Peters had a hand in producing Tim Burton's *Batman* (1989), the film was a success more in spite of him rather than because of him. When he was given the task of bringing Superman back to the silver screen, Peters wanted to give the Man of Steel a makeover. No more "faggy" blue and red suit, no more "overgrown Boy Scout" mentality; Peters wanted a darker and meaner Superman. To that end, Peters chewed through screenwriters at the average rate of one writer and script each year after the WB takeover of *Superman*. Apart from a few successful television ventures (*Lois & Clark: The New Adventures of Superman*, *Smallville*, and several cartoon incarnations), *Superman* couldn't break free of the phantom zone of development, imprisoned by Jon Peters.

These are the incarnations that *Superman* could have taken.

Superman Reborn
(Jonathan Lemkin, circa 1994)
Superman battles Doomsday, only to die by the end of the first act. Lois has been mysteriously impregnated with Superman's spirit. Their hastily gestated heir grows at an incredible rate to adulthood (think *Starman*). Of course, he saves the world from destruction in this campy, stillborn first effort.

Superman Reborn
(Gregory Poirer, December 20, 1995)
Brainiac, credited here as the creator of Doomsday, has infused his creature with Kryptonite blood. Meanwhile, on Earth, Superman tries to deal with being an alien in love with a human woman, via psychiatric help.

Dead by page 23, Superman's corpse is stolen by an alien, Cadmus. A Brainiac victim, Cadmus becomes Superman's sifu after resurrecting him on page 32. His own body deteriorating, Brainiac seeks Superman's body as the perfect corporeal vessel. The baddie threatens the people of Metropolis to aid in the search (along with lame criminals Parasite and Silver Banshee).

Powerless, Superman wears a robotic suit that mimics his old powers until he can learn to use them again on his own (according to the script, they're a mental discipline called "Phin-yar"—not to be confused with "The Force"). Bad guys are defeated and Superman feels at home by the end of Poirer's script.

Superman Lives
(Kevin Smith, March 27, 1997)
It was a fanboy's dream that quickly became a nightmare. Kevin Smith's cornball script suffers from Peters-imposed ideas (polar bears guarding the Fortress of Solitude, a giant spider) and cheesy Smith dialogue.

>   **CLARK**
> I know it sounds silly -- where do I get off
> complaining? He -- the guy who's faster than
> a speeding bullet, more powerful than a
> locomotive... what's the last one?
>
>   **LOIS**
> Something about tall buildings.

This time Superman stays alive until page 38, where he's again defeated by Doomsday. Superman's demise is aided by the lack of sunlight—the result of a merger between Lex Luthor and Brainiac. Their sun blockage isn't as creative as the way Mr. Burns did it on *The Simpsons*, but it's evil nevertheless. Superman is resurrected by Kryptonian robot, The Eradicator, which has lain

Superman: Grounded

dormant at the Fortress of Solitude. (The Eradicator made an appearance in the "Superman: Exile" comic arc as an ancient mystical Kryptonian relic).

Rather than Superman's lifeless body, Brainiac wishes to possess The Eradicator and its technology. Powerless (again), the resurrected Superman (back by page 50) is sheathed in armor (The Eradicator becomes his protective suit) until his powers return, courtesy of some sunbeams. Evil is vanquished and Brainiac's annoying robot lackey, L-Ron, has a pithy closing remark.

Around the time that Smith's script reached completion, Peters continued to act as the architect in Superman's destruction by hiring Tim Burton to direct the new *Superman* film. For a hot second it seemed like a Smith/Burton/Cage *Superman* would really happen. Warner Brothers even had a poster made up for the February 1997 Toy Fair with a silver Superman logo on a field of black with the simple statement "Coming 1998" emblazoned across the bottom.

Had Burton's *Superman* been made, it's certain that the stranger in a strange land aspect of Kal-El on Earth would have been played to the hilt. Burton scrapped Smith's script and brought in Wesley Strick to rework the puzzle pieces (Brainiac, Luthor, Doomsday, etc.). Smith's tales of Peters woe would become part of his stand up routine.

Meanwhile, Burton was trying to cast his film:

Superman	Nicolas Cage (or Ralph Fiennes)
Lois Lane	Cameron Diaz
Jimmy Olsen	Chris Rock
Lex Luthor	Kevin Spacey
Doomsday	Hulk Hogan
Brainiac	Tim Allen (or Jim Carrey)
Batman	Michael Keaton (cameo)
K (formerly The Eradicator)	Jack Nicholson (voice)

During this period of time, there was a flurry of activity. Strick's script was in, until Warner Brothers nixed it. A string of new writers followed:

Superman Reborn
(Wesley Strick, circa 1997/1998)
Going back to some of Poirer's ideas, Strick's script is said to have included Silver Banshee and Parasite as lesser villains again. Strick's version of *Superman* was darker, much to Burton's delight.

Superman: The Man of Steel
(Alex Ford, 9/4/98)
While Hollywood tried to get Superman to straighten up and fly right, fans weren't taking this silver screen hiatus lying down. The better-known fan scripts floating around the internet included *Superman: Last Man of Krypton* by T.J. Grech, *Superman* by Matt Fisher, *Superman Firestorm* by David B. Samuels, and *Superman: The Man of Steel* by Alex Ford. The story of Ford and his script is almost a Hollywood tale in itself. Alex Ford wrote this alternative *Superman* script and, after being encouraged by his wife, he connected with the right people to get it read. He even managed a meeting with Peters and additional *Superman* producer Lorenzo DiBonaventura. Feeling like a work of fan fiction, Ford's script sets up a longer series of films that will include more villains than just Luthor, Brainiac, and Doomsday. Like too many Hollywood stories, Ford's work was rejected and he was given a "don't call us, we'll call you" farewell.

Lexiac fights his way into the Fortress of Solitude

Superman Lives
(Dan Gilroy, 9/20/98)
A pastiche of the previous scripts' lesser elements, Gilroy's draft has Brainiac on the hunt for Kal-El after having destroyed Krypton. Like Smith's draft, we don't see Superman fly—merely hearing a "whoosh" and a blur of color, as would be done a few years later in *Smallville*. When Brainiac reaches Earth, he "merges" with Lex Luthor to form Lexiac (à la Alan Moore's *Superman* story, *Whatever Happened to the Man of Tomorrow?*). He dispatches with Superman by page 61 via the Kryptonite-blooded Doomsday (shades of Poirer).

Typical of the other drafts, it's only a matter of ten to twelve minutes (page 72) before the Man of Steel is resurrected. The Kryptonian device, The Eradicator, goes by "K" in this script. Again, K sheaths Superman and provides him with power as he heals. The majority of the script seems to be Lexiac chatting with Luthor's slimy lawyer, Morris. Meanwhile, Superman goes on a bit of a spiritual journey as he learns to accept his role on Earth in order to regain his powers (page 101). Superman has some horrible lines as he fights Brainiac ("You've been recalled!"), and if Smith's painfully self-reflexive "more powerful than a locomotive" line was bad, Gilroy surpasses this with the old "It's a bird! It's a plane! It's Superman!" on the final page.

Superman: Grounded

It wasn't long after this that Tim Burton was reluctantly fired by Warner Brothers. The reluctance came, no doubt, from Burton's play-or-pay contract, which netted him a significant amount of cash for doing nothing more than wasting time.

After Burton sought greener pastures in *Sleepy Hollow*, Peters approached a number of directors, such as Michael Bay, Shekhar Kapur, and Martin Campbell. They all turned him down, apparently because of Gilroy's lame script. This draft was finally canned and William Wisher was brought in to start anew.

Superman Lives
(William Wisher, 8/23/2000)

In the myriad articles documenting the winding road that *Superman* followed to reach the big screen in 2006, Wisher's script is often described as being influenced by *The Matrix*. Allow me to put that notion to bed. Apart from some Lex Luthor-created wireless internet technology people can wear on their necks, there's no hint of anything remotely similar to *The Matrix* in Wisher's work. The "Lexmen" are a cadre of drones that act like The Matrix "agents" and manage to slow down the Man of Steel for a hot second.

If anything, Wisher's script was a return to the roots of the *Superman* project, resembling the aforementioned Lemkin, Poirer, and Gilroy works. Kal-El, one of the scant few survivors of Krypton, is pursued by his father's creation, Brainiac. He's discovered on Earth just after he's had a fight with Lois Lane about how uncomfortable he feels being an alien among humans. Lex Luthor allies himself with Brainiac in exchange for technology that gives life to his ill-fated "Lexlink" program.

Again, Brainiac employs Doomsday to kill Kal-El by page 60. His body is taken by Mal-ar, last Knight of Krypton, who swore to protect the infant prince before Krypton's King Jor-El was murdered by Brainiac, prior to the destruction of Krypton. Like Jesus, Superman is resurrected after "about three days" (page 79). Waking up a weakling, Kal-El wears a suit of "Krypton Armor": a sleek black outfit that gives him enhanced abilities. Doomsday doesn't have a second shot at Superman—he disappears from the script after he's served his purpose. Rather, Superman easily cuts his way through the Braniac-controlled "Lexmen" with a crystal sword, looking like "a samurai from outer space" (page 98). While Lex Luthor tries to redeem himself as a human being before Earth explodes (Brainiac has a habit of destroying planets), Superman battles Brainiac in a rather anticlimactic scene wherein he regains his powers and, very un-Superman-like, kills the baddie while destroying his talking "skull ship."

Again, wearing black and attacking the Luthor Building doesn't really make Wisher's *Superman Lives* anything like *The Matrix*, either. Oliver Stone was approached at this point to direct Wisher's script, but he didn't take the bait. It was time, too, for Nicholas Cage to cash in his chips after years of practicing wardrobe changes in Tom Jones's phone booth. The new choice for

Superman went to Russell Crowe. With Wisher's moody Superman, Crowe may have been a good choice. The Aussie actor wasn't interested. No director, no stars, and a script that took the project back six years. The wind had gone out of Superman's cape.

Superman Destruction
(Paul Attanasio, 6/27/2001)
There's little known about Attanasio's work on the *Superman* project. Some reports have him utilizing a treatment by DC comics writer Keith Giffen with Superman battling the stellar bad guy Lobo, while others have him turning in a 50-page treatment of his own that rehashes the death/resurrection plot line yet again.

While the Peters-plagued *Superman* project labored on for years, the *Batman* franchise sputtered under the direction of Joel Schumacher. Batman wasn't being killed off in the comics. Instead, he was being recast in *Batman: Year One* in Frank Miller's seminal tome. Miller reinvigorated *Batman*. A movie was said to be quick to follow. By 2002, Wolfgang Peterson was on track to bring *Batman vs. Superman* to the screen. This was to be followed by the long-delayed Peters project, set to be directed by McG.

Asylum
(Andrew Kevin Walker, Revised by Akiva Goldsmith 6/21/02)
When you're a kid, you pit people against each other in imaginary fights. "Who would win: Johnny Socko's Giant Robot or Ultraman?" One of the classic match-ups has to be Batman versus Superman. Now that may sound like a one-sided fight; the man of steel versus the man in a bat suit. How could a mere mortal best Krypton's favorite son? Read Frank Miller's *The Dark Night Returns* to witness this superior throw-down. The question is, why would these two beacons of justice ever face off?

In Andrew Kevin Walker's *Asylum* (also known as *Batman vs. Superman*), Lex Luthor drives a wedge between the champions of Gotham and Metropolis via an elaborate plot that involves cloning The Joker and giving Bruce Wayne the perfect mate, only to take her away. Through his machinations, Batman's desire for revenge comes in direct opposition of Superman's dogmatic protection of his human charges. Simply, Batman wants to murder The Joker and Superman won't let him. The two come to blows in an epic battle that involves a lot of Kryptonite and millions of dollars in property damage.

While the showdown between the caped crusaders wears out its welcome after twenty pages, the rest of the script is incredibly engaging and typical of Andrew Kevin Walker's style. Yet, as is the case with Walker, his best work is often rewritten (*Sleepy Hollow, 8mm*, etc).

Superman: Grounded

Superman: The Man of Steel
(J.J. Abrams, 7/26/02)

If fanboys were excited about Kevin Smith, they were beside themselves with J.J. Abrams. He was on top of the world with TV's *Alias*, and the fervor over his involvement with *Superman* might have been topped only if Joss Whedon has volunteered to pen a script. The height of expectations was only equaled by the depths of disappointment when Abrams script was trashed by the hacks at the *Ain't It Cool News* website.

Also known as *Superman: Flyby*, the Abrams story was a revisionist tale with Krypton besieged by civil war between its King, Jor-El, and his upstart brother, Kata-Zor. The baby Kal-El is sent to Earth partly as a safety measure when Kata-Zor's forces trash the Krypton capital, and also in hopes that he'll fulfill a prophecy to return to Krypton as its savior. When Kal-El arrives on Earth, he's adopted by Martha and Jonathan Kent. When they discover his powers, they try their best to have Kal-El/Clark suppress his abilities. In the process, they make him neurotic.

Isolated, persecuted, and thinking he's the devil's spawn, Clark meets a spitfire young lady named Lois Lane in college. An undeclared senior, he's impressed by her pre-freshman ambition to major in journalism and work in Metropolis at *The Daily Planet*. Creepily, he decides to do the same thing (this "Superman as stalker" theme would be explored in a later incarnation). When he meets up with her again, she remembers him only as the guy who had his zipper down.

Lois doesn't give Clark the time of day. She's more concerned with exposing and humiliating the government agency that's wasting untold time and resources trying to prove the presence of alien beings on Earth. The hard-as-nails beuraucrat in charge of this alien-hunting squad is none other than Agent Lex Luthor. Sporting a brush cut and a massive attitude, Luthor has quite an axe to grind about aliens—so much so that he blows his top at a Congressman and gets canned.

Apart from the framing device of the script that starts out with Superman down and nearly out (a similar frame would be employed in the Abrams-penned *Mission: Impossible 3*), we don't see Superman until nearly an hour into the film. This scene of Superman saving Lois Lane as she's aboard Air Force One interviewing the President is something of a nod to *Superman: The Movie*, in which Superman saves Lois as she's on her way to interview the President. The scene and its aftermath—Superman setting down the saved airplane in a very public place (here, Boston Common)—also finds its roots in the John Byrne-penned *Superman: The Man of Steel* comic series. An amalgamation of these scenes would be found later in *Superman Returns*.

(I'm glad that the President's plane didn't crash. Otherwise, we might find Lois Lane on a mysterious island pursued by a smoke monster for a few years.)

This first appearance of Superman isn't followed up by the montage of him going on a crime-fighting spree. Rather, Clark Kent is so pent-up about his role as Superman that he swears to never wear the costume again. This changes when he learns that Jonathan Kent (who up and died upon hearing the news of his son saving the President) would have wanted him to take the mantle of power and embrace his role as Superman.

News travels pretty fast. Really fast, apparently, as the radio and television waves from Earth reach Krypton in record time. This brings Kata-Zor's son, Ty-Zor, and three other badass Kryptonians to Earth. To say that this brings about a lot of scenes reminiscent of *Superman II* is an understatement.

Again, Superman is defeated and killed. There's a funeral, but the Man of Steel isn't down and out for long. He's visited in death by Jor-El (who committed hara-kiri back on Krypton) and resurrected. With the help of some Kryptonite-fueled weapons, Superman defeats the four known Kryptonians, as well as the secret-lurking Kryptonian, Lex Luthor, before this first chapter of a proposed series is over. There are mentions of characters either slightly seen or unseen in the screenplay, and Superman's messianic return to Krypton is set to happen in the next film.

The changes to the *Superman* mythos infuriated fanboys, who forget that Kryptonite didn't exist until the Siegel and Schuster story was translated to radio. This kind of re-imagining happens all the time in the superhero world; sometimes successfully (*Batman: Begins*), and sometimes not (*Catwoman*). For all of the problems I had with the script, it was something new and not simply a recycling of the old, good ideas from the original *Superman* series.

Wolfgang Peterson stepped out and let *Batman vs. Superman* die in favor of *Troy*. Before the dust could settle, J.J. Abrams delivered his take on the Superman tale to Warner Brothers and everyone was elated, with the possible exceptions of McG and apoplectic *Superman* fans. McG left to direct the sequel to *Charlie's Angels*, and the ever-obnoxious Brett Ratner had his turn in the director's chair.

Ratner hadn't even had time to warm up his seat when the backlash against the Abrams script swelled into a shitstorm. When the opportunity presented itself, the *Rush Hour* auteur fled the sinking Peters ship. Oddly enough, Ratner would go on to direct the third film in the *X-Men* series while its former helmer, Bryan Singer, would defect to the *Superman* camp.

Superman Returns
(Michael Dougherty & Dan Harris, 9/27/2005)
With his super-heroic clout, director Bryan Singer managed to break away from most of the tenets laid down by producer Jon Peters. Gone were Brainiac, Doomsday, and the black suit. Still present was Superman's pathos, a near death, and the red and blue "whooshing" suit (albeit a fairly dingy one).

Superman: Grounded

Singer's *X2* screenwriters Michael Dougherty and Dan Harris made *Superman Returns* a continuation of the Superman story line from the Richard Donner films or, at least, *Superman: The Movie*. There may be no mention of General Zod, Non, or Ursa, but it's apparent that Lois Lane bedded the Man of Steel. The product of their Fortress of Solitude union, Jason, spends the majority of the story as an asthmatic, bespectacled weakling, except for one head-scratching, contrived moment.

The victim of an elaborate ruse, Superman returns to where Krypton ought to be, only to find a deadly meteor field of Kryptonite. He manages to escape and get back to his adopted planet Earth five years after he departed. Instead of finding out how he got tricked and/or looking up his long-time nemesis, Lex Luthor, Superman hangs out in Smallville. Then he goes looking for Lex Luthor, right? Wrong. He goes back to Metropolis to learn that Lois Lane has moved on from Superman, even winning a Pulitzer for her piece "Why the World Doesn't Need Superman." Ouch! Then he doggedly pursues the only man who's come close to defeating Krypton's favorite son… wait, no. He doesn't.

Even after Jimmy Olsen, in his infinite wisdom, suggests, "Why don't you guys track down Lex Luthor?" on page 73, the greatest criminal mind of our time is swept to the wayside. This leaves a lot more time for Superman to mope around and retread dialogue from *Superman: The Movie*. Meanwhile, Lex Luthor seems to be in his own film and pursuing a plot with earmarks of his ideas from *Superman: The Movie* and *Superman II*, only in reverse order. Luthor makes his way to The Fortress of Solitude before revealing his elaborate real estate scheme, paraphrasing his lines from the earlier films along the way, as well. Who came up with this idea—the same guy who thought it'd be smart to build a second Death Star?

Superman finally catches up with Luthor on page 118, and they share all of three pages together in an anticlimactic showdown. Rather than squaring off like Kirk and Khan in *Star Trek II*, Luthor and Superman are more like Hanna and McCauley in *Heat*.

Superman Returns
(Bryan Singer, 2006)

There are few differences between the screenplay of *Superman Returns* and the final theatrical version, except for the lack of explanation in Superman's disappearance and the scenes of Superman flying (in a spaceship) amongst the ruined crags of Kryptonite asteroids.

The cuts between the Superman (Brandon Routh) story line and the Lex Luthor (Kevin Spacey) story line are jarring. The film moves from the moody introspective Kryptonian, who's been dumped by Lois Lane (Kate Bosworth) in favor of the boss's son, Richard White (James Marsden), to the hammy criminal mastermind and his Miss Teschmacher stand-in, Kitty Kowalski (Parker

Posey). The worst character in the film has to be Superman's bastard son, Jason (Tristan Lake Leabu), and his awful Adam Rich haircut.

While I can respect the decision to emulate Donner's *Superman* films, aping these superior movies just made me long to see the originals. The John Williams theme, combined with the unnecessary cameo appearance by Marlon Brando, only reinforced this desire. Overall, I would have rather have seen J.J. Abrams's version of the story, as it strayed the farthest from the Jon Peters directives, divorced itself from Donner, and actually managed to feel like an original take on the *Superman* story.

Even if it hadn't taken over a dozen years and millions of dollars to bring the next chapter of Superman saga to the big screen, *Superman Returns* would epitomize anticlimactic. Rather than breaking new ground or taking the Superman story in a different direction (see *Red Son* by Mark Millar), the film was just a rehash of a better film that predated it by nearly three decades.

Superman: Doomsday
(Lauren Montgomery, Bruce Timm, and Brandon Vietti, 2007)
This is the movie that was promised back in 1993 and, though it's a cartoon, it's far more mature than the Bryan Singer film.

When we first see Superman (Adam Baldwin), he's hanging out at the Fortress of Solitude with Lois Lane (Anne Heche), trying to find a cure for cancer. Though he wants to be more than the Earth's greatest strongman, it's his strength that will save the planet from the marauding Doomsday when the creature shows up for an intense nine-minute battle royale that leaves a crater in Central Park and Superman dead in Lois's arms.

The rest of the story by director Bruce Timm and writer Duane Caprizzi has Lex Luthor (James Marsters) unable to live in a world without Superman. Luthor creates a Superman clone that is without a strong moral compass, but carries a stash of Kryptonite in his head—Luthor's failsafe. The audience first witnesses the new Superman's flawed ethics when he kills the Toy Man (John Di Maggio), beginning a new era in which a Dark Superman sits in judgment of his Earthbound wards.

There are similarities to the comic book story arc, but the movie isn't held captive by the restrictions placed upon previous attempts to bring "Death of Superman" to the screen. While Superman's body is taken to the Fortress of Solitude by a robot servant for some good blasts of "yellow solar energy," the real plot has Jimmy Olsen (Adam Wylie) working as a paparazzi and Lois Lane uncovering the real story about Dark Superman.

There are plenty of clever references to past *Superman* films. The battle with Doomsday recalls Superman fighting Non in *Superman II*, while Superman squaring off against Dark Superman recalls the junkyard battle in *Superman III*. There's even a nod to the Peters-plagued *Superman* attempts, with Kevin Smith making an audio cameo comment about the Toy Man's giant spider transportation: "Like we really needed him to bust up the mechanical spider, right? Lame!"

The only remotely satisfying tale of Superman's death and return, *Superman: Doomsday* fulfilled the promise that had been made and broken repeatedly since 1993.

Superman Flies Again for the Second Time

It's so refreshing when a movie company actually agrees with your opinion and admits that one of its blockbuster hits wasn't quite the right direction that the franchise should have gone. That's the word from Warner Brothers, who pretty much pimped out Bryan Singer on August 22, 2008, saying that *Superman Returns* "didn't quite work as a film in the way that we wanted it to." In other words, it sucked. This could be good news for the next *Superman* film, or it could mean that Warner Brothers will take too many cues from Christopher Nolan's *Batman* films and make Superman the dark, brooding character that Jon Peters and Tim Burton would have had him be back in the early '90s.

The original version of this article ran in *Cashiers du Cinemart* #15.

interviews

Bruce Campbell and his boomstick in *Army of Darkness*

BRUCE CAMPBELL: THE MAN WHO WAS ASH

By Mike White

Born in Royal Oak, Michigan, and raised outside of Birmingham, Michigan, Bruce Campbell has starred in some of the most popular movies ever made: *The Evil Dead* series. Campbell has also been the star of the critically acclaimed television series, *The Adventures of Brisco County Jr.*, as well as directing and starring in the highly rated syndicated show, *Hercules: The Legendary Journeys*.

When he was growing up, Campbell wanted to be either an actor or a cartoonist. He kept a leather case in his closet, filled with everything he could find about these two professions. Campbell has never had any formal acting training, but by the time he was in the first *Evil Dead* he had starred in hundreds of movies for his old chums: "I mainly learned while doing it. I feel, ultimately, that is the most practical way."

Campbell met Sam Raimi in their high school drama class. They also had a radio speech class together, during which they did a weekly Friday morning show for the school on a local radio station. *The Continuing Saga of Captain Nemo* was a radio play done in the vein of the Firesign Theater. In addition, they would play a few songs, and Campbell (as a fan of Harry Chapin, Cat Stevens, and other balladeers) enjoyed messing around with KISS records, putting his finger on the vinyl to slow, and finally stop, the music. At times like this he would make sure that the door to the booth was secure, in the advent of burn-out retribution.

Having already performed in several of Scott Spiegel and Josh Becker movies (two junior high chums he met in study hall), Campbell felt at ease when he began acting in some of Raimi's short Super-8mm movies. Where Spiegel (*Intruder*) made take-offs of Three Stooges, Becker (*Lunatics: A Love Story*) would make movies like *Oedipus Rex*, which Campbell describes as "a heavy drama with subtitles on a chalkboard."

It's a common misconception that Bruce Campbell went to Michigan State University—in reality, he attended Western Michigan University for half a year before dropping out, feeling he had no need for it. He spent a lot of time in East Lansing, though, making movies with Raimi, Becker, and Spiegel. It was during this time that Campbell started doing some professional work. He did a series of commercials, and eventually got his Screen Actor's Guild card doing an industrial film for auto dealers.

Sam Raimi went on to direct all three of the *Evil Dead* movies (the third, *Army of Darkness*, was originally titled *The Medieval Dead*). Raimi and Campbell have one of those director/actor relationships along the lines of Martin Scorcese and Robert De Niro, John Ford and John Wayne, and John Woo and Chow Yun Fat—Campbell has been involved with or starred in nearly all of Raimi's films to date.

Bruce Campbell: The Man Who Was Ash

Evil Dead is low budget and well made, and it got Raimi noticed. The director teamed with *Evil Dead*'s editor, Joel Coen, and his brother, Ethan, to write *The XYZ Murders* (also known as *Broken Hearts and Broken Noses*). Campbell was up for the lead, but the head of production nixed him. "So we beefed up the Heel role. It was a blessing in disguise," meaning that Campbell could avoid being associated with the mess that became *Crimewave*. There were problems with the studio, and even problems with the Detroit police over the movie, which was re-cut before release—and not to the satisfaction of anyone involved; nor to audiences.

Further problems included issues with the Michigan Film Office. There was a meeting between the MFO, an Embassy Pictures rep, Raimi, Campbell, and producer Robert Tapert. The Michigan Film Office told them that the use of Detroit police during filming was free (to control the crowds, block off streets, keep the crew safe, etc.), but at the end of shooting they got a bill for $36,000(!), which they fought, and eventually the MFO conceded that they only needed to pay half.

They attempted to get the remaining $18,000 taken care of by the completion bond holder, but he refused to pay. They then tried to get Embassy to eat it, but Embassy had been at the same meeting, and they outright denied them the funds. "A miscommunication of grand proportions," says Campbell. It never got paid, and for several years they were personas non grata, which is why *Darkman* wasn't shot in Detroit, as originally planned.

After their flop, Raimi and Campbell returned to the woods, with their pal Scott Spiegel in tow, to remake *Evil Dead*—but this time it would be a comedy. Since the original cabin in Morristown, Tennessee had been burned down by squatters, a duplicate of the movie's locale was constructed in Wadesborogh, North Carolina, on the same property where *The Color Purple* was shot.

Evil Dead 2 is one of those movies that has comedy working on every level: from physical gags (at one point, Campbell's hand becomes possessed and tries to kill him), to dramatic irony (after Campbell removes said hand, he puts a bucket over it and weighs it down with a copy of *A Farewell to Arms*), to ingenious and humorous camera movements.

Campbell says of his role, "Ash was the most fun, because I had the most leeway." In *ED2*, Campbell runs the gamut of emotions, from sympathetic doofus to a kick-ass demon killer who, after strapping on a chainsaw to replace his severed hand, has one of the all-time great lines in cinematic history: "Groovy."

After a movie like *Evil Dead 2*, Campbell should have taken Hollywood by storm. Unfortunately, this was not the case. Campbell remained a "low-budget leading man." That's not to say, though, that his roles since then have not been memorable, nor his performances any less stunning.

Campbell may have not been the star of *Darkman*, but he certainly left his mark on the movie. He was involved in a lot of the post-production work, including the sound mix. It was common practice on the *Darkman* set to imitate Liam Neeson's distinctive vocal stylings, and Campbell excelled at this. Instead of calling Neeson back whenever there was an extra line of dialogue needed, Raimi would have Campbell work his magic. Raimi also knew what a fantastic screamer Campbell is and used this to his advantage, having Campbell do all the screams for criminals falling to their deaths.

Bruce Campbell has his moment in the sun with *Darkman*'s final shot. They had shot Neeson too, but Raimi opted to use Campbell as a nod to fans of the *Evil Dead* series. Despite its great "Who is Darkman?" ad campaign, the movie was never quite as successful as it was meant to be, due in part to Raimi's unusual blend of melodrama and comedy.

After *Darkman*'s lack of commercial success, Raimi went back to familiar territory and decided to make the third installment of the *Evil Dead* series. "We looked at each of the movies as if the audience hadn't seen the one before it," said Campbell, explaining the discrepancy between the ending of *Evil Dead 2* and *Army of Darkness*. Of course, *Evil Dead 2* is a remake and not a sequel in the truest sense of the word, because the character of Ash appears to have no recollection that everything has happened to him before.

Army of Darkness was an innocent bystander that suffered almost a year delay because of Dino DeLaurentis's pissing war over the rights to the sequel to *Silence of the Lambs*. During this time, none of DeLaurentis's films were released. *Army* missed its summer date, and was put on the back burner for a few more months. Ultimately, despite Campbell's superb performance, *Army* relied too heavily on Three Stooges-style humor, and looked like it had a lower production value than its predecessors. *Army of Darkness* was fun to watch the first time, but doesn't stand up compared to the other two *Evil Dead*s.

"Who's laughing now?"

After *Crimewave*, the future looked dim for another Coen Brothers and Sam Raimi script called *The Hudsucker Proxy*. Working on *Hudsucker* was, to Bruce Campbell, "a dream." He had been making low-budget movies for over a decade, but now he was involved in a movie being produced by Joel Silver. Finally, Bruce was on a professionally run set. He was used to the chaos and frustration of low-budget movies, where there was little to no time for rehearsing and the crew was always running around like decapitated chickens.

Campbell is a big believer in rehearsing—he feels that it's the best way to reconcile the technical and artistic sides of his profession. There were two solid weeks of rehearsing before shooting began on *The Hudsucker Proxy*, and the Coen Brothers asked Campbell to sit in on all of it and read not only his part, but any other, smaller roles, as well. Doing this, Campbell was able to observe and interact with his co-stars. "Jennifer Jason Leigh is incredible, she's an acting machine," said Campbell. Leigh had memorized all of her extensive dialogue before she even set foot on the set.

Watching *The Hudsucker Proxy*, one realizes how incredible Bruce Campbell really is. The self-taught actor is there alongside such luminaries and seasoned pros as Tim Robbins and Paul Newman, but one would never be able to pick Campbell out as a "low-budget" actor—he's a natural.

It's a sad fact, though, that like *Crimewave*, this second Coen Brothers/Raimi project was doomed to fail. It had a threadbare advertising campaign, was opened in only a few art houses across the country, and had a title most people were afraid to even attempt to say. So instead of being Campbell's salvation, *The Hudsucker Proxy* became Joel Silver's albatross.

Campbell also had a very small role in the Coens' follow-up film, *Fargo*. He can be seen through the snow of a TV screen, in a clip from an old UHF soap opera called *Generations*, which *Fargo*'s antagonists watch in their hideout.

Bruce Campbell really regrets signing any paperwork when he went out to visit Sam Raimi on the set of *The Quick and the Dead* in Tucson, Arizona. Although the role of the priest was written for him, Campbell couldn't be in *Q&D*, since he was starring at that time on Fox's *The Adventures of Brisco County Jr*. It was on one of his few days off from shooting that he decided to visit his old friend while he was shooting his new movie.

Bruce Campbell as Autolycus in *Xena: Warrior Princess*

When Campbell came on the set, Raimi grabbed him and told him he had to be in the next scene. They put him in a costume, put some sores on his lips, messed up his hair, and put him in a scene that was designed only to placate Pat Hingle, who played Horace in the film.

Hingle (*Hang 'Em High, Bloody Mama*) had been pestering Raimi that his character never redeemed himself—Horace remained an emasculated, sniveling dweeb through the whole film, and never got revenge for his daughter's deflowering. It was Campbell's job, then, to go up to the daughter and be a real cad: "Hey darlin', ya wanna do the Devil dance?" Then Hingle came up and threw a headlock on him.

"They never even cut the scene together; if you looked at the footage now it'd still have the slates on it." Yet much to Campbell's chagrin, his name is still in the credits listed as "Wedding Shemp," and he has been badgered with the same question time and again: "Where are you in *The Quick and the Dead*?"

Campbell can be seen, in theory, during one of the gunfights in a shot from about two stories up, but even Bruce has trouble picking himself out of the crowd.

Maybe it was those great screams from *Darkman* that got him hired for *Congo*, because that was almost the entire extent of his role in that film. A lot of people might not remember Campbell in this surprise hit of early '95, since his character was killed off within the first five minutes, but he played quite a crucial role—if not for him, the main character would have never made her expedition.

What first appeared to be a scheduling nightmare soon turned out to be one of the most relaxing shoots Campbell has ever been on. While he's only in the movie for a few minutes, he was on location in Costa Rica for a month, as he was in all the establishing shots. He and the few other guys in the doomed research party would come in and walk by the volcano, then they'd take off as the rest of the cast came in to shoot a bunch of scenes in the same locale for a day, or even a week. He'd have to come back and walk buy a river or whatever, then go back the hotel while the majority of the movie was shot. "I must have taken every river rafting trip around, and would spend a lot of time just taking it easy on the beach."

Along with his television work (*Jack of All Trades*, *Burn Notice*), a series of commercials for Old Spice), he continues to pop up in films in his trademark supporting parts (*Escape from L.A.*), as well as star in vehicles (*The Man with the Screaming Brain*, *Bubba Ho-Tep*, *My Name Is Bruce*). Campbell has also penned two books, including the hilarious *Make Love the Bruce Campbell Way*, with an audio version that reunites the author with long-time collaborator Ted Raimi to create a madcap radio play feel, like a larger-budget *Continuing Saga of Captain Nemo*.

Bruce Campbell is a very busy guy. Despite his hectic schedule, he took time out for an interview with *Cashiers du Cinemart*.

Cashiers du Cinemart: Are there any types of roles you'd like to play?
Bruce Campbell: My dream role would be some kind of tour de force where the character goes through hell and still comes out the other side alive.

CdC: How was it directing *Hercules*?
BC: It was great! The day goes a lot faster as a director, because you are involved in every aspect of the shoot. It was, for me, a natural compilation of everything else I had done.

CdC: How was it doing *American Gothic*?
BC: It was fun to work on because it was so weird. Not the usual bland TV stuff.

CdC: Any good rabid fan stories? Do you get people coming up to you and bugging you to say "Groovy"?
BC: One guy took pictures of my rented house. I was warned about him over the internet.

CdC: What is your favorite movie?
BC: *Bridge on the River Kwai*.

CdC: If you weren't acting, what would you be doing?
BC: Teaching or a forest ranger.

CdC: How was it working with Anthony Hickox (*Sundown*, *Waxwork 2*)? How did you hook up with him?
BC: It was fun with him because he gave me a lot of creative rope to hang myself. He contacted me after he saw *Evil Dead 2*.

CdC: What do you do in your spare time?
BC: Write, backpack, hang with my wife [she was the costume designer on *Mindwarp*], Ida, and my kids, Rebecca and Andy.

CdC: Do you feel you've been "Hollywoodized" since you made the move? Have you ever had a fight with an old friend, where they got to use the "Man, you've *changed*!" line?
BC: Hollywoodized? I'm doing an interview for your cheap rag, aren't I?

The original version of this article ran in *Cashiers du Cinemart* #5.

MONTE HELLMAN: THE INTERVIEW

By Mike White

Long time readers of *Cashiers du Cinemart* might recall my fondness for the works of Monte Hellman. In the past I've reviewed *Cockfighter*, *Two Lane Blacktop*, *Iguana*, and *Flight to Fury*, and I was elated to get the chance to interview him.

Hellman's work is starting to get the recognition it deserves from a new generation of critics and cinephiles.

Cashiers du Cinemart: How did you get your start in film?
Monte Hellman: Roger Corman had been one of the backers of my theatre company, where I directed *Waiting for Godot*, among others, and offered me *Beast from Haunted Cave* when I lost my lease on my theatre. I had always planned to go into film, and was four years into my eight-year apprenticeship as a film editor. (It wasn't necessary to work continuously in the Editor's Guild, just put in eight years from the time you joined.)

CdC: Who would you consider your influences, or who influenced your decision to be a filmmaker?
MH: I think my two strongest influences were John Huston and Carol Reed. I wanted to make films like *The Asphalt Jungle*, *Treasure of the Sierra Madre*, *Fallen Idol*, *Odd Man Out*, and *Outcast of the Islands*. I had studied film as a graduate student at UCLA after I was a theatre undergraduate at Stanford. At UCLA I saw many classic films, and was also strongly influenced by Griffith (*Broken Blossoms*) and Pudovkin (*Storm over Asia*). I was also influenced by Lewis Milestone (*A Walk in the Sun*), but I think the film that most made me want to direct was George Stevens's *A Place in the Sun*, to which I paid homage in *Cockfighter*. I was also influenced by Rivette's *Paris Belongs to Us*.

CdC: My first exposure to your work was *Flight to Fury*. I was impressed with the shot of the old Japanese man flailing around in the bathroom to demonstrate the airplane's engine trouble. Can you tell me what inspired you to use a peripheral character in that way?
MH: It never occurred to us to begin the sequence with a shot of an engine smoking. I wanted to show a sudden and violent jolt, and doing it from the POV of a secondary character seemed like a good idea.

Monte Hellman: The Interview

CdC: How was it shooting *Flight to Fury* back-to-back with *Backdoor to Hell*?
MH: I was editing *Backdoor* at night while I was shooting *Flight*, getting by on three hours sleep. It's the madness of a young man. In general, shooting two three-week movies back-to-back is not much different than shooting a seven- or eight-week single picture. It's more difficult when, as was the case with *Backdoor* and *Flight*, the locations are hundreds of miles apart, and you can't scout both pictures before starting to shoot the first.

CdC: What was your favorite film to shoot?
MH: The most fun I ever had on a shoot was *China 9 Liberty 37*. We were in a great location in the south of Spain, had a fabulous cast and crew (the Italian camera crew cooked pasta for the company every night), and I had a great rapport with DP Giuseppi Rotunno, who has a great sense of humor. And of course I was working with Warren Oates and Fabio Testi, two of the best friends of my life.

The worst shoot was *Iguana*. Again a great location, great food, a fabulous cast and crew, but it was spoiled by a stupid, neurotic producer who couldn't spend money until the last minute (when it was usually too late). Nothing was prepared in advance. We didn't have lights until three weeks into the shoot; essential props frequently didn't arrive until late in the day. Lunch took over two hours because the restaurant could only seat us in two shifts. There were many days when we only were able to shoot for one or two hours. I was in a constant state of anger. But I wound up liking the film a lot.

Warren Oates in *Cockfighter*

CdC: What films are you most and least proud of, and why?
MH: I don't like to show *Beast from Haunted Cave* any more, mostly because it's such primitive work on my part, and the story is silly at best. I find something to like in most of the others, with perhaps *Two Lane*, *Iguana*, *Silent Night*, and *The Shooting* my favorites, and *Cockfighter* one of my least favorites, only because I was not able to do as much work on the script as I would have liked.

CdC: How was it working with Charles Willeford? Was there any discussion of directing any more of his novels?
MH: I didn't work with Willeford on the script. In fact, I hired Earl (Mac) Rauch to re-write many sequences, particularly the ones involving the love story. Charles became an actor in the film at the last minute, when I fired the actor set to play his role the night before shooting was to begin, and had the

idea to read Charles because he was there. I enjoyed working with him as an actor. I was unaware of his later novels until he became a cult writer.

CdC: Do you prefer shooting something you've written, or adapting another person's work?
MH: All the scripts I've worked on as a writer have been adaptations. As a director, it doesn't matter whether the original material was a book or written directly for the screen. In the end, I do a final polish on every script and make it my own.

CdC: You have a reputation of being a "hired gun" when it comes to taking over shoots for other directors. Can you provide some examples?
MH: Between *Two Lane* and *Cockfighter*, I directed about half (all the scenes with European actors) of a film called *Shatter* in Hong Kong. Between *Cockfighter* and *China 9*, I directed half of a TV episode of a series called *Baretta*, and I finished a film called *The Greatest* for deceased director Tom Gries.

After *China 9*, I took over for another deceased director, Mark Robson, on a film called *Avalanche Express*. I shot about 10% of the principal photography, shot all the special effects, and supervised the post production. Then I was hired to direct several pictures that didn't get made, including *Dark Passion*, which I'm finally getting to do, *King of White Lady* for Francis Coppola, *Falling* for Mike Gruskoff, and a film about out-of-body experience for Martin Poll.

CdC: I was curious about the way *Cockfighter* was shot. Were the fights filmed first, with the shots prior done with similar-looking chickens?
MH: Each sequence was filmed chronologically. The fights were all fixed, so we knew which chicken would win. The hardest thing was to get the chickens to walk away from the fight. I seem to recall that we were just lucky on that one.

CdC: This film was re-cut and retitled several times. What was different about the re-cuts?
MH: The re-cut eliminated the porch scene with Mary Elizabeth (one of my favorites) and added several dream sequences of tits-and-ass and car explosions, supposedly to justify their use in trailers. This cut was variously titled *Born to Kill* or *Gamblin' Man*. Any version titled *Cockfighter* is my original cut.

CdC: I recall reading that Lewis Teague was involved in shooting some of *Cockfighter*. Is that true?
MH: I don't recall whether Lewis shot any footage. Roger got someone to shoot some added blood (spattering on shoes, etc.). It's possible that Lewis shot some added extreme close-ups of cocks fighting, since those are the sequences he edited. I edited all non-fight scenes. Someone shot the scene of the man eating chicken at the last cockfight, because I didn't.

CdC: You have a very unique editing style (at least when cutting your own pictures). What do you look for in a shot? What is your rule as far as pacing?
MH: My editing style is unique because I place performance first, regardless of the type of shot. So each scene comes out differently, because at any given moment I'll be on the shot that has the best performance.

CdC: How do you deal with your actors? I was really impressed by the acting in *Beast from Haunted Cave*. It might have been a totally different picture with different performances.
MH: The first thing I do is choose good actors who are suited to the role. This is 90% of directing actors. The second thing I do is give them lots of love, and win their trust. I make them believe (because it's true) that I'm looking out for them, that I will protect them, and that I will never let them look bad. Once they believe that, they'll be free to try things because they know if it doesn't work, I'll shoot it again.

CdC: How did you meet Warren Oates and Sam Peckinpah? Both you and he got such great performances out of Oates.
MH: I met Warren Oates casually beforehand, but essentially became friends during the filming of *The Shooting*. I met Peckinpah while editing *Killer Elite*.

CdC: How did you and Jack Nicholson meet?
MH: We met in the late '50s, when I had a theatre company in L.A. that became a magnet for young actors. We became friends when we worked together on *The Wild Ride* in the summer of 1960. He was the star; I was associate producer and editor.

CdC: What is your opinion of Nicholson as an actor?
MH: I think Jack is a great actor, as does much of the world. I don't think we've always seen great performances, as he is clever enough to give the audience what it wants to see often enough to maintain his position as a movie star.

CdC: As a writer?
MH: I have only experienced him as a writer twice. Both times I thought he gave me good material for the job at hand, and I was able to shoot both scripts with very little modification on my part. I had the advantage, however, of working with him on a day-to-day basis. I would characterize him as a good craftsman, as I would characterize myself. I don't think either of us have the natural brilliance of, say, a Charles Eastman. But Charles requires much more re-working and editing for my purposes.

CdC: I've heard that you and Nicholson wrote a script that was never produced.
MH: We wrote a screenplay called *Epitaph* just before we went to the Philippines [to shoot *Backdoor to Hell* and *Flight to Fury*]. We had an agreement with Roger Corman to finance it but when we came back, Roger had changed his

mind (he thought an abortion story was too "European") and hired us to do *The Shooting* and *Ride in the Whirlwind* instead.

CdC: Do you still maintain contact with Nicholson?
MH: I talk to Jack every few months, and see him about once a year.

CdC: Why wasn't he in your later films?
MH: I have not been able to afford Jack since he became a superstar.

CdC: How was it working with James Taylor and Dennis Wilson on *Two Lane Blacktop*?
MH: James and Dennis were very easy to work with, with James being especially conscientious and professional. In general, they were as easy as most actors (and easier than some temperamental actors).

CdC: What was the size of the crew on that shoot?
MH: We had a somewhat smaller-than-normal crew, by special arrangement with the unions for a low-budget picture, but it was still a fairly large company—35 or 40 on the crew. We still had big vans to move the equipment, props, etc.

CdC: Did you actually shoot on the road, or were all locations in one general area?
MH: We travelled and shot in sequence, starting in Los Angeles and ending up in North Carolina.

CdC: What was your involvement in *The Terror*—I've read of four separate people having their hands in directing that film.
MH: Roger directed for two days on a set left over from a previous production, and without a proper script. He hired Francis Coppola to write a script and finish the picture. After five weeks of shooting, Roger fired Francis, and hired me to finish the picture. Jack Hill was hired to write a new script with me. A lot of what Francis shot was thrown out, except for the stuff with the witch from *The Wizard of Oz* (Dorothy Newman), and I finished the picture in five days of shooting. All of  the interiors are Roger's (with the exception of Francis's witch's lair), and most of the exteriors are mine. To the best of my recollection, and contrary to legend, Jack Nicholson did not direct any of the film.

Monte Hellman: The Interview

CdC: What do you do between projects?
MH: I'm always working on a project (90% of the effort goes into getting a film made, 10% goes into making it). My only holidays are working vacations, usually a film festival I'm invited to. My main hobby is also work related: computing. I'm constantly going on the internet to update my software, etc. I also like travelling with my wife and two grown kids (and dogs whenever possible).

CdC: What was your involvement in the shooting of *Robocop*?
MH: I shot all the second unit in Dallas, which included the van chase, Robocop driving around the city, Robocop going through his old house, parts of the new robot shooting up the conference room, the man going through the plate glass window, etc.

CdC: How did you get involved in producing *Reservoir Dogs*?
MH: Someone sent me the script with the idea of me directing it. I liked it, and met with Quentin. The day we met he sold *True Romance*, so he told me he now could hold out to direct *Reservoir* himself. I was so impressed with Quentin personally, I offered to help get *Reservoir* made. The rest, as they say, is history.

CdC: Are there any more plans to work with Tarantino?
MH: Quentin and I are now planning three pictures, two for me to direct that he would executive produce, and one that I would executive produce for him.

CdC: What's your opinion of the controversy surrounding him in regards to his plagiarism of other films?
MH: Shakespeare "borrowed" most of his plots from other sources.

The original version of this article ran in *Cashiers du Cinemart #7*.

THE RETURN OF *CAPTAIN MILKSHAKE*

By Mike White

There was a time in my youth when it seemed that every week brought another Vietnam movie. There seemed to be a glut of Vietnam tales after the successful release of *Platoon*—*Full Metal Jacket*, *Gardens of Stone*, etc. Like all film genres, war films come in waves (witness the recent releases of *Black Hawk Down*, *Hart's War*, *We Were Soldiers*, *Behind Enemy Lines*). However, mainstream films dealing with the Vietnam War had only a few better offerings of any merit before *Platoon*—*Apocalypse Now*, *Coming Home*, and *The Deer Hunter* come to mind.

Certainly, there were smaller films that dealt with Vietnam, but most of them (along with the aforementioned) were released after the U.S. pulled its troops out of Southeast Asia. The rare film dealt with the war in a non-exploitative manner while it was happening. Richard Crawford directed *Captain Milkshake* six years before the official end of the war, when the fighting was at a fever pitch.

The film stars Geoff Gage as Paul Fredericks, a fresh-faced Marine back from Vietnam on family leave to attend his stepfather's funeral. While he's back, Paul meets Thesp (David Korn) and Melissa (Andrea Cagan), two socially minded hippies who live in a groovy pad with several other cats and chicks. Paul falls for Melissa in a big way. However, their divergent views on the War, along with Thesp's obstreperous banter, put their relationship in peril.

Throughout *Captain Milkshake*, the audience sees Paul struggling to survive in suburbia. He's constantly reminded of events from his tour of duty, which come to light in the form of quick flashbacks that pepper the film. Despite identification with Paul, he remains something of an enigma due to his naïveté. His attitude contrasts well with the starry-eyed idealism of his new chums. None of the characters has ownership on truth, and their flaws make them interesting.

The Return of *Captain Milkshake*

More than being a pioneer Vietnam film, *Captain Milkshake* is a progenitor of counter-culture films. The open drug use, free love, and motorcycle scenes anticipated those of Dennis Hopper's *Easy Rider* by months. Likewise, Crawford employed several avant-garde stylistic devices that would be unusual even in today's cinema. Most notably, Crawford shot the film in color and black & white. For the most part, scenes of Paul in Vietnam, or when his life becomes more intense, are in color. Meanwhile, his life back in the United States is usually monochromatic.

Captain Milkshake was a casualty of a war between Crawford and his distributor. After playing for a few weeks, the film disappeared. It remained a faint memory until nearly thirty years later, when it played at Slam Dunk in Park City, UT. Since then, Crawford's screened it at a few other venues and has spent a great deal of effort trying to locate any remaining prints of the original fifty struck.

The film, while not perfect, remains a forgotten treasure of U.S. cinema. Cinephiles should not mourn the loss of *Captain Milkshake*—the film is available via Crawford's website, captainmilkshake.com.

***Cashiers du Cinemart*: Why the title?**
Richard Crawford: You balance aesthetics with commercialism. I wanted a title that would break through the conservative newspapers, and that kids who saw the title would know that this was not their average Hollywood movie. At that time, all the rock groups were bearing names like "Surrealistic Pillow" or "Vanilla Fudge." In other words, you wouldn't want to have named the thing *A Rose for Paul*.

I thought the imagery was appropriate. This kid was a straight arrow whose father and uncle had been in the military. He pretty much bought the country line that he was going over to Vietnam to save the world from communism. So, even though we didn't explain it in the picture, he was so all-American that he was something like a milkshake. Plus, people would react to the title. They'd try to figure out what the hell it meant and it got people's attention.

Director Richard Crawford

I'm not the kind of person who believes in making an "important film." My job is to entertain people. Let's leave "important" to somebody else. What I make may turn out to be "important film" by giving people insight as to what was going on during that time, but I never set out to make something grandiose. After all, it's all show business.

CdC: What's your background?
RC: I worked for General Dynamics and did film reports on the space

program. I did a lot of writing and directing about the progress of the Mercury and Apollo programs, as well as intercontinental ballistic missile development. That was my first real job out of college. It was a great opportunity. I got to have all this beautiful, expensive equipment that the government paid for, and I would stay around nights and weekends and learn the craft. Within a month or so, I was filming half-hour reports for the Air Force, which was wonderful training as a filmmaker; you've got to learn how to compress time, use music, and so on.

I got out of that and started doing national commercial work for Ford, Kodak, and other companies. Then I got to the point where I had been in the business for ten years and said, "You know what? I want to make a feature film." Everybody reaches that point that's been a filmmaker. And then the quest was to try do something legitimate and trying to find someone to finance it.

I didn't know where to start to raise money and I didn't want to wait around anymore, so I went to the Coronado Yacht Club. I stood on the dock and looked for the biggest boat I could find. I knocked on the side of it and told the guy that came out that I was looking to finance a movie. "You either have money or know someone who does," I said.

After he told me that I had a lot of nerve, he invited me up for a drink, introduced me to some of his buddies and started me on that trail of chasing money. I couldn't get anyone who wanted to make a legitimate picture. They all wanted to make "tits and ass" pictures, and I resisted that for a long time. When I couldn't raise the money I said, "Okay, I'll do a T&A movie." I had a friend who was dating the star of Russ Meyer's *Vixen*, and I got her signed to a picture called *The Teaser*. The guy who was backing it had done some business in pornographic bookstores and was very keen on the idea. I told him that if we were going to do a T&A movie that we should do it in 3-D, and be the very first 3-D T&A movie.

I got everything in place, but my conscience was bothering me that there was no alternative cinema and it was time to do something for the "youth market." Kids were looking for something relative to sex, drugs, and rock & roll, and not another Doris Day movie. I kept feeling that if someone could do a breakthrough movie like that it'd be thematically correct, but it'd also be a great financial idea.

I went to my backer and told him that I understood that he really wanted to do this, but that I had heard that X-rated movies were coming to market and, if that happened, no one would want to see his T&A movie. I told him that we could still use 3-D and make a picture for the youth market. Admittedly, it was all pretty crazy to come to him like that at the last minute, but he gave me four weeks to come up with a script or the whole deal would be off.

I locked myself away in a room with a friend of mine, Barry Leichtling. He knew the "hippie scene" in San Diego. We lived there, having our girlfriends bring us food, and typing pages. We walked into my backer's office four weeks later, plopped this thing on his lap, and called him on it. In the meantime, he had gone around and talked to a lot of people who told him that what I was saying was true; it was time for some kind of youth cinema. We wanted to capture that "head market," those kids that were lining up for the second half of Stanley Kubrick's *2001*.

CdC: What was the political/social atmosphere at the time of *Captain Milkshake*'s release?

RC: It's difficult to imagine a time when the Vietnam War was kept under wraps. We weren't supposed to know too much about it. The idea was to keep people living at Disneyland and not let them think about the war. The Military-Industrial Complex had its purpose of protecting Shell Oil, rubber plantations, and other big corporate interests over there. But it's hard to get Mom and Dad to send their kids overseas to help the rich guys keep their stuff. So, the idea was that this was just a little "police action" and that we were sending over people to be "military advisors."

All of a sudden, these body bags started showing up. In a conservative town like San Diego, the parents were shocked that their kids were coming back dead. There was such a good cover-up of it that no one wanted to hear the truth about it. If you said anything contrary about the war at all, you were deemed an insurrectionist and told to either "love it or leave it." I thought that people should at least see both sides of the story before they go jumping into it.

CdC: How did you manage to get such big-name music acts to lend their talents to the film?

RC: Steve Miller, Country Joe and the Fish, and some of these other bands weren't very well known at the time. They were still "San Francisco groups." In order to get permission to use their music in my film, I had to show them a cut before it was released. That's a tough thing as a filmmaker with a low budget, because if they don't like it, you have to take it out.

The only place I could find to show a 35mm screening in San Francisco was a little company called Zoetrope Studios. When I came into this place, there was some guy upstairs just screaming his head off at some secretary. Turns out it was Francis Ford Coppola; he was having a bad day or something.

I brought in Steve Miller and these guys and ran the film for them. They were knocked out by the movie. Steve told me, "I've got to tell you how much I appreciate the way you used my music. I'm so used to playing smoky bars that to see my music being played while people are outside and being playful was great. You have my blessing." Meanwhile, Francis had seen the screening and told me, "You've got a lot of guts to be making a movie about Vietnam. I thought that maybe someday I'd like to make a movie about Vietnam."

Francis and I talked about shooting *Captain Milkshake*, about the 3-D process and all that. He told me how he was trying to get his funding together for *The Conversation*. I was sitting in his office with him and he keeps getting these phone calls from Paramount. He was angry as hell on the phone and said, "Goddamn it, just because I'm Italian doesn't mean I know about gangsters! Mario Puzo can't write for shit! I hate his book and I don't want to do any goddamn mafia movie!" Then he'd slam the phone down and ten minutes later he'd get another call from Paramount.

Between these frantic phone calls, we talked about Francis possibly distributing *Captain Milkshake*. He was just putting Zoetrope together and wanted to distribute my film with *The Conversation*, when that was finished. About this time, this kid comes into the room with film draped around his neck and said, "Francis, I'm trying to cut this scene together with Bob Duvall. I can't get this close-up. What do you think I should do with it?" So, Francis gave him a couple pointers, and it turns out that this kid is George Lucas, and he's cutting *THX-1138*. I had no idea what I was in the middle of.

I came back two weeks later to talk to Francis and he said, "Richard, I've decided to do this mafia movie. They made me an offer I can't refuse. I need the money to finish *The Conversation* and they offered me so much that I'm going to do it."

CdC: Why the mix of color and b&w film?
RC: I was really struck by how the guys I had talked with who had come back from Vietnam were so shell-shocked. Most of them had left from an Iowa farm and within 21 hours they were thrown into a jungle where there were a bunch of guys crawling around in tunnels killing them. The shock of that shifted reality was so incredible that when they came back to the States, they had a hard time adjusting to the kind of "La-La Disneyland" lifestyle.

The other world was so unreal. As a reality, it was hyper-real. I felt that there had to be some way, cinematically, to show that the Vietnam reality was a more intense reality than this life back here. So, I thought I could use color as an effect, rather than making the whole movie in color. I'd let it be the contrast, the super-reality. So anything in Vietnam—or in the protagonist's life as he becomes more alive—that reality would be in color to make it all the more intense.

That's also when I thought that I'd never seen 3-D used aesthetically, to heighten an image or to isolate it from a flat background. I thought, "Wouldn't it be fun to use 3-D in a way other than just poking spears at the audiences' face?" What could be better than to flash to Vietnam and have it in 3-D and in color, then go back to the kind of bland, black & white American landscape? I got a lot of criticism for my mixing of color and black & white. At that time, it wasn't done except for,

Andrea Cagan as Melissa

The Return of *Captain Milkshake*

say, *The Wizard of Oz*. I had a lot of people giving me grief when the movie came out for various reasons, but a few told me, "It's too bad you ran out of money, kid, and couldn't make the whole thing in color."

CdC: Did you use the standard red/blue 3-D, or were other three-dimensional processes available?
RC: We used polarized filters. That was the next step up from red/blue. It still provided 3-D without affecting the color. However, it never was released in 3-D. That was the plan, but our backer listened to a lot of old projectionists and old farts out in L.A. who complained about how difficult it is to run 3-D and how it would ruin our prints. They didn't want to have to work harder and just wanted to start the movie and read their newspaper. I tried to tell my backer that if we could do this in just the major markets—Dallas, Detroit, L.A.—we could promote the heck out of it and every stony kid in America would want to see this amazing film. But, in the end, when it came down to making the prints of the film, he wouldn't give up the additional money for the 3-D processing. This was after we had to build our own camera rigs for 3-D because they didn't exist at that time. It was so frustrating that we had done so much but the backer wouldn't give us the extra $25K for 3-D. It would have been killer.

Crawford consults with Cagan

CdC: Is it just me, or do the protesters, especially their leader, come off as unsympathetic?
RC: That's part of the reality of that time. I tried to not be too empathetic with anybody. I showed Melissa as kind of a rich kid who was out slumming. There was a lot of that going on: kids getting dirty and grungy so their parents would be upset.

But I modeled Thesp after Jerry Rubin and Abbie Hoffman, who would just be so obnoxious that the press couldn't ignore them. The problem was that the press wouldn't give them any coverage for their protests or marches, so they became so outrageous that they would get the coverage they wanted. I tried to do this with the scene where Thesp demonstrates the "nerve gas" that the protesters are going to use. Maybe I missed the mark by not making him sympathetic, but I didn't want to glorify the hippies or glorify the soldiers. Both sides are human; both have their foibles.

CdC: How was the film received?
RC: It was amazing! Young people just lined up! When we opened in San Diego it was booked for three weeks solid. We sold every ticket. Part of that was

from shooting in San Diego, so we could take advantage of that for promotion. But when the film played other theaters around the country, it was being held over in several theaters. They were double-billing it at the drive-in circuit. The distributors were testing it in the southern market to see if the southerners would stand for it. They couldn't afford to lose their southern market. If they could only play it in the north, they couldn't make as much money.

CdC: What happened after the film was released?
RC: It opened against *Zabriskie Point*, *Joe*, and a couple other Hollywood movies, and it was out-grossing them. I thought, "Wow, we're off to a good start here." And that's when the backer decided that he had a picture that was going to make him a lot of money, and he set out to steal it from me.

It was a classic Hollywood situation. The minute the film looked like it was going to go, then it all moved into legal maneuvering on his part to try to arrest the picture from me and take control of it. He was pretty successful, and this is where I started to get the education they don't teach you at school. It turned out to be a nearly three-year legal battle and I learned a lot of hard lessons. I finally got to the point where I got so frustrated and was so broke that I had to just let go of the picture.

CdC: So what did you do after that?
RC: I ran away to the carnival. It turned out to be a great way to travel around the country and make money. So, I'd do that in the summer, then I'd come back in the winter and do film; commercials or corporate film work.

CdC: What's the state of developments with the film?
RC: I ran *Captain Milkshake* out in Park City a few years ago at Slam Dunk. I got to see that there are a lot of bad pictures being made by inexperienced filmmakers. I hung around with one of the committees from Sundance, and they discussed how disappointed they were with the quality of work from young filmmakers because they all seemed to be kind of college-oriented, without solid stories. I realized that there are a lot of older, experienced filmmakers with stories people will pay to see.

The original version of this article ran in *Cashiers du Cinemart* #13.

The Doctor will see you now

STILL DEMENTED AFTER ALL THESE YEARS: DR. DEMENTO

By Skizz Cyzyk

In the late '60s, disc jockey Barry Hansen got an idea to slip some records from his own collection into his set. Having been an avid fan and collector of many styles of music, Hansen recognized that many bands of the day, like The Beatles, The Rolling Stones, and Led Zeppelin, were covering old R&B songs that most of their fans had never heard. He figured it would be a hoot to play the original versions while everyone else was still playing the more popular cover versions. Interspersed, he would throw in novelty records, such as "The Purple People Eater" and "Does Your Chewing Gum Lose Its Flavor (On the Bedpost Overnight)?" The request line began lighting up and the novelty records quickly became the more popular staples of his show. In 1970, a fellow disc jockey overheard someone describe Hansen as demented for playing Nervous Norvus's "Transfusion" on the air, and thus was born "Dr. Demento." A nationally syndicated radio program quickly followed and thirty years later, the good doctor is still at it, turning young and old audiences alike on to some of the greatest comedy recordings ever made.

Skizz Cyzyk: When you first started, did you have any idea you'd still be doing this thirty years later?
Dr. Demento: No. When I did the first *Dr. Demento Show*, I wasn't even sure I'd be doing one the next week.

SC: And now you have this CD out, *DEMENTIA 2000: The 30th Anniversary Collection*. This is the third collection, isn't it?
DD: It's the third in this series. There was a *20th Anniversary Collection* and a *25th*. Before that there was a single CD and various LPs.

SC: There are so many great songs on this 30th Anniversary CD, but reading the liner notes, you keep mentioning all these other amazing songs. Meanwhile I'm thinking, "Oh yeah, I remember that song," and then you mention that they're on the other anniversary collections, making me think, "Oh man, I gotta go out and get all the other collections now."
DD: Well, we never want to duplicate the earlier ones on the anniversary series.

SC: Any chance there'll ever be a box set of all of them?
DD: It's been talked about.

SC: Over the thirty years, what sort of changes have you noticed in the funny music business?

Still Demented After All These Years: Dr. Demento

DD: Thirty years worth of new stuff has come out. When I started the show, I was playing for an audience of people who had, in many cases, grown up with their parents' Spike Jones records. Now much of my audience barely knows who Cheech & Chong are, and Spike Jones is ancient history. But that doesn't stop me from playing Spike's work fairly often.

SC: I have to admit when I was little I didn't know who Spike Jones was, but I was a huge fan of Cheech & Chong, much to my parents disapproval. But it was your show that turned me on to Spike Jones, who I still love today. It was probably your show where I first heard Ogden Edsl's "Kinko the Clown," too.
DD: Probably so.

SC: Have you had to tone down the material over the years because of the whole politically correct movement?
DD: Oh, there are a few cases of that. "Kinko the Clown" is still on the playlist once in awhile.

SC: Is it? Wow. I used to get tons of complaints for playing that on college radio ten years ago.
DD: Well, I may get more complaints about that than any other song. Outside of that, probably the one I get the most complaints about is "Dead Puppies," by the same artists.

SC: That one? That's hysterical!
DD: Right. That's also our number two most-requested song of all time, right after [Barnes & Barnes's] "Fish Heads," so you can't please everybody. I guess examples of things that I used to play that now you aren't too likely to hear would be, uh, "gay-baiting" humor that was really big in the '70s. Some examples of that are "Big Bruce" (which was actually late '60s), "CB Savage," and "The Ballad of Ben Gay." Those are the sort of the changes I've come to; to realize that those are hurtful to people and they probably just aren't as funny as they used to be. Of course, in the years past, before I even started my show, humor that made fun of black people was extremely popular. *Amos & Andy*, for instance. So times change.

SC: Do you still actively seek out material, or are you just bombarded with submissions? I would imagine that the people making "Demento material" would know enough to send it to you.
DD: I get a lot of it in the mail, but I still do some shopping. I still go to thrift shops, though maybe not quite as often as I used to. And I'll still pick up reissues that come out on CD, and the occasional new comedy album that comes out from one of the major labels.

SC: How much of the stuff that's sent to you do you end up turning down or not using?
DD: Oh, I try to add, on the average, three to four things per week that I've never played before. And we get, oh, fifteen or twenty CDs and tapes every week.

SC: So when you get new stuff, what sort of things are you looking for, and what sort of things make you say, "No, absolutely not"?
DD: I try to stay objective. If I think it's entertaining, then it gets considered. If it bores me, then it probably won't. Of course, I look at other things too. I mean, I may enjoy a piece of music a lot, but somehow feel it isn't quite right for the show.

SC: Something like The Vestibules' "Bulbous Bouffant," if someone had sent that to me, I wouldn't know what to make of it. I mean, personally, it's the sort of thing I would love, but I'd wonder whether other people would get it.
DD: That original album has like 28 tracks on it, and that one's down towards the end. But I'd heard the group before. They'd sent me tapes, so it was an album that I certainly listened to carefully, making sure I heard it all. That particular track, I just heard it and said, "Well, that's different!" It kind of reminds me a little bit, in its pacing, of a couple other things that I play, but I thought I'd take a chance with it. I never thought it would become as popular as it did. I thought there were maybe three or four other things on that CD that were just as strong, but that's the one that caught on. I think it's because it goes a little beyond just being comedy. The hypnotic wordplay just kind of generates a little aura of its own.

SC: It kind of starts off sounding like a Bert & Ernie skit from *Sesame Street*, and then goes way out in left field from there.
DD: I think when I first heard it, the first thing I thought of was The Frantics, a Canadian group from the '80s. Their stuff is still very popular on the show. They did a sketch about two guys waiting in line to buy tickets at a bus station, and the delivery is kind of similar. That was the first thing it reminded me of, but then it went on to an entirely different place.

SC: Are there a lot of particular favorites that you love that just never seem to get requested; that you sort of wish you could get more people to like?
DD: Well, we really don't get that many calls for Spike Jones anymore. There are a few diehards. Or anything from before the rock era, there's a few diehards, but I still love to put that stuff on. The calls tend to be dominated by fans of Weird Al Yankovic and some of the other relatively young people that I play, which is normal; times change.

Still Demented After All These Years: Dr. Demento

SC: You get a lot of credit for being the person who put Weird Al on the map. Are there any other artists from over the years that you thought were really going to make it big and it just didn't happen?

DD: Well, nobody really is in Al's class. He's in a class by himself. So with the others, I'm just happy with the success that they have. I can't think of anybody right off hand who has really disappointed me. I mean, there are good people who put out albums that may be not as good as the previous one; that happens of course. It happens with the best of them. I'd rather not put the finger on anybody, but rather relish the ones who've had some success.

SC: One last question and I'm sure you get asked this all the time…but if you could be any vegetable, which one would it be?

DD: Oh, let's see…maybe I'd be the plant in *The Little Shop of Horrors*—does that count? I mean, I'd rather eat than be eaten, I suppose.

SC: Well, doctor, thanks for talking with me, and thanks for thirty years of very enjoyable entertainment. I hope you have another thirty in you.

DD: My pleasure. I feel pretty good about it and hope that I do. I'll do the show as long as I can lift a CD onto the turntable or whatever form of delivery and storage that we're going to have in the future.

The original version of this article ran in *Cashiers du Cinemart* #12.

OFF THE RECORD WITH JAMES ELLROY

By Mike White

I interviewed James Ellroy while on tour for his book *The Cold Six Thousand* on a beautiful spring day in Ann Arbor, Michigan. The author frequently had me turn off my cassette recorder to make comments about his rocky relationship with Hollywood. I've left the breaks in place.

Cashiers du Cinemart: I just downloaded your eNovel, *Breakneck Pace*. In it you talk a bit about your younger years—
James Ellroy: So, you know the story.

CdC: I've read *My Dark Places*—
JE: Then you know the story.

CdC: So, what's in *Breakneck Pace* is a continuation of what's in *My Dark Places*?
JE: No. Listen, I don't give a shit about ePublishing. Somebody gave me five thousand bucks to compile these things for that, but that will not prevent me from collecting [the stories] into a regular book. ePublishing will go bust. People want to go into a bookstore and pick up a book.

What it is: I wrote a piece and I elaborated on *My Dark Places* about breaking into houses to sniff women's undergarments. That's it. It's called "My Life as a Creep" and it's just a memoir piece. That's one of the four (sic). And I think there's a Danny Getchell short story in there, the third Danny Getchell short story, "The Trouble I Cause." There's a piece I wrote about the "scandal magazines" in the fifties called "I've Got the Goods" and [two others—"Blood Sport" and "Grave Doubt"].

CdC: How did you get into writing?
JE: I just started. Summer of '76, I was caddying at a country club and I had a story that started building in my head for growing up around Western Avenue like I did, my love of classical music, obsession with the Black Dahlia murder case, an alcoholic buddy of mine, my relationship with him, and it co-opted a famous L.A. crime. Or, you might want to call it "semi-famous"—the Club Mecca firebombing of April, 1957. Some lowlifes got ejected from a bar for rude behavior. Came back and torched it; Molotov cocktailed it.

I put it all into an outline in the fall of '78, and I didn't start the writing of the text because I was afraid that I'd fail. The following January, just a few months later, I started writing the book and never looked back.

CdC: You've had no formal writing training?
JE: No.

Off the Record with James Ellroy

CdC: Just wrote from the hip?
JE: Yeah.

CdC: That book ended up being *Brown's Requiem*. What did you think of the movie version of that?
JE: I don't... Turn it off.
>>CLICK<<

>>CLICK<<
JE: *Brown's Requiem* was the autobiographical first novel and *Clandestine* is the autobiographical second novel, because it's a fictional reconstruction of my mother's murder.

CdC: From there you went on to the Lloyd Hopkins books and then returned to the Dudley Smith character.
JE: He does not appear in *The Black Dahlia*. He returns in *The Big Nowhere*.

CdC: James Woods has been in two adaptations of your work: *Cop* and the "Since I Don't Have You" episode of *Fallen Angels*. Have you talked with Woods much?
JE: I met him once for two seconds on the set of *Cop*.

CdC: What did you think of the adaptation of that, *Cop*?
>>CLICK<<

>>CLICK<<
CdC: Can you tell me about *L.A. Sheriff's Homicide*?
JE: They filmed two versions of it; two pilots. They're shelved somewhere. I do this kind of film work between books for money. I hope they never get made because if they do get made they're made imperfectly under the best circumstances, and they'll be completely fucked up otherwise.

CdC: Any movement on *The Night Watchman* at all?
JE: No. And *77*—the thing I'm writing for Paramount—is never going to get made.

CdC: And *Plague Season*?
JE: *Plague Season* was written out from underneath me. They're filming it right now [as *Dark Blue*]. I retained a story credit but gave up the screenplay credit.

CdC: I've read the screenplay for that and it seems to be more of your writing than someone else's.
JE: Not one line of my dialog is in there. I created the characters and it was largely extrapolated by [David Ayer].

CdC: I've read screenplays for *The Big Nowhere* and *The Black Dahlia*. Any hope for those?
JE: Look, here's the take any sane person has. There'll never be another good movie made from one of my books. I got lucky; lightning in a bottle. I got lucky on *L.A. Confidential*; it'll never happen again. Anybody who gets involved in this whole thing is crazy. I would never criticize a bad adaptation of one of my books because nobody forced me to take the money.

CdC: How about *My Dark Places*?
JE: It's in development and it'll never get made. If it happens, it happens.

CdC: Is there anyone in particular you'd like to see playing you?
JE: No.

CdC: Sorry to keep harping on these movies but it's kind of my "thing," you know?
JE: No problem. It's a standard answer.

CdC: There's an early draft of *Blood Moon* floating around—
JE: *L.A. Deathtrip*.

CdC: How and why were changes made to that?
JE: In the end, L.A. blows—I mean, it was a completely uncontrolled work on my part, and I needed to get back to basics and relearn how to write a book. It was just an indulgent bullshit manuscript.

CdC: You've never gotten into any hot water with using real-life people as characters?
JE: If somebody's dead you can say whatever you want to about them in any capacity, fictionally. Everybody's dead. They're all dead.

CdC: How much research do you have to do?
JE: I make most of it up. I hired researchers for *American Tabloid* and *The Cold Six Thousand*. They created fact sheets and chronologies for me so that I could just extrapolate off of established fact.

CdC: When you sit down to write something like *American Tabloid*, do you think, "This is going to be the first of three books or four books?"
JE: I decided that *American Tabloid* would be the first book in a trilogy two-thirds of the way through writing the text.

CdC: You've been synonymous with Los Angeles for years, but now you're living in Kansas City.
JE: I made a conscious decision after I finished the four "L.A. Quartet" books that I would write no more books set in L.A. Nor would I write any more books that could be categorized as mysteries, thrillers, or policiers. It's all historical novels from here on out.

CdC: I notice that a lot of the killers in your novels have homosexual tendencies. Is there anything to that?
JE: Just for the pure shock value.

CdC: That I know of, you've had two documentaries made about you.
JE: Five.

CdC: Five?
JE: *Demon Dog*, an Austrian documentary; a British documentary called *White Jazz*; a French documentary directed by Benoit Cohen for the *Great Writers of the Twentieth Century* TV series in France [also known as *L.A. Confidences* —Ed.]; an *E! True Hollywood Story*; and then this recent one.

CdC: How does that feel to be scrutinized so much?
JE: It's wonderful. The best of them all is the new one, *James Ellroy's Feast of Death*, which is directed by Vikram Jayanti, who co-produced *When We Were Kings* (Leon Gast, 1996).

CdC: *Feast* showed on the BBC and you're also touring with it?
JE: It won't be here tonight at Angell Hall but at some of the book gigs, yeah.

The original version of this article ran in Cashiers du Cinemart #15.

TALES OF GUY MADDIN

By Mike White

Guy Maddin lives in the twenty-first century, near the windswept Icelandic shores of Manitoba's Lake Winnipeg. Maddin's films, however, live in the first few decades of the twentieth century, in a mountainous land outside of Prussia. Maddin's films hearken back to the primordial days of cinema. He shot his first feature, *Tales from the Gimli Hospital*, primarily as a silent film. Described by Maddin as "a tone poem in tribute to ambient crackle," *Gimli* is a beautiful tale of rivalry and pestilence.

Maddin's most accomplished works recall fleeting movie moments. Though made in 1990, *Archangel*, Maddin's second feature, falls neatly into place with films made circa 1929, during the trepidatious transition between silent films and talkies. Like Alfred Hitchcock's *Blackmail*, Maddin's *Archangel* employs its sound subjectively. Characters' voices hover before their lips, aiding in the creation of a world of unreality, perfectly suited to a story populated with amnesiacs.

Archangel tells the stories of Boles (Kyle McCulloch) and Danchak (Sarah Neville), war-torn lovers in the Hun-infested titular town. The characters become increasingly obsessed and forgetful in this moody movie chock full of ironic, dark humor. The inhabitants of *Archangel* have a tenuous grasp on their sanity; likewise, the film teeters between silence and sound, as if the soundtrack might flutter away.

Maddin's subsequent film straddles the crevasse between the monochromatic and harshly hued realm of color cinema. Peppered with tinted black & white stock, Maddin shot the majority of *Careful* in archaic two-strip Technicolor—a process notably used in Chester M. Franklin's 1922 work, *The Toll of the Sea*. Painted with a limited palette, *Careful* can be at once muted and garish. Sweaty, anxious faces shot through lenses smeared with petroleum jelly bare red hues that flutter about their faces.

In the mountain village that is the setting for *Careful*, the constant peril of burial under an avalanche makes residents wary to speak above a whisper. In an attempt to deter obstreperous livestock, the villagers' animals have their vocal cords slit. Now, if only those noisy geese would go away! Living under this burden of silence, the local folk have odd aspirations. Grigorss (Maddin regular McCulloch), the hero of *Careful*, wants nothing more than to successfully complete butler school and serve under the village patriarch, Count Knotkers (Paul Cox). Meanwhile, his brother Johann (Brent Neale) flunks out and, just when it looks like he might be destined to share space in the attic with his shut-in brother Franz (Vince Rimmer), the love of his mother (Gosia Dobrowolska) saves Johann from Franz's haunted fate.

Tales of Guy Maddin

Despite its incest, self-mutilation, and Melvillean dialogue, *Careful* ranks as Maddin's most accessible work that showcases his anachronistic style. Years after *Careful*, Maddin directed *Twilight of the Ice Nymphs*, a film that strayed from his venerable cinema. Shot in 35mm with a cast of familiar faces, *Ice Nymphs* shares Maddin's twisted humor but moves at a sluggish pace, as if bloated by lavish craft services. Despite Maddin's tangible unease about the project (witnessed in Noam Gonick's behind-the-scenes documentary, *Waiting for Twilight*), *Ice Nymphs* should count among Maddin's successes.

Beautifully filmed in a lavish soap factory-cum-movie studio, *Ice Nymphs* has a mood somewhere between a fairy tale and myth. Nigel Whitmey stars as Peter, an ex-con returning to his home—an ostrich farm run by his sister, Amelia (Shelly Duvall), and the crazed handyman, Cain Ball (Frank Gorshin). Along the way, he falls for the evanescent Juliana (Pascale Bussières). Peter longs for Juliana while bedding down with the sylvan Zephyr (Alice Krige). If *Twilight of the Ice Nymphs* lacks the outright experimental use of stock or sound, it shares several motifs with Maddin's other work. More than the eccentric dialogue, lush cinematography, and infirmed characters, *Ice Nymphs* feels as though it comes from another era.

Twilight of the Ice Nymphs came about five years after *Careful*. In the meantime, Maddin shot several shorts and worked on an unrealized project, *The Dikemaster's Daughter*. The aborted film, coupled with a shoot Maddin considered too "big budget," soured the director for a while. It wouldn't be until the end of the twentieth century that Maddin would find his filmic footing again.

Maddin was one of several Canadian filmmakers invited to participate in the 25th anniversary of the Toronto International Film Festival by creating a "prelude" piece to celebrate the festival and, moreover, cinema itself. In Maddin's case, it wasn't so much "film" that he reveled in but "kino." With *Heart of the World*, Maddin rejects all that he found distasteful about his larger budget work. Here, the plucky director returned to cinematic basics—shooting on Super 8mm Tri-X stock. The film is without spoken dialogue, relying on a handful of title cards, a driving score, and fantastic editing. Maddin found inspiration for his short in the fervent era of early Russian cinema. His five-minute piece would make Eisenstein and Kuleshov proud, with its intense editing and daring cinematography. *Heart of the World* reintroduced Maddin to the delight of filmmaking, and stood out as the most loving display of cinema in decades.

Careful

Maddin's follow-up feature proved that he was back on track and playing in the realm of silent, black & white cinema. With its manic editing style and ballet sequences, *Dracula: Pages from a Virgin's Diary* resembles Maddin's *Tales from the Gimli Hospital* in terms of its technology, but displays a maturity far removed from the director's initial cinematic efforts.

Subsequently, Maddin began in earnest a group of semi-fictional autobiographical pictures starting with the nickelodeon art installation, *Cowards Bend the Knee*. This hockey–hairdressing film noir combines Maddin's "favorite aspects of the Greek tragedy *Electra* with some stuff from the French penny-dreadful *The Hands of Orlac*... I've made it as autobiographical as possible, setting all of the action in my two childhood homes: The Winnipeg Arena and our family-run beauty salon." Told in ten chapters, this silent film plays upon themes of voyeurism in its torrid and outlandish narrative.

The Guy Maddin "character" would appear again in *Brand upon the Brain*, "a remembrance in twelve chapters." Erik Steffen Maahs plays Maddin returning to his childhood home—an orphanage his parents ran on a remote island; a gothic setting if ever there was one. Much of the tale is told in flashback, recalling the early days of young Guy (Sullivan Brown) and his Sis (Maya Lawson), who both experience crushes on teen detectives Chance and Wendy Hale (Katherine E. Scharhon). They're embroiled in a mystery surrounding Guy and Sis's parents and the immoral experiments being performed on the orphans. This brooding tale of misbegotten love and overbearing parents is told in split-second edits, cutting in the occasional flash of color into the beautiful black & white. At various times and locations, *Brand upon the Brain* has been narrated by the likes of Isabella Rosselini, Crispin Glover, and Eli Wallach. Scored with live music and foley, the film becomes a cinematic event that morphs into something quite different for home viewers.

My Winnipeg

"Maddin" also appears in the love poem to the director's childhood home in *My Winnipeg*. The film brings together a fanciful past, present, and future. Repeated words and phrases form a hypnotic cadence as Maddin's cinematic stand-in (Darcy Fehr) chugs through the snowy darkness. "Winnipeg, Winnipeg, Winnipeg," is the chant, rising and falling like the locomotive drone of the night train carrying its somnambulistic fares through Manitoba's premiere city.

Winnipeg: heart of the heart of Canada; the place that raised Maddin. Here the director explores the structural arteries of his hometown and revisits the history of himself and his city. Narrated by the filmmaker, the prose of the film (courtesy of long-time Maddin crony George Toles) is an overwrought poem of maniacal hyperbole and enthusiastic linguistic gymnastics—a perfect pitch for the fractured visuals of Maddin's multimedia pastiche. Looking like a daguerreotype picture postcard of this snowbound wonderland, *My Winnipeg* typifies Maddin's mad genius, and captures his sordid relationship with his home.

In the midst of this Maddin-mania, the auteur created a tongue-in-cheek social satire and musical melodrama merges in the expressionistic *The Saddest Music in the World*. The biting cold of winter and the Great Depression have turned 1933 Winnipeg into the most melancholy place on Earth. As a marketing ploy, legless beer baroness Lady Port-Huntley (Isabella Rossellini) stages an international competition to find the saddest music in the world. With $25,000 going to the winner, oddball musicians and two-bit schemers pour into the Canadian town. Among them is smarmy, down-on-his-luck Broadway impresario Chester Kent (Mark McKinney), returning home with his amnesiac girlfriend, Narcissa (Maria de Medeiros). As the contest progresses, Chester finds himself competing against his estranged brother, while also re-igniting a past love triangle involving himself, the baroness, and his own alcoholic, ex-surgeon father. Complicating matters further are the secret identity of Narcissa, and the elder Kent's gift to the baroness—a pair of beer-filled, glass prosthetic legs. Spectacular musical numbers alone can't save the sad characters from fate, and ultimately tragedy strikes as the last note is sounded.

Maddin's signature archaic visual look, his unique sense of humor, and his subplots- and triangles-driven storytelling are all displayed here in abundance. Rather than spotlighting a single romantic triangle, a pair of interlocked trios buttresses this momentous melodrama. Played with wondrous flair, Chester revels in the fact that he's stolen the hearts of the former lovers of his emasculated father and brother. Playing with some of his favorite themes (rival brothers, amnesia, a missing parent) and embracing the trappings of the musical, Maddin has succeeded in creating an accessible, artful, and ambitious film.

***Cashiers du Cinemart*:** Your love of film—at least from the primitive days of filmmaking—is obvious. How much have you studied the early days of cinema?
Guy Maddin: My fellow drones and I found an orphaned 16mm projector—an old Pageant swaddled in newspaper and smelling as if it had soiled itself with burnt mildew or bulb dust. There were cans of film on the floor beside the little unloved one. Among these was Erik Von Stroheim's *Foolish Wives*. We watched this some thousand times at least, until we screamed out in agonized ennui at the over-memorized routines of Maude George, Cesare Gravina, Dale Fuller, and even "retarded, deaf, and dumb" Malvina Polo as they retraced their steps ad infinitum like so many ants in a silent movie ant farm.

Long after any flavor had been sucked out of this movie, the inscrutable chirographies of these long-dead actors entrenched themselves in our brains as lucid language of imperatives. Deeply inscribed behind our sleepy pans was

Stroheim's occult Constitution—his Moral Code! It was with his erectile gait we soon strode about the apartment, our faces rippling with Prussian sneers. Constantly pressing monocles to our eyes, we inspected each other's habiliments, cuirasses, and plumages in an endless mutual pass and muster. Between sips and snoozes, we served deliriously as both master and adjutant in an army without ranks, without much wakefulness, without even the wherewithal to exit the apartment.

I managed a daring escape from the apartment with my life. I never really saw, or needed to see, any other movies before picking up a camera myself. I've since seen other titles, but never more than once.

CdC: How have you managed to see these prototypical films? I know that German mountain movies aren't the du jour of the local multiplex…
GM: I've never seen a "mountain picture" except the one I made myself. I hate research. I need my sleep. When Leni Riefenstahl sent me a fan letter, I didn't even know who she was. I wrote back because she sounded hot to trot, a bit of a floozy. I thought, if I'm ever going to get laid, maybe this'll be the one to do it. We arranged a meeting in her hometown, in one of those German meat taverns, where legendary Bavarian aphrodisiacs like ox breast and deer soup are served. Since I'd never been away from home before, I sent Drone Emu in my stead. One week later, he came back from Riefenstahl shell-shocked and mute. He took what happened to him to his grave.

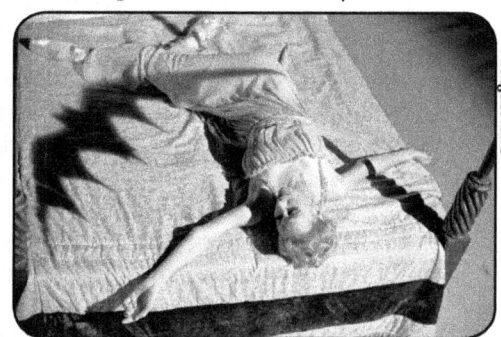
Dracula: Pages from a Virgin's Diary

CdC: What of other modes of cinema? What are other avenues that you have explored, or that you enjoy? Can you turn off your brain and let the latest Joel Schumacher film wash over you?
GM: I like almost anything from Bollywood. I'm afraid I can't abide Schumacher, but I do love Adam Sandler, especially *Little Nicky*.

CdC: You've said that you've had a story lined up to explain the minstrel character in *Gimli*. Can you share this?
GM: Spike Lee said it all, and many times over, with *Bamboozled*, but this middle-class white Icelander is proud to boast he said it a little earlier, albeit differently.

I use an obsolete movie vocabulary. I love this vocabulary, but that doesn't mean I want to live in the era from which it comes, the days before Banting and Best and other medical advances, the days of entrenched segregation and legislated sexism, no matter how great the music, film, and painting from the twenties. I felt it unfair to celebrate the vocabulary of this era without acknowledging other, more shameful movie conventions, the expletives of the language then in common parlance—for one, the blackface.

You'd have to be a complete fucking idiot not to find the use of blackface a heinous insensitivity. At the same time, however (and even Spike found this), the minstrel is an instant way into the attitudes of an era, attitudes that have donned different disguises in order to survive to this day. Anytime one can be made to feel the past so readily, so slap-bracingly, one is perversely exhilarated and excited, hopefully along with being angered or moved. The sight of a burnt-cork minstrel in modern times is strange and sobering, outrageous and funny in an immensely wrong way. It belonged in my movie. Since Buñuel had already sliced open a woman's eyeball, I had to settle for this second-best strategy for achieving all of the above-mentioned effects.

CdC: I experience a sense of malaise when watching *Twilight of the Ice Nymphs*. However, I can't determine if this stems wholly from the film, or if seeing your unhappiness with the project in *Waiting for Twilight* influenced me. What are your feelings about the film now, and what were the critical reactions to this project?

GM: There are things I'm very proud of in *Twilight of the Ice Nymphs*, but I was not happy with much of it (neither were most critics), and it's all my fault.

For a couple years, I blamed my producer for falling short of my hopes, since he's a fatuous and meddlesome moron—like having Ted Baxter of the *Mary Tyler Moore Show* produce your movie. I blamed my director of photography for keeping me away from the camera, for conspiring to shoot in 35mm just for the sake of his résumé, and for working too slowly. I blamed my miserable marriage for keeping me unfocused.

Twilight of the Ice Nymphs

Ultimately, I must accept all blame for the malaise that made it to screen. I was indecisive about what my next movie should be like—whether I should continue in the same primitive vein as I had been, or perhaps make a movie to modernize somewhat. The people who were assigned to the project against my will—I couldn't even get my 18-year-old daughter on as a production assistant trainee—all hated my movies, if they'd seen them at all. They all pushed for modernization, something I should have resisted with all my soul.

I've always made movies that are filmic equivalents to the music from basement bands. I've always averred that it's a tragedy when a good basement band learns to play its instruments. I was surrounded by philistines who knew how to play the instruments. Lawrence Welk's Orchestra knew how to play their instruments in much the same way. I should have had the strength to blow these people away. Then I would have made a break for it, shot the picture even more primitively than *Flaming Creatures*. Had I done this, I wouldn't have done such a grave disservice to the script written for me by George Toles. I'll never make that mistake again!

It took two years to repair my friendship with George after mangling his scenario, hurting his feelings and self-delusionally including him among the blameworthy. Now, George and I are back writing together again and it feels brilliant! I'm very optimistic. But all interlopers beware: it's death to the philistines! Don't tell me you love my vision and then insert your own stuff up my ass. Just tell me you love my vision, please.

CdC: How does it feel to be considered a national treasure of Canadian cinema? Is there a real sense of Canada having a national cinema?
GM: I'd like to firmly establish the notion that I'm a national treasure. Perhaps I'd earn more than 15K a year, somehow. You don't really want me to talk about Canadian national cinema, do you?

CdC: Yes, please, go ahead!
GM: Okay, I'll try, but I run out of gas on this one every time. Any discussion of "our national cinema"—and keep in mind, we're not exactly a politically repressed and perfervid revolutionist band of outlaws fighting for any particular cause up here—always makes me feel like I'm filling out one of those big fat grant applications. Half of the films made here are diluted approximations of the American product, with weak little myth-making impulses where you guys have rope-thick nerve. Characters in Yank pictures are always "bigger than life," in good films and bad, in naturalistic films and in fantasies.

Somehow, Canadian characters seem "smaller than life." We're even scared that naturalism would be implausible. Thank God that De Sica was born in Italy; as a Canadian he'd consider a bike theft farfetched. The other films made here are reactions against American trends, but somehow, by unknowingly garbing ourselves in American film conventions, as we do, we are as rubes standing before a carnival mirror, laughing and pointing at the ugly bumpkins reflecting back to us. We indict ourselves with much slobber flying. Humiliating.

CdC: It seems that only in the last few years has there been recognition of Canadian cinema. Without fail, the works of Atom Egoyan and David Cronenberg are lauded in conversations involving your country's cinematic prowess. How does this make you feel?
GM: I'm proud to know David and Atom a little bit. They're gracious and hilarious. I get a little jealous of Atom sometimes because he's slightly younger than I am, or so he says.

Tales of Guy Maddin

CdC: I've been reading the book of Alejandro Jodorowsky's *El Topo*. Jodorosky cited von Stroheim and Keaton as "filmmakers who make poetry." Meanwhile, you've stated that before making your first short film, *The Dead Father*, you had seen "only a handful of von Stroheim movies and some Keatons." At face value, I can't think of two more dissimilar filmmakers than yourself and Mr. Jodorowsky. What do you think of his work?

GM: I love Jodorowsky! And to further the coincidence, my French distributors say Jodorowsky came into their Paris office one day and bought all my movies on video. A huge thrill and honor. So did Yves St. Laurent. (In other brushes with celebrity, I sent my first movie to Irving Berlin, hoping to coax the 101-year-old out of retirement to score my next picture, but the old grouch kicked the bucket before—or even while—seeing the tape.)

CdC: Titles like *Sissy Boy Slap Party* and *The Cock Crew* sound as if some of your shorts might have some homoerotic overtones. True?

GM: No more than any Watson and Webber gem. *The Cock Crew* is actually an adaptation of Herman Melville's *I and My Chimney*, with a little extra sperm from *Moby Dick* thrown in. I've tried for as much homo-mischief as Melville pulled off—no more, no less.

CdC: Do you have any desire to try to make *The Dikemaster's Daughter* in the future, or has that project's time passed?

GM: I shot a short called *Sea Beggars*, which takes my favorite scenes of that ill-starred feature. I've no use for that sad dalliance with all things Dutch any longer.

The original version of this article ran in *Cashiers du Cinemart* #13.

FROM SHITTER TO AUTEUR: KEITH GORDON

By Mike White

It was a Sunday night in early summer, 1992. A couple of my theater co-workers and I were sitting around, bored, with movie passes burning holes in our pockets. We were allotted two free shows a week, the passes stapled to our paychecks. It wasn't often that we actually found the time to use them. On this particular night, our schedules allowed us a night out, but there wasn't much we wanted to see.

Looking through the newspaper, we narrowed down our choices to three films: *Stephen King's Sleepwalkers*, *Wild Orchid 2: Two Shades of Blue*, or something called *A Midnight Clear*. I was only familiar with *A Midnight Clear* from seeing oblique trailer for it. A preview so vague and ad campaign so myopic are usually signs to steer clear of a film, so we ended up seeing *Stephen King's Sleepwalkers* instead. Big mistake.

After that, I was always a little intrigued about *A Midnight Clear*. It seemed to have an amazing cast, starring some of the brightest up-and-coming talents in Hollywood (Gary Sinise, Peter Berg, Ethan Hawke, Frank Whaley), so why was it just dumped into theaters with little to no support?

When I finally saw *A Midnight Clear*, I was completely blown away. Wonderfully adapted from the novel of the same name by William Wharton (*Birdy*), *A Midnight Clear* is the story of a group of soldiers in World War II who are more concerned about making it home alive than scoring medals and glory. Stunning visuals combined with great performances and strong story make *A Midnight Clear* an incredible film.

After finally chancing a rental, I was then dismayed at the small amount of publicity that went into promoting the film. It was only blind luck that I happened to catch *Mother Night*, the next film by *A Midnight Clear*'s writer/director, Keith Gordon.

Again, Gordon employed a tremendous cast: Nick Nolte, Alan Arkin, Sheryl Lee, etc. And, again, Gordon was directing a movie based on a great book. Kurt Vonnegut Jr.'s *Mother Night* is the story of Howard W. Campbell Jr., a Nazi propagandist who is actually working for the U.S. government, passing information to agents via his venomous radio broadcasts.

After watching *Mother Night*, I explored Keith Gordon's earlier efforts behind the camera: he helped write and produce *Static*, a quirky film

Keith Gordon on the set of *Mother Night*

From Shitter to Auteur: Keith Gordon

in which he starred as Ernie Blick, a genius inventor. Gordon also adapted and directed Robert Cormier's perennial favorite, *The Chocolate War*. Gordon's then helmed an adaptation of Scott Spencer's *Waking the Dead*. Though it was completed in mid-'99, complicated Hollywood production company mergers kept it from being released until early 2000.

Gordon has had a string of great films plagued by bad-to-minimal advertising. After *Waking the Dead* opened in a handful of theaters across the U.S., the director's next film, *The Singing Detective*, shared a similar fate. A remake/condensement of Dennis Potter's epic BBC series, *The Singing Detective* reunited director Gordon with his former *Back to School* co-star, Robert Downey Jr. in a role tailor-made for the mercurial star. Since then, Gordon has directed several episodes of popular television dramas *House* and *Dexter*.

It was a real joy talking to Keith Gordon. He was incredibly personable. I was comfortable enough talking to him that I almost asked him to call me a "Shitter"—the wonderful derogatory term he used so joyously in John Carpenter's *Christine*. I didn't.

Cashiers du Cinemart: Okay, we're rolling.
Keith Gordon: Let me just start by saying that I don't want to discuss any of my legal problems in great detail, but as far as I knew she was eighteen. Or at least sixteen. Or, certainly in anybody's mind, at least fourteen. I also want to say that I did not know that those components could be used to make a bomb. And one has to keep in mind that there's a great difference between third- and first-degree murder. I just wanted to say those things to get them out of the way.

CdC: When I've told people that I've been preparing for an interview with you, I get some blank stares until I associate your name with two roles. Care to take a stab in the dark as to what those might be?
KG: *Christine* and *Back to School*, I'd guess.

CdC: Yup!
KG: Well, that makes sense. Those two have been hugely successful on cable and video. I find it myself that whenever anyone says, "Oh, you look familiar to me, weren't you in that movie?" it was always one of those two, because they've both had a life that's continued up until present day. Some of the other things I've done as an actor have just sort of disappeared more over the years.

CdC: Yeah, it was a coincidence; the other day I ordered *Home Movies* and didn't realize you were in it until I saw it listed on your filmography.
KG: Most people don't even know that that movie exists; much less know that I was in it. That was the first film I did with Brian [De Palma]. It was a very important film for me because not only was it the first film that I had a leading role in, but it was also where I really started to learn about filmmaking in a very concentrated way.

I don't know if you know the story of that movie, but it was made primarily by Brian's filmmaking class at Sarah Lawrence College. The actors were all pros, including Kirk Douglas and Nancy Allen, and De Palma did direct, but almost the entire crew of that film were non-pros. They were all film students. He basically made the film as a lesson on how to make an independent film. Even though I wasn't a student, I desperately wanted to get into filmmaking and directing, and Brian was nice enough that he treated me kind of like I was one of the students. It was a tremendous education in making a film on a budget.

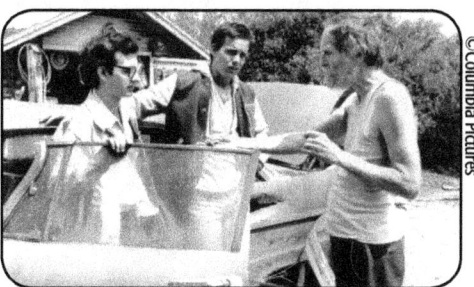

Arnie Finds Christine

CdC: What are you working on?
KG: Right now I'm working on putting together financing for new things that I want to do, which is really the hardest and longest part of my work. Unless you want to make obvious, easy, Hollywood-type movies, the hard part is getting the money together. Basically, I've come to realize that I'm a professional fundraiser, and direct as a hobby.

I've got four or five projects that I'd love to see happen, but I'm in that limbo of being just one actor away, or one piece of financing away. That can still take years to happen, or it could be a phone call tomorrow and suddenly something's going.

The projects range from a character comedy about this guy and his grandmother that got sent to me because I was mentoring some writers for the Independent Feature Project, to a film noir piece that I wrote back a few years ago off of a Jim Thompson novel. They're all in the situation of "being very close" in Hollywood parlance—we just need one big actor to say they want to do it, but of course that's the hardest thing to get.

One of the things you have to learn by going through it a few times is that getting from nowhere to "oh, they really like it, and they'll make it if I just get Johnny Depp" isn't the hard part. The hard part is in getting Johnny Depp. That's why I try to keep a few things in the air, because it's so hard to get one project going that if you have three, four, five going, the odds are much better. It's a strange, nebulous life, because you just never know...

CdC: Which Jim Thompson novel did you adapt?
KG: *Savage Night*, which was given to me by some producers who had it, and I fell in love with it. I did an adaptation of it for free because I wanted to maintain control. So, rather than being paid and have them own the script, I wanted to own it.

From Shitter to Auteur: Keith Gordon

That one's been very tough because, if you know that book, it gets more and more subjective and surreal as it goes along. It starts sort of like normal film noir and by the end it's way into Polanski *Repulsion* sort of territory.

That script is the one where I get phone calls from people saying, "I love the script, but we could never make it." I understand why. The concern is that in the end, this could just be a good "film festival movie." This is a movie that might never cross over to a mainstream audience, and I think that would be a risk. It is a difficult piece of material.

My counter is that it could always be done inexpensively but in the current marketplace, because of how expensive marketing a finished film is, even a couple of million dollars is a big risk to take.

CdC: To be honest, I'm not that familiar with Thompson's work. I've picked up a couple of his books at used bookstores, but they're in my ever-increasing "to-read" pile.
KG: This is actually one of the more obscure ones. People I know who know his work don't know this book, which is one of the reasons why I think that the rights have been floating around. Things like *The Killer Inside Me*, everyone wants to make that book, but this is one that I don't think ever sold really well. It's an interesting book and, as is my want, I stayed very close to it in adapting it. I felt it was very cinematic on the page.

CdC: One of the things that I admired with *A Midnight Clear* was your adaptation. It stayed very faithful to the written word.
KG: I'm a great believer that if you're going to adapt a book, it's because you love it. So why would you end up throwing out what was great about the book? I don't have any big ego about myself as a writer—I don't think of myself primarily as a writer—so I don't feel like I have to prove anything. I'm not going to try to out-write Scott Spencer or William Wharton. These guys are great novelists. I guess what I try to do is edit—try to figure out what works cinematically and what doesn't. If something's too wordy, how do I condense it to its essence, or how do I find an image that's the equivalent. I'm not somebody who goes in with the idea of taking the novel's premise and throwing the rest out. If their dialogue's good or if their imagery is good, then I'm going to use as much of it as I can!

CdC: If you don't think of yourself as a writer, how do you primarily see yourself—as a director?
KG: Well, as a filmmaker. To me that encompasses writing as a discipline and not as a focus or end in itself. The difference is that people who think of themselves as writers tend to have big egos about what they write. I'm happy to say that William Wharton really wrote *A Midnight Clear*; I adapted it for the screen. Scott Spencer wrote *Waking the Dead*, Robert Cromier wrote *The*

Chocolate War, and I think it's a little presumptuous of me to say, "Oh yeah, I wrote those." I wrote the screenplays, but that's very different from someone who sits down and writes an original script from scratch and creates that world. I took worlds that these guys had written and adapted them for another forum.

I feel that I have writing skills and I'm proud of those skills but to me, they fall as part of being a filmmaker, just like knowing something about photographic lenses. It's just part of being what a good filmmaker knows about.

CdC: The only thing from the book *A Midnight Clear* that I remember you changing, other than the elimination of Won't's (the main character) gastrointestinal problems, was your moving of the section regarding Mother sending Won't a check for all those years to the end of the film, where it worked very well—if not better—as a final word about Mother.

KG: There's lot of little changes, like changing Major Love's name to Major Griffin, because I felt that "Major Love" was just too close to *Catch-22* style wordplay. I didn't mind the wordplay with our main characters' names, calling themselves "Mother" and "Father," because the characters are supposed to have made up those names. But the idea of having somebody's real name being that heavily ironic was a little too much.

It was just a lot of editing down and simplifying, but you know, Wharton's a great writer. And that, according to him, was actually a true story. It was something that actually happened to him. He wrote it in a novelistic form, but he swears that there was such an incident that he was part of, and that his squad really did have a "Mother" and a "Father." He was really writing it out of his own memory, and who was I to try to improve on that?

CdC: How does it compare directing something that you've adapted yourself to *Mother Night*, which had been adapted by Robert Weide?

KG: It was a little bit different. I felt a little more distant from the material, but in the case of *Mother Night*, the screenwriter has been my best friend for fifteen years. We developed the project together for a long time, so it was something that I was very intimate with. We came up with the idea of doing the book together. So while the script is one hundred percent Bob's, I was certainly involved through the whole process. It wasn't like somebody handed me a script and said, "Okay, now make this."

If I had adapted it, there are some things I might have probably done differently—I don't know what.

Nick Nolte as Howard W. Campbell

But I just really loved his script and thought it worked as an organic whole. I did very little to that script other than some editing and tightening. My biggest contribution was saying, "Yeah, this is a wonderful scene, and we don't have time to shoot it."

When I've done TV, I'm directing something that I haven't been involved with developing at all. That's very weird, because you're trying to find where to cleave onto it and where to make it your own. Not an uninteresting thing to do,

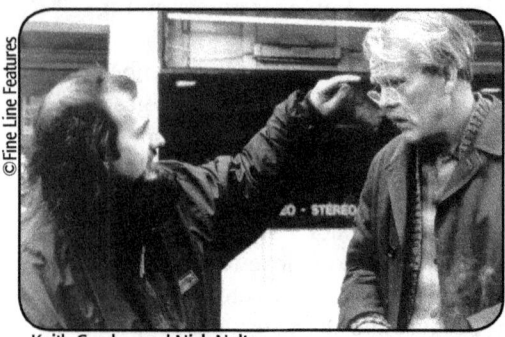

Keith Gordon and Nick Nolte

nor is it unpleasant. It's just different than living with something. By the time we got the money to shoot *Mother Night*, it was as if I had written it, because I had internalized it. But certainly, when I've done TV work, there's a constant feeling of, "Am I missing the point here? Am I not saying what this is about?" You have to have the dialogue constantly with yourself when it's not your own material.

I just had a psychotic experience recently with *Waking the Dead*, where the Writer's Guild, in their infinite wisdom, decided to give writing credit to a guy who had written a script I had never seen, seven years before mine, for a different company. Apparently, I've learned since, that's actually common on adaptations and I've just been very lucky. On *A Midnight Clear*, for example, there were two versions that were written years before mine, but those writers said, "Listen, we weren't involved with it, we don't want any credit." But this guy did, even though our drafts are completely different approaches to the same story. Under Writer's Guild rules all he had to do was show that he wrote one-third of the "elements" (a very loosely defined term, which even includes story points), which of course he did because it comes from the same book! He actually got credit for a movie when none of us involved had ever seen his script. It was the most Kafkaesque thing I've ever been through in my life.

CdC: What was your relationship with Vonnegut?
KG: Really, the relationship was Bob's. He's a documentary filmmaker, and he had gotten to know Vonnegut because Vonnegut had liked some of his early work and had gotten in touch with him. They stayed in contact, and Bob decided that he wanted to make a documentary about Kurt and started filming him over the years. Eventually they developed almost a father–son relationship.

When Bob decided that he wanted to get into features and he and I had been talking about doing something for a long time, he brought me the idea of doing something of Vonnegut's. We discussed which books of Kurt's could be made into good films, and which books could be made well as films for a reasonable sum of money. So, as much as we loved *Cat's Cradle*—first of all, the rights were tied up; but also, you've got to portray the end of the world, and that'd be hard to do on a limited budget. With *Breakfast of Champions* (I haven't seen the film version yet), we thought, "Oh god, that book is so much about being a book. To me, Kurt's drawings were *Breakfast of Champions*. So, how do you translate that and not lose what's special about it?"

We felt that *Mother Night*, being one of Kurt's earlier books where his style was less extreme, was more amenable. It had a beginning, middle, and an end. It wasn't so much about literary style. And, with the nature of Howard Campbell's story, we could make it for a price.

I was lucky enough to get to know Kurt somewhat through the process, and he's been wonderful to me—very kind and supportive. But Bob was the one who got us the rights for free for the years we were trying to get it made, and he got Kurt to be in the film.

CdC: When I first saw *Mother Night* and put your name and Vonnegut's together, I had visions of you two meeting on the set of *Back to School*.
KG: We did, but the reality is that I'm really very shy around people that I admire a great deal. So on *Back to School*, I probably said ten words to the guy. You know, "You've always been one of my heroes." And he mumbled something like, "Oh, thank you." That's probably as much as we talked. It wasn't until I had dinner with Kurt with Bob that I was able to talk to him on sort of a human-to-human basis, and by that point we were already starting to try to put the project together.

CdC: I've heard tales of Nick Nolte being a dogged researcher. What did he do to prepare for the role of Howard W. Campbell Jr. in *Mother Night*?
KG: Oh, man, what didn't he do? From the first rehearsal, Bob Weide and I came in, and Nick had prepared folders of things that he had already put together: a timeline of the novel, the script broken down in chronological order (as opposed to script order), photographs of real German playwrights from the era and biographies about them, photographs and bios of people who would have been involved in the German Arts Ministry, his own biography of Howard Campbell that went beyond what was in the novel, information about spies and propaganda, oh, just all kinds of stuff. Amazing stuff.

Campbell behind bars

From Shitter to Auteur: Keith Gordon

Things came out of that research, like when we started rehearsal I was pushing Nick more towards being very dogmatic when he was doing the radio broadcasts. And Nick said, "I want to play you something." He played me old recordings of Arthur Godfrey: the American, avuncular, nice guy. Nick said, "I want to be the guy who seduces instead of the guys that scream. Let me save the screaming for the one at the end." He was absolutely right—that all came out of him sitting down and listening to the real propagandists who generally were either yelling into the radio or were very monotone. Sometimes research allows you to break with reality for something better, but you're doing it in an intentional, informed way.

Beyond clothes and hairstyles, though, Nick brought a more poetic vision, literally and figuratively, into the rehearsal process. I remember there was one rehearsal where all we did was listen to Nick read some of Anne Sexton's poetry, because somehow her work really spoke to him about the character and the story. It was just breathtaking. The fact that he's not done books on tape is really sad. He has an incredible voice.

He has a very childlike mind—and I mean that in the best sense, in that he's very open to things. He doesn't lock himself into seeing the world one way. New things will hit him all the time.

Then add to that he knows film inside and out, but doesn't let that make him stiff. He's a brilliant technician. We'd be doing a scene and he'd say, "You know, I'm casting a shadow on Sheryl [Lee]'s face here. If I move a bit, she'll cast a shadow on my face, which says much more about what's going on in this scene." And none of us, even the D.P., would even see it. He managed to do that but also be free and improvisational at the same time.

I think a lot of actors treat the medium as their enemy. They resent the camera, they resent the lighting; they just want to play the scene. Having been an actor, I can understand that. The artificiality of it can be very frustrating. Nick would almost never get frustrated. He'd be the one saying, "Listen, if the camera's there, what if I sit this way and kind of turn my back, and you're really just seeing the back of my head. Then on this thing I can turn back into the light." And I just sit there thinking, "Shit, he's smart! This man should be directing!" I'm sort of surprised he hasn't, but it's just not something that interests him on a personal level. He's that sort of actor where he really understands what the shot is doing, what the scene is doing, not just what his part is doing. For a director, that's a blessing. But it's only a blessing as long as the person's as smart and as open-minded as Nick. I'm sure there are other actors out there who think they're that smart, and who use that to drive everyone crazy.

The other thing that was amazing with him (and a big lesson for me) was the subtlety he'd do things with. There were times—some of the best things he does in the film—where I wasn't sure we were getting it. I couldn't see it with my naked eye, but the camera would, and that's how much he knew what cameras could do. My favorite moment of him in *Mother Night* is when he's frozen on the street. Watching it from standing right next to the camera, I was thinking, "I don't think he's doing enough. I don't know if we're going to have a scene." When I saw it in dailies, I thought it was just amazing. He knew what having his face filling the whole screen and what the little stuff behind his eyes was going to do. Luckily, we shot that late enough in the process that I trusted him.

CdC: So, working with Rodney Dangerfield was probably an identical experience, right?
KG: Oh yeah! [Laughs] Rodney and Nick! What can I say? Two of a kind! Rodney's probably the other end of the scale. The only thing I was frustrated about with Rodney (that I also found touching and sad) was that he seemed to be kind of an angry guy. We think of him as such a funny man, but he's had a very rough life. I think he really does feels that he doesn't get any respect. I got along with the guy but he just wasn't the guy I grew up with watching on Johnny Carson. Nick he wasn't.

I think a lot of credit for *Back to School* has to go to Harold Ramis, who came in and did a great rewrite on it. He took the comedy up a whole other level. And I think Alan Metter [the director] did a great job. Alan's sort of disappeared; I don't know what he's doing. But not only was he dealing with Rodney, who was a handful, but Robert Downey Jr., who was a handful…

CdC: How was Downey on the set?
KG: He was great! Funny, inventive, but he was also completely burned out. He was shooting *Saturday Night Live* at the same time; flying back and forth across the country six times a week. So, if he wasn't doing drugs, I don't know how he survived. Robert is very manic and I really like him. I got along with him great. But Robert really was like his character. The thing that Alan had to do was direct that energy. Robert could be brilliantly funny, but if he got off on a tangent he could be not funny at all. Alan had to be very careful not to clamp down Robert's completely improvisational madness, because it was brilliant sometimes. Between that and Rodney, who never liked to do more than one take and was really cranky, Alan had a lot on his plate. I thought he did a great job of balancing all those things and keeping the movie both human and funny. That's something I don't think Rodney's had so much in other things he's done.

Back to School

From Shitter to Auteur: Keith Gordon

CdC: Out of your body of work, in both acting and filmmaking, what are you the most proud of?
KG: I guess I'd have to say the film I just finished, *Waking the Dead*, but that's without the virtue of time. It was certainly the most complete experience—a very emotional experience. I really loved the people I worked with; my cast, my crew. When I look at the film I see a step forward in maturity. But I might not have the same answer in five years from now. My tendency is always to be proud of what I'm doing now, because I see the steps from the things before. In time, I'm sure the flaws will also become clear too.

As an actor, it's much easier to be objective because none of them are "my" films. Probably the best thing I did as an actor was a play that I did in New York that not many people saw (a few thousand at most), done at the Brooklyn Academy of Music called *Gimme Shelter*. It's an English play that Des McEnuff (who's now moved into feature films) directed and it was written by Barry Keeffe, who wrote *The Long Good Friday*, which I love. I thought it was an amazing piece of writing.

In film acting, I think the thing that I'm most proud of is *Christine*. It was a fun mix of everything. It was Jekyll and Hyde, and it was over-the-top in that sort of odd Kubrickian way. Not that it was a very deep piece but then again, most of what I did in film wasn't very deep. I mean, I was proud to be in *All That Jazz*, I think it's a great film, but I didn't have that much to do. Likewise, I was proud to be in *Dressed to Kill*, but it wasn't like I was carrying the movie or anything like that. It really all depends on what lens you look at it through.

How's that for a really long-winded answer to a really simple question? I hope you have a lot of tape. I guess I sit here too quiet all day!

CdC: Conversely, what's the thing that you're least proud of?
KG: I would say, without any hesitation, a little comedy TV movie called *Combat High*. It was just really not funny! And there's really nothing worse than being not funny in a comedy. I didn't have a bad time doing it, but it was really in the category of "I Needed A Job." Like I said, I enjoyed myself, and the good news out of it is that's where I met Wally Ward, who's now Wally Langham, who ended up as one of the leads in *The Chocolate War*.

I'd probably follow that with *The Legend of Billie Jean*, which is not as actively embarrassing. It's too bad, because it was actually a very good script that went through a Hollywoodization process, which turned it from a funky, almost social satire into a way too self-serious (and consequentially kind of laughable) portrait of a rebel movie.

Again, it wasn't miserable to do and I don't think that I'm bad in the movie. I just think it's a movie utterly lacking a theme or coherent vision. It had one but just before shooting started the studio decided that it didn't like what the movie was saying. Even the title—when I read the script originally, it seemed like a joke. Like it was playing off the pomposity of those kind of teen-rebel movies, because Billie Jean was kind of this dimwitted, weird girl who becomes a hero because of the way the media portrays her.

But those aren't my movies, so I don't have to care in the same deep way. That's the benefit of being an actor. You want to do good work and you want to be in good things, but on a certain level, it's not your responsibility. You try to do your job the best you can, and if the movie doesn't come out great, it's not your shame. And, conversely, if the movie is great, you can't really give yourself the credit either. On a career level, of course, you want every movie to be great and to make five hundred million dollars so you can get the next job.

CdC: Did you always want to be an actor, or was filmmaking your ultimate goal?
KG: I think the first passion was about filmmaking. That started for me when I was very young. I think my life started to turn when I saw *2001: A Space Odyssey* on opening day in New York. I was this seven-year-old and I didn't know what the movie was about, but the fact that I saw something so intense and couldn't figure it out drove me crazy (in a good way). And that became a real defining moment in my life. I started watching a lot of movies and reading a lot of books that asked questions that addressed complicated scenes. I found myself drawn to filmmakers like Scorcese, Coppola, and Nick Roeg.

I didn't know how I'd ever get to be a director. Since my father is an actor, I could understand how people did that. But I got really lucky. I was in a school play and somebody who was casting a professional play saw me, and they had me read and gave me the job. Off of that I got an audition for *Jaws 2* and got that job. Suddenly I started working as an actor and it was great, but there was part of me that always tried to think of it as a way to get back to filmmaking.

CdC: How did you finally "make the jump"?
KG: It was a couple-step process. I was always writing scripts and making awful Super-8 films and videos when I as a teenager and as a young actor. Then I met a young guy named Mark Romanek, who's become a huge video and commercial director. He worked as the second assistant director on *Home Movies*, and we struck up a friendship. He showed me his student films and I loved them. He was trying to put together a first feature, and he came from a family where there were enough connections to money to start to piece together some financing. He came to me with an idea that he had and a character for me to play and we wrote this script together. It took about a year to write and another year to put all the casting and financing together. The result was this weird little movie called *Static*.

CdC: ...which is terrific!
KG: Oh, well, thanks! You're one of eleven Americans to ever see that movie. Twelve now that you've seen it. It never really got released in the States. I mean,

it played Film Forum in New York and one week in one theater in L.A., but it never got a true release. It did really well in Europe, though. It played forever in London and got terrific reviews there. In the States the reviews were more mixed. It predated the time of people making lots of those kind of oddball independent movies. I can see both sides with that movie. I see the parts that I'm really proud of, and the parts that are pretentious. Depending on what someone wants to pick up on, it can go either way.

CdC: Not getting a proper release for your films seems to be quite a trend for you!
KG: That seems to be my fate in life. But I wouldn't trade my luck. I've gotten to direct four movies and produce one, all of which have been the films I've wanted them to be. So, I wouldn't trade that for bigger releases. But, would I like to have it all? Sure. If something had to suck in the process, I guess I'd pick that. Because ultimately, whatever the film grosses, it doesn't change the experience of making it and of the film being true to my vision. It's sort of commercial importance and changes how easy it is to get the next one made, but I'd rather have fewer people see something and really get into it than put something bland out there that a lot of people see.

CdC: Being a stuck-up film critic, I was looking at your oeuvre and trying to find some motifs and themes that run throughout. Looking at *Mother Night*, I saw the use of Bing Crosby's "White Christmas," and the setting of *A Midnight Clear* at Christmas time, and even the spot in *Waking the Dead* that I'm at now is going on at Christmas. So, what's the deal?
KG: Well, I'm a big Stanley Kubrick fan and I knew one day he was going to have a lot of Christmas stuff in *Eyes Wide Shut*, so that's just an homage to him. [Laughs]

With a lot of those thematic kinds of things, my experience is that you're always consciously aware of it. I grew up in an Atheist/Jewish family in New York, so it's not like Christmas is a big meaningful thing in my life. A lot of the Christmas themes just come from the stories that I've happened to become involved with.

If I were writing completely original screenplays then I would say, "Yeah, that is weird." But, it so happens that these three books that I fell in love with all have Christmas subthemes. Only in *A Midnight Clear* is it overtly thematic, and even then it's not like I looked at it as a story of Christmas, but more as a story about the insanity of war; my chance to do sort of my version of *Paths of Glory*. With *A Midnight Clear*, Christmas is only a minor ironic subtheme. "White Christmas" wasn't originally going to be over the opening titles. It was only when we were looking for a way to make that opening scene where Nick Nolte's walking through that prison and have that Vonnegut twist. We tried "White Christmas" in the opening. When we saw the Israeli flag with Bing

Crosby crooning over it and these depressing shots of an abandoned prison, it set up a weird schism, so now we had a prison movie about irony.

A Midnight Clear

In *Waking the Dead*, again, Christmas is a tiny subtheme. There's a Christmas tree shown once or twice because it does take place in the winter but, for me, if I were going to talk about a seasonable theme in my work, I'd say it's winter.

It's not that I've chosen to make films about winter, though I do think there is something magical about it. It's a time with snow falling, where it's very hard to see everything. The world is turning cold and blue, people hide inside and hibernate. The themes I'm interested in, which are often about loneliness, are things that show up in stories and things that attract me—those aren't warm, summery themes. The fact that you have Christmas smack dab in the middle of winter just helps the chances that it's going to show up.

CdC: Oh, those film theorists. We're always just reaching for stuff.
KG: Don't get me wrong, I actually think that those theories have a lot of validity. I just think very few filmmakers or artists of any kind are consciously aware of those themes. I don't think very many people set out to make a film on that level, but your subconscious is certainly drawn to things over and over again. I've read some really interesting stuff about people's movies and themes that run through them, but even with someone like Kubrick—I don't know how much he sat around going, "Okay, I'm going to do a lot of symmetrical shots to display my dismay over the attempt to create an ordered approach to the universe that human beings keep making." He probably thought symmetrical shots were cool; he knows instinctively that they were right at the moment. There's no question that they have a meaning when you watch his movies, but

I think most artists work from a more visceral place. At least my experience is that my gut will tell me where to put a camera.

When you've got a crew of seventy or eighty people with art directors and gaffers and all sorts of people who are having subtle influences, things may be happy accidents. I'm a great believer in the general theory of auteur filmmaking in that there is one vision behind it all, but on the specifics, I just know from being on movie sets (certainly De Palma is a very specific filmmaker) that you have a bunch of people around you that are bringing their talents and vision to the film. A lot of the details that people would just ascribe to the filmmaker may not have been the filmmaker's idea at all.

The original version of this article ran in *Cashiers du Cinemart* #10.

STEPHEN HAWKING'S LAB ASSISTANT

By Mike White

Taylor Negron turns cameos into works of art. I first noticed him in *Better Off Dead* ("What's a little boy like you doing with big boy smut like this?"), and then in *One Crazy Summer*. From then on, I was hooked. A movie always had that something extra if Negron had a role in it. Between his book, stage, stand-up, and film work, Negron took some time out for some questions.

Cashiers du Cinemart: What role(s) are you best known for?
Taylor Negron: That depends what neighborhood you're in. If I am in an urban area (or at Puff Daddy's birthday), I am known for *The Last Boy Scout*. But mostly on this planet I am known as the guy who delivered the pizza to Sean Penn in the eternal teen comedy, *Fast Times at Ridgemont High*. I wish I could say I was Stephen Hawking's lab assistant and that I was writing a story filled with insights about time travel, binary quarks, and spectroscopy revealing the expansion of the universe. But, alas, I am no brilliant doctor's protégé about to spill the beans on the universe. I am just "Mr. Pizza Guy."

Taylor Negron

Fast Times has become iconic, and has changed people's lives in tiny little ways. It's interesting because it's a movie that, in current time, seems as if it was made 90 years ago. They would never make a movie like *Fast Times* these days; imagine, underage kids having sex and smoking grass.

So, for me, it's like *Fast Times* is the *Gold Diggers of 1933*, and I might as well be the baby in the carriage going down the steps in *The Battleship Potemkin*. Who ordered the double cheese and sausage?

CdC: How did you get your start?
TN: I was an extra. I loved it. I learned camera, protocol, and technique. I saw up close how to behave on a set and how to focus on excellence. I was plucked out of a crowd scene in *The Main Event* and actually given a part. A month later, I got the lead on an ABC comedy called *Detective School*.

I started very young in the business, taking advantage of being an L.A. local. I was doing stand-up at the Comedy Store at 16 and was a Go-Go dancer opening act for the rock group, The Tubes, at the Whiskey. I was illegal for the first five years of my career.

CdC: You're the second person I have talked to who was on *The Dating Game* back in its heyday (the first being John Daniels). Was that some kind of seedbed for young talent?
TN: It was great! I was on thirteen times. I never had been on TV before. I would go there on my bike. They paid you and gave you bagels. I learned how to pace the laugh because the other bachelors were, generally, boring idiots. I could swoop down for the kill but when I won, the girl was visibly disappointed. We went to Rio de Janeiro on our date and she contracted amebas.

CdC: What projects and/or roles are you most proud of?
TN: I am proud of all the movies I have been in. It's a monumental event to get anything done and released. I am just a working actor, and there is still a thrill about inhabiting a role and playing a scene. The crappy stuff is all in the hands of the writers, directors, and studio executives. I have always been happy with what I do. I pay intense attention—some directors I have worked with haven't.

CdC: You're often noted as being the best thing about *Nothing But Trouble*. Was that a debacle during the making of it, or just after it was released?
TN: Demi Moore and Chevy fought like Osama and Bush. It was like being in a custody battle. The last great mess of a movie at Warner Brothers.

CdC: How about *Easy Money*? I hear that Rodney Dangerfield was on coke during the making of that one.
TN: Crack and steak…and lots of money. That movie is like a fever dream.

CdC: What has been your favorite turn in a "smaller role"?
TN: *Stuart Little*. The scene was with Geena Davis, but, really, I was acting with a ping-pong ball—Stuart's "stand in."

CdC: What's your favorite "cutting room floor" moment?
TN: I was in *Gun Shy* with Liam Neeson. The scene was so disgusting; my character unloads a massive amount of bullets in a man's asshole. This was a Disney movie, and producer Sandra Bullock decided to cut it. But I have to ask here, why did we have to shoot that scene in the first place?

CdC: Can you tell me more about your writing and plays?
TN: I write plays to uncover what really happened. My plays are about things and events in my life. My first play, *Gangster Planet*, was about the Los Angeles Riots, and my new play is called *Yoga Bitch*, which is about me getting kicked out of a fancy yoga retreat in Tuscany. This I turned it into a murder mystery.

The original version of this article ran in *Cashiers du Cinemart* #15.

HELLION

By Mike White

There's something childlike about Crispin Hellion Glover. He's at once a vulnerable lost boy that you want to comfort (George McFly in *Back to the Future*) and the sadistic kid focusing the sun's rays on a colony of ants (Layne in *River's Edge*). In the same way, Glover shifts between quirky independent fare (*The Beaver Trilogy*) and mainstream Hollywood fodder (*Beowulf*). You never know which Crispin Glover you're going to see, but his presence always guarantees a fearless and fully committed performance.

For a number of years, Glover has been toiling away at a proposed trilogy—the *It* series. Funding his directorial efforts via schlocky, albeit entertaining, turns in low-budget horror films (*The Wizard of Gore*; *Simon Says*), Glover has begun a triptych of films that challenge and confound viewers.

Cashiers du Cinemart: How do you go about choosing/accepting your roles/projects?
Crispin Glover: Right now, I am acting in films so I can fund my own films I am making. That being said, if I feel I cannot make a role work in any way, I will not do it.

CdC: How did your folks influence your decision to be an artist?
CG: The fact that both my parents are in the entertainment industry certainly had an influence on me as a young person. I realized at a young age that going into this profession would be something I could make work. It was very much a professional decision I made on my own and then my parents were supportive. I feel like it was a good decision.

CdC: When appearing in remakes, do you try to address the original performances, or do you try to be more insular? I'm thinking specifically of *Willard*, *Bartleby*, and *The Wizard of Gore*.
CG: Coincidentally I did not see *any* of those films before, nor had I read the literature that *Willard* and *Bartleby* were based on previously. In all cases I read the screenplay and got my bearings on the material to play. Then I watched any previous acting versions, and in the case of *Willard* and *Bartleby*, I read the original source material as well. I found that in all of the screenplays, the psychology of the character I was to play had been approached by the writer in a significantly different way from previous versions, so I did what I always do, which is go to the truth of the psychology of that particular character that I was to play, as influenced by the screenplay.

CdC: What spurred your interest in directing?

CG: I have made my own films since I was a young teenager. I started making a longer movie based on one of my books in the mid 1980s. It is called *The Backward Swing* and it is the next project I plan to edit together. *What Is It?* and *It Is Fine! Everything Is Fine* were shot later but have taken precedent.

Really directing is only a part of the whole filmmaking process and probably my favorite parts are the writing and finally the best part is the editing. I particularly like the sound editing. Editing is where the true art of the filmmaking experience comes into play.

CdC: Has this gotten easier or more difficult as your career has progressed? You seem to go from quirkier independent things to some pretty high profile films and back again.

CG: I will explain the questions this way. This goes into some detail as to both going back and forth to my own projects and projects with far more money behind them. One would be able to assess the difficulty in some ways from this:

Steven C. Stewart wrote and is the main actor in part two of the trilogy titled *It Is Fine! Everything Is Fine*. I put Steve in to the cast of *What Is It?* because he had written this screenplay, which I read in 1987. When I turned *What Is It?* from a short film into a feature I realized there were certain thematic elements in the film that related to what Steven C. Stewart's screenplay dealt with. Steve had been locked in a nursing home for about ten years when his mother died. He had been born with a severe case of cerebral palsy and he was very difficult to understand. People that were caring for him in the nursing home would derisively call him an "M.R.," short for "Mental Retard." This is not a nice thing to say to anyone, but Steve was of normal intelligence. When he did get out he wrote his screenplay. Although it is written in the genre of a murder detective thriller, truths of his own existence come through much more clearly than if he had written it as a standard autobiography.

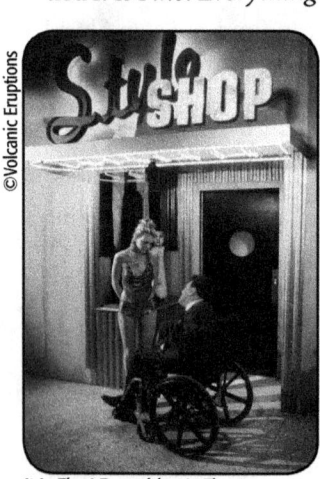

It Is Fine! Everything Is Fine

As I have stated, I put Steven C. Stewart into *What Is It?* when I turned *What Is It?* into a feature film.

Originally, *What Is It?* was going to be a short film to promote the concept to corporate film funding entities of working with a cast wherein most characters are played by actors with Down Syndrome. Steve had written his screenplay in the late 1970s. I read it in 1987, and as soon as I had read it I knew I had to produce the film. Steven C. Stewart died within a month after we finished shooting the film. Cerebral palsy is not generative, but Steve was 62 when we shot the film. One of Steve's lungs had collapsed because he had started choking on his own saliva, and he got pneumonia.

I specifically started funding my own films with the money I make from the films I act in. When Steven C. Stewart's lung collapsed in the year 2000, this was around the same time that the first *Charlie's Angels* film was coming to me. I realized the money I made from that film I could put straight into the Steven C. Stewart film. That is exactly what happened. I finished acting in *Charlie's Angels* and then went to Salt Lake City, where Steven C. Stewart lived. I met with Steve and David Brothers, with whom I co-directed the film. I went back to L.A. and acted in a lower budget film for about five weeks, and David Brothers started building the sets. Then I went straight back to Salt Lake and we completed shooting the film within about six months in three separate, smaller productions. Then Steve died within a month after we finished shooting.

I am relieved to have gotten this film finally completed, because ever since I read the screenplay in 1987, I knew I had to produce the film, and also produce it correctly. I would not have felt right about myself if I had not gotten Steve's film made; I would have felt that I had done something wrong and that I had actually done a bad thing if I had not gotten it made. So I am greatly relieved to have completed it, especially since I am very pleased with how well the film has turned out. We shot *It Is Fine! Everything Is Fine* while I was still completing *What Is It?* and this is partly why *What Is It?* took a long time to complete. I am very proud of the film, as I am of *What Is It?* I feel *It Is Fine! Everything Is Fine* will probably be the best film I will have anything to do with in my entire career.

What Is It?

CdC: Have you gotten any flack for your casting of people with Down Syndrome in *What Is It?*

CG: *What Is It?* is my psychological reaction to the corporate restraints that have happened in the last 20 to 30 years in filmmaking. Specifically anything that can possibly make an audience uncomfortable is necessarily excised or the film will not be corporately funded or distributed. This is damaging to the culture, because it is the very moment when audience members sit back in their chairs, look up at the screen, and think to themselves, "Is this right what I am watching? Is this wrong what I am watching? Should I be here? Should the filmmaker have made this? *What Is It?*"—and that is the title of the film. What is it that is taboo in the culture? What does it mean that taboo has been ubiquitously excised in this culture's media? What does it mean to the culture when it does not properly process taboo in its media? It is a bad thing when questions are not being asked, because these kinds of questions are when people are having a truly educational experience. For the culture to not be able to ask questions leads to a non-educational experience, and that is what is happening in this culture. This stupefies this culture and that is of course a bad thing. So *What Is It?* is a direct reaction to the contents this culture's media.

It is easier for me to show *It Is Fine! Everything Is Fine* than *What Is It?* in terms of when I conduct the Q&A. The films is a very different kind of film from *What Is It?* in terms of having a strong emotional catharsis with the central character. This is not to dismiss *What Is It?* as I am extremely proud of that film as well, but it makes it much easier for me when I conduct the Q&A session. The best way for people to know when I will be where with what film is by signing up for e-mails at CrispinGlover.com and it will email people letting them know when I will be where with what film.

CdC: Please tell me more about the "aesthetic of discomfort."
CG: I really do not use the phrase the "aesthetic of discomfort." I think there is a quote of me using that phrase about something from the '80s or '90s. In any case, there is something related to the films. *What Is It?* is my psychological reaction to the corporate restraints that have happened in the last 20 to 30 years in filmmaking, as I have described above.

Before I show the film I perform a one-hour dramatic narration of eight different books I have made over the years. The books are taken from old books from the 1800s that have been changed into different books from what they originally were. They are heavily illustrated with original drawings and reworked images and photographs. When I first started publishing the books in 1987, people said I should have book readings. But the book are so heavily illustrated and they way the illustrations are used within the books help to tell the story, so the only way for the books to make sense was to have visual representations of the images. This is why I knew a slide show was necessary. It took a while, but in 1992, I started performing what I used to call "Crispin Hellion Glover's Big Slide Show." People get confused as to what that is, so now I always let it be known that it is a one-hour dramatic narration of eight different books that I have made over the years leading up to making *What Is It?* and there are thematic elements that tie the books to the film.

Crispin Hellion Glover

10 QUESTIONS FOR SVENGOOLIE

By Mike White

Detroit has had its fair share of Horror Hosts, those denizens of the Ultra High Frequency channels who would provide a film and a show for your late-night pleasure. The most famous in the Metro area has to be The Ghoul. The most infamous could be Sir Graves Ghastly or Count Scary. Somewhere in the middle was Son of Svengoolie. His stint in Detroit was the result of "a half-assed syndication deal among the then-'Field Communications' stations." This hammy toast of the wee hours came out of his coffin every Saturday night to ward off boredom in the pre-cable TV era with rubber chickens and corny jokes. While his stint in Detroit and the other satellite stations was all too brief, for the good people of Chicago, Svengoolie is still a regular part of their television diet.

Cashiers du Cinemart: What's your background?
Rich Koz: I grew up in the northwest 'burbs of Chicago, where I first got into broadcasting at my high school radio station. When I got into college I would write material (unsolicited) and send it to Jerry Bishop, the original Svengoolie. He eventually hired me on to do writing and voiceover work on his show and—when Svengoolie was cancelled in '73—I went on to be his second banana for his radio show.

Svengoolie and his friends

CdC: What did you want to be when you grew up?
RK: Originally a cartoonist—along the way, such odd sidetrack ideas (all very short-lived) as joining the FBI or being an astronaut!

CdC: How did you become the Son of Svengoolie?
RK: In the late '70s, Jerry moved out to the west coast. He gave me his blessing to carry on the Svengoolie name, and in mid-'79 I managed to get Son of Svengoolie on the air. I'm always amazed to get feedback from people who saw me on the various field stations back in the '80s. I was doing the show from the Chicago station, and we ran on the four other field stations. Most felt the show was forced on them and didn't promote it, rarely giving me any feedback on it. Only now, years later, I run into people who say, "So this is where you came after (Boston, San Francisco, Detroit, etc.). Everybody used to watch!" I never knew there were fans out in the other cities! I ran until January of '86

10 Questions for Svengoolie

in Chicago (when the show was deemed "not suitable" for the station because it was about to join the prestigious Fox network). I went back to that station from '89–'93.

CdC: I remember you as being the Son of Svengoolie—how'd you get the full "Svengoolie" title?
RK: When I joined up with WCIU in '95, Jerry declared that I was all grown up and graciously bequeathed to me the Svengoolie name. I've been using the name and have been on "The U" ever since.

CdC: What does it mean to be Svengoolie?
RK: Actually, it means a lot—not just to me, but to the viewers. After I was fired by Channel 32 in '86, for the next nine years at least, at least once a week somebody would recognize me on the street and ask, "When are you going to do Son of Svengoolie again?" If it meant that much to people, then, obviously, when Channel 26 asked me to do it again, I felt like there was still a public demand for the character, and how could I refuse that? It means a lot that I've become a Chicago TV icon and that the popularity of Sven has crossed generations. For some I symbolize a little of what's left of the old Chicago school of fly-by-the-seat-of-your-pants TV from the '40s and '50s. That and the paycheck…

CdC: Who are your biggest influences?
RK: Wow! My influences include mentors like Jerry G. Bishop (the original Sven), Dick Orkin (a radio and advertising genius who created the *ChickenMan* and *ToothFairy* syndicated radio features, and whom I also had the great opportunity to work with). Then, a lot of old TV and movie comedians: Groucho, Jack Benny, Gleason. Then, side influences of comic books, other radio guys I listened to growing up.

CdC: What have been your favorite movies to host?
RK: It was always fun to do the old Universal Classics, the American-International flicks, and Godzilla-type movies.

CdC: How about your least?
RK: Not all, but some of the Vincent Price/Poe films. I love Vinnie but I remember the network giving me almost two months in a row of his films, and it became physically wearing on me. The absolute worst was a coming-of-age film called *Kenny and Co.* It's about some crappy pre-teens, but the dolt program director at the time thought was a slasher film. I still have nightmares.

CdC: What was the effect on you when *Mystery Science Theater 3000* took off?
RK: Well, at first, I had no idea because it wasn't on my cable system. I remember a guy I worked with saying, "You have to see this; it's your show." I replied,

"Oh, it's my kind of show?" And he said, "No, I mean it's your show! It's a little too similar to Sven!" Personally, it really didn't bother me much. What did bother me was when I went back on in Chicago in '95, and people who never saw my stuff wrote angry letters about how I was ripping off *MST3K*! The story I usually relate is how, on my very first show in '79, the movie we were running was short so the crew grabbed the next week's movie and rolled about ten minutes of it, with me (who had not even seen any of it) super-imposed in the lower corner making wise cracks! (Sound familiar?)

Personally, I never felt they were "ripping me off." They did a great show, and I felt good when about nine months ago, the *Chicago Tribune* did an interview with the guys, and they mentioned Svengoolie as an influence (a couple of them grew up around here). I'm not sure if they meant Jerry (the Original Sven) or me, but it was nice to finally see it in print. People who had been at various conventions would tell me that the *MST3K* guys would talk about Son of Svengoolie, but this was the first concrete verification I ever saw.

CdC: What question have you always wanted to be asked?
RK: Easy: "Is that your final answer?"

The original version of this article ran in *Cashiers du Cinemart* #11.

Star Wars IV: A New Hope

STAR WARS: THE LOST CUT

By Mike White

I have heard about the seven-hour cut of *The Magnificent Ambersons* that RKO butchered and burned for the nitrates. I have read about the five-hour cut of *Once Upon a Time in the West* discovered at Sergio Leone's estate after his death. I have watched alternate cuts of *Heavenly Creatures, Freaked, Hard Target, Touch of Evil*, and all of Terry Gilliam and James Cameron's films. I have to admit that with each unveiling of a different version of a film, I get a giddy feeling. It is not that alternate cuts are necessarily better (*Blade Runner*), or that extra scenes necessarily add anything of interest (*1941*). Instead, these versions offer viewers a chance to witness the progression of the films from their origins to the finished product.

Looking at the aforementioned films and offering up other films that have been released on video, in the theater, or on television in an altered state (*Amazon Women on the Moon, Superman, Jaws, Dune, The Exorcist*—in other words, the fodder of feature articles for *Video Watchdog*), one would be hard pressed to find another film with a history as unique and outrageous as *Star Wars*. Few films have been tinkered with as much since their initial release. Even before 1997's "Special Edition," *Star Wars* underwent minor retooling (adding the subtitle "Episode IV" during the preamble scroll, removing and re-adding C3-PO's "The tractor beam is coupled to the main reactor in seven locations. A power loss at one of the terminals will allow the ship to leave," and the Stormtroopers' "Open the blast doors!" lines). But more than inserting alternate takes and excised scenes, George Lucas created entirely new shots and changed the tone and intent of scenes—not necessarily entirely due to budgetary and technological limits, but because Lucas had simply changed his mind about some things over the years.

Lucas needs to learn to put a project to bed when the time is due. Can you imagine the mess that a director could make if his obsessive tinkering got the best of his work? What kind of damage could Orson Welles do to *Citizen Kane* if he were alive and decided that he really would rather have the story told in a linear fashion? Not to suggest that George Lucas should have passed on after *The Empire Strikes Back*, but it seems that his meddling is more damaging than helpful.

What is more important than what Lucas added to *Star Wars: Special Edition* is what he kept out. Lucas put in the scene of Han Solo talking to Jabba the Hutt, and justified it by saying that it tied in with Jabba's appearance in *Return of the Jedi*. However, using that same logic, wouldn't it also have made sense to put in the scenes early in *Star Wars* with Biggs Darklighter and Luke, so that Biggs's death is given proper weight when he dies in the assault on the Death Star? Isn't this inter-film connection even more important because of Biggs's mysterious appearance of the moon of Yavin? Would it not answer the question of who this mustachioed guy is, and why the music swells after his death? If there was a time to put the Biggs Darklighter scenes (and others) back in, *Star Wars: Special Edition* was it. Lucas's excuse for their continued absence? They are said to detract from the pacing of the film. If that is the case, then the Wampa material and the shot of Darth Vadar's shuttle returning to his Star Destroyer in *The Empire Strikes Back: Special Edition* should never have been shot and crudely stuffed into that film.

So what is the truth for why these scenes remain out of the public eye?

The last decade has seen four major releases of the *Star Wars* trilogy: "The Definitive Collection," the digitally remastered collection, and the Special Edition's theatrical and subsequent video releases. It seems that Lucas's marketing strategy is a combination of Disney's release and withdraw scheme and his old pal Francis Ford Coppola's re-edit and release ploy that he's been using for years with The *Godfather* films (*The Complete Godfather, The Godfather Epic,* the digitally remastered *Godfather*, etc.). As long as there is a dime to squeeze out of the *Star Wars* franchise, Lucas is going to do it. And the best way to milk his cash cow is to dole out extras every few years. In this way, Lucas will continue to release various versions of *Star Wars* in various formats well into the next millennium.

What could the future of *Star Wars* re-releases hold? The Lucasfilm archives contain a treasure trove of material that may or may not ever see the light of a projector bulb again. Sure, there are plenty of embarrassing moments: *The Star Wars Holiday Special* is proof of that. Nevertheless, as cheesy as it is, it still culturally significant and would need to be part of a truly definitive *Star Wars* collection.

It's not that Jefferson Starship's stunning performance of "Light the Sky on Fire" really adds to the overall history of *Star Wars*, but the special played host to the introduction of Boba Fett through the cartoon that Chewbacca's son Waroo watched. Moreover, the "Life on Tatooine" sequence contains shots that were originally in *Star Wars*, but not released in any other format.

When an alternate cut of Howard Hawks's *The Big Sleep* was re-released in 1998, audiences were made privy to a view of an American classic in progress. There is a myriad of reasons why this event was not widely heralded. *The Big Sleep* had a small re-release and virtually no marketing, especially when compared to another classic film noir that had a revival the same year: *Touch of Evil*. Moreover, if *The Big Sleep* is famous for anything, it's for its convoluted plot, begging the question of why it wasn't as big of a draw as a film directed by "the wine guy." In both cases, however, the stories of both of these films' discoveries and re-releases were hot news among cinephiles, and even made waves in the mainstream media.

Try to imagine another film that, if an alternate version were unearthed, might have more significance than *Star Wars*.

News of this kind could generate enough hype that it might even overshadow the fervor that *The Phantom Menace* has created. Being more than a new chapter in the *Star Wars* story, another version of *Star Wars* would put the original film in a new light, by enriching its history and giving us a glimpse into the creation of this cultural phenomenon.

Instead of burning up the internet, at the time this story was written few folks have heard the news: there is a "lost cut" of *Star Wars*. I still find it difficult to believe that the write-up of the lost cut was delegated to the back of *The Star Wars Insider* #41 instead of being the cover story!

So, what's different about the lost cut?

It's a given that the scenes of Luke watching the battle between the Rebel blockade runner and Star Destroyer, Luke at Tosche Station, and the original Jabba the Hutt scenes are in place. It's not too much of a stretch of the imagination to know that most of the special effects shots are a lot rougher, as rear projection was used instead of blue-screen shots. It's also very interesting that there are alternate takes in which familiar lines are said, but with different inflections. But when looking at the lost cut, the most startling thing is that the film has an entirely different tone than the version that has become an integral part of American culture.

According to David West Reynolds's *Revolution of Star Wars*, geography plays a much larger role in the lost cut. Viewers get a real sense of the layout of both Tatooine and the Death Star. This, in addition to a larger cast of minor characters and longer, more realistically paced scenes, gives the film a much more documentary-like feel, putting it in line with Lucas's previous feature, *American Graffiti*, and its quasi-documentary style.

Will this version ever be readily available to the public? I think that one would have a better chance at getting the full Warren Commission Report and President Kennedy's brain than getting Lucas to ever release the lost cut, as it doesn't match his "artistic vision."

I hope that Lucas can see the importance of preserving a part of filmic history and eventually allows it to be studied.

The original version of this article ran in *Cashiers du Cinemart* #9.

Boba Fett

DA JAR JAR DONE GONE

By Mike White

A No-Confidence Vote in George Lucas

Rather than just grousing about *The Phantom Menace*, a few folks took matters into their own able hands and edited this abhorrent film to suit their tastes. This phenomenon came to light in mid-2001 and, via the internet, word spread like wildfire about the various alternative takes on George Lucas's justly maligned film. Reaction to the idea of re-cutting someone else's work was an odd mix of righteous indignation about artistic license (a topic readers of *CdC* should be familiar with), celebration for the correction of the flawed film, and panicked desperation from fans trying to get their hands on a copy of one or more of these alternative versions.

Within days of initial reports, digitized versions of one of these alternate cuts started popping up on servers across the land. This version became known as *The Phantom Edit 1.1*. Some dubbed it "The L.A. Cut," due to its origin and to differentiate it from another version that received some press: *The Phantom Re-edit*. Numerous people jettisoned this title in favor of "The NY Cut." Allegedly, *The Phantom Re-edit* came into being some months before *The Phantom Edit 1.1*. However, it seemed far more elusive to fans, and more extensive in its changes.

Enter the bootleggers. Reviled on message boards, these entrepreneurs aided the technologically and bandwidth impaired by selling VCD and VHS copies of *The Phantom Edit 1.1*. As for *The Phantom Re-edit*, this seemed to remain tight in the clutches of scurrilous "dot-com journalists" who refused to give them up lest they lose their scoop. Luckily, patience provided a few bootleggers who managed to stock *The Phantom Re-edit* by hook or by crook.

The Phantom Re-edit

The most offensive characters of *The Phantom Menace* are the aliens. Toydarians, Nemoidians, and Gungans recall racist stereotypes of Jews, Asians, and African Americans. *The Phantom Re-edit* takes great pains to rework the narrative of *The Phantom Menace* and play down the "massah" intonation of Jar Jar Binks, the space-age Stepin Fetchit. Here the Jar Jar character no longer serves as comic relief. Instead, he is portrayed as a Jedi Knight!

Via removal of Jar Jar's sillier slapstick antics and scrambling his dialogue, the creators of *The Phantom Re-edit* employ subtitles to provide a more sagacious stature to this buffoon. Indeed, Jedi Jar Jar runs off at the mouth with profundity far too often. Waxing philosophically at the drop of the hat, Jar Jar forgets the Taoist principle that "those who say don't know and those who know don't say."

Da Jar Jar Done Gone

Despite his new words, it is difficult to accept Jar Jar as anything but a fool due to the attitude of those around him. Qui-Gon Jin and Obi-Wan Kenobi still treat Jar Jar with contempt ("pathetic lifeform") and C3-PO's remarks about Jar Jar being "a little odd" don't make sense. You wouldn't hear anyone saying that Yoda is a goof, even if he does talk backwards with a voice like Grover from *Sesame Street*.

The Gungans aren't the only race whose dialogue is scrambled and subtitled. The Nemoidians also receive this treatment. However, the Nemodians say nothing new: their words are unintelligible, but their dialogue remains intact. The Nemodians are still completely subservient to Darth Sidious. The subtitles only aid in downplaying the poor initial dubbing of these characters and eliminate their Charlie Chan elocution. Alas, nothing has been done to lessen the "hook-nosed greedy shopkeeper" image of Watuu, poster child for *The Protocols of Zion*.

Jar Jar Binks

The Phantom Re-edit chucks a few bits of unneeded action and dialogue, but not nearly enough. The cuts are far from seamless due to wipe effects that are meant to mimic those of *The Phantom Menace*, but bring unneeded attention to themselves. Finally, due to the unyielding original source material, *The Phantom Re-edit* feels like a good idea gone awry.

The Phantom Edit 1.1

Running 119 minutes (23 minutes shorter than the original), *The Phantom Edit 1.1* is remarkable in its nearly flawless editing. After not having watched *The Phantom Menace* since its initial theatrical run, I found myself confounded to recall anything missing from *Edit*, save for the overlong ocean journey from the Gungan Kingdom to the surface of Naboo. Some viewers felt that this trip was symbolic in its "there's always a bigger fish" metaphor of the Republic swallowing Naboo, but others felt it merely bogged down the narrative, drawing out the film to an even more uncomfortable length. Edit eases the malaise felt by fans of the original *Star Wars* by trimming comedic scenes of Jar Jar (isn't stepping in poop always funny?) and whiny lines from Anakin (truly his son's father—I could almost hear little Ani crying, "I wanted to go to Tosche Station to pick up some power converters!").

To someone admittedly unfamiliar with *The Phantom Menace*, the extent of the editing of *The Phantom Edit 1.1* cannot be determined unless suffering through the original multiple times. Discarded scenes soon number in the dozens, with nary a one necessary to the plot. They are not missed, merely absent. *The Phantom 1.1* weeds out superfluous action and redundancies in the plot. Likewise, The Phantom Editor, Mike J. Nichols, heightens the drama of several scenes with rearrangement of shots and sound.

Nichols told *CdC*, "Watch the scene where Queen Amidala and Jar Jar are at the window after the Senate meeting. In my cut Jar Jar says that the Gungans have 'a grand army' and, visually, we see the Queen juxtaposed. This is the basis for the film's climax. Her paying attention to Jar Jar's ramblings helps her plan the ending battle…Compare that to how Lucas lost track of the scene in *Menace*—and he's the guy who actually wanted Jar Jar in the movie. My way is more effective storytelling."

A list all of the frames, scenes, shots, and lines eliminated might rival a similar list of those that remain. If I have one complaint about *The Phantom Edit 1.1*, it's that Nichols didn't go far enough! While tightening the plotting and action, many annoying aspects of Lucas's original film remain.

There Is Another

The best thing to come from the discovery of *The Phantom Edit 1.1* and *The Phantom Re-edit* is the reclamation of the D.I.Y. spirit of film. The dissemination of these alternate cuts prodded others into admitting that they had also taken matters into their own hands.

Postings began popping up on the occasional newsgroup about cuts from London to Singapore. At the time of this initial printing, these postings remain unsubstantiated. However, Andrew Pagana's "corrector's edition" certainly exists. Dubbed *The Phantom's New Hope*, Pagana's cut runs 116 minutes and moves at a pace reminiscent of the original *Star Wars*.

Tightened with a socket wrench, Pagana has cut *The Phantom Menace* with a surgical skill, removing several of the items that *The Phantom Edit 1.1* left sticking in my craw:

> <SNIP> Queen Amidala giving praise to R2-D2 for being a "brave little droid." Sure, it introduces the R2-D2 character by name, but why praise a machine for just doing its job? Does George Lucas thank his toaster each morning for browning his bread evenly?
>
> <SNIP> Thank you, Mr. Pagana, for eliminating the embarrassing "Are you an angel?" question from Anakin to Padme.
>
> <SNIP> Like *The Phantom Edit 1.1*, Pagana eliminates the midichlorians—the blood-borne organisms that appear to endow humanoids with The Force (making Jedi Knights more of a biologically elite society than a mental and spiritual discipline). However, *The Phantom's New Hope* removes the solitary blood reference that remained in *The Phantom Edit 1.1*.

<SNIP> Again, blood and fate have undue weight, especially with the "virgin birth" of Anakin. Thoroughly ridiculous, Pagana eliminates this silly and overtly biblical notion.

<SNIP> Anakin's not the only annoying kid in *The Phantom Menace*. All of his friends are troublesome, as well. One quick cut eliminates their meeting around Anakin's pod racer.

<SNIP> A few seconds later Jar Jar lifts some comedy from Bill Cosby's old routine about going to the dentist. There's no need to see the goofy Gungan get zapped by Anakin's pod and have his tongue go numb.

<SNIP> Out go the two C3-PO lines about Jar Jar being an "odd creature." It's best not to draw attention to him. Maybe if we just ignore him, he'll go away.

Quite a few other annoying lines are blissfully sacrificed in *The Phantom's New Hope*. Only a handful of references to Anakin as "Ani" remain, while the battle droids' cutesy "Roger, Roger" has wound up in the dustbin. The battle droids remain a weak threat at best but the less they speak, the more menacing they appear. (Has anyone noticed that the few shielded "destroyer droids" appear invincible, while the legions of battle droids are virtually ineffective? Perhaps budget restrictions prevented the Nemoidians from mass-producing these hardier droids.)

As with *The Phantom Edit 1.1*, *The Phantom's New Hope* is not without its flaws. There are a few missteps with the sound (courtesy of John Williams's ever-present score) and an occasional rough edge (the scene of Anakin leaving his mother), but otherwise, *The Phantom's New Hope* stands out as a remarkable alternative to Lucas's original film.

Send in the Clones

Ideally, Pagana, Nichols, or some third party (or parties) will study the aforementioned alternative cuts, and use the best ideas to produce the definitive emendation. I thought that I had found this "final cut" with the discovery of *The Phantom Edit Version 1.14* (versions 1.11, 1.12, and 1.13 have yet to show up), but this was not to be.

Where Nichols and Pagana used a scalpel to pare down *The Phantom Menace*, the creator of *TPE v1.14* appears to have used a machete. Instead of frames, shots, or scenes finding their way onto the cutting room floor, *The Phantom Menace* shares the fate of Darth Maul by being hacked in half. Going so far as to dispense with the opening scroll, title theme, and end credits, this version of *The Phantom Menace* has the scant running time of 84 minutes! Relying on The Persistence of Plot, *TPE v1.14* runs like a choppy overlong preview rather than any sort of cohesive, albeit portentous and silly, narrative.

A Thousand Terrible Things

Only so much can be done to *The Phantom Menace* with cutting, rearranging, and redubbing. Inherent flaws in the original remain beyond rectification. For example, a moment of anticlimax comes from the revelation of Padme as the true Queen of Naboo, an event that need not have happened when it did, if at all. The conceit of Padme as the true Queen never goes anywhere except as a pale parallel to the dual existence of Senator Palpatine as a man of honor and Lord of the Sith (way to go, catching those subtleties, Jedi Knights!).

In addition, no matter how one cuts it (literally or figuratively), the long-winded pod race and piss-poor acting of Jake Lloyd (Anakin) cannot be completely deleted. And of course, there will always be too much Jar Jar and not enough Darth Maul.

Be Mindful of the Future

The beauty of the Nichols and Pagana edits comes from the adroit use of editing—one of the most under-appreciated disciplines in filmmaking. Neither editor cleaves away scenes out of spite, but only to make *The Phantom Menace* a more effective film. When placed in context, will Lucas's *Episode II* and *III* contradict the changes that Nichols, Pagana, and other editors have made? Does it really matter?

George Lucas seems bent on self-destruction with the needless (and mindless) meddling he's done to the three original *Star Wars* films (though little could make *Return of the Jedi* any worse, save yet another musical number). Lucas must unlearn what he's learned during his idle years. The editing of *The Phantom Menace* should serve as a wake-up call to Lucas (and his ardent admirers). Lucas is not infallible. The *Star Wars* films aren't sacred texts. Where Lucas has been intrusive in tweaking the original *Star Wars* films, changes to *The Phantom Menace* have been insightful.

While Nichols has taken the subsequent *Star Wars* films into consideration with *The Phantom Edit 1.1*, Pagana's work (with its lack of midichlorians) may leave some viewers scratching their heads if these contemptuous globules make an unwanted appearance in future Lucas work. Rather than getting bent out of shape (as some decriers of the re-edits have done), the solution looms large. Instead of bringing the mountain to Muhammad, take *Episode II* and *III* to the chopping block and continue to correct Lucas's mistakes.

Why should audiences continue to suffer for the foolishness of megalomaniacal directors? Optimistically, the edits of *The Phantom Menace* will edify other directors to rein themselves in, and give inspiration to other would-be editors that might make pre-existing material better. Please, feel free to include a film's extra scenes when it's released on DVD, but leave the original theatrical version intact.

Da Jar Jar Done Gone

The glimmer that directors might be able to tone down their excesses comes in the re-release of a shorter version of the Coen Brothers' *Blood Simple*. Conversely, George Lucas's crony, Francis Ford Coppola, continues to misjudge the extent of his talent by releasing *Apocalypse Now Redux*. The inclusion of the infamous "French plantation scene" does his film far more harm than good. Certainly, a better cut of *Apocalypse Now* could have been culled from the bootleg versions of the film that run up to five hours!

Outside of Hollywood, there is a tide in the affairs of fans: stirrings of dissension. Whether they ever reach fruition or merely remain good ideas, rumors of alternate cuts of *Superman II* and *Star Trek V* flourish. Instead of special director's cuts that add unneeded plodding and padding to films' plotlines, perhaps there will be a rash of cuts that abrogate abuses and trim films to concise refinement.

Think of all the near misses over the years that could be made new with a honed blade. Say goodbye to circuitous subplots and extra scenes for the sake of extra scenes! Say hello to reasonable running times and logical narratives. At least we can hope.

The original version of this article ran in *Cashiers du Cinemart* #13.

TRIUMPH OF THE WHILLS

By Mike White

As I sat down to put together all of the *Star Wars*-related pieces that I'd penned over the years, I realized that I have basically been saying the same thing, rephrasing it over time. The first section, "I Have a Boba Fettish," comes from *Cashiers du Cinemart* #4, 1995. This was a reaction to the announcement of the *Star Wars* prequels, and a plea for sanity in a world insane enough to allow *Return of the Jedi*. Next, "Dude, That's Your Sister!" (*CdC* #7, 1997) examined the incestuous nature of the Skywalker siblings, tracing its roots back to previous work by *Star Wars* creator George Lucas. I had yet to experience *The Phantom Menace* at this point.

I remained oddly mute about *The Phantom Menace* upon its release. I think I was in denial, or too much pain. It wasn't until some jackass in an "online community" started spouting off about Lucas having an overarching plan for his grand vision of the *Star Wars* saga that I lost it. "Everyone Knows It's Windu" (*CdC* #15, 2007) was the same rant some ten years after "I Have a Boba Fettish." Perhaps more eloquently expressed (or not), the frustrations of my eleven-year-old self have yet to be laid to rest and are only stoked by every inane, revisionist, money-grubbing move George Lucas makes.

I Have a Boba Fettish

I haven't seen *Return of the Jedi* in a few years. And you're lucky for that, because I could go through it and give a step-by-step analysis of why I hate every scene in that film. But we'll keep this at a general overview.

Go back and watch *Star Wars* and tell me what you feel. When I watch it, I feel like I'm watching a huge Japanese epic that is truly galactic in scope and delivers all that it promises. Some might accuse it of simply being a pastiche of familiar scenes and universal themes just set in a galaxy far, far away, but even if it is, it works.

I love that in *Star Wars*, characters don't explain every little thing, nor do the sets and special effects overshadow the characters. In *Star Wars*, the story is king.

Return of the Jedi falls victim to the "Well, we can do all these neat effects; build a story around them" phenomena.

When I look at *Return of the Jedi*, I see a film that is pandering to the lowest common denominator. A bunch of scenes that proved popular in the first two films: space battles, aliens, sword fights. When I look at *ROTJ*, I think that there's no way George Lucas had any of it in mind when he came up with *Star Wars*. Either that or he's the biggest money whore I've ever seen, taking a series from the highest of the high to these depths.

Triumph of the Whills

Just the idea of building another Death Star was the start of the big cop-out. And don't tell me they had Leia in mind as Luke's sister the whole time, or I'll vomit when I see her slip him the tongue on the ice planet of Hoth in *The Empire Strikes Back*.

Then there's the Ewoks—yeah, we've been fighting the Empire for all these years, guess we just needed some sticks and rocks to defeat them forever. A marketer's dream—cute, cuddly, and with the name *Star Wars* on it, they'll sell like crazy.

Yeah. Sell *out*.

And since when did the Empire (do you know what that word means—empire?) become so tiny? When did Lord Vader move from one of many Lords of the Sith—one of many bureaucratic governors (like Grand Moff Tarkin)—to "The Shit"? Were all of the governors on that original Death Star?

And when did C3-PO change from a used-car salesman (as he frequently seemed to be in Star Wars) to the bumbling booby Dr. Smith impersonator that he became in *ROTJ*?

I really like *The Empire Strikes Back* a lot, but there were some bad seeds planted there. But I place all the blame on *ROTJ* for taking the ball and running with it.

From the very beginning of *ROTJ*, we are introduced to funny creatures (keep the kids happy) and dumb-ass comic relief. We have Luke returning home without a second glance at his former world and trying the front-door approach at Jabba's palace that might have worked—if he were a real Jedi Knight.

Up until this point in the article, I have tried to keep my perspective as a 23-year-old cinephile looking back on one of the sourest notes in movie threequels (which might even put *Superman III* to shame), when comparing *ROTJ* to the two films that came before it. Damn, I hate that film.

But now it's time to unleash that 11-year-old who saw *ROTJ* three times at the theater and hear what his biggest complaint was:

> Those creeps killed off BOBA FETT! Boba is only the coolest of all the bounty hunters and he dies in a totally dumb way that's supposed to be like a joke or something?! Get real! The whole Sarlac pit was just dumb and I can't believe Boba Fett died. He was a total badass who could, like, kill anyone, anytime, but he gets hit by Han (who is temporarily blind from the carbon freezing) and falls into the pit. At least the comic book of *Star Wars* brought him back for an issue, but he's still dead. That's just wrong! What was he doing fighting for Jabba, anyway? He was just a bounty hunter who only cared about money, and he would have said, "See ya!" right after he got his money.

Man, like I said, it's a good thing *Return of the Jedi* isn't on right now, or you'd get a whole zine dedicated to how utterly repulsive I think that is. It's as entertaining as a turd in a punch bowl.

Now my skin is crawling to think that Lucas might be bringing us another lamefest with the new series. What's next? A whole movie that takes place on the moon of Endor with those cuddly Ewoks? Be afraid.

Dude, That's Your Sister!

The other day I thought of yet another reason why *Return of the Jedi* stinks—aside from a lousy story and some the bad acting (Mark Hamill, Carrie Fisher). It offends me on a more Jungian level by breaking the nearly universal taboo of incest.

I don't think that Luke and Leia consummated their relationship, but there was that little peck on the cheek in *Star Wars* (which some people on the internet are calling *A New Hope*—isn't that lame?) and that big ole sloppy tongue kiss in *Empire*—which nauseates me every time I see it, knowing that their kinship is revealed in *Jedi*.

I could see Luke maybe having a sister, but as a completely different character. I used to be fairly certain that Leia being the "other" to which Yoda refers was a last-minute ditch to give some unneeded closure to a terrible screenplay. But then I remembered Lucas's *American Graffiti*, and the strange exchange that happens when Stephen (Ron Howard) and Laurie (Cindy Williams) are making out in her car:

STEPHEN
Well, what's wrong? You're just sitting there!

LAURIE
Well, you want to, go ahead!

STEPHEN
Not like that!

LAURIE
If you're not going to remember me for anything else, why don't you just go ahead!

STEPHEN
Aw, come on! You want it and you know it. Don't be so damned self-righteous with me. After all that stuff you told me about watching your brother.

> **LAURIE**
> You're disgusting! Get out of my car! Get out!
>
> **STEPHEN**
> Laurie!
>
> **LAURIE**
> Get out! I told you never to mention that!

It doesn't sound like Laurie and her brother (Curt, as played by Richard Dreyfuss) actually did anything sexual together, but what in the world was she watching him do? Masturbate? Fornicate? Regardless, it sounds like our friend Laurie's little voyeuristic escapade was a little out of the realm of open societal acceptance.

In the three films that Lucas has directed, two of them feature suspect siblings, and if one was inclined to think of Indiana Jones (who was treated as a son by Professor Ravenwood) messing around with Marion as strange, chalk up another bizarre sister–brother relationship in Lucas's oeuvre.

Certainly Lucas isn't the only director to explore filial lust on screen, but Lucas isn't just any other director—I grew up on *Star Wars* and it's pretty damn unsettling to look at these films, movies that shaped my life, and catch a glimpse of the seamy underbelly of Lucas's psyche.

What other evil lurks in the mind of George Lucas?

It's George's World… We Just Live Here

There are some who have completely shunned the idea of the *Star Wars: Special Edition*, saying that it tarnishes the memory of a once-great film, that it is a plundering of an American film classic. Then there are others who would argue that it's George's film—he can do what he likes with it.

It's all of four frames, but those four frames change so much. If you haven't seen it yet, here's the lowdown: you'll remember that during Han Solo's confrontation with Greedo, the bounty hunter pretty much admits that he's going to kill Han Solo ("Over my dead body," says Han. "That's the idea," says Greedo). So, Solo secretly removes his blaster from its holster and shoots this scumbag from under the table. Cool!

Han Solo is a smuggler, an admitted scoundrel, and works for the biggest gangster in the galaxy—he ain't no hero romping around the galaxy on damn fool idealistic crusades…not yet, anyway. But now the scene plays out with Greedo shooting and missing at point-blank range before Solo kills him in self defense!

It was self defense in the first version—just not as clear-cut. Within these four friggin' frames, George has successfully changed the makeup of Han Solo.

He's removed a layer of grey and cleared up any doubts that Solo's really just a nice guy with a tough exterior. What a load of crap!

It sucks not only because of the changes of character in Han Solo—but because it looks shitty, too! The action needed to be longer than four frames and the continuity blows: when Solo gets up to pay for his drink, there's no hole in the wall as there was in the previous shot.

Everyone Knows It's Windu

While a vast improvement from *The Phantom Menace*, *Attack of the Clones* is not free of flaws. Of all the disappointments in the movie, the greatest has to be not living up to its potential. The most interesting character, Count Dooku (Christopher Lee)—the only Jedi who truly knows the score—alerts Obi-Wan Kenobi (Ewan McGregor) to the presence of Darth Sidious (Ian McDiarmid). Wouldn't it have been far more interesting if Dooku were the lone visionary? The longer the *Star Wars* saga goes on, the dumber Jedis appear. Not only do they not believe Dooku, the Jedi Council can't grasp that if there are only "good" Jedis around, "bringing balance to the force" means an expansion of the Dark Side! (Apparently, they haven't read Louise Cooper's *Time Master* Trilogy.)

Midway through *Attack of the Clones* I was terribly bored, listening to Anakin's "stalker wooing" of Padme. Apparently the way to her heart is through appealing to her with constant jabber, digs at her profession, and psychotically slaughtering Tusken Raiders.

Is this what Lucas had planned all along?

According to Laurent Bouzerau's *Star Wars: The Annotated Screenplays*, "It all began in 1973, when Lucas sat down and wrote a forty-page outline entitled 'Journal of the Whills.'" Later, this phrase would be re-used as subtitle for a few of Lucas's drafts of the original *Star Wars* screenplay ("From 'The Adventures of Luke Starkiller,' as taken from the 'Journal of the Whills'"). In these later instances, the "Journal of the Whills" served only as a fictional tome that contained the entire history of Lucas's intergalactic setting. In this way, Lucas's "Journal of the Whills" became a nod to the many books to which Frank Herbert referred in his *Dune* series. Often, chapters in *Dune* begin with quotes from more official historical records of the known universe, making Herbert's story feel like the inside scoop on the life of Muad'dib.

The original "Journal of the Whills" featured "Mace Windy, a revered Jedi Bendu of Ophuchi as told by C.J. Thorpe, Padawaan learner of the famed Jedi." From this proximal incarnation of the Mace Windu name, one might begin to get the impression that Lucas had his six films laid out some four years before the release of *Star Wars*. I opine that Lucas has been myopically struggling to piece together his grand scheme for the last three decades, and will continue to do so long after his two trilogies are complete.

Triumph of the Whills

When Lucas announced that *Star Wars: A New Hope* (a title not widely used until the late '90s) was the fourth film—his first of many changes to his completed work—he stated that there were to be nine films in the *Star Wars* saga, and that only three characters would be in all nine films: C3-PO, R2-D2, and Chewbacca.

Now George Lucas seems to have amnesia in regard to the nine films. His "original vision" called for six and that's all he's going to create. Meanwhile, Yoda has replaced Chewbacca as the third recurring character (most likely at the behest of Hasbro). Rather than being an expansive tale starring the droids, the *Star Wars* films have become the creation and unraveling of the Skywalker family, turning the "space opera" into a soap opera.

The expanding universe has been contracting. Lucas has been narrowing the scope of his tales with each subsequent film (and will revise his earlier films to fit this new vision). On the surface, it is "cute" to have cameo appearances in the newer films by characters who will show up in the original trilogy. But what Lucas doesn't seem to realize is that he's making the universe a very small place.

Did the fate of the Fett family really need to intertwine with the Skywalkers? Does this enrich the narrative, or merely cheapen it? Perhaps the only benefit of introducing Boba Fett's father for the film series is making the death of Boba less embarrassing in *Return of the Jedi*. Instead of being a cool, competent bounty hunter, Boba seems sired from rather inept stock. In *Attack of the Clones*, the senior Fett, Jango (Temuera Morrison), subcontracts a simple job that gets botched twice, allows himself to be sought out twice, and dies with less of a bang than a whimper.

It's understandable that some of the character and place names in the *Star Wars* universe might have shifted and mutated from the earliest outlines to later drafts. Lucas tended to grab onto words and move them about until they fit his fancy. For example, the aforementioned Mace Windy was to become Windy Starkiller—seven-year-old twin brother of Biggs Starkiller. It wouldn't be until *The Phantom Menace* that Mace Windu (Samuel L. Jackson) made his appearance, and it wasn't until *Attack of the Clones* that this character actually did anything.

Apparently, names and places weren't nailed down until the shooting of *Star Wars* began. In auditions for Luke Skywalker, Han Solo, and Princess Leia Organa, the dialogue has a familiar ring, but is oddly skewed. Instead of Alderaan being destroyed by the Death Star, Han and Luke visit the remains of Organa Major. Meanwhile, they discuss the plausibility of venturing to the Alderaan system, as if it were the heart of the Empire.

I lost my faith in George Lucas's ability when he undoubtedly felt that he was coming into his own. Lucas apparently bought into his own hype and felt that he could do no wrong. The resulting travesty was *Return of the Jedi*. This film serves as the most damning evidence that Lucas may have had some vague notion of the larger scheme of things, but no clue about the execution of the later films.

If Lucas had known that Luke and Leia were siblings, he might have reconsidered the romantic overtones of their relationship. (That newlyweds Anakin and Padme are framed nearly identically at the end of *Attack of the Clones* as Luke and Leia were in *The Empire Strikes Back* serves as an eerie reminder of their children's potential romance.) Likewise, did Lucas's grand scheme include multiple reincarnations of the Death Star? And were missing limbs a motif?

After *Return of the Jedi*, Lucas's self-delusion spiraled out of control back at Skywalker (not Starkiller) ranch. It's obvious that Lucas didn't spend the years between *Episode VI* and *Episode I* boning up on his writing skills or cementing the details of the first three *Star Wars* films. Despite claims to the contrary, Lucas still doesn't have a firm hand on these new films. The mercurial nature is best evidenced by Lucas's heeding of public opinion about *The Phantom Menace*. Nowhere in *Attack of the Clones* do midichlorians rear their ugly head. Likewise, Lucas diminished the role of the universally execrated Jar Jar Binks.

For someone who claims to have had *Star Wars* plotted out to the last details, I contend that Lucas is stumbling through the dark when it comes to these new films. He knows where he needs to get these characters, but he's clueless about how to get them there.

Recalling the unneeded additional bits to the "special editions" of Lucas's original trilogy, the extra scenes and shots constitute nothing more than bitter eye candy. Lucas seems more intent on examining what he can show via special effects than what he can do with a solid story. Rather than enhance the films, Lucas has built in unnecessary distractions and destroyed pacing.

Like those new scenes, *Episodes I–III* of the *Star Wars* saga are extrinsic. While Lucas may not have nailed down enough about this universe to produce convincing storylines for *Episodes I–III*, his early work, with his myriad drafts and notes, provided the original *Star Wars* with a rich back story. The events outside of Luke Skywalker's little world made for a narrative that felt truly galactic. By strip mining the pre-history of *Star Wars* and dealing solely with the life and loves of Anakin Skywalker, Lucas has devitalized his work.

Luke Skywalker (Mark Hamill) and Biggs Darklighter (Garrick Hagon) in *Star Wars*

Rather than showing some panache and making films that broke new ground, creating the first three episodes took all the skill of shooting fish in a barrel. If the filmmaker and the audience are painfully aware of how these characters end up, the journey from Point A to Point

Triumph of the Whills

B should at least be interesting. Thus far Lucas has yet to recapture the imagination or accommodate the attention span of his audience. Lucas appears under the delusion that the only prerequisite for a grandiose film is that it have a running time over two hours.

Lucas will wrap up the events of these first movies and make sure that they tie into his original works. He'll initially snip off every loose end, and then cement the relationship by further digital augmentation of the first three episodes with the last three. Don't be surprised to see Bail Organa (Jimmy Smits) have a tearful reunion with his daughter, Princess Leia (Carrie Fisher), when she safely returns to the moon of Yavin in *A New Hope*. I mean, we've already got Temuera Morrison and Ian McDiarmid coming back to redub Boba Fett and the Emperor, and Hayden Christensen showing up as a ghost in *Return of the Jedi*. The madness won't end here.

Portions of this article originally ran in *Cashiers du Cinemart* #4, #7, & #15.

cashiers du cinemart

black shampoo

The CdC Manifesto

Mary is not a ~~~ Anymore

The Truth About Black Shampoo

$2

© 1997 Nathan Kane

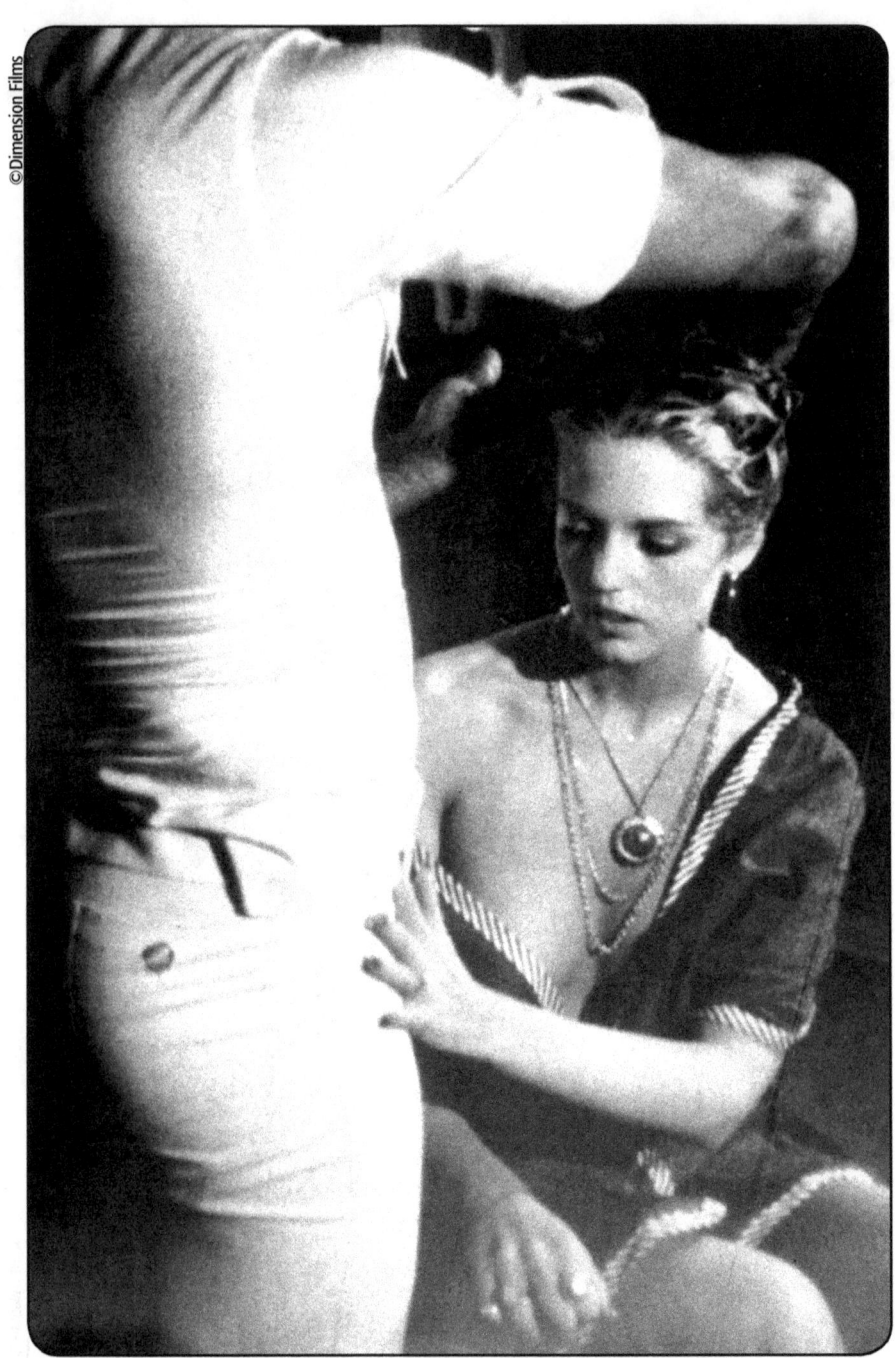

Mrs. Carruthers really enjoys her wash and rinse in *Black Shampoo*

A FEW NOTES ON *BLACK SHAMPOO*

By Leon Chase

What always sticks out in my mind is that spectacular opening build-up. The crackle of damaged film, the name of the production company and then—two notes on an electric bass (open E to F#, I believe)—simple, bottom-heavy, sure, and sticky thick, with the promise of the sexual ballet to come. Remember, please, that we had no idea what we were in for—us, the Original Three—all bored, sixteen, and virginal (well, at least I was, anyway…)

We had braved blizzard conditions and nard-choking automotive tailspins just to procure this tape. Mike, the brave Malibu pilot; Leon, the unwitting discoverer; and Steve.…what did Steve do? Why, it was in his otherwise wholesome family room that our eyes were opened, our loins awakened, and our souls forever stained with a new filthy joy. I recall, at the onset of the aforementioned bass strains, remarking, "With bass like that, it's gotta be good." Oh, the understatement! The cosmic Zen ironies at work in that nondescript suburban home that night! Only an unbridled naïveté like ours could make a person so willingly plunge into such immeasurable libidic depths!

I still shiver at those two notes, repeating themselves as the screen melts, psychedelia-style, into the image of Mrs. Carruthers, about to get her hair washed, cinematic surrogate for our own anticipation. The images stick with me like a primordial dream…a glint of light on the earthtone sink, the base sensuality of running water, the sure and mighty twist of a shampoo cap, and a new, tenser sound: the first staccato licks of a potent wah guitar, careful—testing the waters, so to speak.

One visual is conspicuously lacking, though—who, we ask ourselves, is doing the shampooing? Even as the shampooee begins writhing in her seat, an obvious slave to both the sexuality of her wash-and-rinse and the quickening funk guitar, we see the man only in pieces—at once a clever suspense tactic and implied comment on his larger-than-life persona. A manly brown hand caressing blonde locks. White jeans, impossibly tight. The bass quickens slightly, the guitar steadies, the two reconcile themselves into a leisurely yet popping groove. A woman's voice, slinky and steeped in echo, slips into the mix and gives name to this faceless, follicle-fingering phenomenon: "Jonathan," she purrs. And then (as if we didn't know by now) she adds, "He's a real man."

More rinsing, more booty shaking, the woman drags her fingers down her own increasingly exposed body until, finally, neither she nor her experiential audience can stand it any longer. She sits straight up in her seat. Her frantic bony hand traces abundant fields of black chest so bursting with virility that not even a polyester shirt can quite cover them. The hand winds down to the zippers, struggles to clear the obvious girth beneath, and next we see her hand

A Few Notes on *Black Shampoo*

on the white clad buttocks, the music breaks down into a single, repetitive four-four kick drum, and all of our greatest hopes and fears are realized.

"Oh my god! Mr. Jonathan! It is bigger and better!"

At this point one can clearly envision composer Gerald Lee bringing his baton down hard, signaling the whole PCP-laced crew to jam with abandon—the bassist unleashing an arsenal of fills, the guitarist's wah-foot working overtime, and the vocals driven into a frenzy of trance-like repetition: "He's a real man… He's a real man… He's a real man…"

One can also imagine the enormity of the collective "Holy Shit!" that exploded from our awed mouths at this moment, and which only grew as the camera slowly tilted up from the gut to the chest to the stone-cool glare of Mr. Jonathan himself, confident yet disinterested, face framed by an as-yet-immeasurable afro, unwavering even as the groove-soaked chorus sings his praises, the timeless portrait of a sex machine.

He looked into our souls then, as he does now, and as he always will for anyone with the blind luck or guts enough to sit back and let him grace their once chaste screen. And here, in my veteran opinion, is where the true beauty of this hallowed film lies. My fellow pioneers can no doubt sing the praises of its complex storylines or the subtleties of its dialogue or the raw force of its realistic contributions to the great canon of action cinematography—and I would be a fool to argue them. But for me, the greatest thrill—whether in my own memory or in the vicarious joy in the faces of the traditional new converts—will always be in that first sublime, sexually charged, playful and—dare I say—artful initiation into the sweet place in our hearts called *Black Shampoo*.

The original version of this article ran in *Cashiers du Cinemart* #8.

CAN YOU FEEL THE LOVE?

By Mike White

Of all the films I've written about in my years of doing *Cashiers du Cinemart*, I'm not sure why it took me eight issues to give proper coverage to my favorite film. I guess I just didn't want to do it half-assed. I wanted to devote the proper amount of time and energy to passing along information about and admiration of this movie.

I don't know how we—Leon Chase, Steve Chesney, and I—could have missed it all those times we came into Blockbuster—maybe we were New Release addicts. How could we have passed by a cover box boasting about a man who's mad, mean, and both a lovin' and killin' machine? Who wouldn't want to see a movie about a black, ballsy hairdresser? I'm not sure who spotted it first—it's all a blur—I just remember walking out as a new man, with a copy of *Black Shampoo* in my hands.

Seeing *Black Shampoo* was a revelation. I'm not a religious man, but I have witnessed the power and the glory of the universe. Like most converts, I wanted to spread the gospel. After our initial viewing, we agreed not to rest until all of our other friends shared our experience.

Thus was born the tradition of sharing the wealth of *Black Shampoo*. Each year when we get together to celebrate the anniversary of our first night with Mr. Jonathan, we all attempt to bring someone new into the fold, so that their eyes may be opened as ours have!

Since December 26, 1988, I must have seen this movie over five hundred times. In those first few weeks of 1989, we watched it at least once a day. We got to know the storyline a bit better and we began to analyze it. Every scene, every shot, every line, and every musical cue: we watched, listened, and learned.

We all latched on to certain characters as our favorites, and then designated other people as other characters by their similarities. Looking back at a 1990 Riverview Community High School Yearbook, you'd see "Freddie," "Brenda," and "Chuck Barris" listed among the nicknames for myself, Aimee Chorkey, and Leon Chase (Jeff Dunlap didn't claim "Black Baboon Butt," for some odd reason). Steve Chesney even strutted his stuff in the annual "Mr. Riverview" contest under the name of Mr. Jonathan. And, somehow, *Black Shampoo* was listed in our yearbook's section, "Students' Favorite Films."

No character went unnoticed. We didn't go so far as to actually act out the film, as fans of *The Rocky Horror Picture Show* would, but, as sad as it sounds, our lives revolved around this movie for the better part of two years, and it's still with us today.

Can You Feel the Love?

MR. JONATHAN (John Daniels): Is that Mr. Jonathan-something? Or Mr. Something-Jonathan? The answer can be found on the back of the video box. It's Jonathan Knight, owner and operator of his own salon on the Sunset Strip. He likes doing hair, but his female clients like him to do a lot more. All of this changes when he falls in love with his new receptionist in one of the most heartfelt montages of all time. Jonathan does everything right—paddle boat rides, dinner, and a walk through the botanical gardens. But don't cross him. This smooth hairdresser packs a punch when the going gets rough. He's the master of the right hook, the chainsaw, and the pool cue.

The jig is up, Mr. Jonathan

Favorite Lines: "Hey! Gimme that, I make my living with that!" "They came at me like sharks." "She did, Artie. I know because I just left her and she's happy as hell where she is." "I'll take my own car, if you don't mind." "Right on both counts, if Mrs. Simpson is your mother." "Okay, have it your way, bought and paid for. But your hair looks like shit that way."

Filmography: No other films in John Daniels's oeuvre will even begin to compare with *Black Shampoo*, but he has had memorable roles as Baron, the meanest pimp on the Sunset Strip in *Candy Tangerine Man*, and Mike Barnett, president of Impossible Funky records in *Getting Over*. His other films include *Tender Loving Care*; *Bare Knuckles*; and *Mean Dog Blues*.

BRENDA ST. JOHN (Tanya Boyd): This former mob moll is the ever-so-pleasant new receptionist at Mr. Jonathan's salon, until Mr. Wilson (a real Mafioso name) returns and his goons find her. Through a clever ruse (and a nice wig), Brenda eventually gets the upper hand by stealing Wilson's McGuffin.

Favorite Lines: "Full." "Then you tell Mr. Wilson I decided to go for a ride, messenger boy!"

Filmography: Her other films include *Jo Jo Dancer, Your Life Is Calling*; *Ilsa: Harem Keeper of the Oil Sheiks*; and *Black Heat*. She's also appeared on *The Ted Knight Show*; *Roots*; *Walking through the Fire*; and *Good Times*, as one of J.J.'s many girlfriends. Tanya Boyd is best known for her long running performance on *Days of Our Lives*.

ARTIE (Skip E. Lowe): He's the kind-hearted assistant to Mr. Jonathan. In actuality, Artie pretty much runs the show. He's in charge of the salon when Jonathan's out making house calls, and he places himself at the helm of the cleanup when the shop is trashed by Wilson's thugs. Artie's got some problems, though. He has a strange way of belching at pretty women like Brenda, and his tips just aren't what they used to be, even when women pinch his butt (foreshadowing).

Favorite Lines: "That bitch, she pinched my cheek, honey, and she didn't even tip me." "It's a Western-style Bar-B-Q!" "He's as straight as an arrow." "She'll never drown, believe me!" "Oh, that poor fella!" "My mirrors! My lovely, lovely mirrors." "Put that thing down!"

Filmography: Skip appeared in such films as *Sunny Side Up*; *The World's Greatest Lover* (not as the title character, unfortunately); and *Bare Knuckles* (that's right…a second appearance with John Daniels!). Skip also hosted his own public access show *Skip E. Lowe Looks at Hollywood* in San Francisco for many years.

RICHARD (Gary Allan): Artie's pal and confidant. Richard is the id to Artie's superego, the yang to Artie's yin, the coffee to Artie's cream. Richard is easily upset but he's a good guy at heart. And, he throws one hell of a Bar-B-Q. If only Richard's intense drive could find its way into his enthusiasms over drying hair.

Favorite Lines: "I wouldn't bet on it, honey!" "What do you think you're doing? Put him down!" "You black baboon butt!" "This is deplorable, this is utterly deplorable!" "You're right, Artie Baby, her hair is a fright!"

MR. WILSON (Joe Ortiz/Joseph Carlo): The cold-as-ice underworld boss who doesn't like to talk on the phone or share his books and papers with anyone. We're not really sure what he does, but the IRS would probably be willing to give a year's refund to get their hands on some incriminating evidence about him. You know he's mean by the way he treats Brenda like a six-pack, but you don't know the extent of his vileness until he gives Artie the thrill of a lifetime.

Favorite Lines: "I told you before—Schmuck!" "I don't want to talk about this over the telephone." "Young men can be so impetuous…but then maturity has its moments, too." "That's a good little pussycat." "I can take that as your own personal guarantee."

Filmography: Credited as Joe Ortiz, Joseph Carlo worked with director Greydon Clark on *Satan's Cheerleaders*.

MADDOX (Jack Mehoff/William Bonner): Maddox, AKA "Schmuck" (see above), is the right-hand man of Mr. Wilson. He's not very good at his job, however, and is constantly being admonished.

Favorite Lines: "Your move." "Don't be a dead hero." "Mr. Wilson? I don't know anyone by that name." "God damn you people; shut up!" "I could get it out of him." "I'm coming for you, you son of a bitch! You're gonna die!" "Look, she said she'd call. There were people around. You told me not to…"

Filmography: Credited as "Jack Mehoff," William Bonner has a classic exploitation résumé (*Satan's Sadists*; *The Hard Ride*; *Soul Hustler*, etc.).

JACKSON (Bruce Kerley): I don't think he's ever called Jackson in the film, and we usually refer to him as "Black Baboon Butt" (see above). Jackson's the strong, silent type (he has only two lines), but he says them with so much conviction that his performance is one of the most memorable in film history.

Favorite (and only) lines: "I'll get you for this, you son of a bitch." "Okay, let's go, everybody in the backroom."

CHAUFFEUR (Salvatore Bennissimo/Sheldon Lee): "Chuck Barris" (he wears his hat low, like Barris used to do at the end of *The Gong Show*) and "Black Baboon Butt" have a relationship similar to that of Artie and Richard, in that he is the more verbose and excitable of the two. I wouldn't rule out undercurrents of homosexuality between them, either, since he gets such a thrill from yanking down Artie's drawers.

Favorite Lines: "So I was grabbin' a little ass, so what?" "Kiss this, sweetie." "What's the matter, stud, you losin' your touch?"

Filmography: In addition to acting, Sheldon Lee was a production manager, makeup artist, writer, producer, and composer on a wide array of films. He even starred in *Hell's Bloody Devils* with William Bonner.

FREDDIE (Fred Scott): Jonathan's caretaker and sensei. Freddie is a man of nature and wisdom. His latest discovery is a well from whence waters pour that make men speak their minds twice over. Above all that, Freddie is the film's deus ex machina—whatta guy!

Favorite Lines: "Jonathan!" "Oh, fine, fine, fine, fine." "Well, everything's coming along pretty good, pretty good." "Care for a drink of water?"

Filmography: The most cultured of the cast, Fred Scott worked continuously in film and television from 1972 until his death in 2002.

MRS. SIMPSON (Diana St. Clair/Heather Leigh): She hasn't had her hair done in months, and needs to see Jonathan so badly that she convinces Brenda to set up a housecall. Unfortunately, she's got two jailbait daughters in need of a wash and rinse, as well.

Favorite Line: "Funny farm? Why, I ought to call the police."

Filmography: The statuesque beauty went under the name Diana St. Clair for *Black Shampoo*. She made a handful of other soft and hardcore films under the name Heather Leigh.

MEG (Kelly Beau) AND PEG (Marl Pero): Never referred to by name, they're just called "a couple of pushy little chicks" by Mr. Jonathan when they try to seduce him. You see, they've shared a guy before—wait, no, my mistake. They've shared at least two guys before. Let's just say that their mother hasn't imbued them with many family values.

"They came at me like sharks."

Favorite Lines: "Oh, let me." "Tools of the trade, handle with care." "Yeah, come on in, Mom, we'll help ya swim." "Yeah, we'll help you swim right to the bottom!" "Nyah nyah nyah nyah nyah nyah."

RUBY (Ruby Williams): Affectionately known as "Ruby Baby," we're not really sure of her duties around the salon, but she's quick with a broom.

Favorite Lines: "What're you gonna do with that gun?" "Watch out, Mr. Jonathan!"

THE MANICURIST (Helene Farber): She doesn't like to make her presence known around the salon too much, but she's quick to point out anything amiss.

Favorite Line: "You don't look like any god-damned health department to me."

Filmography: Farber didn't burn up a hot path to the top of the box office after *Black Shampoo*. Apart from her role in the exploitation classic *Teenage Mother*, she also had a small role in Alex Cox's *Walker*.

NEW RECEPTIONIST (Edith Wheeler/Jacqueline Cole): A familiar face to Greydon Clark fans, as she also starred in *Angel's Brigade* and *Satan's Cheerleaders*. Her role is small but memorable, and we love that she's wearing a "Mr. Jonathan's" T-shirt!

Filmography: Credited as "Edith Wheeler," Jacqueline Cole starred in a bevy of Greydon Clark films, as well as starring in Clark's life as his wife.

MRS. PHILLIPS (Anne Gaybis): Boy, is she mad! Mrs. Phillips really wants her hair done, but she catches Jonathan at a bad time. Unfortunately, she feels that Artie just doesn't have the equipment to help her out of her predicament.

Filmography: Gaybis had quite a career after *Black Shampoo*. Her roles have included *Hollywood Zap*; *The Lost Empire*; *Bachelor Party*; *10 Violent Women*; *Friday the 13th Part 3*; *Beyond Evil*; and *Fairy Tales*.

SALLY CARRUTHERS (?): The woman who introduces us to the magic of Mr. Jonathan's caress, and she doesn't even get a credit at the end? Injustice (or embarrassment)! And what's up with her medallion—isn't that the same one worn by the woman in the photograph with "nice tits" and frightful hair?

Favorite Lines: "Mr. Jonathan, it is bigger and better!" "Oh, Jonathan, it feels so good." "What interruptions?"

WESTERN-STYLE BAR-B-Q PLAYERS: This must have been one hell of a shindig! How come I've never been to a party with a ballet dancer and guy from the Australian outback? Some of our other favorite party guests include Ben, "The Crazy Running-around Dude," "Freddie Krueger," and the woman in the overalls. Alas, the big pie fight at the Bar-B-Q was relegated to the cutting room floor.

The original version of this article ran in Cashiers du Cinemart #8.

MUSIC IS THEIR WAY OF LIFE

By Mike White

Before the picture even comes up the soulful bass begins. This is the first indication that the music of *Black Shampoo* is going to be a major player in the film. From the rollicking sounds of the Western Style BBQ, to the sultry, sudsy song played when Jonathan and Brenda make love, to the ceaseless strains of the cross-country chase through the California wilds, the score from musician brothers Gerald and Gary Lee keep *Black Shampoo* funky.

***Cashiers du Cinemart*:** How did you get your start in music?
Gary Lee: Our mother was a concert pianist who would get up in the morning and play Chopin preludes. Whenever guests came to the house, each of us performed a musical number. In the '50s, it seemed like everyone had a piano and everyone knew how to play something, even if they couldn't read music.
Gerald Lee: Church was very important in our lives as kids. I think we must have gone to every service a Sunday could provide. My mother played and sang in the choirs and we were taught to use our talents in a Godly manner.

I was quite rebellious with my piano instruction and would drive my mother crazy playing boogie-woogie and jive songs. I really didn't want to learn to read music, as I had somewhat of a gift to play what I heard without music. I also had a bad experience in a recital, when I about 10 years old, where I had studied to perform only to get nervous and forget where I was on the page. From that point on I played by ear.

Through the years I became the church youth music director where the late Billy Preston played the organ and his sister Rodena played piano. I loved gospel music and still do. At UCLA I minored in music and, once graduated, went to work for Disneyland as one of the original "kids of the kingdom" in the park singing groups. Over 1,500 kids auditioned, yet my sister Lady Lee, Gary, and I made the group of only twelve performers.

***CdC*:** How did you get into film scoring?
Gerald: Arranging music and composition were passionate twins in my life in the '70s. Quincy Jones had just finished scoring *The Pawnbroker* and I was mesmerized by the music. I was also greatly influenced by Henry Mancini and his *Pink Panther* scores. Sitting at the piano and making up ways to play Mancini songs like "Moon River" was almost an everyday occurrence.
Gary: Gerald hooked up with a company that expected overnight lead sheets and arrangements from nothing more than a tape. We had to listen to the tape hundreds of times to pull out the words, melody, and chords. After the lead sheet was finished, we had to arrange the music for a recording session. Later we found out that some of the lead sheets we wrote were for Barry White! We

continued to supply this company music and it grew into film scores. I thought about writing for TV shows and had bought a book by Earl Hagen, who was writing for several TV shows back then. This book explained timing the action with click tracks, etc., and turned out to be a great investment later.

CdC: Can you tell me a bit about writing the music for *Black Shampoo*?
Gerald: While out pitching some original songs, I came across an ad in *The Hollywood Reporter* looking for a film composer for a new Greydon Clark film. The ad recommended that interested composers come to a screening of the unfinished film. I got invited based almost solely on my work in the record industry. I knew I would get the film because the after-screening questions were a breeze for me. Over the years I had learned to read music and had studied with one of the great arrangers of the day, Herb Mickman. I had misgivings about doing a black exploitation film, but it was an opportunity to get my feet wet, so to speak.
Gary: When *Black Shampoo* came along, I had just graduated from Cal State Fullerton. Gerald was singing and playing piano professionally before that, getting more connected with decision makers in the industry, while I was teaching music in the public school system. I had taken only one orchestration class, but I knew how to write and transpose for all of the instruments.

Gerald watched movies and timed all of his music and "hits" for action on the screen. He had a simple score that showed when the action happened—on the beat—and what the mood of the music should be at that time. We wrote around those notations, trying to make the music match the action on the screen, but remember—all we had was Gerald's notes on paper. I never saw the film until it was finished! Gerald came up with the great ideas and remarkable melodies. My job was to write the parts correctly for the instruments to reproduce Gerald's ideas into the sounds he had imagined. We called in musician friends from everywhere to help us record; in fact, I played trumpet on the sound track.
Gerald: Different from today's film composers, when composing for low budget films in those days we had to time out all the scenes and where all the significant hits or actions were to take place. This cue sheet became my bible. Watching scenes over and over again to get the flavor of the scene and listening to the director to get the mood of the scenes, all important stuff. Finally, we went into the studio to record the music, using click tracks to measure exact timings and having the music engineer work with you in the process. It was great fun.

Writing for any film is quite challenging and, this being my first, I almost gave up. Thanks to Gary and his orchestral background we got through it. Gary's book by Earle Hagen helped. Also, I had purchased Henry Mancini's book on film scoring and, between the two, everything I wanted to know about film scoring was answered. See how important it is to learn to read!

Gary: We wrote all night, several nights in a row. We would get an idea, start to write it down, and then accidentally fall asleep for 10 minutes, only to wake up and try to rework the idea. We could have written all of the music in no time at all if back then we had some of today's technology and software programs. Heck, Finale or Cakewalk would have made it child's play.

CdC: I would love to know what specific guitars, effects, and/or amps they were using on the soundtrack, particularly the opening song ("He's a Real Man") and "Liquid Love."

Gary: Gerald hired a great guitar player. I don't remember his name. Was it Roland?

Gerald: Roland Bautista.

Gary: He took direction from Gerald with regards to different types of sounds. Looking back now, those guitar sounds really make you think of the 1970s!

Gerald: He was a great innovator of sounds and could make sounds like no one else. He was also a terrific rhythm guitarist. We used Wah-Wah pedals made famous by the great Wah Wah Watson, who played on Isaac Hayes's *Shaft* score. We also used Echo-plex machines with lots of reverb. Earth Wind & Fire were leaders in this new sound. I love the sound of the piano clavinet and I played the clavinet parts in the scoring of the movie. The sound is biting and funky.

CdC: When it came to "The Chase," was this all pre-scored or was this improvised at all?

Gary: I remember writing every measure of "The Chase" because we were writing to the click track hits. Gerald counted and conducted every measure of "The Chase" in the recording session, accenting those hits.

Gerald: The scene went on for about nine minutes. At the time I thought this was the longest chase scene on record. I had a couple of brass players improvise some lines, but it was still under the confines of musical moods and theatrical events within the scenes.

Gary: The guitar player was given the freedom to adlib above the structured parts, too.

CdC: What other films have you worked on?

Gerald: *The Hi-Riders, Seven from Heaven* (also known as *Angel's Revenge*) and *Satan's Cheerleaders*, to name a few. *Satan's Cheerleaders* is still being played every Halloween and is about as campy as you can get. It's very much a favorite of Elvira.

Gary: We also worked together on *The Big Bus* and *Van Nuys Blvd*. On my own, I wrote a marching band scene for the TV Show *Maude*. I also helped Gerald with a live musical starring Eartha Kitt in Hollywood at the Aquarius Theater, *Bread, Beans, and Things*.

Music Is Their Way of Life

CdC: Your names are associated with "Disco Orchestration." Can you help my younger readers understand what that is and what you had to do with that movement?

Gary: Well, to me, disco orchestration was dance music of the '70s. The string section was featured with hip-funky melodies or appealing smooth sounds that fit well with the disco beat. They would race up and down in high fast-moving parts while the rhythm section kept a driving beat. One of the best examples of the sound was from the movie *Car Wash*. That song is still cool! Another one was the song "The Hustle," with the smooth counter melody from the strings. The normal R&B dance sound was very popular, but when you featured the string section, it also gave the music a touch of class.

Gerald: Instruments associated with classical music were now being cleverly positioned inside a rhythmic setting. Disco music used these instruments in new ways where the strings would dance and play more percussive elements. When needed, the strings would add orchestral beauty on top of a driving dance beat.

Gary: At a recording session, Gerald and I met Gene Page, who was writing orchestra parts for Barry White's Love Unlimited Orchestra. He showed us how to write simple string lines that sounded amazing. I was greatly influenced by that day and I still use the style he showed us back then.

Gerald: The arrangers during this period were classically trained and had the musical chops to write out and direct great string orchestras. Gene Page, in my opinion, was the genius behind Barry White's music. He also arranged for Diana Ross, Elton John, and a host of others. Gene was a musical pioneer in this genre.

My contribution came in several ways. Utilizing my Gene Page knowledge, I was privy to arranging several albums during the disco period, such as Candi Staton's "Nights on Broadway" (which was a number-one Bee Gees song). I danced the strings around fairly well on that album. With that success I started the Gerald Lee String Company and did more arrangements, including Tina Turner's first solo album and the Eddie Harris album *That Is Why You're Overweight*.

My greatest accomplishment during this time was a song I wrote and was recorded by Patti Labelle called "Music Is My Way of Life." I had the good fortune of working with one of the great lyric writers of our time, Marti Sharron, who went on to write "Jump" for the Pointer Sisters and had several songs on the Anita Baker classic *Rhapsody* album. I still get royalties from this song, as it is still being played all over the world. It was arranged by the late Skip Scarborough. Wow, what an arrangement! It is disco epitomized.

Gary: I remember getting into computerized music when the piano player from *The Arsenio Hall Show*, Starr Parodi, performed a recording session for us in her apartment by hooking up twelve keyboards to her computer! She had each keyboard play a different sound-drums, guitar, brass, strings, woodwinds—it was incredible.

Gerald and I wrote music for a Shrine Auditorium Tribute to Quincy Jones after he was released from the hospital for brain surgery. Gerald was writing for an all-girl group called The Love Machine. We stayed up all night writing the music and then arrived an hour early, before any other performers, to have our music played first by the house big band at the Musicians Union. Because we were unknown, our music was played last. I was angry at first; however, as we sat there patiently, Sarah Vaughn rehearsed in front of us. Billy Eckstein was next. And then, I couldn't believe it, Ray Charles came in and started playing the piano right in front of me! When it was finally time to have our music played by the house big band, the lead trumpeter stopped playing-again because we were unknown. However, our music still sounded great and a rumor started that Gerald and I were two great writers from either Chicago or New York.

CdC: The Love Machine, is that the Gwen Brisco group?
Gary: I don't remember. Gerald went on tour with them to Paris and Vegas.
Gerald: The Love Machine was a group managed by John Daniels, the male lead in *Black Shampoo*. The group was patterned after the go-go dancers of the time. However, they could also sing. I'm not sure if Gwen was in the group, as I was not familiar with the names of the girls. It was my distinct honor to be the music director for their Vegas Act and overseas performances. The group opened for Tom Jones in Las Vegas with me as conductor, and we were featured on the *Merv Griffin Live from Vegas* TV show. An album of The Love Machine's music was co-produced and arranged by myself, along with John Daniels. It was geared more toward the European market. [The Love Machine members included "Bernice, Kathy, Mary, Paulette, Renee, Sandy, & Sheila" according to the sleeve of their eponymous album. —Ed.]

CdC: What have you been up to lately?
Gerald: A few years ago I was privileged to be the Gospel music director for Cottonwood Christian church in Los Alamitos, California. I am currently the Music Director for Destiny House Ministries in Long Beach, CA.
Gary: I'm teaching private students and playing in Gerald's church band. We have a great time playing Gerald's church arrangements. I still write music for public schools and will soon publish a how-to music-arranging book for band directors.
Gerald: I've started back writing, not only gospel music, but also some jazz selections. Don't look now, but very soon you may be hearing another song or music by Gerald and Gary Lee.

Brenda (Tanya Boyd) and Jonathan (John Daniels) survey the damage to the shop

HAVE YOU SEEN BRENDA?

By Mike White

Since her role as Brenda St. John in *Black Shampoo*, fellow Detroiter Tanya Boyd went on to notable roles in *Jo Jo Dancer, Your Life Is Calling*; TV's *Roots*; and *Days of Our Lives*. All the while, Boyd continued to satiate her love of the theater. In 1998, Boyd fulfilled a longtime dream and moved from one side of the camera to the other, directing *The Gift*—available on Quickband's *Afrocentricity* DVD release. While the rest of Afrocentricity isn't "all that," Boyd's piece is standout. A remarkable first film, *The Gift* is a rich black & white short about a blind sculptor who refuses an operation to regain his sight.

Boyd took time to speak to me from her Gold Dust Production offices.

Cashiers du Cinemart: Are you directing and writing your new feature?
Tanya Boyd: I brought in another writer who I really like. I wanted a fresh, young approach. I met a writer; her name is Joanne Morris. She is just great. We're going to collaborate on this one as far as the writing goes. Hopefully, I'll direct it. I came up with the idea so that I'd have another project to direct. But because I've never directed a feature, that makes it a little difficult, because *The Gift* was the first film project I had ever done as a director. So, people still aren't very sure about me. They liked the film—so far I've gotten a lot of good response from it—but they're saying, "But can you do a feature?"

I feel I can do it. Right now I'm over at *Days of Our Lives*, preparing to do some directing over there. That is the hardest medium there is, that multi-camera setup. It's so fast and so technical. I feel that once I have that to add to my director's reel, then hopefully, it'll be easier to convince people that I can do a feature.

CdC: I read that before *The Gift*, you directed some plays.
TB: Yes, my background as an actor is in theater. Then I started directing theater by a fluke. I didn't set out to direct; it just happened. I was working with a theater company where one of the directors walked off of her project. They were trying to get the production ready for a festival. Suddenly I got a call from the artistic director of the company, saying, "What am I going to do? I've got ten actors looking at me and I don't have a director!" I told her, "Don't worry about it. Tell everybody to come back to the theater tomorrow, and I'll direct it." After I hung up the phone, I asked myself, "What did I just do? Okay, calm down, there are no accidents; obviously I'm supposed to look into this."

The next day I went to the theater and had ten professional actors looking at me like, "Okay, what are you going to do?" And it just happened. It happened and it did very well. In fact, they said that the play was one of the best of the festival. From that the artistic director trusted me—I didn't dare tell her that I didn't know what I was doing when I got there!

I found that I really liked it. I mean, acting had always been my passion, but there was something about this that went even deeper. I know it sounds really corny, but I've always been able to see beyond what's in front of me—the potential of something. And I was just able to see the outcome from the moment that I accepted that play. It was the same thing with *The Gift* and all the other theater projects that I directed; I felt very comfortable. I think a lot of it had to do with that I was an actor. I know the process that actors need to go through. I know how I want things to be as an actor. I mean, I don't have all the answers, but I pretend like I do! And things usually work out and let everything reveal itself.

Brenda and Jonathan get steamy

CdC: When was this first play that you directed?
TB: Around '93.

CdC: That was about the time that you got onto *Days of Our Lives*, yes?
TB: I got onto *Days* in '94. At the time, I belonged to a great theater company in Hollywood, The Mojo Theater Ensemble. I was directed by our artistic director, Michelle Martin—a great director in her own right. I did a couple of plays for the company and, during that time, I was also working on *Days of Our Lives*. I'm kind of a workaholic. I'm a singer also and there were times where I'd go to one session, leave that and go to another session, leave that and do a performance on stage. That's just the way it is, and the way it's always been.

CdC: Are you still acting in *Days*?
TB: Yes—as a matter of fact, I was on the show yesterday. I was under contract for five years, but now I have a reoccurring role, once every few months or so. That was a blessing in disguise because I wanted to do other things. Now I can go in as a director, which is what I'm doing. They're teaching me multi-camera and allowing me to learn at their facilities. I'm loving it because I have everything available to me, and it's free! I don't have to pay college tuition and I'm learning from some of the best teachers in the business! It's been wonderful for me to learn lighting and to go to editing. I love to edit; I said that if I wasn't going to be a director that I'd definitely want to be an editor.

CdC: When did you get into acting?
TB: I guess it really clicked for me when I was about seven. I knew it was what I wanted; I just didn't know how I was going to get there. My mom and my

aunts really had an interest in the arts. At one point my mother had a radio show—this is years ago—where she did poetry, some of the things she wrote. She'd recite on the show. My aunts were very involved in drama all through high school and college, but they all were married and had kids and that was that. But my mother would always take me to the movies when I was a kid. So I grew up with movies and television; I'm of that era. As a child I was extremely shy, and I opened up the most when I'd go to the movies. That was my escape, I guess.

I would sneak out of school and go to the movies. In those days you could go to the movies and stay all day; they didn't make people come out and leave like they do now. I'd sit there and learn all the lines of the lead actress. All of the winos who hung out and slept in the theater at night would still be there in the morning, and they were my audience. I'd get up and say the lead actress' lines, and it was really something. They would applaud me, they got to know me and they'd cheer me on.

I'll never forget when I left Detroit. The last words I said to some people that I knew, who had tried to tell me what I could or could not do, "The next time you see me, I'm gonna be in the movies!" Sure enough, a year and a half or two years later, I was. I was on a television show that was very popular and people all over looked at it. When I went home these same people said to me, "Girl, you said you

Jonathan and Brenda comtemplate their fate

were going to be in the movies! I'll be damned!" I mean, I was just as shocked as they were, believe me. I knew it was what I wanted to do. It was just…how do I go about getting there? So, I went from Michigan to New York and New York to Los Angeles.

CdC: What was it that you were on, on TV?
TB: Roots. It was my first big project. I was on about two episodes.

CdC: But before that, you were in a couple movies…
TB: Let's see, did I do film? Well, yeah, but we don't really talk about those movies. We don't talk about those. They were "B" black exploitation that were really kind of tacky.

CdC: I have to tell you, I'm a huge fan of *Black Shampoo*.
TB: Oh my god, I could kill you! That wasn't me; that was my twin! [Laughs]

CdC: My friends and I get together every year and watch it on December 26th. This year will be our twelfth year.
TB: Are you serious? What is it about that film that you like so much?

CdC: It was one of my first blaxploitation films and it's just so…offbeat. I've never seen another film like it.

TB: Thank God! Wow. That's really something. You know, a friend of mine came to my house about a year ago with a tape of that movie. I hadn't seen it since I did it. That was when I first came to Los Angeles.

CdC: Now, did you do *Black Shampoo* first or *Black Heat*?

TB: I never did a film called *Black Heat*.

CdC: Sorry, it was probably known by a different name. It was originally called *The Murder Gang*, *U.S. Vice*, or *Girl's Hotel*. You played a reporter named "Stephanie" and your boyfriend was "Kicks Carter."

TB: Oh my goodness, yes! I never saw it! I never saw that film. I don't regret doing those things because they were the first things that I had ever done. In those days, being an African-American female, those roles were the only things available. My whole goal was to get my Screen Actor's Guild card. Once I got my card that was that. I didn't look back and started doing other things. I guess that just shows you that your past will catch up with you!

The original version of this article ran in *Cashiers du Cinemart* #12.

JONATHAN'S RIGHT-HAND MAN

By Mike White

Little did I know that Skip E. Lowe was such a celebrity! For years he's been the host of *Skip E. Lowe Looks at Hollywood*, a San Franciscan treat. He's also held a host of other jobs before acting as Mr. Jonathan's right-hand man, Artie, in *Black Shampoo*. His myriad adventures are chronicled in the book *The Boy with the Betty Grable Legs*.

I bought Skip E. Lowe's memoir with the idea that it would be a horrendous hack-job full of celebrity ass-kissing and rampant name-dropping. I was floored when *The Boy with the Betty Grable Legs* turned out to be a compelling autobiography written with panache and a good deal of humility.

Lowe's book is difficult to put down. He does well to balance his personal tragedies (Lowe seemed to attract molestation the way flowers attract bees) with his career as an entertainer. While his brief mention of his part in *Black Shampoo* is akin to Orson Welles skipping over *Citizen Kane*, Lowe's book manages to stand tall on its own shapely legs.

Cashiers du Cinemart: So tell me all about your book! First off, what's with that title?
Skip E. Lowe: It's called *The Boy with the Betty Grable Legs*, and it's subtitled *From Here to Hollywood*. I used to work strip clubs when I was a kid at seventeen, eighteen years old. I worked in Chicago, for the Mafia. I used to work as an M.C. You'd come home at like four in the morning because the clubs are open late.

Then I worked in Cicero and Calumet City. That was really raw—they had the girls take off everything there. I used to have a lot to do with the girls because I was the "head man," watching the girls at night. Evidently what happened when I used to work for them—it's all about that in the book.

And, also, I worked for the military. I didn't work *for* them. I entertained the troops in Vietnam and Germany. I was with the Everly Brothers, Phil and Don, for about six or seven years as an M.C. and comedian. I worked with Johnny Ray, Joanie James, Sheckie Green (he's also from Chicago). I worked with a lot of big singers.

Then I stayed in Europe a long time, hanging around there. I went all over Europe, working the military bases so I could see Europe. Then, finally, Vietnam came and I went to Saigon. I stayed in Saigon and I worked in Da Nang and Le Trang and all the bases. This is where I met Martha Raye and Mamie Van Doren. Martha wasn't entertaining there—she was working as a nurse—and I stayed with her there.

Jonathan's Right-Hand Man

CdC: What timeframe are we talking here?
SEL: I was living in New York and I left there in about 1960 to visit Paris. Then I was in London at the time that John F. Kennedy was assassinated. I was working the Blue Angel with Noel Harrison (Rex Harrison's son). And I met the Beatles. Paul McCartney—he was going with an actress by the name of Jane Asher. A lot of chic people used to come there. Then the night that President Kennedy was shot I was with a girl there, a singer, and we both decided to go back to Paris.

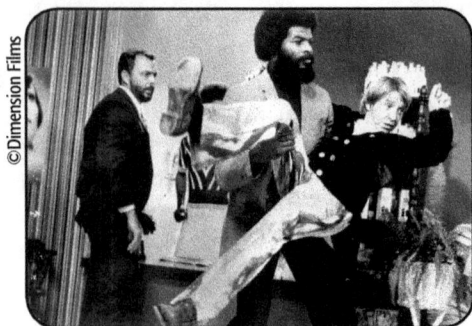

Jackson about to put Artie (Skip E. Lowe) down

Back in Paris I worked with Josephine Baker. She was slipping at the time. From there we went to Germany, and then I started doing the bases there. The war in Vietnam started getting hot then. I went over there about…1967, and stayed there until 1972. After I left there I landed in San Francisco, and wound up staying in California.

CdC: What did you do once you got to the west coast?
SEL: I did showcases. You present singers and comedians. Some of my finds were Michael Feinstein and Yakov Smirnoff—you remember Michael Feinstein? He used to work for me. He came from Ohio. There are a lot of good singers; I can't even think of all the names of people I helped along the line.

So, anyway, I did the *Skip E. Lowe's Talent Showcase*. It became very popular around L.A. I worked all the clubs and hotels. I still do it every once in a while. I just closed the Passion and I'll probably open at the Roosevelt.

CdC: Then you got involved with Roger Corman's studio for a while?
SEL: Yes, I did for a while. I met Edy Williams and her husband, Russ Meyer, was doing a movie. I met Christian Brando through her—Marlon's son. Marlon and I got very close. It's in my book.

CdC: I really enjoyed some of your films from the seventies, like *Capone* and *Crazy Mama*. My favorite, though, has to be *Black Shampoo*.
SEL: That's your favorite? Wow! I have never really seen the film, you know. I do a lot of movies that I've never seen. I did about four of them just recently and I don't even remember the names of them. I just go and do them, you know. I heard the music is great in that.

CdC: How did you get involved with your cable access show?
SEL: Some man saw me do my show at the Hyatt and said to me, "Why don't you do a public access show?" When I started I was the very first in Hollywood.

The very, very first. I started with the close-ups. My shows are filled with tight close-ups.

CdC: What was it like being a child star?
SEL: I came out to Hollywood when I was nine years old. It's all in my book. It's all the odysseys of my life. I did *Best Foot Forward*; that was my first movie. Then I did a movie with Jane Powell—it was her first movie—*Song of the Open Road*.

CdC: Did your parents push you into show business?
SEL: My mother did. My mother was very mothery, tough lady. You see, I'm half Jewish and half Italian. My mother was Jewish and she really wanted to push me. I stayed in Hollywood until I was twelve, and then my mother took me to New York and I stayed with my Aunt Sadie, who worked at a club called Sammy's Bowery Follies. I worked there for a while as a singing newsboy. When I got to be about sixteen or seventeen, I worked up at the Catskills in the mountains. Then I got booked into Pittsburgh, and from there I went to Chicago and I started working strip clubs.

CdC: When you were overseas, what kind of material would you do?
SEL: I was doing very, very clean material. Singing, I do singing. I'm an Irish Tenor. I used to sing songs like "Yankee Doodle Dandy," you know, George M. Cohan. "Danny Boy" was my big, big thing in Vietnam. No dirty material. That's why the military loved me.

CdC: How did you get involved in Fellini's *La Dolce Vita*?
SEL: That was when I was working in Rome. I played a cameraman. I had blond hair and a scarf and I looked like one of those guys running around. Do you remember when she got off the plane? I was one of the paparazzi.

CdC: You still haven't answered my question about the name of the book.
SEL: The girls in the clubs in Chicago, backstage I used to have boxers and I used to take my pants off and run around the backstage. And the girls used to make fun of me: "Oh, here he comes, the boy with the Betty Grable legs!" I have great legs and that's it.

The original version of this article ran in *Cashiers du Cinemart* #12.

"I HATE THE HOLLYWOOD BAG"

By Mike White

I was gushing like a little schoolgirl as I talked to John Daniels. It felt as if the last decade had been building up to this moment. Back when I first put finger to keyboard for my first paltry issue of *Cashiers du Cinemart*, I had dreamed of interviewing the star of my favorite film, *Black Shampoo*. It was in honor of John Daniels that I initially chose the nom de plume of "Mike Barnett," after his character in *Getting Over*.

Going back and listening to the interview with Daniels, I find myself slightly embarrassed by how astonishingly giddy I sound. Here's hoping that the printed version might find my effervescent enthusiasm a bit muted.

Cashiers du Cinemart: It's a great pleasure to finally talk to you.
John Daniels: I'm flattered that anybody is interested in [talking to me] at this time, because I had refocused my life away from film. What I really do and where my passion has always been is producing shows. Maverick's Flat is where I do most of the work. I'm there for rehearsals and production business, but I don't spend any time in the club when it's open. I haven't been there at night in eons. But I am there, running my rehearsals.

Producing shows is a multifaceted situation because I also write and produce music. That goes along with the shows, they're all musical shows. As a producer, I've put on shows in 80 countries.

CdC: You must be doing something right.
JD: I've played all of the major venues in the world: the London Palladium, the Budokan in Tokyo—you name it.

CdC: What acts are you working with in your shows?
JD: My wife (Gwen Brisco) is an entertainer. She's a dynamite person on stage and used to carry a big live review with her. Just to give you an idea of what she's like: we were in Australia when Tina Turner was touring Australia, and the paper said to go see Gwen.

I've always produced her shows. And I've written and produced her music for CDs. We haven't had a mega-hit in this country, but we've had them in other parts of the world. She's had about ten CDs so far, and she's getting ready to release another one.

CdC: How long have you been doing that?
JD: Interestingly enough, that's what I came to California for. I was basically a songwriter and singer. I ended up getting signed to a record company and I went to a celebratory so-called party in the executive's house in the Sunset

"I Hate the Hollywood Bag"

Hills. He had some other ideas that I just didn't agree with (see *Badazz Mofo* #7 for details); I threw the brother though a plate glass window, and that was the end of my career.

I could have reasserted myself in many ways, but I found out that even though I enjoyed entertaining and being on stage, I was much more comfortable working with other people and creating the music for them. I found my passion and my real calling. So, I deprived the world of my entertainment skills and came off the stage to work behind the scenes.

CdC: How did you get into acting?

JD: I had been successful acting in high school. They had a nationwide talent search for a picture called *Take a Giant Step*. The producer and director came to my high school in Gary, Indiana. The director thought I was pretty damn good, but he ended up taking Johnny Nash for the part. Nash had appeared on Arthur Godfrey's show and had national attention at that time. It was before Nash did "I Can See Clearly Now."

When I came to California, I already had the experience and the acting bug, but I was really into music. I left college to pursue the music, and the acting thing just happened to present itself. I didn't go anywhere looking for a part and did absolutely nothing to seek out involvement in films. It just happened. It just fell in my lap. It was amusing, but I always did it on the run—when I could—and catch the next plane. My shows were really hot at that time. I opened up an office in Paris and we were importing bands to the tune of three and four a month. It was a heady time. The movies lost in a dead heat to other things.

CdC: It's ironic that while you weren't looking for film roles, you managed to get some plum ones. Certainly, you did films like *Hitman* or *Tender Loving Care* where you had some scenes here and then—bam—you're in starring roles in *Candy Tangerine Man*, *Black Shampoo*, and *Getting Over*.

JD: I think that it was just fate. The notoriety of Maverick's Flat at that time was so hot, and the social life of Los Angeles was focused in that place. It was kind of like a mini Studio 54. It was the only place that stayed open until four in the morning and was frequented by high echelon people, both black and white. We had dress and conduct codes and never had bouncers. The biggest difficulties we had were people getting a little tipsy, but they got that way on their own, because we didn't sell any liquor at Maverick's. We put it in at the beginning because it was expected, but when we found out that a liquor license was $25,000 we decided to just sell ice-cold Coca-Cola. We got known all over the United States for only selling Coca-Cola. That was in the first six months that we were open. Now, at thirty-six years old, we've never changed. I think we're the only club that has been able to survive with Coca-Cola.

Those days we had everybody that was doing anything in television and film down there. So, you were kind of in an environment where you'd see people—*The Addam's Family* is on TV and you're seeing Carolyn Jones in the club that night. After so much of that environment, my friend started telling me that I should go into the movies. I told him that he was crazy and that I was too busy to even think of anything like that. But he was a talent coordinator for the *The Dating Game* and he got me on there. I was on there twice and they brought me back for a third time for the nighttime game, which was in color. I won all three times and after that it felt like I was, I don't know, in demand.

CdC: Here's hoping you can finally settle something for me. I've seen so many ad mats and other materials with varying dates; I was hoping you could finally tell me when *Candy Tangerine Man* and *Black Shampoo* were out.
JD: *Candy Tangerine Man* came out in 1974 and *Black Shampoo* in 1975. In fact, they were both in *Variety*'s top fifty at the same time, which was flattering. To me, there wasn't any ego involved. I was just having a good time and moving on to the next thing. My wife and I were in London and I took her to Leicester Square and, while we had been together for over a year, I had never told her that I had been in movies. I didn't want it to get in the way of her knowing me as a person. So we're walking, hand in hand, and here's a thirty-foot picture of me with *Black Shampoo*. She looked at it, looked at me, and said, "Is that you?" The manager comes out of the theater and says, "I can't believe it!" The manager pulls me into the theater and stopped the movie to announce that they had the star of the movie there. She looked at me and said, "What are you involved in?" The cat was out of the bag.

CdC: Tell me more about the book you're working on. Is there a projected release date?
JD: As a magazine editor, I used to do a lot of writing for my magazine like you do.

CdC: Right, but it sounds like you had your act together a bit more than I do. I know you'll be talking a lot about your music career, but I just hope you don't give short shrift to the films.
JD: I don't intend to be short-changing, but the thing is that it's been a long time. *Getting Over* was 1980.

Let me tell you about *Getting Over*. With that, I was trying to make a feel-good film. I had had enough of the "kick ass" films. I was qualified for "kick ass," but only half of me was really in love with that. The other half was in love with romance and good taste; things that were beautiful. When I finally had a chance to make my own movie, I wanted to make something that was uplifting. It was made at a strange time. It came at the end of the blaxploitation era and before movies like it were accepted by the distribution establishment. Most of the distributors wanted me to reprise the roles that had made them money, like *Candy Tangerine Man*. When they saw *Getting Over* and it didn't have any shooting or fighting or anything like that, at that time they just hadn't

"I Hate the Hollywood Bag"

got that out of their system. The deals I got still took it along those tracks, but it wasn't that product. So I just kept it and didn't allow it to be released in that capacity. I took it around the world and it did well in select locations, but I wouldn't submit it to that "Black track distribution" because there was a lot of trash during that time, and they wanted to put it in with the rest of the trash.

CdC: Any chance of it coming out on DVD anytime soon?
JD: I don't know. I haven't had contact with the company that I sold it to in years. It'd be their decision, I suppose. I think I had a clause in the contract that allowed it to revert to me after so long, but I haven't really looked into it. With the glut of movies in the market, I don't think it'd kick up a storm. If they happen to do it, fine. Or if the world suddenly decides that it needs *Getting Over*.

CdC: Was that your last movie, or was that *Mean Dog Blues*?
JD: *Getting Over* was my final film. I got paid well for *Mean Dog Blues*, but I got cut out of most of that. I didn't see it until years later, not knowing that I had rescinded my fame to the cutting room floor.

CdC: Do you keep in touch with any of the folks from the movies you've been in?
JD: No. But I was going to the L.A. County Museum and the young lady who played my interest in *Black Shampoo*—

CdC: Tanya Boyd.

JD: I'm going to tell you how Tanya Boyd got into *Black Shampoo*. Greydon Clark told me that I could choose anyone to star opposite me. A whole lot of young ladies auditioned that were more beautiful than her and willing to do anything on God's green earth, but I just never registered with that thing. I went with Tanya Boyd because I felt that she was the most serious actress. So, we did the film and later Tanya's on television on a soap opera [*Days of Our Lives*], where she has a recurring role.

So, we're in line at the L.A. County Museum and Tanya Boyd is in line, too. She did not know me. I think it was intentional. I don't think she was comfortable being associated with *Black Shampoo*. She was standing there, looking through me, and I recognized what was happening. She had moved up to the networks. It was a funny thing, and I had a similar thing happen with Cheech & Chong.

Tommy Chong was playing guitar in the band that backed up Bobby Taylor & the Vancouvers. They had a big hit out at that time, "Does Your Momma Know about Me?" [Co-written by Chong and Tom Baird —Ed]. We booked them into the club, and after the show Tommy came upstairs and said, "Hey, man, I've got a partner and we do comedy—would you give us a chance?" I was known for taking a chance on something new. They came in and stayed at the club for a long time. And, boom, Lou Adler signs them eventually and the rest is history. So, I'm standing in a theater line, and who should be standing at the front of the line but Tommy Chong. I went up to him and said, "Hey, do you know me?" He said, "Do I know you? I wouldn't be who I am if it wasn't for you. I know you very well!" I never take it for granted if people know you, because a lot of them can make it heartbreaking.

The original version of this article ran in *Cashiers du Cinemart* #14.

SHADES OF GREYDON CLARK

By Mike White

Fellow Michigander Greydon Clark is a master of Exploitation films, First noticed in the Al Adamson biker flick *Satan's Sadists*, Clark held a supporting role as well as writing the picture. Often combining incongruous subgenres in unique and often challenging ways, Clark moved on to write and direct hybrid works like *Satan's Cheerleaders* (playing off the popularity of possession films and soft-core cheerleader flix), *Joy Sticks* (*Porky's* meets *WarGames*), and *Black Shampoo* (*Shampoo* filtered through a blaxploitation lens). Clark's unique interpretations of generic conventions lead to some strange films that never fail to entertain.

Cashiers du Cinemart: How did you get your start in film?
Greydon Clark: I came to Los Angeles in 1965, no experience, didn't know a soul. I wanted to be a "movie actor" and found the name of an acting coach in a book, *The Young Actors' Guide to Hollywood*. I attended classes for a couple of years. I sold various items door to door to put food on the table and pay for acting lessons. I met Al Adamson in 1967, through an actress I'd met in class. We became friends and he gave me my first role, a very small part in *The Fakers*.

Al owned the rights to a western short story he wanted written into a full-length script. I volunteered to write it. I'd never written anything before, but after a few months, I presented the final script, and it was very well received. Robert Taylor, a superstar from MGM's heyday, agreed to star. ABC agreed to finance as one of their first "Movie of the Week." We were set to begin production in Spain in the spring of 1968, when Mr. Taylor suddenly entered the hospital with cancer. He died in a very short time and the project was never produced. A financier approached Al with $50,000 to produce a movie. We couldn't begin to do the western for that amount, but I convinced Al that I could write a script that could be done on that budget.

Greydon Clark calls the shots on *Black Shampoo*

Motorcycle pictures were very popular at the time. This was just prior to *Easy Rider*. The picture was made in Indio, California, a desert community near Palm Springs. This was my first real picture-making experience, and I loved it. I had met Jackie in the same acting class and was instrumental in her being cast as the female star in *Satan's Sadists*.

The picture was an enormous success and played all over the world. I wrote a script about a Vietnam vet who returns to the States and rebels against the establishment. I decided I wanted to direct as well as act. Jackie and I starred in that picture, *Mothers, Fathers, and Lovers*. We made that picture on a record low budget—$12,500! It had modest success. I'd like to think it was ahead of its time.

I was active in the civil rights movement of the late '60s and decided to write a story about a well-meaning white guy who gets involved in the inner city. *The Bad Bunch* also had a degree of success, and we played in most major markets. The year was 1975, and I wanted to make another picture looking at the black experience, but did not want to make one where the hero was a pimp, pusher, cop, etc. I got the idea to make the hero a successful black businessman. *Shampoo* was about to come out, with a ton of publicity.

Black Shampoo—a businessman who innocently gets involved with mobsters—it seemed like a good idea at the time. The picture played all over the world and was quite successful. From there, I was fortunate enough to make seventeen more pictures, and still counting!

CdC: So *Mothers, Fathers, and Lovers* is not the same as *The Bad Bunch*? I had read that they were the same movie.
GC: I consider *Mothers, Fathers, and Lovers* to be a separate film from *The Bad Bunch*. They do share some of the same cast and a few scenes.

CdC: Can you tell me about some of the cast of *Black Shampoo*? I've always wondered about some of the actors with some of the more outrageous screen names such as Jack Mehoff and Salvator Benissimo.
GC: Salvator Benissimo was Sheldon Lee. Sheldon worked in several of my earlier movies. The actor playing Jack Mehoff was a good friend, who also was in those early pictures I've mentioned above. His name was Bill Bonner. Unfortunately, tragedy struck Bill very early in his life. In early 1976, not long after *Black Shampoo*, while filming in the Midwest, Bill was involved in an automobile accident and paralyzed. Jackie and I visited him for several months in the hospital. One day, he checked himself out without notice and literally disappeared. Bill was an exceptional actor and good friend. We tried to find him, but were unable to. Nobody ever saw him again.

CdC: Was that Jackie Cole from *Satan's Cheerleaders* and *Angel's Brigade* (also known as *Angel's Revenge*)?
GC: Jackie and I were together for more than 34 years. She was my wife and the mother of our two boys. She starred in *Satan's Sadists* under the name Jackie Taylor. I wrote and acted in *Satan's Sadists* for Al Adamson in 1968, and that's

when Jackie and I first got together. She starred in the first movie I directed in 1970, *Mothers, Fathers, and Lovers*, and my second in 1973, *The Bad Bunch*.

Black Shampoo was my third movie and was made in 1975. It was not a SAG picture; therefore, many of the actors used alternate names. She used the name "Edith Wheeler." I've made twenty movies in my career, and she was in many of them.

Jackie passed away in February of this year [2007]. She is loved and missed by all who knew her.

CdC: You definitely were ahead of the times with your horror parody *Wacko*. A lot of the elements in it seemed to echo through *Student Bodies*, *Scary Movie*, etc.

GC: *Wacko* was my first picture with Joe Don Baker. When I was making the deal with him, I could only afford him for two weeks. He asked how I could film him in two weeks. I explained that I would use a double for two weeks when he was in the "pumpkin head." He agreed to do the movie, but only if he was the only actor playing the Halloween Killer.... And he'd do it for the two-week price.

Joe Don is a terrific actor and wonderful person. We did three films together, and I have nothing but fond memories of our days together. Our last picture was *Final Justice*. Filmed entirely in Malta, it was a unique experience. Unfortunately, we've sort of lost contact over the years.

CdC: You've worked with a lot of "name" actors: George Kennedy, Jack Palance, Martin Landau, Tony Curtis, etc. How is it managing "bigger" and "smaller" actors all on the same set?

GC: I've been very lucky regarding my relationships with actors. I've never really had difficulty, especially with "name" actors. I remember when I hired Jack Palance for the first time in *Angel's Brigade*. There were stories that he was difficult to work with. Nothing could be further from the truth. He was extremely well prepared, very cooperative and helpful with some of the young actors he was working with. Same is true with George Kennedy and Martin Landau. I remember on *Without Warning*, Marty worked almost 20 hours straight and never complained. George Kennedy agreed to come in for a quick shot on a day that he was not even paid for!

Wings Hauser came in after he was wrapped to do off-camera lines for Susan Blakely's close-up on *Sight Unseen*. These guys and many like them always put the picture before anything else. Their success is deserved, all real pros. I loved making all my pictures. Some were more successful than others, but all were a joy to make. I've been very fortunate in my career and have worked with many people who have gone on to wonderful careers.

Shades of Greydon Clark

CdC: What are you working on currently?
GC: I've got a couple of projects, but nothing definite at this time. I don't like to talk about a project until it's an absolute "go."

In the last decade or so I've made four movies in Russia and one in Bulgaria. After doing *The Forbidden Dance* for Menachem Golan, this in itself was quite an experience. Ninety days from our first meeting (without even a story) to a Columbia Pictures national release. Menachem then asked me to go to Russia, where I made *Dance Macabre* and *Mad Dog Coll* (aka *Killer Instinct*) for him. I made *Russian Holiday* and *Dark Future* for my own company in St. Petersburg. *Star Games* was made in Bulgaria for my own company. It is very interesting shooting overseas, especially in former communist nations. I also made two episodes of *The New Mike Hammer*.

CdC: Do you have anything you can share with other diehard *Black Shampoo* fans?
GC: A day before shooting began, my cameraman was in an automobile accident. Nothing too serious, but he received a blow to his face. He insisted he was okay, but within the first few hours of shooting he came to me and said he couldn't continue. He suggested that the gaffer could shoot the film. The gaffer was Dean Cundey. He'd never shot a movie before. Necessity, being that mother, I gave him a chance. Dean ended up shooting *Satan's Cheerleaders*, *The Hi-Riders*, *Angel's Brigade*, and *Without Warning* for me. As you know, Dean is one of the most successful directors of photography in the last two decades, with credits on major films too numerous to mention.

CdC: Of all your work, what film are you the most proud of?
GC: I'm proud of all my work and it would be impossible to pick a favorite. If pushed, I'd say, "The next one."

The original version of this article ran in *Cashiers du Cinemart* #14.

FEEL THE LOVE...ON DVD

By Mike White

I was fortunate enough to be invited to write liner notes for the DVD release of *Black Shampoo* when VCI released it in 2005. Since then, I've gotten several emails from folks whose DVDs were missing those notes. Here's a reprint of what I wrote:

> I grew up on movies like *Star Wars*, *Blade Runner*, and *The Blues Brothers*; I had heard "Theme from Shaft" but hadn't seen the movie, or even *Sweet Sweetback's Baadasssss Song*. My education in so-called "blaxploitation" films had yet to begin.
>
> We always remember our first. *Black Shampoo* was my initial exposure to Black Action films. It opened a whole new world to me. My high school cronies and I were hooked from the outset—from those first two notes of Gerald Lee's phenomenally funky score. In the weeks and months following our initial viewing on a snowy December 26, 1988, we must have watched *Black Shampoo* a few hundred times. It was our *Rocky Horror Picture Show*—we latched onto characters, we memorized dialogue, and we picked apart every nuance the film had to offer.
>
> When does an obsession become fanaticism? Somewhere just north of five years of annual get-togethers. While watching yet another John Daniels film, *Getting Over*, I began work on a movie fanzine, *Cashiers du Cinemart*, which would help me celebrate *Black Shampoo* with a wider audience. Eventually, I would score my dream interviews—talking to Artie (Skip E. Lowe), Brenda St. John (Tanya Boyd), Mr. Jonathan (John Daniels), and the film's director, Greydon Clark.
>
> "In 1975 I wanted to make another picture looking at the black experience, but did not want to make one where the hero was a pimp, pusher, cop, etc. I got the idea to make the hero a successful black businessman," says Clark.
>
> Capitalizing on the rampant publicity of Hal Ashby's *Shampoo*, Clark set his tale in a hair salon. Named after its proprietor, Jonathan Knight (John Daniels), Mr. Jonathan's is the hottest beauty spot on the Sunset Strip. The popularity of the salon stems not from the busy scissors of Artie (Skip E. Lowe) or Richard (Gary Allen), but from special attention Mr. Jonathan pays to his clientele's more intimate needs.

Feel the Love…on DVD

For the first half of the film, we witness Mr. Jonathan as a Los Angeles Lothario, albeit a reluctant one. "I just came to do your hair," he bemoans, as he's used like a slab of meat by Mrs. Simpson (Diana St. Clair). Luckily, true love sits behind his receptionist desk.

After just three days at the salon, Jonathan finally takes notice of his latest employee, Brenda St. John (Tanya Boyd). Unfortunately, Brenda is haunted by a troubled past. She's on the run from the mob and when her former flame, the short-tempered Mr. Wilson (Joe Ortiz), learns her whereabouts, he fights to get her back. But Mr. Jonathan, the "loving machine," exchanges his blow dryer for a chainsaw to become a "killing machine," in order to keep true love by his side.

Unlike the aforementioned films of my youth, VCI presents an uncut and beautifully restored version of Black Shampoo for all to enjoy. Rest assured that somewhere this December 26th, a handful of wayward cinephiles from Michigan will be enjoying this. We hope you do too.

The irony here is that I was careful to mention *Star Wars*, *Blade Runner*, and *The Blues Brothers*, as all three films had been mangled in their DVD releases. I didn't know that *Black Shampoo* would not be free of tampering. While VCI utilized a terrific-looking print courtesy of director Greydon Clark, the DVD had a rather strange scene midway through the movie. After Mr. Jonathan confronts Brenda by the pool, he goes not back to the salon, but over to visit Mrs. Phillips (Anne Gaybis) in an attempt to reinstate his manhood. What's truly odd is that this scene is without its original audio track. The dialogue was lost over the years, as was the script. In an attempt to salvage this scene, VCI utilized other bits of music and dialogue from the movie. The results are less than satisfying, and mar an otherwise flawless presentation of my favorite film.

This "poodle kick" scene (named after the way Mr. Jonathan treats Mrs. Phillips's dog) should have been relegated to the section of the disc with the other scenes that were without audio (more scenes of the Western-style Bar-B-Q, including a pie fight), instead of being crowbarred into the film. I couldn't watch this now-flawed gem and have since created my own fan edit of the film, sans poodle kick.

The original version of this article ran in Cashiers du Cinemart *#15.*

THEATER DAZE

By Mike White

I originally conceived the idea for *Cashiers du Cinemart* when I was working at a movie theater—tearing tickets, sweeping theater floors, and dousing hot popcorn with butter-flavored soybean oil. Much has changed since then: I have long since been fired from the theater, started the zine, and not written a lick about my days at the Star Theater–Taylor. However, the name I came up with then stuck, and it is high time I try to live up to it.

My original goal was to let the downtrodden theater workers know that they were not alone in their struggles with the Great Unwashed: people complaining about the high concession prices, going into the wrong theaters, old people saying how cold they were, rowdy teens, gang fights, lousy previews, and breaking films. It can be a thankless job at times.

"But you get to see free movies!" Sure, the one place I want to be on my day off is the place I spend all of my time. The late night pre-screenings are cool, but we would have to beg and plead for those.

No, the most enjoyment I got from my job came from my co-workers and making fun of the customers. The easiest targets showed their true colors at the box office, where people either had no idea what time the movie they wanted to see started, what movies were showing, or what the name of the movie was that they were seeing.

I still cringe when I look in the paper every Friday to see some of the names of films opening. I shuddered at *The Shawshank Redemption*, cringed at *The Hudsucker Proxy*, reeled at *It Could Happen to You*, and choked at *Johnny Mnemonic*.

I once got *The Search for Orange September* for *The Hunt for Red October*. To "Far-out Granny" (as she was unaffectionately known), *Men Don't Leave* became *Men Don't Leave Me, Please*. *The Usual Suspects* netted alternatives like *The Unusual Suspects* and *Those Suspicious Characters*. That's just the tip of the iceberg.

Part One: Box Office Boredom

Going back to my days at the Star Theater, I'm really thankful that I was allowed to work all three of the jobs allowed to the "cast members": those of usher, concessionaire, and box-office person. Cross training was not only encouraged; it was required—you had to work X number of shifts at each position before you could get a raise. Of course, there were some who would try to avoid one of the positions even if it cost them fifty cents an hour. Each job had its pros and cons, but the biggest gripe everyone had was the customers.

Being in the box office meant that you had to have direct contact with everyone. This wasn't bad at all, if the person coming in knew exactly what they

Theatre Daze

wanted to see and didn't have a gripe with the price. But, oh, that was a rare customer indeed. Most people walking through the door either had no idea what time their movie was, or even what was playing. And then there were those who needed a synopsis of everything, the rating, the justification of this rating, and a recommendation or condemnation of its entertainment value. The concept of not knowing what you're going to see and when it starts is completely alien to me, but it seemed commonplace among those who just kind of dropped by the theater to see what was shaking or to buy a box of popcorn.

I must have seen at least two dozen people walk in, buy a medium or large popcorn with extra, extra butter, and walk out again. "Nothing tastes like movie theater popcorn." Yeah, but nothing costs as much, either. Not even a whole fifty-pound bag of unpopped corn fresh off the truck costs as much as your large buttered.

It was here that I learned that my opinion meant nothing to the common man. "That *Short Time*, is that any good?" "Not that I've heard." "Okay, I'll take one ticket to that." And invariably, I'd hear, "What? Six dollars?!"

I didn't mind the little old ladies who demanded a refund, despite my earlier warnings that they would probably not enjoy *Whore*. I didn't mind the idiots who said I had pointed them in the wrong direction when they left the box office and ended up sitting in an empty theater for two hours waiting for their movie to start. I didn't even mind (too much) the people who would come up and ask for a movie by actor or concept instead of by name.

I really was expecting too much from people for them to remember the name of the movie they were going to see. My favorite day came when I had two sets of patrons who both asked for "Act." I sent the old ladies to *Class Act* and the young rabble-rousers to *Sister Act*. I never felt so good giving a refund and telling them the importance of being clear on requesting a title. Sure, I could tell exactly what most people were going to see as soon as they walked in the door, but it was so much fun making them say the title. Sometimes it might have been obvious that the kids with black nail polish were not here to see *Boyz N the Hood*, and the kids with half of their overalls falling down under their Triple Fat Goose coats were not likely to want to see *Fire Walk with Me*. But I was slick, man: if I worked too many box-office shifts in a row, I knew what tickets every plain Jane and John Doe were going to request when they stepped up to the plate.

The people I minded the most at the box office were the jokesters. I once wrote a screenplay about what it was like to work in the movie theater business, and started it off with a scene like this:

FADE IN:
A young thick-necked man and his wisp of a girlfriend stand in front of the box office, staring at the big screen listing

today's show times. Finally, as if waking from a dream, the man steps up.

HIM
Yeah, one adult and one child for <u>Pretty Woman</u>.

The girl giggles and lightly slaps the man's arm as a shit-eating grin covers his face and the box-office worker's night of eye rolling begins.

ME
That'll be twelve dollars, please.

HIM
Twelve bucks?!

FADE OUT.

Part Two: Would You Like Butter Flavoring on That?
"If people are dumb enough to pay it, we'll keep charging it," was my pat response when I worked in the concession stand. I heard more complaining in The Stand about prices than I could ever imagine hearing in the box office. Also, my nerves were more worn and I was more likely to go off on people when they gave me shit.

"Can I have *that* popcorn?" (Pointing to the popcorn being made at the moment.) "Sure…" I would say, knowing what a complete pain in the ass it is to have to stop my regular routine, walk over to the popper, wait for the corn to be done, and then walk back to a butter machine. I got my revenge, though. The popcorn was certainly fresh. So fresh that the popper hadn't had time to sift out the seeds. And, it wasn't like the sifted popcorn wasn't going directly into my warmer in a matter of seconds. It never sat around, except for the first corn put in the warmers in the morning.

I would return to the front of The Stand with a big ole bucket of some popcorn and a lot of seeds. "Can I have extra butter on that? I mean, just soak it." Okay, you asked for it. There's your soggy bucket o' seeds; anything else?

We were never allowed to say just "butter" in The Stand. It was a old tale of housewifery passed on from one worker to another that some new employee somewhere called it just "butter" and a woman had an allergic reaction to the soybean oil that it really is. So it became mandatory to ask, "Would you like Butter Flavoring on that?" The "flavoring" was our caveat emptor.

You've got to remember that I was working at a time before the big oil scare. We had no qualms about cooking the corn in coconut oil and dousing it with a bit of the sodium-concentrated "Savor-all." It became a real pain when we would have to make a batch of non-Savor-all corn because we had to remember to do it first (before the popper was tainted), and no one bought the foul-tasting plain corn, anyway.

To me, people wanting popcorn without Savor-all—popcorn in a manner that we just didn't fix it—should have learned to go without popcorn at all. Where did they grow up? That, to me, was like wanting a fried egg at McDonalds when the eggs just don't come that way. Star Theater's motto was not "Your way, right away." No, it was something really lame like, "Love, Laugh, Live." I mocked the motto so much that I can't even remember the real deal.

In the concession stand, the biggest problem was people complaining about the prices. The second biggest was that customers expected us to know exactly where and at what time their movie was showing. That's not the job of the concessionaire. Time and again I'd have to say, "Do you have your ticket?" and then proceed to read the information to them off of it.

Working in The Stand had its perks: a busy night went by fast and there was always pop to drink and leftover hot dogs to eat at the end of the night. But it was the worst in terms of end-of-the-night hassle. All those cups and buckets to be put away, the popper to be scrubbed out, the warmers to be left sparkling. As time went on we also had to worry about the hot dog warmer, the nacho cheese dispenser, the frozen coke machine, and the pretzel turner. And, also, there were those not-so-busy day shifts where one had to look busy. The Stand was in the middle of the theater—right in the line of sight of the manager's kiosk. So if you had some dicky manager sitting there talking on the phone all day, the people in The Stand were stuck out in the open. No slacking allowed. "If you've got time to lean, you've got time to clean."

Being an usher, though, was a slacker's paradise. There were guys who fell asleep on the job, fer chrissake. Years before "Where's Waldo?" we used to play our own little game of "Where's Cornell?" Usually in Theater Five, sleeping.

The customers generally left you alone as an usher. You'd tear their tickets, tell them where to go, watch them, making sure they knew the difference between right and left, and sweep your little area a bit. That was the state of being known as Post. Some nights it felt like all I did since I was born was stand Post. "Welcome to the Star, that's in Theater Three, which is the second theater to your right. Enjoy your show." If I were to say these words one more time, I would attain some sort of oneness with the universe. But luckily, just at the time I thought I would crack, someone would relieve me of my duties and allow me to slack off and do an aisle check. Oh, those glorious aisle checks. That's a euphemism for standing in the back of a theater and watching a movie for a few minutes. Sure, you were supposed to walk down the aisle, looking for nogoodniks with their feet on the back of the chairs, but in an empty house, who cares? The only people I loved to bust were drinkers and smokers. What the hell do smokers think? That I can't smell it and see it? I just love enforcing those federal laws!

Part Three: Adventures in Slacking

The grunt work of being an usher came in cleaning theaters. Walking up and down the rows, picking up popcorn buckets and cups of pop. I didn't mind this. The only time it got gross was when people would bring their chaw o' tobacky into the theater and use their cup to spit in. On a nice, busy night there might be upwards of eight people cleaning one theater, and we would move like a well-oiled machine. On a nice, slow day there might be two guys cleaning and chewing the fat all the while. We ushers, when we could get into groups of two or more, could talk up a storm. And if you held the "break schedule" just right, it would look like we were discussing the next few movies letting out and who would stand Post while the other cleaned, instead of mulling over the implications of the works of Sam Cooke. We discovered that one could make a never-ending medley of all of Sam's songs, as long as it kept going back into "Chain Gang" every twelve to sixteen measures.

Other fun times while cleaning theaters were found in complaining about end-credit music. My top three all-time worst closing credit themes would have to be from *Suburban Commando*, *Loose Cannons*, and *Spaced Invaders*. The best? *Boyz N the Hood*, *Men Don't Leave*, and *The Hunt for Red October*. Heck, I hate to admit this, but I even had a fun time mocking Axl Rose during the end of *Terminator 2*.

Another plus of cleaning theaters was all the money to be found. If it was a wallet I was honest and gave it to the manager to put in the lost and found drawer (after we went through and looked at the guy's family photos and whatnot). If it was loose money, I'm sad to say that it was divided up amongst those cleaning (never mentioning it to the people on Post). One busy night my friend was cleaning a theater with a pair of dweebs. As they were finishing, my friend was up front pulling out the brooms from behind the screen. The two dweebs bid their fond adieu—"See ya, sucker!"—and left him to sweep the rows all by his lonesome. The happy ending to this story is that he found a big ole wad of money in one of the rows and, since he was by himself, he didn't have to cut anyone in on his take.

As fate would have it, Cornell was always luckiest at finding full wallets on a Friday night, which he would then empty and throw above the doors of the theater where no one would ever look, nor should have any reason to. This was rumor, of course, and I doubt it sometimes, since I never once saw Cornell clean a theater.

There were two different Posts to stand at: One through Four and Five through Eight. At the first, you had the advantage of being hidden from the manager's kiosk and the ability to stand around and talk for long stretches. The spoiler was that you were alone and forced to watch the televisions in the back lobby for long periods of time.

There were six or seven big-screen TVs right in the line of sight of that 1–4 Post stander, and our eyes were drawn to them. They showed an unending loop of previews. When the new tape came in at the beginning of the month, everyone was excited to see the new previews. The usher standing Post that day was looked at in envy by the box-office and concession-stand workers, who were denied visual access to the TVs. By the end of the month, a tear would come to my eye when I saw some poor sap stuck over there for hours on end, watching the same trailers over and over.

Unlike my days at Blockbuster, there was no way to block out the TVs or play something else. Those previews ran all the time. They were just a constant drone to every worker, except the guy who kept watching and memorizing every line.

"I want you to meet my sistah, goddess of fiah." These words from the *Marked for Death* preview still haunt me. And why is space being taken up in my brain with the knowledge that a lot of the scenes in *Gremlins 2* had different angles?

One advantage of seeing all the previews was that it also allowed one to judge how good a movie was in regards to how long ago the preview was first seen. Sure, there are "teasers" like *Terminator 2* (with its cool Terminator factory stuff that was later cut) and the infinitely cooler-than-the-movie *Alien3* teaser, but I'm talking about full-fledged trailers that seemed to go away and come back and go away again for a long time before the movie either came out or showed up at Blockbuster. The best example of this was *Swing Kids*—just because it looked so fucking stupid. Another good couple of previews that became MIA movies were *Where the Heart Is* with Dabney Coleman and *Coupe de Ville* with Daniel Stern. Either these were "blink and you'll miss it," or just never made it to wide release.

The second Post, by the way, was fun or horrible, depending on who was managing and projecting that day. The Post was only a few feet away from the manager's kiosk, and

Impossibly Funky

on a good day a lot of time could be spent with one's elbows up on the counter shooting the breeze and deciding who to "trade out" lunch with (movie passes are gold when bartering for food). On a bad day, I would bissel a lot (Bissel is the brand name for those carpet sweeper things and can be used as an noun or verb, and even sometimes as an adjective, but then it's spelled "abysmal") and try to overhear where the management was going to get lunch from, while leaving everyone else to eat popcorn and stale hot dogs.

A lot depended on the management. With the right managers, the job was a dream. Work got done, but after the last of the patrons were shown the door, the theater might become the scene of a killer laser tag match, a drunken night of video game and card playing revelry, or we might simply have an employee showing of a print to be released the following day.

Watching a movie in the company of just your fellow employees was quite a treat. We would be as loud and obnoxious as the movie merited and inside jokes were yelled instead of whispered. I still remember *Flatliners* fondly, not just as a link for the Kevin Bacon game, but because of the great time we had hooting and hollering when little Billy Mahoney (Joshua Rudoy) came back to kick Kiefer Sutherland's ass. "Yeah, get him, Billy!" Though there may not have ever been more than forty people watching these after-hours screenings, we made more of a ruckus than a packed house on a Saturday night, and we were proud of it.

The most successful employee screening was probably *Terminator 2*, since everyone was so psyched to see it—and it lived up to its hype. The least successful honors wpi;d have to go to *Fire Walk with Me*. I had been part of the committee to decorate the lobby for that film. We had arranged a trade-out with a donut place, who gave free coffee to anyone with a *FWWM* ticket stub. We also had a huge display, complete with a "corpse" wrapped in plastic. The guys who worked on the display were so excited that it must have been contagious, because the Thursday before the movie opened, some of the other employees stated that they wanted to have a showing of it. "You're not going to like this movie," I told them. They blew me off and we proceeded to have the showing (since the manager was a big *Twin Peaks* fan, too). By the time Agent Cooper finally showed up, half of the audience was gone.

Theatre Daze

I think the only other movie that drove people away as quickly must have been *Dutch*.

There were quite a number of films that came to the theater and were never heard from again. You'd be surprised how many so-called "straight to video" releases have had a theatrical run. *Brain Dead* is one I distinctly remember watching in Theater 6, and I did an aisle check or two on *Class of 1999* and *Wild Orchid*. We even had a big gala premier for *Mirror Mirror*, that cheesy horror movie with Karen Black. I was amazed when I read about the sequel finally coming out so many years later, since all of the promotional material had said, "*Mirror Mirror 2*, coming soon!" There must have been some major kickbacks going on, since the movie opened in our largest theater and we had posters for it all over the place. But by Saturday morning, *Mirror Mirror* was safely tucked away in Theater 7, the place where movies go before they die.

Most of the time, that job was a pain. But I also had a lot of fun, singing, hanging out in the back room eating raw popcorn, and pasting the extra "t" onto all of our *The Pope Must Die* posters.

Two Tickets For…

What the heck's a Cinemart? Hell if I know. Sounds to me kind of like a cinema crossed with a mini-mart. I couldn't call the magazine "Cashiers du Cineplex," since the word "cineplex" is a licensed trademark of the National Amusements Company. Betcha didn't know that one, did you?

I found out that juicy little tidbit when I was in training at the Showcase Theater in Ann Arbor. I had been working at Blockbuster (my job after Star Taylor) and was getting really sick of the customers (I'm just not made for retail) and lack of hours, so I went back to the profession I knew best: a theater worker. I had spent three years working at the Star Taylor, and felt I had the job down to a science.

I went around to all the theaters in Ann Arbor putting in my application. I found out some unpleasant truths in my quest for a better job: the Michigan Theater, since it's kind of a charity operation, doesn't pay dick. I also learned that the United Artists at Briarwood Mall has some sort of weird schedule where one has to work full time for two weeks and then get two days off and then work three shifts of part time or something equally ridiculous. It was almost like they didn't want people to work there—especially people going to school or with social lives. And I found out that it's too far to walk to the Goodrich Ann Arbor 1&2, and that parking is nonexistent.

But the saddest truths of all I learned while actually working at Showcase Cinema Ann Arbor.

I felt like an undercover agent going in there, comparing and contrasting everything they did at their theater with what I did at mine, trying to see if they did anything better or more efficiently. Nope.

The Star Theater might not have been a full-time party, but at least it was clean. My first night at the Showcase, I was put in the concession stand in my dumb-ass uniform (complete with visor and apron), and when the time came to clean the popcorn warmers, I almost shrieked in terror at how dirty the bottoms were. When I popped open the bottom to clean out the tray underneath, my co-workers stood around in amazement: "I never knew that came out," one of them said. How could I have guessed? What was my first clue? Was it the layer upon layer of grit and grease?

That first night I was also scolded for tainting the popcorn I took out of the warmer with my dirty paper towels. You see, I'm used to throwing out that crumbly mess left in a warmer after a busy night. My mistake. At Showcase, they like to reuse that refuse. So in essence, you could be eating a piece of popcorn today that was popped the first day the theater opened. Maybe a few more squirts of butter flavoring would help you swallow that bit of info.

The cleanliness thing really got under my skin, especially those day shifts during which we were waging a constant battle with flies. I remember seeing a few flies at the Star and quickly disposing of them in a sanitary manner. But it was like the wrap party for *The Amityville Horror* was taking place in the Showcase lobby every day. I don't know where they were coming from, and frankly, I'd rather remain ignorant.

After a week I put in my notice at Showcase. I couldn't handle the dirt, the clientele, my co-workers, the management, and my low, low pay. The first Saturday I worked, I went to an early morning meeting, where the topic was upselling.

For those lucky bastards out there who have never had to work retail, let me fill you in on the insidious concept of upselling. "Would you like a large? It's only a quarter more." That's it in a nutshell. Any candy or nachos with that?

Upselling is all fine and good in a job where you can make commission. I made it at the Star, so I didn't really mind selling the better-priced "Superbucket Special" when I got that big ole check at the end of the week. Of course the owners weren't losing money by me making money, so everyone was happy. At Showcase, on the other hand, the more I sold the same I got. If I made the National Amusements Company a thousand dollars a night, I still got dick. I still got my quarter more than minimum wage. That really is incentive, now isn't it?

Incentive for what? To steal.

This is the part of the article where morality goes out the window, so, please, if you've never been guilty of ripping off your cheap-ass boss, please stop reading now.

Showcase was run by a bunch of tight wads. That embarrassing uniform I mentioned earlier had no pockets of any kind. I couldn't even carry my wallet down to the concession stand (where I found I was stuck for the rest of my

Theatre Daze

life—no cross training at this job and, since I had half a brain, I got to handle the toughest task—lucky me).

Also, I had to keep a personal inventory of everything I sold. At the beginning of the shift I had to count out all my popcorn bags, cups, and candy (each bag). This process took at least fifteen minutes after I counted it and my supervisor double checked it. I was always being double checked. I felt like a criminal. So I became one.

After a few days I found out which items I wasn't responsible for. I couldn't sell a pop off the register since I would be missing a cup at the end of my shift. But hot dogs, nachos, and ice cream—those were another story altogether.

This is where my math skills paid off. I would ring up the item but never total it. Then I would take my cut from the booty, stick it in my sock, take if off the register, and then total it out.

Unfortunately, not too many people bought these items compared to pop and popcorn but, oh, it felt so good to skim that extra money off the top. An extra twenty dollars a night isn't much compared to the amount of money I made for the theater, but it helps bring that minimum wage plus a quarter up a notch—and, hey, it was tax free!

Yeah, go ahead, call me a monster for being so flagrant in my pilfering of petty cash, but make sure it's because you morally object to it, and not because you're jealous for not having done the same in any number of dead-end jobs you might have worked. I look back with great happiness that I managed to get away with something, because that company didn't give a shit about its workers. It was something right out of Marx & Engels.

Sure, there are some perks to working at a movie theater—all the free movies you could watch…well, kind of. You can't see anything less than three weeks old for free on a Friday or Saturday night (maybe you actually got one of those off for a change), and you had to call and get permission before you came to watch anything. Then when you did finally sign the last of the twenty-seven forms, took a urine test, and coughed twice for Mr. Brown, the manager, you got to watch a movie presented in only the way Showcase can show it. A scratched, out-of-focus print with bad sound. Ahhh…all that hard work and upselling was worth it just for these two hours of bliss…

I never actually got to see anything while I worked my two weeks at Showcase. I had, luckily, kept my job at Blockbuster and was working both every day. You had better believe I enjoyed Blockbuster a whole hell of a lot more after my ordeal at Showcase was over.

Portions of this article ran in *Cashiers du Cinemart* #6.

GHOTI OUT OF WATER

By Andrea White

Few people that know that "ghoti" is a phonetic way to spell "fish": the "gh" in tough, "o" in women and "ti" in motion. In the balmy month of June, Mike and I attended the Underground Publishing Conference as an alleged "birthday weekend getaway," and here I felt like the proverbial ghoti out of water.

We got to Bowling Green, Ohio the night before the conference began. We had reserved a hotel room, despite the availability of dorm rooms, a lovely church floor, and ample campsites. After stowing our bags, we went over to the local campus, looking for the conference building to drop off all the stuff Mike had brought. Here we met up with another person looking to do the same thing. Dressed in his jean shorts and Hawaiian-type shirt, this fellow led me to believe, wrongly, that I was going to be okay with this weekend event.

Saturday morning we were up bright and too early. We got to the conference building and started hauling in the numerous boxes of stuff that we had brought to sell or give away. Once our table was loaded, we were all set to begin the two-day event, or so I thought.

It wasn't long before I committed my first punk rock faux pas by asking the dread-locked, safety-pinned, pierced young man what the "A in a circle" tattoo on his arm meant. After that, things only got worse. It didn't take long before I realized that I didn't conform to the informal dress code. My clothes were quite conservative: no tights, tank shirts, slip worn as a dress, overalls, or Bettie Page look on me. And though my hair was dyed red (light auburn, according to the box), it did not compare to the bright pinks, blues, purples, and stoplight reds that adorned other tresses in those rooms. The hairstyles were incomparable: multiple pigtails, dreadlocks, numerous barrettes, and shaved heads were de rigueur. If the hair on my head wasn't enough, shaving also separated me from the other women in the crowd. Most leaned toward the hirsute lifestyle, a fact made easily discernable via tank-style shirts, overalls, and skirts.

The first day of the conference I stuck close to the table. I sold what I could, traded zines, and tried to answer questions about all the swag and wares we'd brought. Easier said than done, I'm afraid, as I had no idea what half of the things we had brought were for or about.

I got brave a couple of times and circled the room, looking at the zines, drawings, books, pamphlets, and other chotchkes on the tables. Later in the day, I enjoyed sampling the "donations accepted" vegan offerings provided by a group of women friends of the conference presenters. I especially enjoyed the cookies. I even bought a couple of vegan cookbooks, although Mike and I include eggs, dairy, and seafood in our diet. I had a tense moment late in the day when I realized I was eating Baskin-Robbins ice cream among this group of strict vegans. I thought it best to turn around and hide what I was doing. Who knows how many "laws" I was breaking by enjoying real dairy!

I also hid what I was reading from other eyes. The book was a spy story, and didn't support the prevailing anarchy theme of the room (yes, I found out what the "A in a circle" tattoo meant). Thinking about it, I suppose I should've been reading some of the zines we had traded for. I perused a couple at some point, but they just didn't hold my interest like the book I brought.

That night we went to showings of *Godass* and *Acne*. Both were great! I especially enjoyed Rusty Nails—director, writer, and star of *Acne*. After the show I stuck my foot in my mouth when I said we were going back to our hotel room to use the Jacuzzi, instead of going to a bar and listening to a band (whose members were also part of the conference). Comfort over punk rock? Say it isn't so!

On Sunday I changed my tactic, electing to go to a presentation enticingly titled "Fuck Western Medicine." I mistakenly thought that the presenters would offer alternatives to traditional medical practices, like using holistic medicine instead of pharmaceuticals. Instead, I learned how to do a menstrual extraction with homemade holistic RU468. The gals also recommended the use of sea sponges in lieu of tampons or pads. Per the presenters, "you just have to get used to rinsing [the sponge] in public restrooms." And let's not forget the advice that women should not wash their perineum area with soap and water. I simply couldn't support that theory and respect myself afterwards.

My head was reeling and my neck was tense from watching my back. I kept wondering when someone would point at me and shout: "She doesn't belong here!" I was biding my time, hoping to last the remaining hours before we could make our escape. I had figured out that this gathering was not a part of my milieu.

I am a self-realized government worker who prefers a hotel room with a king-sized bed and Jacuzzi to a spartan dorm room, dusty church floor, or muddy campsite. I prefer dairy, eggs, and fish to true vegan offerings. In general, I just did not fit well with an anarchy-supporting conference. We left Bowling Green with less to pack up than when we started, and I suppose that means the event was an overall success. I can't begin to relate how relieved I was to put the last box of stuff into the car and head back to my "normal" life.

The original version of this article ran in *Cashiers du Cinemart* #12.

ANDREA AND MIKE GO TO BREAKFAST

By Andrea White

We had watched *Harold and Kumar Go to White Castle* the night before. Anyone who has a White Castle nearby knows that after a night of drinking, nothing satisfies the munchies cravings like a "slider" (though, personally, I vote for Taco Bell).

It was one of those mornings that nothing other than breakfast at Waffle House would satisfy my cravings.

I persuaded Mike that we could be up and at the closest Waffle House in less than an hour. I had gone to wafflehouse.com to scout locations, and the nearest one was at Exit 15 off of Interstate 75. No problem. We're only forty miles from the Michigan-Ohio border: what's an extra fifteen miles?

Off we went. The thought of a pecan waffle with smothered and covered hash browns was causing me to salivate. A half hour later we were seeing the "Welcome to Ohio" sign—it should only be a few more minutes until we were sitting down to our breakfast. Then I noticed a mile marker—What!?!—#258. I really goofed: the Waffle House I looked up was at the southern border of Ohio, about 243 miles away. Now what?

We were in the Toledo area and I knew there were two Toledo Waffle House locations. We got on the phone and called. The girl on the phone was directionally challenged; it was a waste of time talking to her. We decided to just keep driving south. There would be signs or billboards, right? After another forty minutes we saw a sign and ended up at a Waffle House in Bowling Green, Ohio, some eighty miles further south.

It was worth it.

I learned my lesson, though—the next time I suggested going to Toledo for breakfast, I mapped it first.

BRENDAN FRASER + MONKEY = FUN!

By Skizz Cyzyk

Take any movie, replace the male lead with Brendan Fraser, and replace the female lead with a monkey—Voila!—more interesting movie. Try it. It can be any movie, good or bad. *Shanghai Surprise*: replace Sean Penn with Brendan Fraser, and replace Madonna with a monkey. *Citizen Kane*: replace Orson Welles's Charles Foster Kane character with Brendan Fraser, and replace Dorothy Comingore's Susan Alexander character (or Ruth Warrick's Emily Norton) with a monkey. *The Happening*: replace Mark Wahlberg with Brendan Fraser, and replace Zooey Deschanel with a monkey. A lot of times, a bad movie gets better, while a good movie just gets more interesting. Fraser and the monkey don't have to necessarily play the characters according to the script; they can just be themselves (which is certainly easier for the monkey). Either way, it works.

Some naysayers are probably trying to think of exceptions to the rule. What about movies Brendan Fraser is already in, particularly ones featuring a monkey? What about *Monkeybone* or *George of the Jungle*? (My cheap sense of humor is trying really hard not to make an *Encino Man* joke right now, equating Pauly Shore with a monkey.) And why Brendan Fraser? Why not?

Fraser is a good-looking, likeable everyman, and he's not afraid to take on roles that a lot of other actors would deem "career suicide." He is at his best when he plays the straight man/victim of bad luck. It's conceivable that Fraser would actually co-star with a monkey in a remake of any movie. Why a monkey? Who doesn't love a monkey? Any movie with a monkey in it is already on the right track to being a better movie than any movie without a monkey in it. It's almost as good as a film with a creepy dwarf for entertainment value.

I don't know—what do you want? This is just some stupid game I play at dinner with other film geeks.

Credits

Cashiers du Cinemart — Issue #4 — One Dollar

Secrets of Dolemite Revealed · Sacred Cow Slaughter · Movies Reviewed · Plus Beat Box · Bill Morrison · And Much, Much More...

"WOULD YOU LIKE BUTTER-FLAVORING ON THAT?"

AFTERWORD

For a while I was really tempted to call this book *Rock 'N Soul Pt. 2*, in reference to the 1983 Hall & Oates album. This was one of several "greatest hits" collections with an initial entry that never had a sequel. Kind of like *Remo Williams The Adventure Begins*. It's an obtuse and somewhat obscure reference and that's what this book is all about. I also added a couple "bonus tracks" with revamped articles and a few bits that never made it into the pages of *Cashiers du Cinemart*. Hopefully, they'll be a bit better than the ubiquitous filler songs stuffed onto a "greatest hits" record (Billy Joel's "You're Only Human (Second Wind)" springs to mind).

I'm not a writer. I've never claimed to be such. What I tend to do is put a lot of words down on paper and sometimes find sentences amongst them—like the monkeys typing Shakespeare. I'd be lucky to be one monkey banging out piss-poor prose. If I had to put a name to my style, I'd call it "hackademic." However, I've included notes about which issues what stories came from in the hope that some kind of improvement can be found.

I got the idea for *Cashiers du Cinemart* in the early '90s as I was standing in the box office at the Star Taylor. I had been reading *Factsheet Five*—the Bible of zine reviews—and loved the idea of starting a rag compiling work stories: butchered titles, concession trends, failed romances, and other drama that rivaled the Hollywood fare being showcased in the auditoriums. It'd be a few years after I had moved on from the Star that a wealth of time on my hands and too many opinions in my head forced the issue.

All-nighter shifts with access to cable television, a Xerox machine, a postage meter, and a rudimentary word processing program can lead to some interesting results. It definitely led to *Cashiers du Cinemart* #1. With the original idea of writing about theater workers, including cashiers, and Detroit being the Paris of the Midwest, the title "*Cashiers du Cinemart*" was only natural. Yet you'd be amazed at how few people got the joke.

From there things just kept getting bigger and better. With each issue I strove to improve the look of my primitive publication, and the content to boot. When I began, even doing a simple screen capture was nearly impossible. Before long I was investing in basic layout software and trying my hand at desktop publishing, working hard to add that "maga" look to my zine while maintaining my limited indie cred.

Actor Bruce Campbell and artist Nathan Kane helped push *Cashiers du Cinemart* along. The fifth issue was the first to be desktop published. It hosted my first interview (with Mr. Campbell) and a snazzy cover designed by Mr. Kane. Nathan remained the resident *Cashiers du Cinemart* cover artist up to the thirteenth issue. He provided a bevy of bodacious babes as eye candy covers.

Afterword

Over the years, I've been joined by a cast of amazing characters who have provided some great prose in the pages of my little hobby publication. Uncool stuff like "work" and "real life" would often derail the steady release of issues, but my friends, co-writers, and readers were always there for me, buoying me and the zine right along.

—Mike White

ABOUT THE CONTRIBUTORS

Leon Chase lives in Brooklyn, New York, but still smells like southeast Michigan. He is the author of the stage play *The Last Carburetor*, which enjoyed two runs in New York City and was published in the anthology *Plays and Playwrights 2003*. His story "Acetylene" won second place in the San Francisco Bay *Guardian*'s 1997 Summer Fiction Contest, and he has penned sloppy comics and obsessive pop-culture rants for various small publications. He is the co-creator of "Don't Come Knockin'" (rockinvan.com), a Web site celebrating custom-vanning culture, as well as the founder of Brooklyn Country (brooklyncountry.com), an online celebration of New York City's surprisingly fertile country music scene. He is also the twisted mastermind behind cult cowpunk group Uncle Leon and the Alibis, and currently plays bass in the rock band Sister Anne. When he's not making music, he watches a shit-ton of movies, hangs out at the roller derby, does his best to avoid gainful employment, and claims to be working on a novel.

Chris Cummins is a Philadelphia-based freelance writer/pop culture savant whose writings have appeared in *Philadelphia City Paper*, *Philadelphia Weekly*, *High Maintenance*, *Topless Robot*, and other wonderful publications and online destinations. He is a gentle giant of a man who will be sporting a different configuration of facial hair each time you see him.

Skizz Cyzyk first made a name for himself in Baltimore, Maryland's early-'80s hardcore scene, playing in pioneering punk bands like TRUD, Burried Droog, Slug Log 3, Braille Party, and Berserk. He became a filmmaker in 1983, and has since made more than 50 short films and videos, including the *Night Flight* classic *Bad Aliens From Another Planet*, the animated *Four Films In Five Minutes: A Trilogy*, the Formstone documentary *Little Castles*, the YouTube favorite *Managers Corner*, and music videos for Young Fresh Fellows, Meatjack, The Moaners, and Beach House. In 1989, Baltimore's City Paper named him Baltimore's Best FM Disc Jockey for his work at college station WCVT. In the early '90s, he moved into a former funeral home, turning it into The Mansion Theater, a microcinema where he spent most of the decade hosting film screenings for countless underground, experimental, and touring filmmakers. In 1997, he founded MicroCineFest, an annual underground film festival dedicated to low-budget, off-beat, cinematic oddities. In the meantime, he has maintained involvements with Utah's Slamdance Film Festival, the Maryland Film Festival, the Atlanta Film Festival, Alabama's Sidewalk Moving Picture Festival, and many other festivals. He serves on the Maryland Lawyers for the Arts' Board of Directors, and has been a frequent contributor to publications like *Cashiers du Cinemart* and *Go Metric!* He continues to play music, currently supplying electric ukulele for The Go Pills, and drums for legendary surf/garage act, Garage Sale, as well as indie-rock sensations, The Jennifers.

About the Contributors

Chris Gore is a self-described Nerdlebrity who writes books, makes films, and speaks on TV. He owes Mike White a beer…and a hug.

Andrew Grant is a film critic who runs the popular film blog "Like Anna Karina's Sweater" (filmbrain.com), and has written for *Premiere, Cineaste, TheReeler* and Greencine.com. He is also the President of Benten Films (bentenfilms.com), the first US DVD label run by film critics. A proud citizen of Brooklyn, NY, he counts ranting about the sad state of independent cinema amongst his favorite hobbies.

Reared on the mean streets of Detroit, **Nathan Kane** now lives in Los Angeles. He's worked as a colorist in the comic book industry since 1993 and has done freelance illustration for just as long. He did some background paint on the (very) short lived Clerks animated series and appeared as himself in the Mark Hamill-directed mockumentary, *Comic Book: The Movie*. Mr. Kane is currently the Art Director for Bongo Comics and has decided that writing this biography is depressing.

Jonathan Higgins works in southeast Michigan as a freelance medical and scientific illustrator, contributing to encyclopedias, college textbooks, surgical manuals, scientific journals, and anatomical atlases. For fun he draws pictures of his family, his animals, and his favorite Meifumado-traversing devices.

Lori Hubbard Higgins is a copy editor/proofreader/graphic designer by day, an evil-fighting, pen-toting, letter-writing activist by night. With her master's degree and university teaching assignment in hand, she set out to rid the world of improper grammar, misspellings, and sentence fragments, while turning the conservative freshman in her classes into raging liberals. Lori has since given up teaching in favor of design and freelance work, where she has been more of a behind-the-scenes doer of good.

Clifton Howard is a professor of semiology at a western university. He's been with *Cashiers du Cinemart* since the beginning, opposing the editorial staff at every turn. He likes monkeys and ponies.

Pat Lehnerer is a crazy philosopher with a lot of creative energy and not enough hours in the day. He makes his living as a graphic designer in Chicago. Currently he is in the infant stages of making animated shorts again. Someday he'll be on stage in a band with a horn section and learn how to ride a motorcycle. Sporting one of the coolest nicknames ever, **Herschell Gordon Lewis** is also known as "The Godfather of Gore," thanks to his series of '60s and '70s splatter films. Seeming to anticipate or set trends in cinema, Lewis wrote, produced, and directed the first wave of "nudie cutie" films before taking the world by storm with *Blood Feast*. Some of his other films include *She Devils on Wheels*, *Year of the Yahoo*, *Just for the Hell of It*, and *The Wizard of Gore*. Lewis is also a pioneer at advertising and direct marketing. Visit his website at herschellgordonlewis.com.

A veteran of the early-nineties zine boom, **Rich Osmond** was co-editor (along with Jordan Oakes) of the power pop fanzine Yellow Pills before starting the teen exploitation movie zine *Teenage Rampage*, where he interviewed such filmmakers as *Rock 'n Roll High School* director Allan Arkush and *Switchblade Sisters* auteur Jack Hill. He has been a contributor to *Cashiers du Cinemart* since issue #3.

Jim Rugg is a cartoonist/illustrator best known for *Street Angel*, *Afrodisiac*, and *The Plain Janes*. See more of his work at jimrugg.com.

Dean Stahl is a freelance illustrator and Central Michigan University graduate. He is a big fan and follower of comic books, role-playing games and pro-wrestling. He constantly strives to improve his art, while refusing to ever grow up. More of his work can be found at steelhorse-studios.com or wookiee71.deviantart.com.

Mike Thompson still lives in Michigan with his wife and sons.

Andrea White, the somewhat vanilla wife of Mike White, curiously keeps ending up in Bowling Green, Ohio.

Often mistaken for the ginger director/screenwriter/actor of the same name, **Mike White** has been a frequent contributor to other publications including Paracinema, Detroit's *Metro Times*, WildSideCinema.com, Detour-Mag.com, and *CinemaScope*. He's been rejected by several magazines for being too lowbrow and several others for being too highbrow. Apparently, he's midbrow. He has served on juries at the Slamdance, Cinekink, and MicroCineFest film festival, and has appeared in *David Goodis: To a Pulp* and *The People vs. George Lucas*. Keep up with White at impossiblefunky.com

www.ingramcontent.com/pod-product-compliance
Lightning Source LLC
Chambersburg PA
CBHW071648160426
43195CB00012B/1392